Hennrietta Quinnel at Drizzlecombe, Dartmoor, 1992.

Recent Archaeological Work in South-Western Britain

Papers in Honour of Henrietta Quinnell

Edited by

Susan Pearce

BAR British Series 548
2011

Published by

Archaeopress
Publishers of British Archaeological Reports
Gordon House
276 Banbury Road
Oxford OX2 7ED
England
bar@archaeopress.com
www.archaeopress.com

BAR 548

Recent Archaeological Work in South-Western Britain: Papers in Honour of Henrietta Quinnell

© Archaeopress and the individual authors 2011

ISBN 978 1 4073 0884 5

Printed in England by Blenheim Colour Ltd

All BAR titles are available from:

Hadrian Books Ltd
122 Banbury Road
Oxford
OX2 7BP
England
www.hadrianbooks.co.uk

The current BAR catalogue with details of all titles in print, prices and means of payment is available free from Hadrian Books or may be downloaded from www.archaeopress.com

Contents

Hennrietta Quinnell: Rescue Archaeology, Adult Education and South West Britain 1
Susan Pearce

South Western Hunter-Gather Landscapes 7
Paula Gardiner

The Early Neolithic of South Western Britain: New Insights and New Questions 21
Alison Sheridan

Pseudo-Quoits to Propped Stones 41
Tony Blackman

Between the Channel and the Chalk: A Regional Perspective on
the Grooved Ware and Beaker Pottery from the Mendip Hills, Somerset .... 49.
Jodie Lewis and David Mullin

Without Wessex: the Local Character of the Early Bronze Age in the South West Peninsula 61
Andy M. Jones

Earlier Bronze Age Cemetery Mounds and the Multiple Cremation Burial Rite in Western Britain 75
Paul Bonnington

Interpreting the Dartmoor Reaves 93
Andrew Fleming

Telling Tales from the Round House. Researching Bronze Age Buildings in Cornwall 101
Jacqueline Nowakowski

In the Footsteps of Pioneering Women: Some Recent Work on Devon Hillforts 121
F.M.Griffith and E.M.Wilkes

Romano-British Brooches of Cornish Origin? 139
Anna Tyacke, Justine Bayley, and Sarnia Butcher

The Early Medieval Native Pottery of Cornwall. AD c.400-1066 151
C.M.Thorpe

Multiple Identities in Cornwall 159
Peter Herring

A Guinea Pig's Testimony 169
Judith Cosford

A Student's Progress 171
Susan Watts

Bibliography of Henrietta Quinnell's Published Work, to 2011 173

Henrietta Quinnell:
Rescue Archaeology, Adult Education, and South Western Britain

Susan Pearce

Introduction

In 2009 a conference entitled 'Current Research in the Prehistory of South West England' was held at Tavistock under the joint auspices of the Devon Archaeological Society and the Cornwall Archaeological Society, to celebrate Henrietta's sixty-fifth birthday and her achievements in archaeology over her working life so far. It was attended by some 140 people, almost all of whom knew Henrietta personally, and whose lives had been touched by her work. Since she first came to the southwest, in 1968, Henrietta has dedicated herself to her twin roles of working practical archaeologist and archaeological teacher, and during this time, she has gathered around her a large band of devoted friends, who hold her in great regard and affection, amply manifested at the Tavistock Conference. This volume is the outcome of that meeting, and it is appropriate that its opening paper should explore how Henrietta has shaped archaeological practice in the southwest, and how this relates to the broader context of archaeology as it has unfolded through her life.

Discovering Archaeology

Henrietta was born a war baby in 1944, and spent her early years during the period of austerity and high socialist hopes. Her father, Henry, after whom she was named, was the first member of his family to attend a university, and did so in style, achieving scholarships to Christchurch, Oxford, where, in 1932, he took a First in Philosophy, Politics and Economics. In 1947, he became Vice-President of Ruskin College, Oxford, one of the places where Labour Party political thinking was formed. Her mother, Margaret, also a socialist economist, similarly followed the adult education route to a university post at Bristol. In 1949, they bought a run-down cottage in the Cotswolds, and their elder daughter, soon joined by her sister, Catherine, went to the local primary school and Witney Grammar School. The young Henrietta imbibed a strong sense of social responsibility, particularly in relation to educational opportunities, and in the need for collective care for what was just beginning to be known as 'the heritage'; these convictions were to shape her working life.

Both were deeply significant contemporary issues. The development of new universities was to wait until the nineteen-sixties, but the pre-war network of Ruskin, Workers Education Association classes, and external degrees, from which the new institutions would come, flourished in post-war Britain. A conference in London to discuss the destruction of archaeological sites, which the huge development of the military was causing, and what might be done, had already met in 1943, probably largely at the instigation of O.G.S. Crawford, who had become the first archaeology officer at the Ordnance Survey (OS) in 1920. At the OS, Charles Philips had already begun the massive task of creating the modern OS Record of British archaeological sites. Meanwhile, Bryan O'Neil, on behalf of the then Ministry of Works (MoW), was carrying out emergency excavations ahead of the Army, particularly on the southern chalk lands, and Cyril Fox was similarly digging. This needed substantial numbers of volunteer diggers, for whose benefit Richard Atkinson, already a veteran excavator, wrote Field Archaeology in 1946. This was a practical, hands-on manual of how to do digs, which guided generations of excavators.

By the time she was eight years old, Henrietta knew that her life's interest would lie in the past and its interpretation; by then she had discovered, and fallen in love with, Homer's Odyssey, read in Rieu's Penguin translation. It was clear that she needed more than her grammar school could provide, particularly in Classics, and so arrangements were made for her to study Greek and Latin privately, while her mother taught her geology and history herself. When she was fifteen, she made contact with Oxford University Archaeological Society, and began her career in archaeology by digging with them regularly for two years. A bad road accident in 1961 necessitated a break, and when she returned to action, Henrietta started excavating on what became known as 'the circuit', the sequence of excavations, generally in advance of site destruction, carried out by an itinerant but close-knit body of site directors, supervisors, and diggers, funded (to a modest degree, which made little or no provision for write-up and publication) by MoW. She dug on the circuit for three years.

The pre-war network created by Crawford was still effectively controlling archaeological thinking, particularly at the most senior levels. Its members embraced Gordon Childe in London, Cyril and Aileen Fox at Cardiff, Christopher Hawkes in London and then Oxford, Clarke at Cambridge, and Stuart Piggott at Edinburgh. Overwhelmingly, archaeology was seen as a form of history, in which the course of events could be understood by defining 'cultures', assemblages of similar material culture plotted over space and given chronological depth by typological studies. Cultures acted in the place of the unknown individuals, moving about Europe and taking over new areas by displacing their existing cultures, creating an historical framework, based on what has become known as the 'invasion theory'. Following Childe and Hawkes, the thrust of this was employed to create an over-arching narrative of early European prehistory, in which the perceived uniqueness of Europe and its especial significance for the rest of the world could be explored and explained.

The 'Excavation Circuit'.

The pressure of the new wave of excavation the circuit represented was bringing new people to the fore, but the majority of these were linked to the old network. Atkinson had dug with Crawford at Dorchester henge and was Hawkes's cousin; Sonia Chadwick was to marry Hawkes; Paul Ashbee combined excavation and teaching until 1969; Philip Rahtz gave up his photographic and teaching work and dug full time for the Ministry between 1953 to 1963, at the request of O'Neil. While Henrietta was on the circuit, she excavated with Chadwick, Ashbee and Rahtz, and became a supervisor on sites like Staines and Alcester. She remembers three archaeologists from this period as providing significantly to her practice and thinking. Paul Ashbee had been meticulous in the proper and appropriate use of equipment. George Boon at Caerleon spent much time teaching her surveying and the basic elements of the study of ceramics. Philip Rahtz provided great insights into the understanding of stratigraphy and the beginnings of modern contextual recording; he also used machinery to strip large scale sites skilfully and to great affect. Henrietta was amused to find that she had lived until the age of three in the same street in Bristol as Philip and that all the early photographs of her sister and herself were taken by 'Studio Rahtz'!

In 1963, the Robbins Report into higher education was published, and it triggered the foundation of new universities like East Anglia and York, and new Departments of Archaeology in universities, in which most of the senior people running the circuit found academic posts, and many of those working as diggers became students. By 1965, Henrietta knew she wanted a career in British practical archaeology, and she chose to go to the Department of Archaeology, University of Wales (University College, Cardiff), which at the time, under Richard Atkinson, promised the best education for such a career. In preparation she took Greek, Latin, and Ancient History at A Level, achieving three Grade As: this classical background was central to archaeological thinking as it then stood. She was awarded the Sir Alfred Thomas Prize after her first year examinations, and a first class single honours degree in 1968; the external examiner was Aileen Fox. While at Cardiff she started on a ten year association with the then Principal Inspector of Ancient Monuments, Andrew Saunders, as main supervisor of work at Launceston Castle, Cornwall. She married Trevor Miles while still an undergraduate in 1967; they divorced in 1975.

Atkinson wanted Henrietta to do a doctorate on aspects of stone axe production, the subject of her undergraduate dissertation, but, characteristically, she decided to become involved again in excavation. She particularly wanted to widen the scope of sites she was familiar with and to put into practice ideas gained digging on circuit and built on during her University days and the excavations, especially those at the Roman Fortress at Usk under William Manning, with which she had been involved. She directed excavations for the Inspectorate of Ancient Monumentsat, among other sites, the Iron Age settlement at Westonzoyland, Somerset, Roman villas at Cosgrove, Northamptonshire, and Seaton, Devon, and the multi-period site at Rhuddlan, Clwyd. This directorial experience encouraged imaginative use of earth moving machinery, and, more importantly, showed that few sites were limited to the periods and features initially expected. At Rhuddlan the site as initially stated was that of a Norman borough; in fact it produced in addition extensive evidence for the Mesolithic, the Roman and the Early Medieval periods. At Fisherwick, Staffordshire, a rural Roman settlement proved to overlie a Late Neolithic structure. Henrietta could see that rescue excavation, if sufficiently extensive and adequately financed, would continually provide totally new classes of site and data. This made careful targeted 'research excavations' – something she never undertook herself – appear somewhat limited in their scope. Research excavations also absorbed resources that could, in her view, often be better expended on sites about to be destroyed.

In January 1970 Henrietta came to Exeter to take up the newly established post of Staff Tutor in Archaeology in the Department of Extra-Mural Studies at the University of Exeter. Exeter, one of the new universities of the then recent wave, was the only university in the south-western peninsula, and therefore the remit of the Department of Extra-Mural Studies covered the counties of Devon and Cornwall.

The region into which Henrietta had moved rejoices in its particular character. It is bounded by the sea on all sides except the east, and geomorphically it takes the form of a series of upland areas, mostly granitic, beginning with Exmoor in the east, followed by Dartmoor, and then, west of the Tamar, Bodmin Moor, Hensbarrow, Carnmenellis, Penwith and finally the Isles of Scilly. All of these areas, together with much of the better agricultural land around them, are replete with surviving ancient field systems, monuments and settlements. The principle risks to these sites are, and always have been, mineral extraction, forestry, and modern arable farming. The area has historically been difficult of access to the rest of Britain, but it is set at the heart of seaways, which run south down the Atlantic coast into the Mediterranean, west to Ireland, east to Brittany and beyond, and north to Wales, the Irish Sea coastlands, and the Scottish peninsulas and islands. In its own history, archaeology has tended swing back and forth between stressing the significance of this Atlantic/Irish Sea cultural province, and emphasising connections between eastern Britain and continental Europe. The area has a strong sense of itself as 'the South West', but within this, there is a rivalry between Devon, which sees itself as the western land of milk and honey, and Cornwall, which identifies itself as one of the ancient Celtic lands distinct from England to the east.

In 1970, the region already had an impressive history of antiquarian and archaeological enquiry. In the1930s the excavation by Dorothy Liddell of Hembury hillfort in east Devon, which first demonstrated hill top Neolithic, as well as Iron Age, use, was a major landmark, and so later were the excavations carried out by Aileen Fox in war damaged Exeter. In Cornwall there had been the excavation by C. A. R. Radford at the hillfort of Castle Dore and extensive rescue work by Dorothy Dudley. The present past, visible throughout the peninsula, had stimulated a great deal of smaller scale archaeological work, much of it of considerable value, and had resulted in an exceptionally strong local structure. The Royal Institution of Cornwall, founded in1818, had set up its Library and Museum in Truro, as major resources and repositories; by the 1970s the Museum held, and displayed, very substantial archaeological collections. In Devon, the County Museum Service and the two City Museums of Plymouth and Exeter, were doing the same. The Devon Archaeological Society, founded in 1929, has carried out excavations and field work, and published its Proceedings more-or-less yearly since then. In 1961 the West Cornwall Field Club turned itself into the Cornish Archaeological Society, and since then has done the same.

When Henrietta came to her new Staff Tutor post in 1970, this was the structure within which she quickly found her natural place, and she continued to work hard in many offices for both Societies throughout her career, eventually becoming President of the Devon Society in 1987-9 and of the Cornwall Society in 2004-7. In particular she had been Editor for Cornish Archaeology 1975-81, a post she enjoyed as much of it then involved solving problems with the publication of long-overdue excavation reports. These were the heady days of the later sixties and seventies, and hers was not the only new post. Aileen Fox, now appointed to a position in the new Archaeological Section within the History Department at the University of Exeter, was the force behind the creation of the Staff Tutorship, of additional lectureships in Archaeology in the University, and of the Curatorship of Archaeology at Exeter City Museum. Interestingly, all of these posts were filled by women, from which a number of conclusions might be drawn. Charles Thomas was the prime force in Cornish archaeology, working from the Universities of Edinburgh and Leicester, until he returned to Cornwall to the Chair of Cornish Studies at the Institute of the same name, part of Exeter University, in 1971.

Teaching and 'Rescue'.

For Henrietta, there followed three crucial developments. When she accepted the Extramural Department Staff Tutorship, she was briefed (in both senses) in her duties by Tom Daveney, then Head of the Department. He said simply that she should give three or four weekly classes, which were usually based in Exeter and Truro, in the two Winter terms, a Summer School, and should arrange for other tutors to give classes as she saw fit. This gave her tremendous freedom to harness the local enthusiasm for archaeology, and organize it productively. It put her squarely in her family tradition of working within openly available education, which offered personal fulfilment and the chance to significant work to all comers. It is the philosophy of 'giving something back', perhaps the greatest of the British traditions. In practical terms lecturing and digging were to feed into one another. Extra-mural students were keen to assist with rescue excavation work, while well-publicized excavations increased the audience for lecture classes and several special series were set up to accompany excavations.

Secondly, at that time Extra-Mural work was closely linked with rescue archaeology, and the pressure group Rescue, formally founded in 1971, arose from beginnings at the annual meetings of Staff Tutors. Rescue was created by the then younger generation – Charles Thomas, Barry Cunliffe, Paul Ashbee, Peter Fowler, Philip Rahtz- all of whom were descended from the old Crawford network, and with all of whom Henrietta had worked closely. The group identified the twin needs as a comprehensive listing of data about existing archaeological sites region by region, and the creation of a network of field archaeology units, who could carry out excavation in advance of development, all funded by central government. Bit by bit, this structure emerged. In Devon soon after her arrival in 1970 Henrietta became secretary for a 'Roads' sub-committee of the Devon Archaeological Society set up to continue the pioneering work of the M5 Committee under Peter Fowler further north. The work of the DAS Roads Committee continually expanded and became in 1975 the Devon Committee for Rescue Archaeology (DCRA), with Henrietta still its Secretary and guiding light. DCRA employed Field Officers and established one of the first County Sites and Monuments Registers in the country. Out of this eventually came the present County Archaeology Service and Historic Environment Record. In both Devon and Cornwall, where the equivalent body was the Cornish Committee for Rescue Archaeology, connections with the county Archaeological Societies were exceptionally close, and this did much to relieve the differences between amateurs and professions, which has proved so corrosive in some other parts of the country. The way in which a good deal of archaeological activity was organised around the two societies in the two counties had always meant that high quality volunteers were usually available; or, to put it another way, the relationship between 'amateurs' and 'professionals' was much kinder in the south west than in some other parts of the country. Rescue archaeology was very close to Henrietta's heart, and she threw herself into its very considerable demands in both counties with great skill and enormous enthusiasm.

Finally, archaeology itself was changing. In the Archaeology Departments of the new universities, people were less interested in broad European historical narratives and were developing new ideas drawn from post-modern thinking and were stressing the probability of indigenous development rather than the influence of wise men from afar. New universities also promoted methodologies for new scientific dating and analytical techniques. The new Field Units soaked up the archaeology graduates from the newly founded universities, and created the second wave of insecure, itinerant diggers. Hard men and women, these, with dirt under their finger nails and wanting little truck with theory, but they were interested in the notions of local and regional development, and in archaeology as a practice which could unravel the landscapes within which local pasts had been embodied. Henrietta's deepest archaeological instincts had always centred upon the landscape and its capacity to reveal the pasts of individual communities through time.

Henrietta brought together landscape, rescue, and outreach education in an outstanding series of excavations during the seventies. There were the barrows on the china clay area near St. Austell at Cocksbarrow, Caerloggas, Trenance Downs and Watch Hill between 1970 and 1973. The ring cairn at Shallowmead on Exmoor followed in 1977. In these early years in the south west Henrietta was gradually beginning to concentrate on prehistory, and in particular the importance of local traditions and practices in the formation of material culture. This found clear expression in her reports on barrow excavation, where both monument form and ceremonial activities were interpreted as based in their local backgrounds and not, as in the current literature, merely offshoots from Wessex.

Trethurgy Round on the china clay followed in 1973. This site had been found by a local archaeologist Peter Sheppard who had initially failed to get its potential recognised. Henrietta was able to make the case for funds for the complete excavation of its interior to the Inspectorate of Ancient Monuments: no interior of enclosed settlement in Cornwall had previously been excavated. It had been expected, prior to excavation, that the site belonged to the Iron Age. It belonged in fact to the Roman period and to the immediate post-Roman centuries. Its interior buildings, very well preserved, were new to the county, but have since been recognised as typical of the period. Henrietta, in working toward the publication of the site, carried out a complete review of Roman period sites and artefacts in Cornwall. This revealed among other things that courtyard houses were of Roman, not prehistoric date. The excavation report still the forms the basic work of reference on Roman Cornwall.

Hillforts had first been addressed with the long line of road widening through Woodbury, East Devon in 1971. In 1975-6, the continued damage caused by the extensions to a pig farm – outside the remit of planning leglislation - led to work Killibury, near Wadebridge, and this excavation was set up as a training exercise. This was necessarily taken at a slower pace than general for excavations and enabled considerable refinements in recording and methodology. Killibury was, for example, the first site in the southwest in which wet sieving for charred plant remains was carried out. Henrietta regards the Killibury excavation, and the innovatory follow-up classes on the preparation of the excavation report as one of the greatest satisfactions of her teaching life, and a glance at the publication in Cornish Archaeology for 1977 shows why. Six members of the Cornish Archaeological Society are listed in the Acknowledgements, several of whom contributed to the publication. Moreover, the same section includes this unusual note:

> The contributors to this report would like to express their gratitude to Mrs Miles for all the help, criticism and encouragement she has given them; they appreciate more than any one else could the difficulties of the unprecedented task she undertook, of coordinating the efforts of a dozen individualists scattered over the county from the Tamar to the Lizard (p. 120).

Just so; it was an enormously generous enterprise on Henrietta's part, which created a life –changing opportunity for those who took part, some of whom, like Daphne Harris, went on to become excavating archaeologists in their own right. And this process locally blurred any specious distinctions between 'professionals' and 'amateurs'.

By 1978, continuous over-work took its toll, and Henrietta needed a two-year break to recover. She started to teach again in 1980, and went part-time in 1987. Meanwhile, she began the serious work on her excavation publication backlog, which she had not had space to do before. In the 1970s and 80s excavation finance did not normally include finance for publication work and this inevitably led to worrying backlogs for many energetic excavators. By 1991, the ethos in the former Extra-Mural Department, now Continuing and Adult Education, encouraged more formal study and allowed a two-year Certificate in Archaeology, something which Henrietta had had wanted to initiate since the late 1970s. The first three intakes of the Certificate, 1991/2 to 1995/6, covered methodology and British prehistory in great depth and demanded a great deal from both tutor and students. These, after Killibury, provided the second great satisfaction of Henrietta's teaching career. The course attracted groups of highly dedicated students, which made the teaching a great joy. Henrietta retired formally in 1999, but continued to teach for the Department until 2005. She was appointed an Honorary Research Fellow at the University of Exeter in 2001, a position that she still holds.

Henrietta has always been a brilliant teacher, one of the rare band who can hold a fee-paying class not merely for one year, but for years in succession. For her, also, teaching has been a highly rewarding experience. During the first run of the Archaeological Certificate, the students bonded as a group, and called themselves 'HQ's Guinea Pigs' because they were aware that they were the trial run for the course. They still meet as a group. The flavour of those two years can best be appreciated by the accounts contributed by one of the Guinea Pigs, Judith Cosford. From 1996 the format of the content of the Archaeology Certificate underwent changes in line with Department policies. One advantage was that at long last students were allowed the credit of one year's full time study towards an Exeter degree in archaeology. Sue Watts was a certificate student in the late 90s and her contribution (below) provides an additional view of the certificate experience.

Henrietta's post-excavation work came to fruition in 2004, with the major publication of the excavation at Trethurgy. Trethurgy: Excavations at Trethurgy Round, St. Austell: Community and Status in Roman and Post-Roman Cornwall, some three hundred pages long and published by Cornwall County Council, was chosen by Current Archaeology as one of its Books of the Year. Another important publication, with Jacqueline Nowakowski, is planned for 2011, also to be published by Cornwall County Council. This will cover the results of C. K. Croft Andrew's 1939 excavations at Trevelgue Cliff Castle, and will contain a major review of Middle Iron Age ceramics in the region.

Regional Patterns.

One consequence of the shift of interest away from the grand European narrative and towards indigenous developments was a resurgent focus on the region as a topic of study in its own right, with its own characteristic role in the broader scheme of things. As already set out, the southwest in general, and perhaps Cornwall in particular, is so constituted as to make this approach especially fruitful. This local distinctiveness was fully apparent in prehistoric ceramics but, until the 1990s, south west regional studies had lacked resident specialist. This was the role Henrietta took up after her retirement from the University and still carries out today. She is concerned both to establish a clear chronological sequence from the Early Neolithic through to the Cornish local ceramics, and to define regionally distinctive patterns and the individuality of local traditions. This period coincided with expansion of developer funded excavations, undertaken by field archaeology units, especially the Historic Environment Service, Cornwall Council and Exeter Archaeology. Henrietta no longer directs excavations but collaboration with archaeologists such as Andrew M Jones and Jacqueline Nowakowski has proved both fruitful and enjoyable. She would also, I know, wish to acknowledge her great debt to her geologist colleague, Dr Roger T. Taylor formerly of the British Geological Survey, who works with her on petrology and sourcing. Now, in 2011, the chronological sequences are nearly complete – some gaps remaining for the Middle Neolithic and for the Late Bronze Age/Early Iron Age, but much of Henrietta and Roger's work is still 'forthcoming', fully prepared for, but awaiting publication.

Henrietta first published a paper on distinctive artefacts, in this case stone objects, in the Cornish Roman and post-Roman periods in the *Festschrift* for Philip Rahtz in 1993, and her further illumination of the south-west as a regional theatre will be extremely interesting. But if archaeology can cast light on Cornwall and Devon as peripheral to a Mediterranean or European centre, it can also show how this must be balanced by its particular status as core in other respects. Tin production and distribution, illusive though it often is in the record, is a case in point, and the peninsula's role in the post-Roman exchange system, which bound together the Irish Sea and the eastern Mediterranean, is another. Henrietta and her collaborator, Roger Taylor, are currently unravelling another distribution pattern, involving the sources of pot clays. It has long been known, through David Peacock's pioneering work, that the pots made from Lizard gabbroic clays were moved long distances. Now work on the distinctive Bronze Age Trevisker material is demonstrating that much gabbroic clay was moved before potting and mixed with local materials, both within Cornwall and right up onto Dartmoor. Other important and intriguing work on sourcing has located the precise sources of some clays used for the Iron Age South Western Decorated (Glastonbury) wares are in Devon. There is much food for thought here, at a number of levels.

I know that Henrietta would wish me to write about Norman Quinnell, who became her partner in 1975. They married in 1980, and lived together in Exeter until his death in 2008. Norman had a reputation as a very fine archaeological surveyor, who made a considerable contribution to the record of the Ordnance Survey. His own *Festschrift, From Caithness to Cornwall*, was published by British Archaeological Reports, on his retirement. Norman always supported Henrietta's archaeological work, and provided many of the drawings for her reports and input into the more practical aspects of certificate teaching. His children and grandchildren have become important to Henrietta, and travel with Norman was always a great joy.

The range, not only of subject but also of author, of the papers in this volume demonstrates the breath and depth of Henrietta's archaeological attachment to the region. Some of the chapters are by nationally respected, professional experts in their fields; and some are by members of the voluntary archaeological community, who are so dear to Henrietta's heart, and who have unrivalled understanding of local monuments. Others are by younger archaeologists, to whom Henrietta has always been so generous with time and encouragement; and I particularly welcome the two pieces that describe what it was like being one of her students. The volume reflects Henrietta's life and work in archaeology, her great contribution to the discipline, and the very many friends she has made along the way. It is offered to her by those same friends, with gratitude, admiration, and the very best of good wishes for the future.

South Western Hunter-Gather Landscapes

Paula Gardiner

Abstract

Hunter-gatherers of the Mesolithic are traditionally seen as principally transient groups surviving on a subsistence diet of hazelnuts and venison. Those on the coast were regarded as being dependent on shellfish and other seafood and were constantly on the move. Although Star Carr (Clark 1954; Mellars and Dark, 1998) has gone some way to shifting our vision of hunter-gatherer activity in this period, much of the British database has had to rely on flint scatters alone in order to put forward hypotheses of social evolution. Recent excavations at East Barns, Scotland and Howick, Northumberland (Waddington and Pedersen, 2007) have shown that substantial houses were being built and renewed by Mesolithic people, who may have stayed in one place for much longer than previously thought. The paucity of large scale excavation being carried out on Mesolithic sites in south west England has biased the archaeological record, because we have had to rely on flint scatters alone. Extensive fieldwork by the author in Somerset, has allowed a consideration of the landscape to be taken into account, which suggests that hunter-gatherers of the late Mesolithic may not necessarily have had to travel large distances, but that access to a coastal-upland ecotone may have provided sufficient resources to enable them to occupy sites on a much more permanent basis (Gardiner 2000; 2007b; 2009).

Introduction

Throughout the Mesolithic period, hunter-gatherers had to cope with a constantly changing environment. The large land mass that was lost in the North Sea Basin due to sea level rise in the ninth millennium BP, had a direct effect upon hunting accessibility (Bell and Walker 1992; Coles 1998). Rising temperatures affected both the existing land mass and the distribution of vegetation and animals and by the time Britain was separated from the Continent, around 8000 BP, a new island status has been created, with hundreds of kilometres of new coastal and estuarine environments. Small herding animals such as red and roe deer, wild pig, and aurochs were widespread throughout Britain (Jarman 1972; Jochim 1976) and there was an abundance of marine mammals within a variety of wetland environments (Fischer 1995).

This post-glacial period should be seen as one of instability with ecosystems susceptible to fluctuation, and by the Atlantic period (5500 BP) coastlines and river courses were more accessible for hunter-gatherers than the more densely wooded areas inland (Bell and Walker 1992). By the end of the Mesolithic, woodland on both sides of the Severn Estuary, shows evidence of the encroaching sea level with forests becoming submerged.

At Porlock Weir and Minehead, flint has been recovered from what was once an area of woodland used by hunter-gatherers (Wymer 1977, 248) and which is now submerged at high tide. The Mesolithic footprints in the clays of the intertidal zone at Uskmouth shows that vital evidence has been lost in an area now covered by the sea (Aldhouse-Green *et al.* 1992). On the Gwent Levels there is evidence in the clays and silts of the Wentlooge Formation of red deer, aurochs and wolf footprints (Bell and Neuman 1997, 24). Unstratified finds of tranchet axes from Goldcliff East, together with animal footprints, suggest use of an intertidal strip on the coastal edge (Bell and Neuman 1997, 24). Mesolithic flints have also been found in the intertidal zone of blue clay at Yelland Stone Row in Devon (Grinsell 1970, 43). Further inland, Mesolithic evidence is often deeply buried due to alluviation or colluviation processes, for example at Birdcombe, North Somerset (Gardiner 2001, 88) or simply eroded and ploughed away. Discovery of sites is opportunistic, rather than predictable.

There is, therefore, an imbalance between the evidence that we do have and our expectations of what we hope to discover. The surviving evidence from Scandinavia tantalises us with its quantity and sheer quality, showing extensive settlement and cemetery evidence from Skateholm (Larsson, 1989) and logboats, paddles and fishing equipment elsewhere in Denmark (Fischer, 1995; Andersen 1987). At sites such as Kinlock (Rhum), Scotland (Wickham-Jones 1990) or Eskmeals, Cumbria (Bonsall *et al.* 1989) flint tools have been recovered in their thousands. They are believed to be the components of a wide range of hunting tools (Mithen 1999), although Clarke (1976) suggests they may also have been used for processing plant foods. Zvelebil stresses the importance of plant food in the diet (Zvelebil 1995, 86) and suggests that as much as 30-40% of the Mesolithic diet is made up of plant material (Zvelebil 1994, 58). Nevertheless, the palaeobotanical evidence from sites such as Mount Sandel in Northern Ireland of a wild pear/crab apple pip and seeds of white waterlily (Woodman 1985, 79), and the fruit seeds from the Westward Ho! midden in Devon (Balamm *et al.* 1982) are exceptional, although these were probably a common resource in the Mesolithic. Generaly, in south west England we lack such detailed artefactual information, apart from Bell's extensive work on the Welsh side of the Severn Estuary (2007).

Flint tools, therefore, are often all we have to work with. The diagnostic tools from the early Mesolithic period, the "broad blade assemblage" (Clark 1934) and Jacobi (1976) usually include obliquely blunted points and relatively large microliths such as isosceles triangles. From about 8500 BP a 'narrow blade industry' containing smaller microliths, appear in the archaeological record with no parallels outside Britain. The reasons for this change are not clear, but Jacobi suggests that it was Britain's isolation from Europe which allowed tool typology to develop (Jacobi 1976). Mithen suggests that the increasing growth of dense deciduous woodland would have required different hunting tools and strategies (Mithen 1999, 38). Microliths, therefore, are the diagnostic tool of the late Mesolithic in Britain and are rarely, if at all, found in later Neolithic contexts (Gardiner, 2001). This suggests that the late Mesolithic were a distinct cultural group, leading complex and successful lives until the arrival of the Neolithic at the beginning of the fifth millennium BC (Gardiner, 2001).

The Mesolithic period is equated with the use of the bow and arrow and sharp tipped microliths, as these are the most important tools for hunting and killing within a woodland environment (Rozoy 1989, 14). Although it is tempting to suggest that microliths appeared in response to the changing environment, Rozoy points out that the 'microlithisation' of armatures in Europe occurred over a long period of time, perhaps as much as a millennium, beginning in the pre-Boreal period, and that this technical innovation started before any climatic change (Rozoy 1989).

Fischer's experiments with a variety of microlithic armatures from Scandinavian industries has shown that an arrow shot using a fifty pound bow could penetrate a wild boar's rib-cage and prove lethal. He suggests that flint points evolved typologically in an effort to produce an armature that would have optimum penetrative qualities, together with the sharpest cut to induce bleeding, as well as creating the maximum stability for the arrow. Manufacturing a microlith using the microburin technique produced a stable tip far sharper than earlier retouched ones (Fischer 1989).

There can be do doubt that hunting with bows would have been extremely effective in the dense forests of Britain and Europe throughout the Mesolithic. It allowed hunters to stalk prey from a considerable distance, with the virtually silent firing of arrows allowing a second shot if necessary (Gardiner 2001). Lightweight microlithic armatures efficiently penetrated the hides of large game such as deer and aurochs (Rozoy 1989).

Stone tools, as we have seen, represent a fraction of the material that would probably have been available on

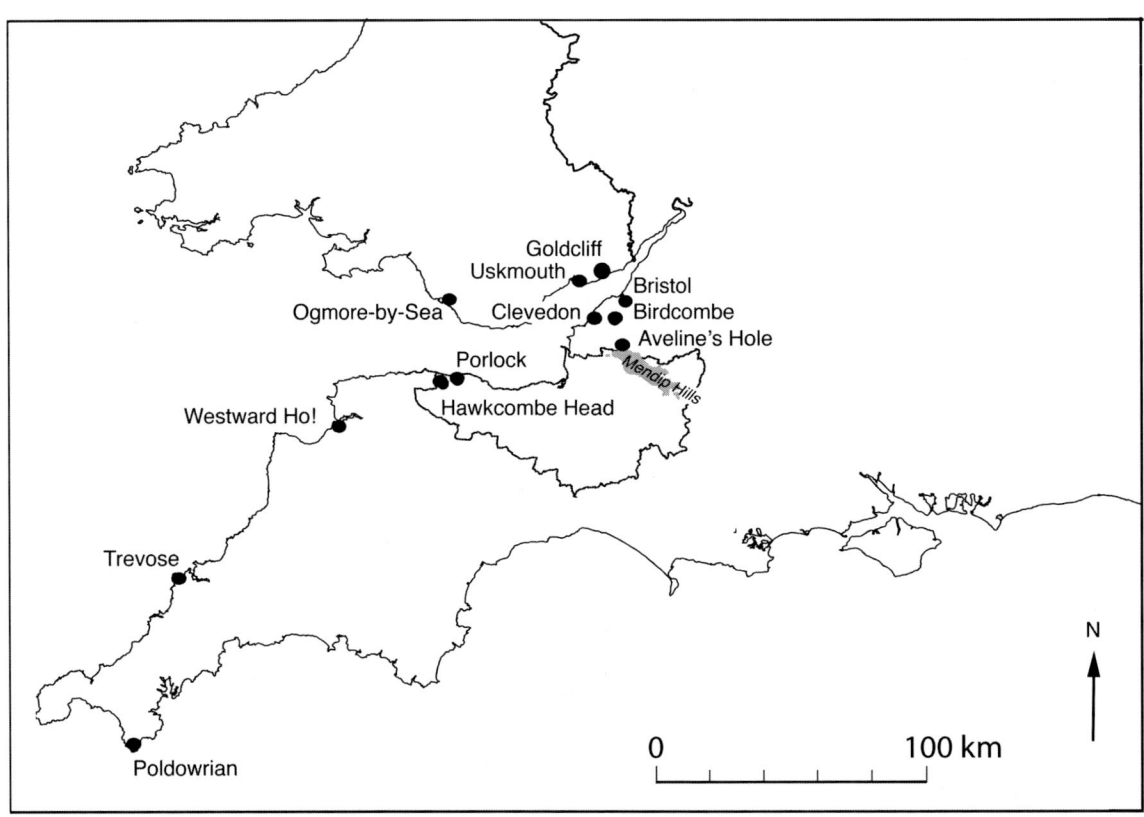

FIG. 2.1 LOCATION MAP OF SITES DISCUSSED IN THE TEXT

hunter-gatherer sites and Clarke's suggestion (1976) that microliths were used for plant processing should not be ignored. The presence of scrapers does not *only* imply skin working as the micro-wear analyses from Star Carr showed (Dumont 1989). Many different functions could be allocated to different tool types and the function of the majority of the microliths from Star Carr remains unclear (Dumont 1989). Whilst large lithic assemblages and features such as hearths, pits and postholes may suggest repeated visits to a site by hunter-gatherer groups, we need more secure radiocarbon dates from within sites to be able to make close chronological distinctions.

Attempts have been made to derive site activities and settlement patterns from the distribution of tool types and debitage (Mellars 1976; Mithen 1999). Mellars' data did not include sites from the south west peninsula. It has been suggested that tool types can be distinguished in relation to site function and topography with more diverse toolkits from lowland sites and hunting equipment coming from higher ground (Mithen 1999). This is a reasonable assumption if Binford's 'logistical mobility' model is applied (Binford 1983, 358) where small hunting groups might move out from a 'home base/residential camp' for periods of time on a seasonal basis following deer. However, categories such as these can be constraining when considering the wider landscape implications of an occupation site and this will be discussed further below.

The Mesolithic in South West England

It was the late Roger Jacobi's extensive study of the flint from late Mesolithic sites in south west England (fig 2.1) that allowed him to put forward the idea of a "Southern English" social grouping, based on the percentage of microlithic types from places that include Baggy Point, Devon, Culverwell, Dorset and Roskestal Cliff, Cornwall (Jacobi 1979; Jacobi and Tebbutt 1981). Jacobi suggested that there was a pattern of seasonal occupation of clifftop sites, often where there was access to raw material (beach pebble). Some sites, such as Trevose Head, Cornwall, which have around six thousand pieces of flint, were

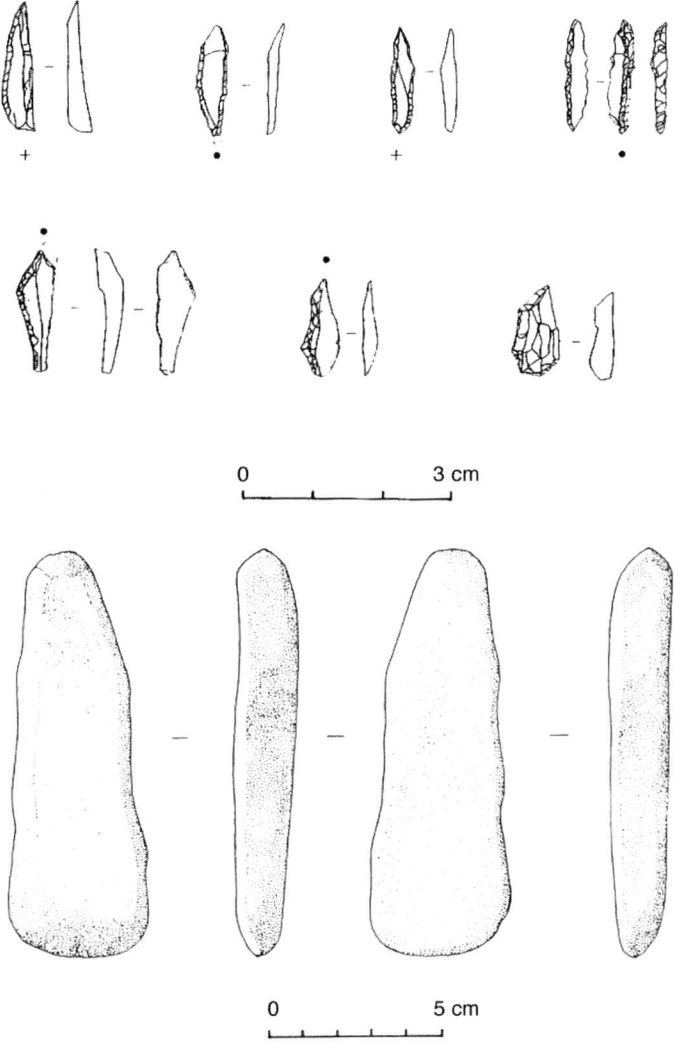

Fig. 2.2 Microliths and pebble tools from Poldowrian, Cornwall (after Smith and Harris 1982)

interpreted as being places repeatedly visited over a considerable period (Jacobi 1979, 76-78).

The site at Poldowrian on the Lizard, demonstrated a distinct late Mesolithic presence on the cliffs above the coastline at 60m OD (6450 ± 110 BP; 5618 – 5149 cal. BC - HAR-4568, Smith and Harris, 1982). Although this was a multi-period site with later Neolithic and Bronze Age features, no hearths and postholes are associated with the Mesolithic phase. There was, however, a ready supply of beach pebble below the cliffs at Poldowrian, accessible some 700m further along the coastline. The excavation recovered 308 microliths and a large number of pebble tools (370) that suggested a diverse range of activities were being carried out there, not just hunting (fig 2.2). The unusually high number of microburins (923) led the excavators to interpret the site as being used for microlith manufacture, possibly outside of the 'hunting season' (Smith and Harris, 1982). Jacobi, however, believed that the presence of hazelnuts showed an Autumn and early Winter use (Jacobi 1979). He reinforced his idea by adding that limpets were best harvested at this time (Jacobi, 1979), but this assumes that the pebble tools are used as 'limpet scoops'. This interpretation is by no means conclusive and the wear marks on some of the pebble tools from Poldowrian, may not necessarily have been used for limpet extraction (Smith and Harris, 1982).

While Jacobi's study suggests that many of Cornwall's coastal sites would have been used seasonally (Jacobi 1979), Poldowrian's topographic location, in a small spring-fed valley, and situated on high ground with access to both coastal and terrestrial resources, suggests that it could have been occupied for longer periods of time. Sea level rise has prevented us linking Poldowrian with other possible submerged sites nearby, but Poldowrian illustrates the interaction that many of these so-called 'coastal' groups may have had in exploiting marine and terrestrial resources within a specific topographical location. Waddington and Pedersen (200, 2) emphasise that we must now look beyond lithic industries if we are to compare settlement patterns and push forward our interpretations of social organisation.

The following case studies of Birdcombe and Hawkcombe Head in Somerset, show that they are sites that are set back from, but within striking distance of a coastline, but are situated within a diverse range of resources: Birdcombe with access to the coast, immediate wetland resources and nearby hunting; Hawkcombe Head at the point on

FIG. 2.3 BIRDCOMBE VALLEY SHOWING THE POSITION OF THE MESOLIHTIC SITE AT X; THE WOODLAND OF THE FAILAND RIDGE AND THE VALLEY BOTTOM BELOW THE WHIRLY POOL (PHOTO: AUTHOR 2007)

the moorland, where two springheads have cut natural routeways to the coast (Gardiner, 2001; 2007a 24; 2007b; 2009).

Birdcombe, Somerset

Birdcombe (fig. 2.3) lies at the foot of a south facing slope which forms part of the Failand Ridge and adjacent valley, 8km south of Bristol. Behind the site is woodland on the limestone ridge and below this is a line of springs that follow the valley bottom from Tickenham Hill to Belmont Hill, with two springs immediately adjacent to the site (Gardiner 2001; 2007a,24).

Excavations in the 1950s (Sykes and Whittle 1960) and more recently in 1997 (Gardiner 2000; 2001; 2007a, 24) have established the Mesolithic nature of the site. The flint collections from both excavations contained approximately 750 retouched pieces and includes microliths and microburins (fig. 2.4). The tool typology and radiocarbon dates, have established Birdcombe as spanning both the early and the later Mesolithic periods, before it was abandoned abruptly at the end of the late Mesolithic (Gardiner, 2001; 2007a,29).

Environmental coring from the site can reconstruct the local environment and this shows the presence of oak and hazel on a steep valley slope, leading to a deep, wet

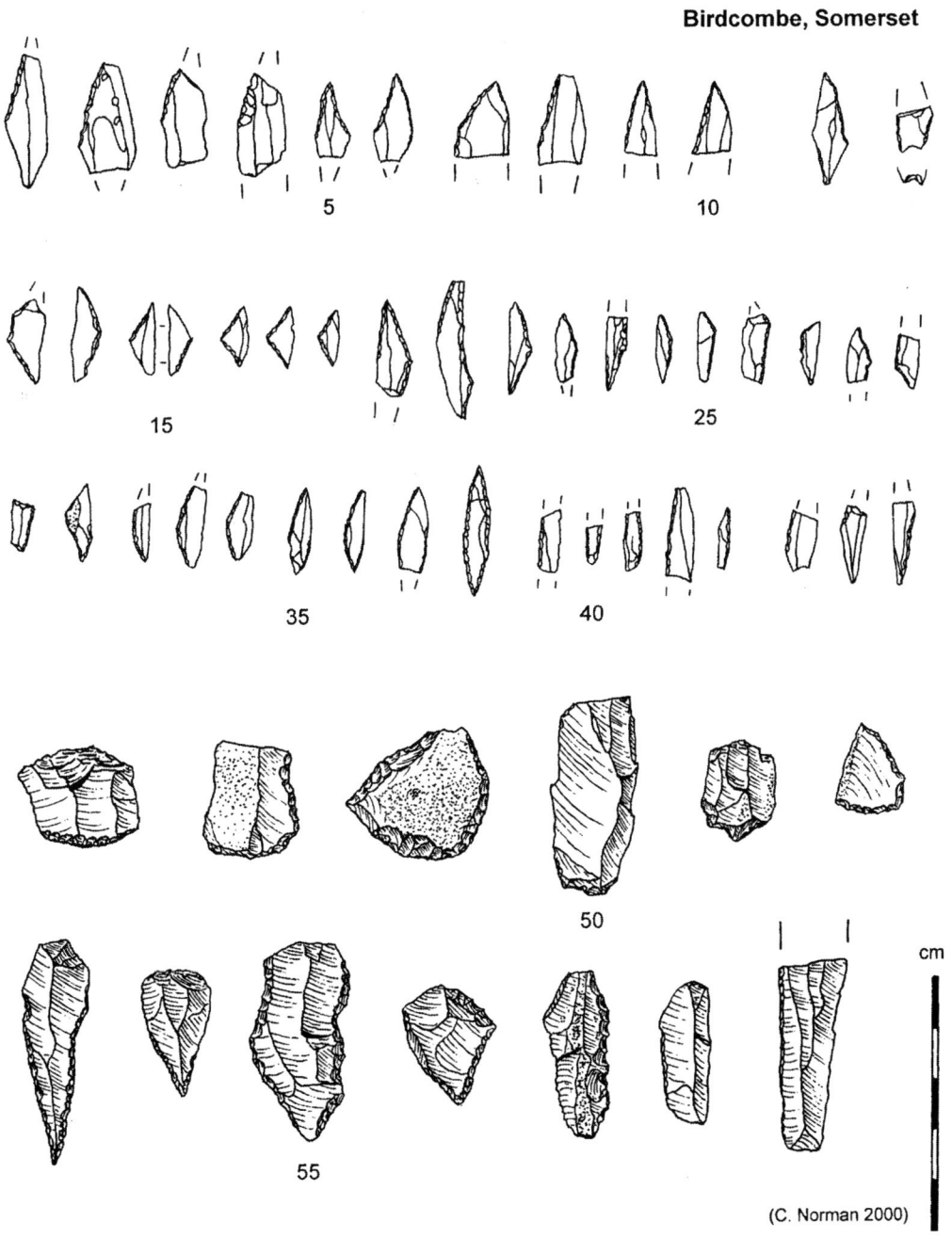

FIG. 2.4 MICROLITHS FROM THE 1997 BIRDCOMBE EXCAVATIONS: EARLY MESOLITHIC 1-11; HORSHAM BASE 12; LATER MESOLITHIC 13-46; LARGER PIECES 47-59 (GARDINER 2001; 2007A; 2009).

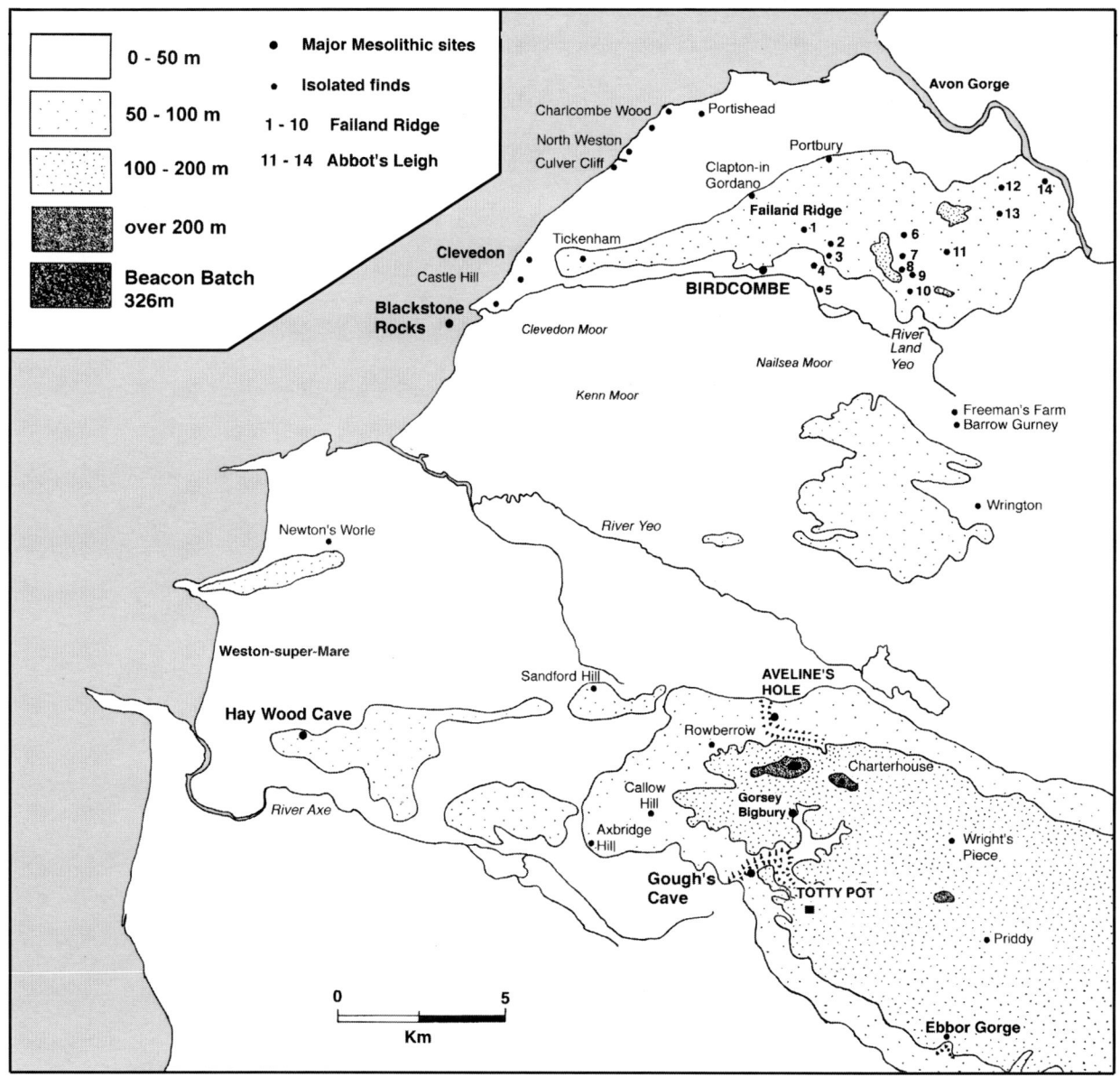

FIG. 2.5 MESOLITHIC FINDSPOTS ON THE FAIL RIDGE AND MENDIP HILLS (GARDINER 2001; 2007A; 2008).

valley bottom (Gardiner 2001, 104). Although the high proportion of microliths to other retouched pieces suggests that there were repeated, relatively brief phases of activity at Birdcombe, the topographical location and availability of resources could suggest otherwise.

The Birdcombe valley runs west-east in a south-facing sheltered position as far as Clevedon the west. Studies at Kenn Moor, 4.8Km to the south west and the Gordano Valley, 3Km to the north west, suggest that between the Atlantic and Sub-Boreal periods the area was much wetter with fluctuations between saltmarsh and fresh-water conditions (Jefferies *et al.* 1968; Butler 1987; Gilbertson *et al.* 1990). This environment would produce an abundance of wetland resources in the area and this may have been one of the attractions of the site in the Mesolithic. To the west at Blackstone Rocks, Clevedon, now only accessible at low tide (Sykes, 1938) and at Clevedon and Portishead, Mesolithic flint has been recovered. There may be further evidence for the Mesolithic on this coastline, but it may now be permanently submerged.

Hunter-gatherers at Birdcombe are in the prime position of having a link with these coastal sites, but also of having access immediately around Birdcombe to wetland resources created by the springs and saltmarsh conditions. Hunting could take place on the limestone ridge immediately behind the site, or less than a day's walk up on to the Mendip Hills (fig. 2.5). This would be an easily accessible hunting round from Birdcombe, offering a further range of resources (Gardiner, 2001; 2007a, 32). The Birdcombe site, therefore, is located in a pivotal position within the landscape, for access to a diversity of resources. This suggests that the site could have been occupied on a much more permanent basis (Gardiner, 2001; 2007a, 32) which outweighs the earlier suggestion that the high proportion of microliths suggests short, frequent visits (Gardiner 2001).

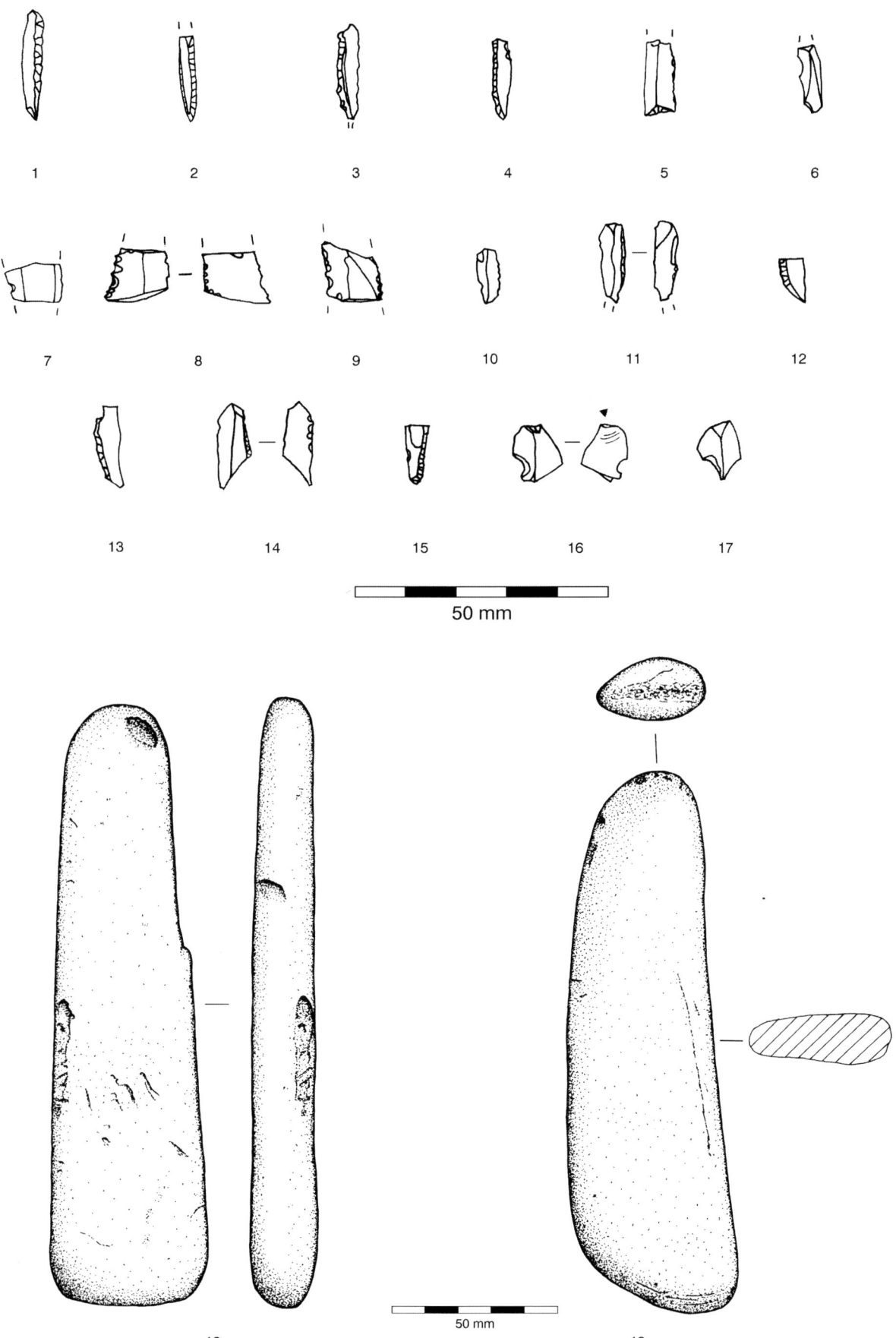

Fig. 2.6 Hawkcombe Head flint: elongated scalenes 1-3; backed bladelets 4-6; blade with notch 7; snapped blade end 8; trapedoid 9; microliths 10, 11; convex backed 12, 13; triangles 14, 15; pebble tools 18, 19 (A.George 2010)

Hawkcombe Head, Exmoor, Somerset

Hawkcombe Head is located at a high point of the moorland above Porlock Bay at 415mOD. There is a submerged forest, visible at low tide at Porlock Weir 3Km away. Palaeoenvironmental evidence indicates that the present pebble beach was woodland in the Mesolithic (Riley and Wilson-North 2001;) and flint has been recovered from clay deposits under the remains of the forest in 1890 (Wymer 1977, 248) and more recently by staff at Exmoor National Park (R. Wilson-North pers. comm.). The site has been known as a late Mesolithic site for over fifty years due to the number of flint finds (now in their thousands, fig 2.6) that have been indiscriminately collected from the ground surface around the Hawkcombe Head springhead (Wymer 1977). These finds contain hundreds of microliths from the later Mesolithic period, together with flint debitage. This together with flint recovered from recent fieldwork and excavation puts the number in excess of around 10,000 pieces. Fieldwork, continuing excavation and radiocarbon dates (Gardiner, 2007a; 2007b; 2009) has revealed detailed activity by late Mesolithic hunter-gatherers and established Hawkcombe Head as the earliest occupation site within Exmoor National Park (Gardiner 2007a; 2007b; 2009, 491).

The flint collection contains hundreds of microliths that are dominated by elonged scalene triangles and backed bladelets, with an overall presence of micro-cores and miroburins. Fifteen pebble tools, similar to those at

FIG. 2.7 SECTION THROUGH CLAY FLOOR.

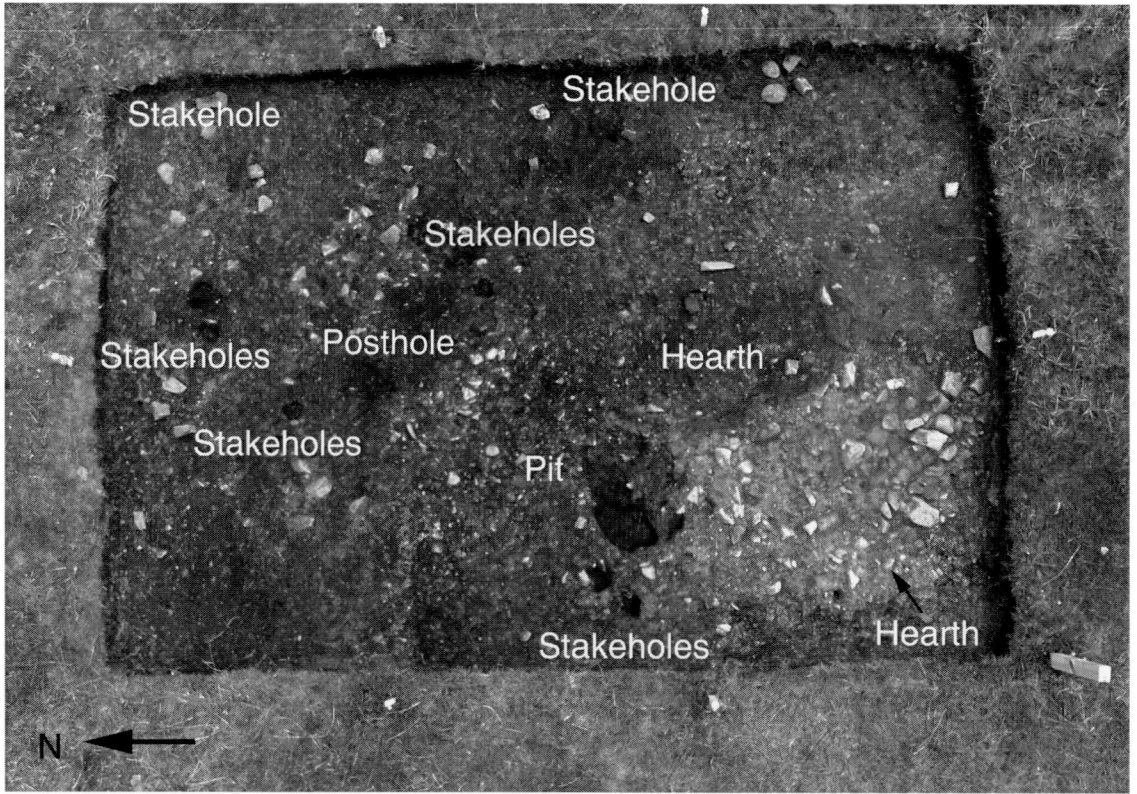

FIG. 2.8 PHOTOGRAPH OF FEATURES IN TRENCH 11 FROM 2010 EXCAVATION (PHOTO: A. HAWKINS 2010)

Poldowrian (Smith and Harris, 1982) have been recovered, some of which show wear marks or polishing, together with a small collection of hammer stones. A clay floor with postholes (fig. 2.7) together with a hearth in the Ven Combe area has been dated to 6390-62120 cal.BC (SUERC-2970 9GU-11979 7420 ± 25BP, Gardiner 2007a) and numerous features from the 2008-10 excavations have shown lines of postholes and stakeholes cut into the old ground surface, together with further hearths and shallow pits (fig 2.8). Hawkcombe Head's diversity of features show a range of activities, that are not necessarily restricted solely to hunting (Gardiner, 2009, 492).

Hawkcombe Head and its Landscape Context

The spring from Hawkcombe Head cuts a natural routeway from the moorland down to Porlock Beach, giving easy access to hunter-gatherers exploiting both the foreshore, the now submerged woodland and the moorland. The spring at Ven Combe cuts another routeway to Lynton, which would give hunter-gatherers two natural routeways that lead from the lower coastal zone up on to the high moorland for hunting. The raw material on site is predominantly beach pebble, that may have been derived in the Mesolithic from Porlock Beach, although there is little evidence of it today (Gardiner 2009, 492), or from further afield at Baggy Point, Croyde further down the coast.

Hawkcombe Head is located in a significant position within the landscape where two combes have created a natural routeway up on to the moor, that could easily be found within a wooded landscape (fig. 2.9). The moorland, the woodland and its adjoining coastal strip should be considered as a rich ecotone for hunter-gatherers who were able to exploit a variety of resources within a few square kilometres of Hawkcombe Head and possibly even further across the estuary to Ogmore-by-Sea, Vale of Glamorgan.

Ogmore-by-Sea is a coastal site today, that is 30Km across the estuary from Porlock Weir. It was excavated by Stephen Aldhouse-Green and colleagues (fig. 2.10) in the late 19990s when hundreds of flint tools from the late Mesolithic were recovered from sandy contexts on the beach. The raw material is beach pebble that was knapped on site. The site is unpublished, but there are a few pieces from the John Tucker private collection held by the author (fig. 2.11), that suggest that it was the same group of hunter-gatherers that were crossing between Hawkcombe Head and Ogmore-by-Sea, who were possibly sharing a raw material source and flint tool tradition (Gardiner 2011 *in preparation*).

The coastline in the Early Holocene would have been much further out into the Estuary in the Mesolithic (Allen *et al.* 1997, 108) with narrow, well-vegetated saltmarshes (Haslett *et al.* 2000, 49). The intertidal zone was probably

FIG. 2.9 AERIAL PHOTOGRAPH OF THE AREAS EXCAVATED AT HAWKCOMBE HEAD (REPRODUCED BY PERMISSION OF ENGLISH HERITAGE NMR 21521/32 2003).

Fig. 2.10 Photograph of the Ogmore-by-Sea Mesolithic site excavation
(Photo: Author 1999)

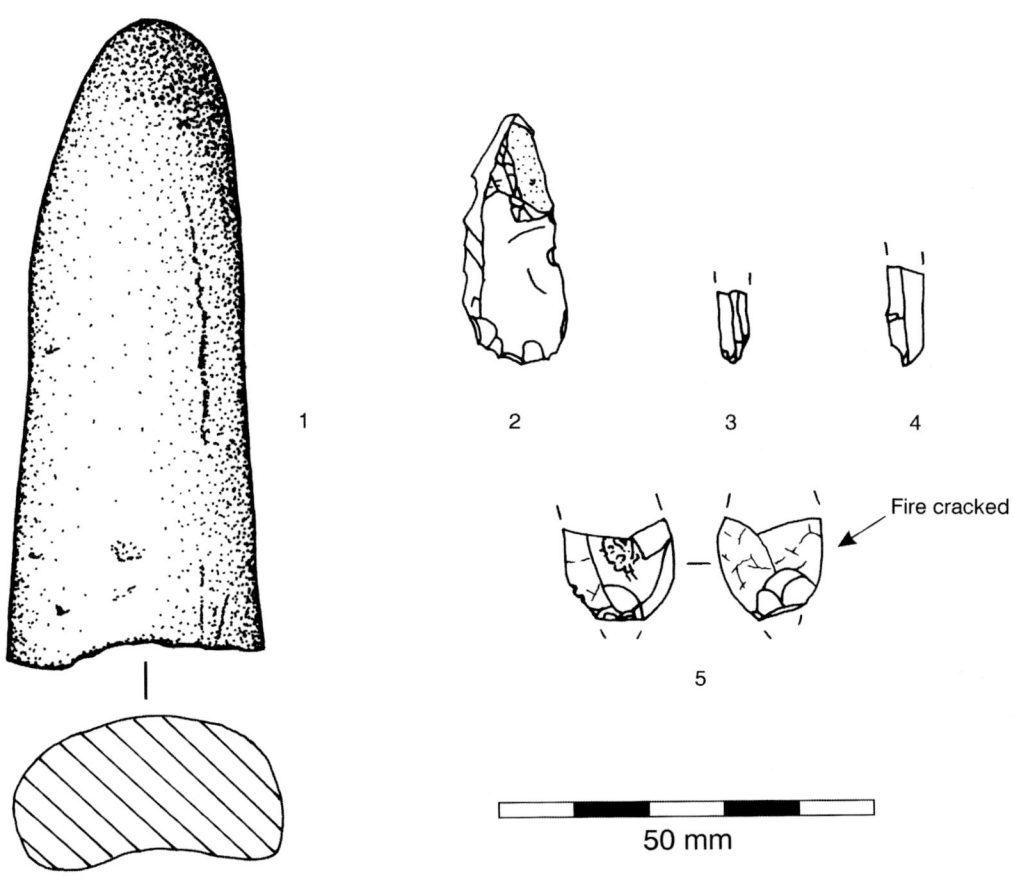

Fig. 2.11 Drawing of Ogmore flint and broken pebble tool from the unprovenanced surface collection of John Tucker (A. George 2010)

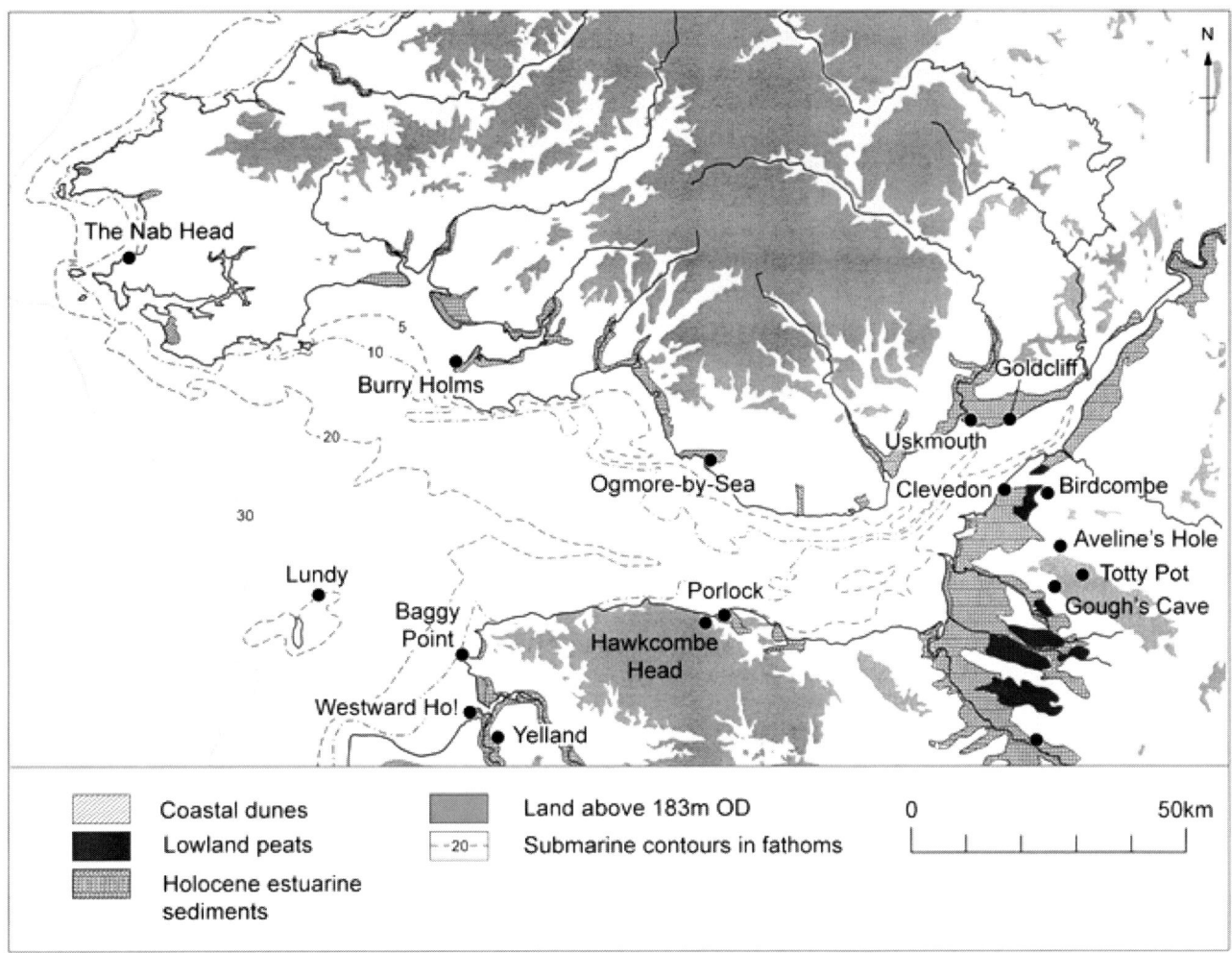

Fig. 2.12 Map of Severn Estuary showing position of Hawkcombe Head and Ogmore-by-Sea adapted from an original drawing by S. Allen (Bell 2007, 9).

a dangerous mudflat as it is today, but the major tidal creeks would have enabled access by boat for fishing (Haslett *et al.* 2000, 49). These saltmarsh and mudflat environments would have been available to hunter-gatherers in the Mesolithic, but the rapid rise in sea level between 10,000 and 7,000 cal. BP at a rate of 5-6mm per year (Haslett *et al.* 2000, 44) would have meant diminishing access to certain resources in the Estuary (fig 2.12).

From around the middle to the later Mesolithic, there was a slowing down of relative sea-level rise and the high marsh areas of the earlier Mesolithic would have expanded seawards creating a very distinctive landscape (Haslett *et al.* 2000, 49) that was attractive to deer and other animals, as can be seen in both the fossil animal and human footprints on the Welsh side of the Estuary (Aldhouse-Green *et al.* 1992; Bell and Neumann 1997, 24) The presence of continued woodland up to the land-sea interface offers an ecotone with a wide range of resources for hunter-gatherers on both sides of the Estuary and Bristol Channel, particularly if the intervening stretch of water was navigable by dug-out or raft. Permanent settlement in the immediate intertidal zone may have been unlikely due to frequent flooding, but by having a connection with a more permanent site further inland, for example Hawkcombe Head, would have afforded hunter-gatherers a variety of more stable resources.

Mesolithic sites often characterised as 'coastal' may in fact have had access to a broader range of resources than previously thought and hunter-gatherers, may not have needed to be constantly on the move. From a topographical perspective, the area of Ogmore-by-Sea is visible from the cliffs above Porlock Beach on a clear day, but perhaps as importantly, it is the high moorland above Porlock Weir that would be the highest point on the horizon from the Welsh side, that may have enticed hunter-gathers over the water for hunting.

Bell's map of the estuary that models the submarine contours between 9,500-4000 cal.BC (Bell, 2007, 9) suggests to the author that there is a likelihood that hunter-gatherer groups could cross the estuary in the later Mesolithic if they had sufficient knowledge and good watercraft. The similarities in raw material and tool typology suggests that there might have been a link between groups at Hawkcombe Head and Ogmore-by-Sea (Gardiner 2011 *in prep*).

Discussion

The territories of sites that were previously thought of as being purely coastal and transient with a limited range of marine resources, should not necessarily be restricted to the intertidal zone. Hunter-gatherers appear to have a much wider range of landscapes available to them if they are moving between the coast at Blackstone Rocks/Clevedon towards Birdcome and up on to the Mendip Hills for hunting and burial (Gardiner 2000). With Birdcombe being situated in a pivotal position and having access to both marine and terrestrial resources, this strengthens the possibility that the site might have been occupied on a more permanent basis that previously thought (Fig. 6).

Similarly, the annual round of Ogmore-by-Sea could be even wider if there is the possibility of crossing the Severn Estuary, to a resource-rich area on the other side of the channel, that offered both marine and hunting resources. Although we use the term 'coastal' site, in reality the landscapes available would have been much more extensive, particularly if an erratic sea level rise at certain stages forced hunter-gatherers to forage for their resources in different environments. This model from the Severn Estuary could be applied elsewhere in the south west peninsula and sites like Poldowrian and those on the North Cornish coast warrant further fieldwork to widen interpretations of the activities that might have been carried out there. Some occupation sites could perhaps be regarded as having a much more permanent foothold, but within a wide and diverse landscape that does not necessarily lock hunter-gatherers into a limited seasonal round. We will, however, only be able to advance models like these for south west England, if further fieldwork and excavation is undertaken on a large scale.

Bibliography

Aldhouse-Green, S.H.R., Whittle, A., Allen, J.R.L.., Caseldine, A.E., Culver, S.J., Day, M. H., Lundqvist, J. and Upton, D., 1992, 'Prehistoric human footprints from the Severn Estuary at Uskmouth and Major Pill, Gwent, Wales, *Archaeologia Cambrensis,* CXLI, 14-55.

Allen, J.R.L., Bradley, R.J., Fulford, M.G., Mithen, S.J., Rippon, S.J. and Tyson, H.J. in M. Fulford, T. Champion and A. Long (eds), 1997, *England's Coastal Heritage. A survey for English Heritage and the RCHME.* Archaeological Report 15. RCHME and English Heritage.

Andersen, S.H. 1987, 'Tybrind Vig: A Submerged Ertebolle Settlement in Denmark', in J.M Coles and A.J. Lawson (eds.) *European Wetlands in Prehistory.* Oxford: Clarendon Press.

Balaam, N.D., Bell, M. David, A., Levitan, B., Macphail, R.I. Robinson, M.A. and Scaife, R.G., 1987, 'Prehistoric and Romano-British sites at Westward Ho! Devon: Archaeological and palaeoenvironmental surveys 1983 and 1984, in N.D. Balaam, B. Levitan and V. Straker (eds) *Studies in palaeoeconomy and environment in South West England.* Oxford: British Archaeological Reports, BS 181, Oxford, 163-264.

Balaam, N.D., Levitan, B. and Straker, V (eds) 1987. *Studies in palaeoeconomy and environment in South West England.* Oxford: British Archaeological Reports, BS 181, Oxford.

Bell, M. 2007. *Prehistoric Coastal Communities: The Mesolithic in western Britain.* CBA Research Report 149. Council for British Archaeology.

Bell, M. and Neumann, H., 1997, ' Intertidal Survey in the Welsh Severn Estuary 1997', *Archaeology in the Severn Estuary,* Vol. 8, 13-18.

Bell, M. and Walker, M.J.C. 1992. *Late Quaternary Environmental Change: Physical and Human Perspectives (1st edition).* Harlow: Longman.

Binford, L. 1983, *Working at Archaeology.* New York: Academic Press.

Bonsall, C., Sutherland, D. Tipping, R. and Cherry, J., 1990. 'The Eskmeals Project: Late Mesolithic settlement and environment in North-West England, in C. Bonsall (ed) *The Mesolithic in Europe.* Edinburgh: John Donald Publishers Ltd., 175-205.

Butler, S., 1987. 'Coastal Change since 6000 BP and the Presence of Man at Kenn Moor, Avon', *Proceedings of the Somerset and Natural History Society,* 131. 1-11.

Coles, B. 1998. 'Doggerland: a Speculative Survey', *Proceedings of the Prehistoric Society,* 64, 45-81.

Clark, J.G.D., 1934, 'The Classification of a Microlithic Culture: The Tardenoisian of Horsham', *Archaeological Journal,* Vol. XC, 52-75.

Clark, J.G.D., 1954. *Excavations at Star Carr,* Cambridge: Cambridge University Press.

Clarke, D., 1976. 'Mesolithic Europe: the economic basis', in G. de Sieveking, I.H. Longworth And K.E. Wilson (eds) *Problems in Economic and Social Archaeology.* London: Duckworth, 449-81.

Dumont, J.V. 1989. 'Star Carr: the Results of a Micro-Wear Study', in C. Bonsall (ed) *The Mesolithic in Europe.* Edinburgh: John Donald Publishers Ltd., 231-240.

Fischer, A., 1989. 'Hunting with Flint-Tipped Arrows: Results and Experiences from Practical Experiments', in C. Bonsall (ed) *The Mesolithic in Europe. Papers presented at the Third International Symposium, Edinburgh 1985.* Edinburgh: John Donald Publishers Ltd., 29-39.

Fischer, A. (ed) 1995. *Man and Sea in the Mesolithic: coastal settlement above and below present sea level : proceedings of the international symposium, Kalundborg, Denmark 1993.* Oxford: Oxvow Monograph, 53.

Gardiner, P.J. 2000. "Excavations at Birdcombe, Somerset: Mesolithic Settlement, Subsistence and Landscape Use in the South West of England", in R. Young (ed) *Mesolithic Lifeways. Current Research from Britain and Ireland.* Leicester Archaeology Monographs No.7, University of Leicester, 119-207.

Gardiner, P.J. 2001. *The Mesolithic-Neolithic Transition in South West England.* Unpublished PhD Thesis, University of Bristol.

Gardiner, P. 2007a, 'Chasing the Tails of Hunter-gatherers in South West England', in M. Costen (ed) *People and Places: Essays in Honour of Michael Aston.* Oxford: Oxbow Books, 23-52.

Gardiner, P. 2007b. Mesolithic Activity at Hawkcombe Head, Somerset. Interim Report of Excavations 2002-3, in C. Waddington and K. Pedersen (eds) *Mesolithic Studies in the North Sea Basin and Beyond.* Proceedings of a Conference held at Newcastle in 2003. Oxford: Oxbow, 81-95.

Gardiner, P.J. 2009. 'South Western Regional Identities: Birdcombe, Totty Pot and Hawkcombe Head', in McCartan, S., Schulting, R., Warren, G., and Woodman, P. (eds). *Mesolithic Horizons: Papers presented at the Seventh International Conference on the Mesolithic in Europe, Belfast 2005.* Oxford: Oxbow Books, 485-493.

Gooder, J. 2007, 'Excavation of a Mesolithic House at East Barns, East Lothian, Scotland: an interim view' in C. Waddington and K. Pedersen (eds) *Mesolithic Studies in the North Sea Basin and Beyond. Proceedings of a conference held at Newcastle in 2003.* Oxford: Oxbow Books, 49-59.

Gilbertson, D.D., Hawkins, A.B., Mills, C.M., Harkness, D.D. and Hunt, C.O. 1990. 'The Late Devensian and Holocene of Industrial Severnside and the Vale of Gordano: stratigraphy, radiocarbon dating and palaeoecology', *Proceedings of the Usher Society,* 7, 279-284.

Grinsell, L.V., 1970, *The Archaeology of Exmoor.* Newton Abbot: David & Charles.

Haslett, S.K., Davies, P., Davies, C.F.C., Margetts, A.J., Scotnet, K.H., Thorpe, D.J. and Williams, H.O., 2000, 'The Changing Estuarine Environment in Relation to Holocene Sea-Level and the Archaeological Implications', in S.J. Rippon (ed), *Estuarine Archaeology: The Severn and Beyond. Archaeology in the Severn Estuary 11 (for 2000) Annual Report of the Severn Estuary Levels Research Committee.*

Jacobi, R.M. 1976. 'Britain Inside and Outside Mesolithic Europe', *Proceedings of the Prehistoric Society,* 42, 67-84.

Jacobi, R.M. 1979. 'Early Flandrian Hunters in the South West', *Devon Archaeological Society,* 37, 48-93.

Jacobi, R.M. and Tebbutt, C.F., 1981. 'A Late Mesolithic Rock-Shelter Site at High Hurstwood, Sussex', *Sussex Archaeological Collections,* 119, 1-36.

Jarman, M.R. 1972. 'European Deer Economies and the Advent of the Neolithic', in Higgs, E.S. (ed) *Papers in Economic Prehistory.* Cambridge: Cambridge University Press, 125-147.

Jefferies, R.L., Willis, A.J. and Yemm, E.W., 1968. 'The Late and Post-Glacial History of the Gordano Valley, North Somerset;'. *New Phytologist,* 67, 335-348.

Jochim, M.A. 1976. *Hunter-Gatherer Subsistence and Settlement. A Predictive Model.* London: Academic Press.

Larsson, L., 1989. 'Late Mesolithic Settlements and Cemeteries at Skateholm, Southern Sweden', in C. Bonsall (ed) *The Mesolithic in Europe. Papers presented at the Third International Symposium, Edinburgh 1985.* Edinburgh: John Donald Publishers Ltd., 367-378.

Mellars, P., 1976. 'Settlement patterns and industrial variability in the British Mesolithic', in G. de Sieveking, I.H. Longworth And K.E. Wilson (eds) *Problems in Economic and Social Archaeology.* London: Duckworth, 375-399.

Mellars, P. and Dark, P., 1998. *Star Carr in Context.* McDonald Institute for Archaeological Research, University of Cambridge.

Mithen, S. 1999. 'Hunter-Gatherers of the Mesolithic', in J. Hunter and I. Ralston (eds) *The Archaeology of Britain. An introduction from the Upper Palaeolithic to the Industrial Revolution.* London & New York: Routledge, 35-57.

Riley, H. and Wilson-North, R., 2001. *The Field Archaeology of Exmoor.* Swindon: English Heritage.

Rozoy, J.G. 1989. 'The Revolution of the Bowmen in Europe', in C. Bonsall (ed) *The Mesolithic in Europe. Papers presented at the Third International Symposium, Edinburgh 1985.* Edinburgh: John Donald Publishers Ltd., 13-28.

Smith, G. and Harris, D., 1982. 'The Excavation of Mesolithic, Neolithic and Bronze Age Settlements at Poldowrian, St. Deverne, 1980', *Cornish Archaeology,* No.21, 23-60.

Sykes, C.M. 1938. 'Some Flint Implements from the Blackstone Rocks, Clevedon', *Proceedings of the University of Bristol Spelaeological Society,* No.1, Vol 5, 75-79.

Sykes, C.M. and Whittle, S.L. 1960. 'The Birdcombe Mesolithic Site, Wraxall', *Proceedings of the Somerset Archaeological and Natural History Society,* 104, 106-122.

Waddington, C., 2007. 'Rethinking Mesolithic Settlement and a Case Study from Howick' in C. Waddington and K. Pedersen (eds) *Mesolithic Studies in the North Sea Basin and Beyond. Proceedings of a conference held at Newcastle in 2003.* Oxford: Oxbow Books, 101-113.

Waddington, C. and Pedersen, K. 2007 (eds) *Mesolithic Studies in the North Sea Basin and Beyond. Proceedings of a conference held at Newcastle in 2003.* Oxford: Oxbow Books.

Wickham-Jones, C.R. 1990. *Rhum: Mesolithic and Later Sites at Kinlock. Excavations 1984-86.* Society of Antiquaries of Scotland Monograph Series No.7.

Woodman, P.C., 1985. *Excavations at Mount Sandel 1973-77.* Northern Ireland Archaeological Monographs: No.2. Belfast: Her Majesty's Stationery Office.

Wymer, J.J. (ed) 1977. *Gazetteer of Mesolithic Sites in England and Wales*. CBA Research Report No.22. London: Council for British Archaeology.

Zvelebil, M., 1994, 'Plant Use in the Mesolithic and the Implications for the Transition to Farming', *Proceedings of the Prehistoric Society,* 60: 95-134.

Zvelebil, M., 1995. 'Hunting, Gathering, or Husbandry? Management of Food Resources by the Late Mesolithic Communities of Temperate Europe', *MASCA RESEARCH Papers in Science and Archaeology* Vol. 12 Supplement (1995): 79-104.

Acknowledgements

I would like to thank the following people: Sue Grice and Anne Leaver (University of Bristol) for their time and skill on the illustrations; Abby George for her drawings of the Hawkcombe Head and Ogmore-by-Sea flint; Martin Bell for permission to adapt his submarine contours map (fig.1.12) which was from an original drawing by S. Allen; Mark Blathwayt and Porlock Manor Estate for permission to carry out fieldwork and excavation at Hawkcombe Head; Rob Wilson-North and Exmoor National Park for funding radiocarbon dates and supporting the Hawkcombe Head excavations; John Tucker for the Ogmore-by-Sea flint from his private collection; English Heritage for permission to use the air photograph of Porlock; Nick Saunders for his helpful comments on the text. The views expressed in this paper are entirely the author's.

The Early Neolithic of south-west England: new insights and new questions

Alison Sheridan

Abstract

This contribution reviews the current models for the Neolithisation of south-west England in the light of recent advances in our knowledge, and explains why the version featuring one or more small-scale episodes of colonisation from Normandy (and perhaps also northern Brittany) around the 39th century BC seems to offer the best fit for the data. Subsequent developments during the first half of the fourth millennium BC are reviewed, and some outstanding research questions are set out.

Introduction

The aim of this contribution is to draw attention to some recent and current research that is helping to shed new light on a fascinating period in the prehistory of south-west England, namely the Early Neolithic. Our understanding of this period owes much to the research work of Henrietta Quinnell, whose no-nonsense approach to the characterisation of ceramic and lithic finds has done so much to set Neolithic Peninsular studies on a firm footing, and it is a pleasure to offer some new insights and some new questions to Henrietta, along with thanks for many kindnesses.

This paper will start by sketching the current models that have been proposed to account for the Mesolithic-Neolithic transition in south-west England (and elsewhere in Britain and Ireland), and will go on to consider the nature of the earliest Neolithic in the South West, and the possibility that its appearance may relate to developments in Normandy (and perhaps also northern Armorica) around the 39th century BC. The contribution made by a recent international research project on Alpine axeheads to the question of French connections will be highlighted. Subsequent developments during the early Neolithic will then be discussed briefly, before reviewing the outstanding questions that remain to be answered about the early to mid-fourth millennium BC inhabitants of south-west England.

The Mesolithic-Neolithic transition: the Big Picture

The question of when, how and why a new way of life, principally based on the tending of domesticated animals and the raising of cereals (as opposed to the exclusive use of wild resources, as in previous millennia) became established in Britain and Ireland has been debated for well over half a century. In his influential book, *The Prehistoric Cultures of the British Isles* (1954), Stuart Piggott argued for 'the arrival at various points of the long coastline of the British Isles of smaller or larger groups of colonists from varied regions of the Atlantic and Channel coasts of western Europe' (Piggott 1954, 15). From the early 1990s this 'colonisation' model was challenged, most notably by Julian Thomas, who postulates that the prime movers for the change were not immigrant farmers, but rather the indigenous Mesolithic communities of Britain and Ireland who, he argues, must have been in contact with the Continent, where farming had been established for over a millennium before it was practised here (Thomas 1991; 1999; 2003; 2004; 2007; 2008). Thomas' model regards early farming and its associated lifestyle in Britain and Ireland as being semi-nomadic in nature, showing strong continuity from the traditional hunting, gathering and fishing way of life. It downplays the evidence for cereal cultivation, and points to the paucity of early Neolithic houses in Britain as evidence for a non-sedentary lifestyle (Thomas 1996). While popular in some quarters, this model has undergone vigorous criticism (e.g. Cooney 1997; Rowley-Conwy 2004; Schulting 2000; 2004), not least from the current author (e.g. Sheridan 2010a).

Today, in 2011, at least four competing models for the Mesolithic-Neolithic transition are being debated: in addition to Thomas' 'proactive indigenous acculturation' model (with Bonsall *et al.* 2002 adding that environmental change around 4000 BC may have been responsible for the selective adoption of farming and other Neolithic traits from the Continent), there are three versions of the 'colonisation' model. The first is that proposed by Alasdair Whittle, Frances Healy and Alex Bayliss (2011), based on their meticulous reappraisal and re-dating of the enclosures and long barrows of southern Britain (and of other early Neolithic material from Britain and Ireland). This argues for an initial arrival, from the near Continent, of immigrant farmers in south-east England – specifically Kent and the lower Thames Valley – around 4000 BC, followed by a northwards and westwards expansion from there. The

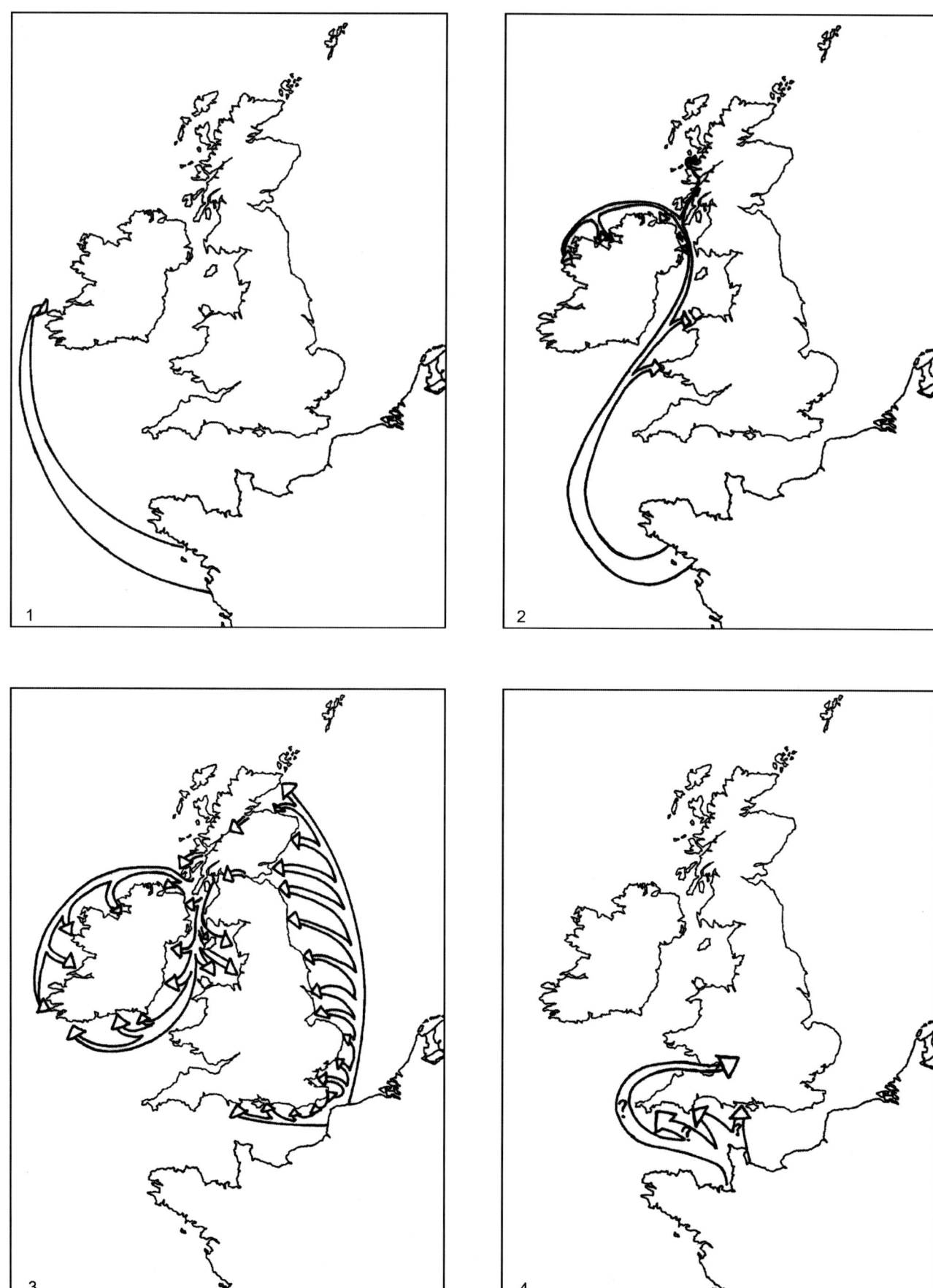

FIGURE 3.1 THE AUTHOR'S MULTI-STRAND MODEL FOR THE NEOLITHISATION OF BRITAIN AND IRELAND

second, proposed by Mark Collard and colleagues in 2010 (Collard *et al.* 2010), relies exclusively on radiocarbon dating. Using date density as a proxy for population size, this posits an initial arrival in and around Wessex during the 40th century BC, with subsequent expansion from there. The third is the current author's (e.g. Sheridan 2010a), and is based on a consideration of material culture, structures, faunal and plant material and evidence for practices and beliefs, as well as on radiocarbon dates. This proposes a multi-strand model of colonisation (Fig. 3.1), in which different, small groups of people arrived in different parts of Britain and Ireland, from different parts of northern France, at various times between c 4300 BC and the 39th century BC. The reasons for their arrival, the success (or otherwise) of their implantation of a new way of life and the response of the indigenous groups varied considerably. The earliest of these 'strands' may have involved the arrival, in south-west Ireland, of a small number of people (along with their farming supplies) from north-west France around 4300 BC, and is attested by just seven bones of domestic cattle, found at the late Mesolithic camp site at Ferriter's Cove, Co. Kerry (Woodman *et al.* 1999; Woodman and McCarthy 2003). The cattle must have been imported, since aurochsen did not exist in Ireland. The presence of these bones has been interpreted as evidence for the hunting and eating of the farmers' precious cattle by the local indigenes, and the absence of other evidence for the presence of farming communities in the area might indicate that they (and their stock) failed to reach a critical mass, sufficient to set down roots.

The second strand of Neolithisation seems to have involved northwards movement up the Atlantic façade from the Morbihan region of south-east Brittany, some time between 4300 and 4000 BC, at a time of significant social change in the Morbihan (but also as part of a longer-term, complex pattern of long-distance movements from the Morbihan: Cassen and François 2009, 535-6; Cassen *et al.* in press; Pétrequin *et al.* in press a). It is attested by the construction of Breton-style megalithic closed chambers and simple passage tombs in south-west and north-west Wales, west Scotland and various points around the northern coast of Ireland. (See also below regarding the suggestion that this phenomenon might also be attested in West Penwith.) Breton 'Middle Neolithic II' (MN II) pottery, including a decorated bowl of Late Castellic style, has been found in one such tomb in Scotland (Achnacreebeag, Argyll and Bute) and the unusual large bowl found at Carreg Samson in Wales can also be compared with Breton MN II pottery. This strand of Neolithisation took root in Scotland and Ireland, but apparently did not thrive in Wales.

The third, and even more extensive strand, probably resulted ultimately from population expansion in northern France and brought what is termed the 'Carinated Bowl Neolithic' to much of Britain and Ireland (Sheridan 2007), arriving from the far north of France (i.e. the Nord-Pas de Calais region) during the 40th and 39th centuries BC. The fourth strand, which this author has termed 'trans-Manche ouest', involved one or more episodes of small-scale cross-Channel movement from Normandy (and perhaps adjacent parts of northern Brittany) to south-west England around the 39th century BC, bringing the practice of building drystone-built closed chambers and simple passage tombs and the use of north-west French MN II pottery, *inter alia*.

With the exception of this last strand of Neolithisation, it is not proposed to describe the models more fully here, or to offer a detailed critique of the three not proposed by this author, as this has been done exhaustively in several previous publications (most recently Sheridan 2010a; Sheridan and Pailler 2011. See also Bishop *et al.* 2009, Lancaster *et al.* 2009, Monk 2000 and Rowley-Conwy 2004 for discussion of one element of the debate, that of cereal cultivation). Instead, the aim is to focus on the earliest and early Neolithic in south-west England (especially Devon and Cornwall, but occasionally straying as far east as the Cotswolds and Wiltshire), and to examine how recent and current research is helping us to clarify its nature and to pose new questions. This contribution does not purport to offer a comprehensive discussion of the late Mesolithic and early Neolithic periods in the South West – others are better placed to comment on late Mesolithic evidence (e.g. Barton and Roberts 2004; cf. Mercer 2003), while the staff of the Cornwall and Devon Historic Environment Services maintain the most up-to-date perspective on the Neolithic (e.g. Jones and Reed 2006) – but instead to highlight several interesting developments and useful lines of enquiry.

The nature of the earliest Neolithic in the south-west

Until recently, it was long assumed that the earliest Neolithic in south-west England is that represented by enclosures such as Hembury (Liddell 1935) and Raddon Hill (Gent and Quinnell 1999) in Devon, Carn Brea (Mercer 1981) and Helman Tor (Mercer 1997; 2003) in Cornwall, and Maiden Castle (Sharples 1991) and Windmill Hill (Whittle *et* al. 1999) in Dorset and Wiltshire respectively; by funerary practices featuring non-megalithic and megalithic long barrows (including Severn-Cotswold tombs), mostly located east of Devon, and portal tombs in Cornwall; and by the use of 'Hembury ware' and 'Windmill Hill ware', or 'South-Western style' and 'Decorated style' pottery, to use the respective terminologies of Isobel Smith (1956) and Alasdair Whittle (1977). Several developments have, however, caused this view to be revised.

Firstly, and on the one hand, Whittle *et al.*'s re-evaluation of the dating of southern English long barrows (Bayliss and Whittle 2007) and enclosures (Whittle *et al.* 2011) – aided by the systematic re-dating of the Hambledon Hill causewayed enclosure (Bayliss *et al.* 2008) – has clarified their chronology, establishing that they do not appear to pre-date the 38th century BC (although see below on the Fussell's Lodge 'curated' remains). Furthermore, the radiocarbon dates obtained for South-Western style pottery from recent developer-funded excavations (e.g. at Portscatho, Cornwall: Jones and Reed 2006) are consistent with the view that 'classic' examples of this pottery tradition are unlikely to pre-date the 38th century, with the *floruit* suspected to fall between 3700 and 3500 BC (Jones and Reed 2006, fig. 6). And although the recently-obtained radiocarbon dates for Sperris and Zennor Quoits (Kytmannow 2008) date only the use, and not the construction of these portal tombs, it is likely that these monuments, with their markedly Irish Sea distribution, are also no earlier than the 38th century. (See Sheridan 2004 for a discussion of this monument type.)

Secondly, and on the other hand, there are growing indications that there had been Neolithic activity – as defined in terms of the use of domesticates and/or of the use of novel technologies and traditions, alien to the preceding indigenous lifestyle – in south-west England prior to the 38th century. Of course, the dendro-dating of the famous Sweet Track wooden trackway in the Somerset Levels to 3807/3806 BC (preceded, incidentally, by another trackway, the Post Track, built 3838 BC: Coles and Coles 1986) had already long ago demonstrated the presence of 'Neolithic' traits during the 39th century – here in the form of a magnificent Alpine jadeitite axehead (Fig. 3.7), a mint-condition axehead of mined flint, probably from Sussex, and sherds of several fine carinated bowls, all found beside the trackway. We shall return to these below. To this can be added the traces of occupation activity found underneath the lateral-chambered Cotswold-Severn long barrows at Hazleton North, Gloucestershire (Saville 1990), Ascott-under-Wychwood, Oxfordshire (Benson and Whittle 2007), Gwernvale, Powys (Britnell 1984: here a rectangular timber house seems to be involved) and in the mound of another probable example at Cow Common long barrow, Gloucestershire (Smith and Darvill 1990,

150). Having Bayesian-modelled the radiocarbon dates relating to the material from the first two sites, Whittle *et al.* (2007, 127-8 and fig. 3) concluded that the activity belongs to the 39th century, and may extend as far back as the 40th century at Ascott-under-Wychwood. Elsewhere, other pottery that cannot be regarded as 'classic' 'South-Western' or 'Decorated' style assemblages, and which definitely or probably pre-dates these traditions, has been recognised at several sites in south-west England and Wiltshire. Furthermore, as regards funerary practices, the recent dating of human remains from the small passage tomb at Broadsands, Devon (Sheridan *et al.* 2008) has concluded that that monument may have been in existence as early as the 39th century BC. Other research into early Neolithic funerary practices in the South West has been shedding new light on their diversity, and also on the diet of the individuals in question. This ceramic and funerary evidence will be reviewed briefly below.

The earliest Neolithic pottery in south-west England (and Wiltshire)

In Rosamund Cleal's review of the earliest Neolithic pottery in Wiltshire and south-west England (Cleal 2004), attention was drawn to an unusual ceramic assemblage from a large pit called the Coneybury Anomaly, Wiltshire, with forms including long-necked carinated bowls, shallow uncarinated bowls or dishes, and a closed bowl/jar with vertically-perforated lugs (Fig. 3.2; Cleal 1990; 2004). Some of the pots had been made from gabbroic clay, suggesting their importation from Cornwall. Also present in the pit were bones of domesticated cattle and of wild animals, carbonised cereal grains (probably emmer

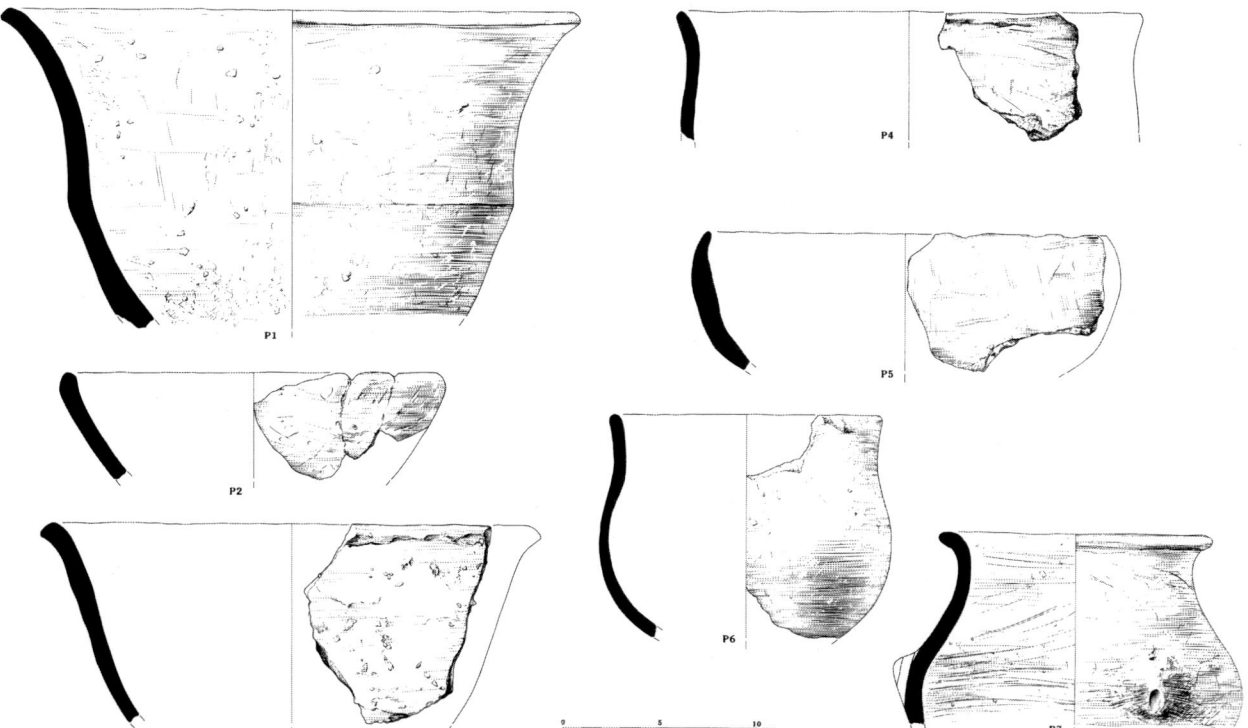

FIGURE 3.2 EARLY NEOLITHIC POTTERY FROM CONEYBURY ANOMALY, WILTSHIRE (FROM CLEAL 1990; COPYRIGHT HBMCE); ILLUSTRATION BY ROB READ

FIGURE 3.3 EARLY NEOLITHIC POTTERY FROM ROUGHRIDGE HILL, WILTSHIRE
(PHOTO COURTESY OF ALISTAIR BARCLAY)

wheat), and wild plant remains. A sample of animal bone produced a date of 5050±100 BP (OxA-1402, 3960-3715 cal BC at 1σ, 4040-3650 cal BC at 2σ; Richards 1990, 259 and table 37; Lawson 2007, 44-5). *Prima facie*, this date raises the possibility that this distinctive ceramic assemblage could date to before 3800 BC, although its large standard deviation is unhelpful. New radiocarbon dating, currently being undertaken by Alistair Barclay as part of his 'Early Pits and Pottery' project, should clarify matters (Barclay pers. comm.).

The number of other ceramic assemblages which are, or could be, of pre-38th century BC date in Wiltshire and the South West has been steadily growing. Elsewhere in Wiltshire, apparently early assemblages including those from a pit at Roughridge Hill (Fig. 3.3) and from a possible quarry at Cherhill (Evans and Smith 1983) are currently being investigated by Alistair Barclay as part of his aforementioned research project, the results of which are eagerly awaited. As he had previously noted (Barclay and Case 2007, 279), there are similarities between the pottery from Cherhill, Ascott-under-Wychwood, Hazleton North and elements of the Coneybury Anomaly assemblage. A further assemblage including sherds of plain fine carinated bowls has recently been excavated at Woodhenge, as part of the Stonehenge Riverside Project (Josh Pollard pers. comm.). In Dorset, in the weathering cone of a remarkable natural shaft, the Fir Tree Field shaft on Down Farm, was found a sherd of similarly fine, undecorated pottery, along with a domesticated cattle scapula, a hearth, a roughout stone axehead and two fragments of polished flint axeheads (Green and Allen 1997; 1998; Green 2000,

fig. 23). Material from this layer produced three dates, of which two (namely OxA-8009, 5045±45 BP and OxA-8010, 5150±45 BP) calibrate at 2σ to 3960-3715 cal BC and 4045-3800 cal BC respectively. (A third, slightly earlier date may well be from residual material: Barclay pers. comm.) Also in Dorset, excavation of a group of four pits found at Bestwall gravel quarry, within Poole harbour, yielded a small but important ceramic assemblage (Fig. 3.4). This included sherds from deep baggy vessels with solid knob-lugs, a horizontal loop lug, a necked lugged jar and a mid-depth open bowl; encrusted organic residue from one pot has produced a radiocarbon date of 4955±40 BP (GrA-28428, 3900-3650 cal BC at 2σ: Woodward 2009). However, while this assemblage differs in several respects from 'classic' South-Western style pottery, the fact that its 1σ cal BC date range falls firmly within the 38th-37th century BC date bracket suggests that it could have been in contemporary use with such pottery. Current research by Ann and Peter Woodward on other early assemblages in southern Dorset (e.g. at Pamphill: Field *et al.* 1964) promises to clarify the picture, in the same way as Alistair Barclay's work is shedding new light on the Wiltshire material.

Progressing south-westwards into Devon, the fine carinated bowls from the simple passage tomb at Broadsands (Fig. 3.5) have been discussed elsewhere (Sheridan *et al.* 2008); less well known is a collection of sherds of similar-looking fine pottery from a submerged forest nearby, found on the seabed near Victoria Park, Paignton and curated in Torquay Museum (Rick Schulting pers. comm.). These intriguing sherds, which demand closer attention, remind

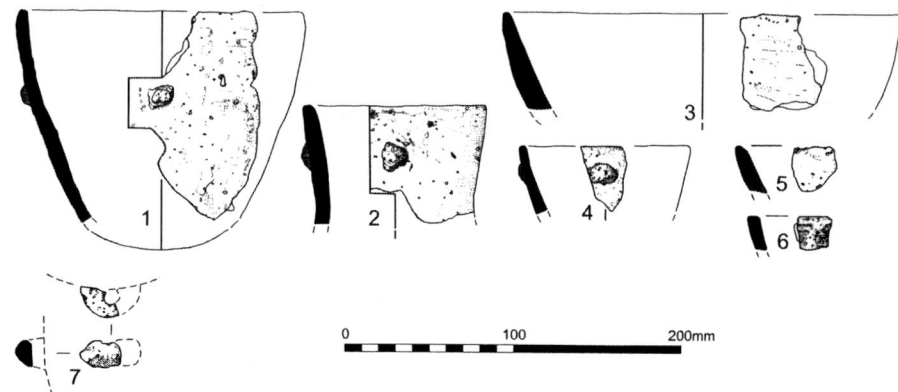

FIGURE 3.4 EARLY NEOLITHIC POTTERY FROM BESTWALL QUARRY, DORSET (FROM WOODWARD 2009; REPRODUCED BY PERMISSION OF ANN WOODWARD, LILIAN LADLE AND VAL KINSLER)

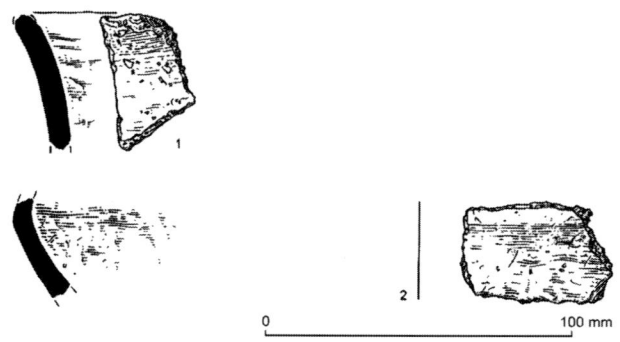

FIGURE 3.5 EARLY NEOLITHIC POTTERY FROM BROADSANDS, DEVON (FROM SHERIDAN ET AL. 2008; DRAWN BY JANE READ)

us that some of our evidence for the earliest Neolithic and late Mesolithic may well have been destroyed, or at least submerged, through rising sea levels. Other assemblages of potentially pre-38th century BC pottery in Devon have been found in recent years through developer-funded excavations. These are generally small, and while that from Nymet Barton was found sealed under the bank of an enclosure (Caseldine *et al.* 2000), the others come mostly from pits (as in the case of Waylands, Tiverton; Four Ways Cross, Willand; and the Sidmouth Donkey Sanctuary – all assemblages that Henrietta Quinnell has examined and is far better placed than the present author to discuss). One pit find, from Long Range in east Devon, produced pottery which could either be regarded as falling within the South-Western style (as argued by Laidlaw 1999, 148), or else as a precursor to this style; the number of identifiable pots in the assemblage (three) is too small to offer a detailed impression of the ceramic repertoire.

In Cornwall, while several assemblages clearly identifiable as belonging to the South-Western style have recently been found during developer-funded excavations (e.g. Tregarrick Farm, Roche: Quinnell 2003, and Portscatho: Quinnell 2006), there seems to be a dearth of pre-3800 BC material, as Henrietta Quinnell has pointed out (Quinnell 2003, 119-20). There is, however, one possible candidate site, at Penhale Round, Fraddon. Excavations here in 1993 revealed traces of two structures, one of which – a large, sub-rectangular post-built house, at least 19 m long by 7 m wide – produced markedly fine carinated bowls and AMS dates of 5001±75 BP (WK9839, 3910-3650 cal BC at 2σ, from charred wheat grains) and 4951±61 BP (WK9840, 3940-3640 cal BC at 2σ, from alder/hazel charcoal: Nowakowski pers. comm.; Jones and Reed 2006, table 7; Nowakowski and Johns forthcoming. A second, circular post-built structure nearby produced a slightly later date.) The pottery from Penhale Round differs from 'classic' South-Western style assemblages in having a high proportion of markedly fine, thin-walled pottery; it also has a relatively high proportion of carinated vessels. However, one feature shared with South-Western style pottery (e.g. at Carn Brea and Tregarrick Farm, and on the gabbroic fineware bowls from Maiden Castle, Dorset: Smith 1981; Quinnell 2003; Cleal *et al.* 1991) – and also with the late 39th century BC pottery from the Sweet Track – is its deliberate black surface treatment. According to Coles and Orme (1984, 44, on the Sweet Track pots), this black finish could have been '... a carbon-based paint applied to a vessel still hot or subsequently heated...Although further analysis and experimentation is needed, examination of ethnographic material shows that one method which could yield the same result involves coating with crushed tree bark and then smoking the pot over a slow fire for 2–3 days. The result is a shiny black coating of organic composition, which helps make the vessel waterproof'. Analysis of the material on some of the Carn Brea vessels, revealing 'charred organic matter which has partially decomposed to carbon', is consistent with this suggestion (Tite in Smith 1981, 170). It may well be that the Penhale Round assemblage, like the Sweet Track pottery, represents the forerunner of the South-Western tradition, and that the use of this distinctive surface finish had been present from the start, continuing in use over several centuries.

The affinities of this early pottery – and more specifically, its connection with north-west French Middle Neolithic II pottery – will be considered below.

The earliest Neolithic funerary practices in the south-west

The question of what constitutes the earliest Neolithic funerary practices in south-west England has been thrown into focus by three pieces of recent research. The first is the dating of human remains from the simple, mostly drystone-built passage tomb at Broadsands in Devon (Fig. 3.6), along with a study of the diet of the deceased through carbon and nitrogen isotope analysis (Sheridan *et al.* 2008). The second is a similar dating exercise, undertaken by Martin Smith and Megan Brickley on bones from drystone-built and other funerary structures in the Cotswold-Severn region (Smith and Brickley 2006; cf. Smith and Brickley 2009); this complements Tim Darvill's long-standing research into the drystone-built Neolithic round mounds ('*rotundae*') of this region (most recently published as Darvill 2010), and also complements Whittle *et al.*'s aforementioned dating work on southern English long barrows. The third is Rick Schulting's dating and isotopic analysis of individuals buried in caves in Devon (Sheridan *et al.* 2008), which forms part of his broader research on the use of caves for burial (e.g. Schulting

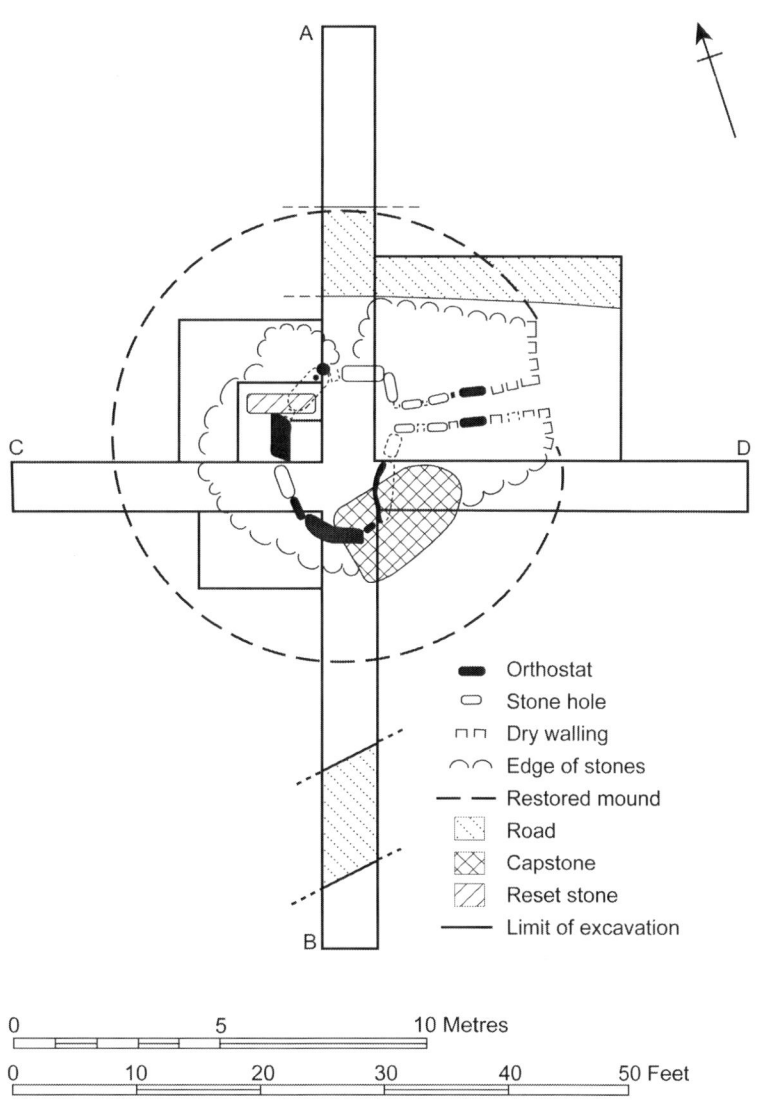

FIGURE 3.6 PLAN OF SIMPLE PASSAGE TOMB AT BROADSANDS, DEVON. FROM SHERIDAN *ET AL.* 2008; DRAWN BY FLOSS WILKINS

2007). Since all of these have been fully published, only the key findings and issues will be discussed here.

The recent dating of individuals within the simple, mostly drystone-built passage tomb at Broadsands indicates that this monument may have been in existence as early as the 39th century BC: Bayesian modelling has produced an estimated date range for the earliest dated depositions of *3845–3726 cal BC at 68% probability*, and of *4121–3712 cal BC at 95% probability* (Sheridan *et al.* 2008, 15). There is no reason to suspect that the bones from the two or three individuals that were dated to this initial use of the tomb had been brought in from elsewhere, following a period of curation, and so it would therefore appear that the Broadsands passage tomb is the earliest funerary monument in the south-west Peninsula (although see below regarding claims for three quoits in West Penwith, Cornwall). Furthermore, carbon and nitrogen isotope analysis of the bones has shown that the individuals' diet was predominantly, or totally, terrestrial in nature despite the tomb's proximity to the sea (Sheridan *et al.* 2008, 10-12). The dating of the superficially-similar *rotundae* in the Cotswolds has been more problematic, since in the case of Notgrove, where the closed chamber had subsequently been incorporated within a Severn-Cotswold chamber tomb, the very earliest bone (inside the closed chamber) was too weathered to provide a radiocarbon date, while other bone found in that chamber and on top of the circular cairn – which produced a date comparable to that of bones in the Severn-Cotswold monument – could easily have been placed there when the monument was converted into a Severn-Cotswold chamber tomb around the 37th century BC (Smith and Brickley 2006, 343-5). While the dates obtained for the Sale's Lot *rotunda* suggest that it might not have been in use before the 37th century (Smith and Brickley 2006, 345-8), nevertheless Darvill has rightly commented that 'the overall chronology of these monuments is weak' (Darvill 2010, 136) and one cannot rule out the possibility that at least some of the Cotswold *rotundae* were built as early as Broadsands, and belong to the same architectural tradition. (It should be noted in passing that Bayliss *et al.*'s contention (2007, 43) that *rotundae* 'may not be particularly early. Rather than starting as free-standing, earlier, constructions in their own right, rotundae could be seen as a formalization in stone of the concentrated middens found at Ascott-under-Wychwood and Hazleton…' is wholly unconvincing, at least to this author.)

As regards the question of how Broadsands and the *rotundae* compare chronologically with the architecturally-different, free-standing rectangular timber 'linear zone' mortuary structures in southern England as studied and dated by Whittle *et al.* (Bayliss and Whittle 2007; cf. Kinnes 1992), this partly depends on which Bayesian model one chooses to accept. While the dating of the mortuary structure and its oval mound at Wayland's Smithy I to the early 36th century seems to be well established (Whittle *et al.* 2007, 128), the evidence from Fussell's Lodge is more open to debate. Whittle *et al.* preferred to regard the bones in the mortuary structure as representing curated ancestral relics, and hence to date the construction of the mortuary structure to *3755-3660 cal BC (95% probability;* here, as previously, the use of italics indicates that these dates are Bayesian-modelled), while an alternative model, not predicated on the curation of remains, had produced an earlier date of its construction at *3840-3710 cal BC (95% probability*; Wysocki *et al.* 2007, 76-7*)*. Thus, under one reading of the evidence, it may be that the Fussell's Lodge mortuary structure could have been built around the same time as the Broadsands passage tomb, while under another reading, it may have post-dated it. Either way, the main point to make is that *two* monumental funerary traditions were in use in southern and south-west England during the early fourth millennium BC, with the 'linear zone mortuary structure' tradition apparently not represented in the Peninsular south-west. (That said, we shall never know whether such a structure ever existed beneath a long barrow at Long Burrow near Tiverton, Devon, since the monument was destroyed around 20 years ago: Smith 1990 and Griffith pers. comm..)

As for the third piece of new research referred to above, Rick Schulting's study of human remains found in south Devon caves has concluded that the practice of depositing the dead in caves could well have been contemporary with (or not long post-date) the initial use of the Broadsands passage tomb, at least as far as Cow Cave, Chudleigh is concerned (Sheridan *et al.* 2008, 9-10; cf. Schulting 2007). Furthermore, like the Broadsands individuals, there was no evidence to suggest that the diet of the deceased had included a significant marine element, despite the proximity of the caves to the coast. Such Early Neolithic 'interments' post-date the earlier funerary use of caves in southern Britain by nearly two millennia, so that it would be hard to argue that the practice represents a continuation of an indigenous Mesolithic tradition.

It therefore appears that three funerary traditions characterise the Early Neolithic in the South West, as follows:

i) the use of simple passage tombs and closed chambers, principally of drystone construction, as attested at Broadsands and in the Cotswolds;

ii) the use of timber 'linear zone' mortuary structures, some associated with oval mounds and succeeded by long barrows of various designs; the mortuary structures may not extend further west than Wessex, while the subsequent use of long barrows seems to have extended as far as Devon (not just to Long Burrow, but also to Corringdon Ball, Cuckoo Ball and possibly another one or two locations: Griffith pers. comm.), with a few further long or oval barrows in Cornwall (Mercer 1986, 57) which may or may not be associated with portal tombs; and

iii) the use of caves.

To these traditions, and probably not earlier than the 38th century BC as discussed above, was subsequently added the practice of building portal tombs (quoits). These are limited to Cornwall and represent the adoption of a tradition that developed around the Irish Sea (Kytmannow 2008; Sheridan 2004).

It should be noted that Kytmannow has raised the intriguing possibility that a group of three monuments in West Penwith – Chun Quoit, Mulfra Quoit and Bosporthennis Quoit – might belong to the family of Breton-style closed megalithic chambers and simple passage tombs as mentioned above in the discussion of the Breton, Atlantic façade strand of Neolithisation (Kytmannow 2008; cf. Kirkham 2011, 102-3); they differ from portal tombs in details of design and location. (Note, however, that excavations in 2009 by Andy Jones at Bosporthennis Quoit led to the conclusion that this is more likely to be a badly damaged Entrance Grave, and thus unrelated to Breton-type monuments). If the Chun and Mulfra Quoits do turn out to belong to the Breton, Atlantic façade Neolithisation strand, then they would pre-date all the other types of south-west English funerary monument described above by at least one century, and perhaps up to four centuries. In the absence of firm corroborative evidence, however, this must be left as a question demanding further research.

The origin of the earliest Neolithic in south-west England: a French, 'trans-Manche ouest' connection?

If the aforementioned West Penwith tombs are set to one side, then as argued elsewhere (e.g. Sheridan *et al.* 2008), a north-west French, 'trans-Manche ouest' origin can plausibly be proposed to account for the appearance of the novel technology (i.e. pottery manufacture) and at least one element of the novel funerary traditions (i.e. the mainly dry-stone built passage tombs and closed chambers) described above.

Regarding the earliest Neolithic pottery in the south-west, despite the fact that the presence of undecorated, thin-walled, fine-textured carinated bowls in many of the aforementioned assemblages might initially lead one to assume a connection with the Carinated Bowl ceramic tradition – and indeed, it is a moot point as to whether some of the assemblages east of Devon might indeed belong to that tradition – nevertheless there are good reasons for looking towards north-west France, and in particular Lower Normandy as the area of origin for this tradition, rather than to the far north of France (where the Carinated Bowl tradition is believed to have emerged). Firstly, the use of thin-walled, fine-textured carinated bowls is a characteristic of the early fourth millennium pottery not only in northern France but also across north-west France, albeit declining in frequency westwards. (See Chancerel and Marcigny 2006 and Marcigny *et al.* 2007 for accounts of ceramic developments in Lower Normandy and northern Armorica, and Cassen and François 2009 on Armorican developments in general). A major reason for its widespread occurrence is that it is a characteristic feature of the northern (and particularly Paris Basin) Chassey ceramic tradition, and this tradition influenced ceramic design both to the north east and to the west of the Paris Basin. The numerous *comparanda* for the south-west English fine carinated bowls in north-west France include the northern Chassey assemblage from the promontory enclosure at Soumont-St-Quentin 'Mont Joly', Lower Normandy (Chancerel *et al.* 2006, fig. 51). Secondly, some of the pottery in south-west England and Wessex has features that are either rare or absent from the Carinated Bowl tradition, but are found in the Middle Neolithic II (MN II) pottery of north-west France (and in particular, Lower Normandy). For example, the globular-bellied bowl with vertically-perforated lugs from the Coneybury Anomaly (Fig. 3.2, P7) can be paralleled at Saint-Martin-de-Fontenay (Clément-Sauleau *et al.* 2010, fig. 4), while the S-profiled bowl from the same assemblage (Fig. 3.2, P6) can be paralleled at Grentheville (Chancerel *et al.* 2006, fig. 42.1), both French sites being in Lower Normandy. The wide shallow bowls in the Coneybury Anomaly assemblage (Fig. 3.2, P2, P5) are a widespread feature of north-west French MN II ceramic traditions, as are globular jars with narrow collars (as seen in the Bestwall assemblage, Fig. 3.4, no. 2; lugged versions, as here, tend to be found in northern Chassey pottery, as at Boury-en-Vexin: Marcigny *et al.* 2007, 92). Casting the comparative net a little wider both geographically and chronologically, there are features in the South-Western style tradition (which seems to have evolved from the earliest Neolithic pottery in the South West) which reinforce the north-west French connection: these include the rare presence of flat 'plats à pain' baking plates (as at Carn Brea, Cornwall: Smith 1981) and the abundance of deep lugged baggy jars (e.g. at Hembury, Devon: Liddell 1935), for which excellent parallels are offered, for example, by the assemblage from Louviers 'La Villette' in the Eure valley, Upper Normandy (Giligny 2005, fig. 180; Marcigny *et al.* 2007, 110).

As far as funerary monuments are concerned, the striking similarity between the Broadsands passage tomb and its counterparts in lower Normandy, northern Armorica and Jersey (at La Sergenté) has already been emphasised elsewhere (Sheridan *et al.* 2008), and the dating evidence from north-west France confirms that simple, drystone-built passage tombs were constructed and used from the last few centuries of the 5th millennium into the first couple of centuries of the fourth (e.g. Chancerel and Marcigny 2006; Clément-Sauleau *et al.* 2003, 96; Marcigny *et al.* 2007, 128-143 *passim*). The simple passage tomb *rotundae* of the Cotswolds are sufficiently similar to Broadsands to be considered as belonging to the same funerary tradition and, like their counterparts in Lower Normandy and northern Armorica, they may have served as monuments and territorial markers for individual lineages (cf. Marcigny *et al.* 2007, 135). By contrast, the timber linear zone mortuary chambers of Wessex are not echoed in north-west France and seem more to be a feature of the 'Carinated Bowl Neolithic' (Sheridan 2007). As for the use of caves for funerary purposes, despite the paucity of caves in north-west France, there is actually evidence for deposition of corpses in a cave/rock shelter, at Mestreville, Saint-Pierre-d'Autils, Lower Normandy (Billard 2007). The associated material culture belongs to the Middle Neolithic, and a skull fragment has been radiocarbon-dated to the third quarter of the fifth millennium.

Other evidence points towards a 'trans-Manche ouest' connection for the earliest Neolithic in south-west England. The large rectangular timber house at Penhale Round, for example, finds echoes in a slightly earlier house at Cairon, Calvados (Lower Normandy: Ghesquière and Marcigny 2011) and, in a slightly later context, at Saint-Vigor-d'Ymonville, Lower Normandy (Marcigny pers. comm.). Similarly, the practice of using promontory and hilltop enclosures, which seems to have emerged in south-west England during the 38th century (Mercer 2003; Whittle *et al.* 2011), can be seen as a continuation of a tradition that is well-attested in north-west France (e.g. at Soumont-St-Quentin, Saint-Martin-de-Fontenay and Lillemer in Lower Normandy). A further piece of evidence in support of the 'trans-Manche ouest' hypothesis comes from the study of stone axeheads, and in particular from a recent major international research project, *Projet JADE* (Pétrequin *et al.* 2008; 2011; in press b). Before exploring the possible reasons for our hypothetical episode/s of colonisation from north-west France, we shall examine the axehead evidence in a little more detail.

Alpine axeheads in south-west England: further evidence of a French connection

Projet JADE, led by Pierre Pétrequin and undertaken between 2007 and 2010, focused on axeheads made of jadeitite and other Alpine rocks, at a pan-European scale of analysis. (For details of the project see, *inter alia*, Pétrequin *et al.* 2008; 2011; and in press b, especially Chapter 11). Having located the source areas of the rocks and the working sites in the high north Italian Alps, the team used the non-destructive technique of spectroradiometry to source individual axeheads by comparing them with their large reference collection of raw material samples, working débitage and finished axeheads from across Europe. Furthermore, the team collated information about the dating of Alpine axeheads, and have been able to construct a regionally-variable typochronology across Europe and to trace the complex life histories of individual axeheads. As a result, we are able to say much more about the origin and prior history of the specimens found in Britain than we were before.

FIGURE 3.7 AXEHEAD OF OMPHACITITIC JADEITITE, AN ALPINE ROCK, FOUND BESIDE THE SWEET TRACK, SOMERSET. PHOTO: PIERRE PÉTREQUIN, PROJET JADE

FIGURE 3.8 AXEHEAD OF JADEITITE FROM BREAMORE, HAMPSHIRE. PHOTO: NATIONAL MUSEUMS SCOTLAND

Thus, for example, we can now say that the magnificent axehead made of omphacititic jadeitite that was found beside the Sweet Track in Somerset (Fig. 3.7), and which was deposited in 3807/6 BC or in the succeeding dozen or so years of the track's use-life (Coles and Orme 1984; Coles *et al.* 1974), had started its life several centuries beforehand in the north Italian Alps, most probably in the Mont Viso massif (Pétrequin pers. comm.). Thereafter it had a complex history: having arrived in the Morbihan area of southern Brittany, its shape was altered there at some point between 4300/4200 and 3900 BC, and then it circulated around north-west/northern France before being brought to south-west England – arguably as a treasured possession of a group of early immigrant farmers, complete with legends about its ancient distant origin and its history. Its deposition in a watery environment, thereby returning this precious object to the realm of the gods and spirits from whence it had ultimately originated, is in line with depositional practices for Alpine axeheads in north-west and northern France (Pétrequin *et al.* in press c) and suggests a continuity of belief. As with so many other aspects of the Neolithic in Britain, there is no Mesolithic precedent for the ritualised deposition of axeheads in south-west England, or indeed for the use of exotic axeheads (save for some possible movement of flint in the south-west: Mercer 2003, 58); instead, everything about the Sweet Track axehead points towards traditions and beliefs that were current in Middle Neolithic France.

Other Alpine axeheads in south-west England have similarly complex life histories. An exquisite example of jadeitite found at Breamore in Hampshire (Fig. 3.8; Sheridan *et al.* 2010) had also been reshaped in the Morbihan, as had a fragmentary axehead of Tumiac type (according to the *Projet JADE* classificatory system) found at High Peak near Sidmouth, Devon (Sheridan *et al.* 2011, fig. 5.3). In the latter case, an attempt had been made, then abandoned, to perforate the butt (a Morbihan characteristic), and the axehead had been deliberately broken before its deposition. Although this particular specimen had been found in an Early Neolithic enclosure that is likely to date to the 38th or 37th century, its association with the enclosure is not definite. Thought to have eroded from an area of activity on the hilltop, the axehead fragment could theoretically have been deposited before the enclosure was constructed.

The other axeheads (and other objects) from south-west England that have been shown by *Projet JADE* or by previous analyses to have originated in the Alps are mapped in Fig. 3.9. The concentration on and near the

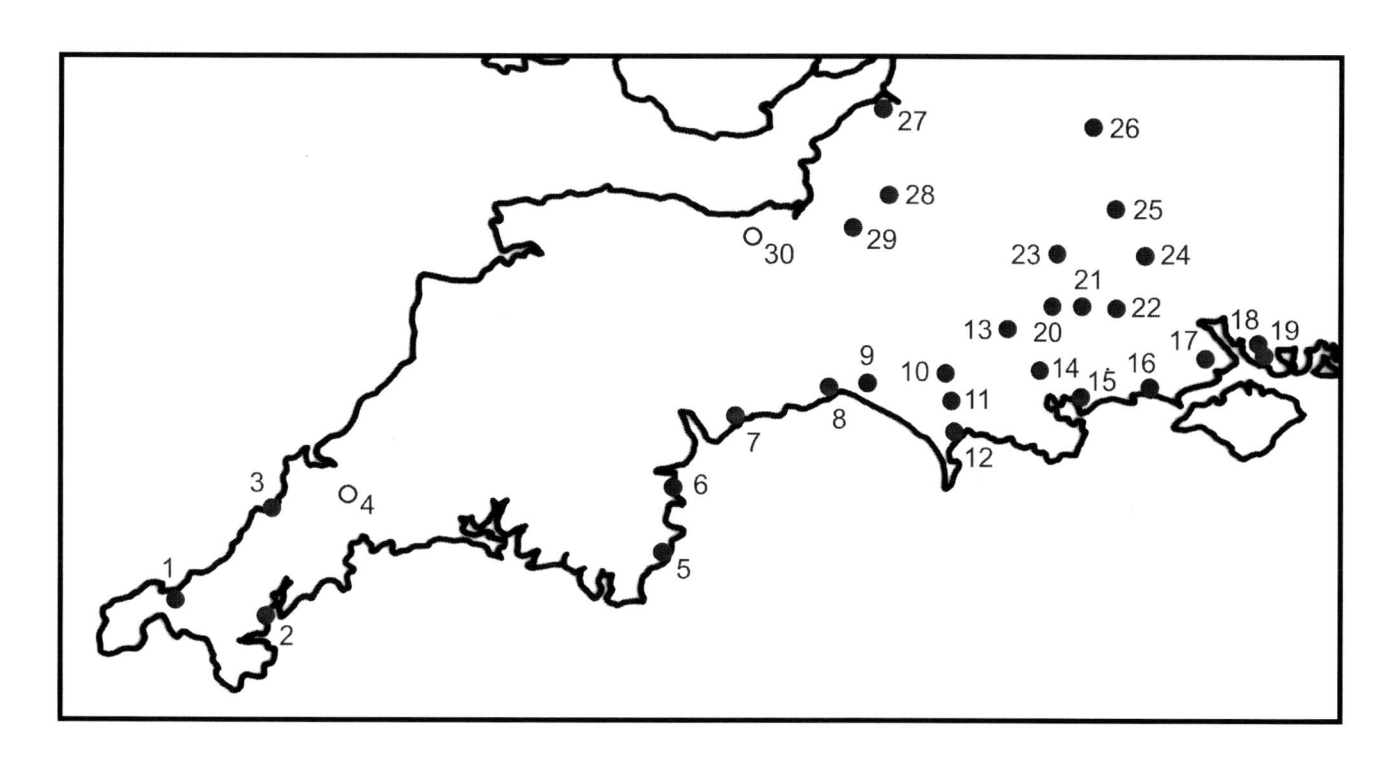

FIGURE 3.9. DISTRIBUTION OF OBJECTS OF ALPINE ROCK IN SOUTH-WEST ENGLAND (ALL AXEHEADS UNLESS SPECIFIED OTHERWISE). KEY: 1. HAYLE, TREVASSACK FARM, CORNWALL; 2. NEAR FALMOUTH, CORNWALL; 3. NEWQUAY, CORNWALL; 4. 'CORNWALL'; 5. BROWNSTONE FARM, DEVON (EARLY BRONZE AGE CHISEL); 6. ?TORQUAY AREA, DEVON (EARLY BRONZE AGE CHISEL); 7. HIGH PEAK, SIDMOUTH, DEVON; 8. WOOTTON FITZPAINE, DORSET (AXEHEAD-PENDANT); 9. NETHERBURY, DORSET; 10. NETHER CERNE, DORSET; 11. DORCHESTER, DORSET; 12. PRESTON, DORSET (AXEHEAD-PENDANT); 13. HAMBLEDON HILL, DORSET; 14. NEWTON PEVERILL, DORSET; 15. PARKSTONE, DORSET; 16. BETWEEN BARTON AND MILFORD, HAMPSHIRE; 17. NEAR BEAULIEU, HAMPSHIRE; 18. TITCHFIELD, HAMPSHIRE; 19. HILLHEAD, HAMPSHIRE; 20. HANDLEY COMMON, DORSET; 21. PENTRIDGE DOWN, DORSET; 22. BREAMORE, HAMPSHIRE; 23. TEFFONT MAGNA DOWN, WILTSHIRE; 24. WINTERBOURNE, WILTSHIRE; 25. FIGHELDEAN ('A BARROW NEAR STONEHENGE'), WILTSHIRE; 26. BECKHAMPTON, WILTSHIRE; 27. WRAXALL, SOMERSET; 28. ST. CUTHBERT OUT, EBBOR GORGE, SOMERSET; 29. SWEET TRACK, SOMERSET; 30. QUANTOCK HILLS, SOMERSET

Wessex and Devon coasts has previously been remarked upon (Sheridan *et al.* 2010); also of note are the clusters in Cornwall and in Somerset. (A small jadeitite axehead recently brought to the attention of the author, and said to have been found at Frenchay, is a potential addition to the latter cluster.) Not all of the objects date to the Early Neolithic: two axehead-pendants from the Dorset coast were probably imported from north-west France between 3200 and 2800 BC, while a pair of chisels, one from Brownstone Farm, Kingswear, Devon and the other possibly from the Torquay district, are of Early Bronze Age date (Sheridan *et al.* 2011, 415, 417, fig. 6).

We cannot say for certain whether the early fourth millennium Alpine imports in south-west England and Wessex had come via the 'trans-Manche ouest' route as opposed to the north French, 'Carinated Bowl Neolithic' route (which seems to have been the main conduit for Alpine axeheads). However, to judge from what we know about the circulation of the various types of Alpine axehead around France, the 'trans-Manche ouest' route is perfectly plausible (as shown, for example, by the overall distribution of Tumiac-type axeheads: Pétrequin *et al.* in press c, fig. 89). It is only the flat, 'Greenlaw/Altenstadt'-type axeheads from near Falmouth and in Wessex which are perhaps more likely to have entered England via northern France and then to have circulated down to the south-west, given the comparative rarity of this axehead type in north-west France (Pétrequin *et al.* in press c, fig. 117). However, one cannot altogether rule out their importation from Normandy.

Other imports of axeheads from France will be considered briefly below. Before leaving *Projet JADE*, however, it should be added that the project was able to discount one Peninsular axehead which had previously been claimed as an Alpine import, namely a magnificent axehead of nephrite or serpentinite found at Lower Down near Bovey Tracey, Devon (Sheridan *et al.* 2011, fig. 13.4). Found in 1930, when a new path was being cut 'through a mound of unknown character, and a few feet from an ancient trackway...' (Anon 1932; Smith 1963, 158), its most likely origin is, however, New Zealand or New Caledonia. Other ethnographic manuports are known from Britain, with some turning up in extraordinary locations (Sheridan *et al.* 2011); it may be that this example had been brought to Devon by a sailor, and subsequently discarded. The project was also able to rule out an Alpine origin for another axehead, from the causewayed enclosure at Raddon in Devon (Gent and Quinnell 1999, fig. 16.1), which had been the subject of differing identifications following microscopic examination and thin-sectioning during the 1990s. (The source of its rock remains a topic of debate: Vin Davis and Mik Markham pers. comm..)

A possible explanation for the hypothesised episode/s of colonisation from north-west France to south-west England

As repeatedly argued elsewhere (e.g. Sheridan 2010a), the Neolithisation of Britain and Ireland cannot be understood without understanding the dynamics of demography and social change on the near Continent, and the 'trans-Manche ouest' phenomenon proposed above is no exception. In tracing the history of late 5th and early 4th millennium developments in north-west France, Marcigny *et al.* (2007, 93; cf. Chancerel and Marcigny 2006, 184) have argued for some kind of significant change around 3800 BC, after more than a millennium of presumed population expansion following the establishment of farming as a way of life in this part of France. A contraction and regroupment of the population is proposed, with the use of defensible hilltop or promontory sites; drystone-built passage tombs continued to be used in the west of the area (and silo graves in the east). Some kind of socio-economic or demographic stress is assumed to have occurred – and this is consistent with the demographic 'boom-and-bust'-type changes in agricultural communities as proposed by Shennan and his colleagues (Shennan and Edinborough 2007) – but the shortage of evidence makes it hard to establish its nature in detail. Nevertheless, at such a time of change, the desire of some people to seek a new life elsewhere is understandable, and this could well be the reason for the appearance of the 'package' of novelties seen in south-west England and parts of Wessex from the 39th century, as sketched above.

Subsequent developments in south-west England

Having become established in south-west England, farming communities appear to have flourished over the following centuries, rapidly establishing networks of contacts over which gabbroic pottery (e.g. Quinnell and Taylor 1999; Peacock 1988) and Cornish axeheads (Clough and Cummins 1988, maps 2-5 and 15; Markham 2009) were exchanged eastwards. The Sweet Track finds remind us that westwards movement also occurred, in this case featuring a mint-condition axehead of mined flint, almost certainly from a Sussex mine. The appearance of portal tombs in the west of the Peninsula indicates that some groups were also now engaging in an Irish Sea network of contacts, other evidence for which includes the presence of South-Western style deep lugged bowls in south-west Scotland and north-east Ireland (Sheridan 2004). Farming communities also seem to have grown large enough to feel the need to construct hilltop enclosures, and the evidence for violent attack at Carn Brea (Mercer 1981, 2003), along with other evidence from other Peninsular enclosures, suggests that inter-group relations were not always peaceful.

Maintenance (or re-establishment) of links with north-west France after the 38th century BC is indicated in several ways. While the development of the South-Western style of pottery can be seen as a regional example of 'style drift' from the initial, Earliest Neolithic ceramic tradition – analogous to the evolution of the Decorated style further to the east – the use of trumpet lugs on the finest bowls is a feature that may well have been adopted from contemporary north-west French pottery. More concrete evidence for links is provided by the presence, at Maiden Castle, of a saddle quern fragment made from silicified leucocratic flint conglomerate from near Evreux in Normandy (Peacock *et al.* 2009). If the pit in which this had been found is contemporary with the main use of the causewayed enclosure at Maiden Castle, the quern is likely to have been imported during the 36th century BC (according to Whittle *et al.*'s 2011 re-evaluation of the dating of this enclosure). Some of the handful of imported axeheads of Type A metadolerite from the quarries at Plussulien in central Armorica (le Roux 1979) could also have been imported to southern and south-western England around that time (if not slightly earlier), while the distinctively-shaped *hache à bouton* found at Pulborough, West Sussex probably arrived during the second half of the fourth millennium (Le Roux 1999, 146). Two fibrolite axeheads found in west Cornwall – one from St. Levan, Raftra, the other from Wendron, both sadly lost – were also imports, most probably from Brittany (Evens *et al.* 1972; Smith 1963, 171). At what point they arrived is impossible to tell; Yvan Pailler's research into fibrolite exploitation in Brittany has shown that production of fibrolite axeheads occurred, on varying scales and at different times, from around 4800 BC to around 3000 BC, reaching a peak during the late 5th – early 4th millennium (Pailler 2009). (Incidentally, a claimed major hoard of old and worn fibrolite axeheads from St. Buryan (Pitts 2009) has since been dismissed as being a 20th century collection that may have been amassed in Spain: Varndell pers. comm..) The late fourth/early third-millennium importation to Dorset, from France, of axehead-pendants of Alpine rock, has already been mentioned above. Finally, the much later chisels of Alpine stone mentioned above suggest that links with France continued into (or resumed during) the early second millennium; there may also have been Chalcolithic, Beaker-related contact with north-west France around the mid-third millennium, as suggested by the 'Boscombe Bowmen' grave and its associated grave goods in Wiltshire (Fitzpatrick in press).

As far as the fourth millennium, post-earliest Neolithic contact between south-west England (including Wessex) and north-west France is concerned, it should be noted that this phenomenon of continuing or renewed links with the Continent is not echoed elsewhere in Britain and Ireland. The only possible exception concerns Louwe Kooijmans' claim (1976) that some early fourth-millennium pottery from Swifterbant and Hazendonk in the Netherlands could have been influenced by Carinated Bowl pottery from south-east England, but this needs to be revisited in view of the recognition of similar-looking, locally-evolved pottery in the Group de Spiere (Vanmontfort 2006) and at Étaples (Philippe *et al.* in press).

Conclusions, and some outstanding questions

It is hoped that this review of some new information about the establishment, and subsequent development, of 'the Neolithic' in south-west England will have helped to enhance our understanding of developments during the first half of the fourth millennium (cf. Mercer 1986). The evidence supporting the 'trans-Manche ouest' hypothesis of Neolithisation is growing and, along with our developing understanding of processes on the other side of the channel (thanks to the research of Cyril Marcigny and his colleagues), a plausible explanation as to why some people from north-west France should seek to relocate to south-west England around the 39th century BC has been proposed. An understanding of the prevailing sea currents (Cunliffe 2008; Garrow and Sturt 2011; Mercer 2003) helps us to understand the geographical patterning of the links; whether climate change during the preceding centuries had also influenced matters is open to debate. The dynamics of developments subsequent to the 39th century reminds us of the complex and far-reaching networks of contact, and movements of ideas, people and objects, that rapidly developed after the initial implantation of a farming mode of life.

Of course, there is much that remains to be clarified, and there are some key gaps in our knowledge. As Jones and Reed have emphasised (2006), even though we have some idea of the domesticated resources that were used by these early farming communities – with flax being present alongside emmer and spelt wheat and barley (Gent and Quinnell 1999) – the nature and scale of cereal cultivation, especially in Cornwall, remains poorly understood. Similarly, the poor survival of bone in the acidic environment of the Peninsula makes it hard to reconstruct patterns of animal management. The nature of hilltop enclosures could be investigated further, with Roger Mercer already having identified a number of candidates for excavation several years ago (Mercer 2003; cf. Davies 2010). The whole question of the acculturation of the indigenous hunter-fisher-foragers remains a largely closed book, although rapid acculturation (rather than population replacement) seems to this author to be the most likely scenario. Underwater excavation of submerged Mesolithic and Early Neolithic sites (as in the case of the aforementioned pottery found off Paignton) might conceivably yield relevant information.

There are also outstanding questions about the French links. In terms of ceramics, the absence of *vase-supports* from the English assemblages is slightly curious as they are present in MN II ceramic traditions in north-west France; in mitigation, however, one should emphasise that many of the earliest Neolithic English assemblages are very small. Likewise, it remains to be established whether there are north-west French parallels for the distinctive black surface treatment seen on the Sweet Track pottery, the Penhale Round pottery and on some South-West style vessels. As regards the importation of metadolerite and fibrolite axeheads from Brittany, there remains uncertainty as to when most of these crossed the Channel; and it may be that further French imports of axeheads remain to be recognized in Britain, just as there may be unrecognized British axehead exports to France. And as regards funerary monuments, although the drystone simple passage tombs of south-west England are easy to parallel in north-west France and Jersey, the closed chambers of the Cotswold *rotundae* do not seem to be paralleled, even though their structural similarities with the passage tombs strongly suggest that they formed part of the same funerary tradition. It may be that the investigation of a newly-discovered potential *rotunda* at Hinckley Point, Somerset may shed new light on this kind of monument (Darvill pers. comm.). Other questions that remain to be resolved regarding the Early Neolithic funerary traditions of the south west include the date and character of the few long barrows in Devon and Cornwall (and particularly whether the latter may be associated with portal tombs), and the question of whether the aforementioned Chun and Mulfra Quoits really do belong to the Breton, Atlantic façade of Neolithisation, as Kytmannow has proposed (2008; cf. Kirkham 2011, 102-3).

In terms of the regional identity of the earliest Neolithic communities and their successors, the question of the 'boundary' between pioneering communities from the 'Carinated Bowl Neolithic' and from the 'trans-Manche ouest Neolithic' remains to be established; it is suspected to lie within Wessex, although one is not dealing with neat territorial divisions or firm boundaries (cf. Davies 2010). The perpetuation of distinct identities between south-west and south-central England can, however, be traced with the differing choices of funerary monument and in the emergence of the 'South-Western' and 'Decorated' styles of pottery (with each showing regional variability, and with some interchange of design ideas and of vessels). Similarly, locally-specific identities within the South West can be traced, especially with regard to the tip of the Peninsula at West Penwith (Kirkham 2011).

There are also gaps in our understanding of where whole classes of evidence may fit within our overall Neolithic picture, although the situation is improving. Andy Jones' and Charles Thomas' recent re-evaluation of Cornish Entrance Graves (2010) lends weight to the suggestion that this funerary tradition, with its close links with south-east Ireland and perhaps elsewhere around the Irish Sea, is likely to be of late 3rd or early 2nd millennium date (i.e. Chalcolithic or Early Bronze Age) and thus not part of our Neolithic narrative. The recent dating of a stone alignment buried in peat at Cut Hill on Dartmoor to some time between the 34th/32nd century BC and the 25th/23rd century BC (Fyfe and Greeves 2010), suggesting that some stone settings are probably of Late Neolithic date, is not inconsistent with the evidence from the submerged double stone row at Yelland, in the Taw estuary, currently 3 metres below sea level (Mercer 2003, 58). How such sites fit in with our sketchy understanding of the Late Neolithic in this part of England, and where individual standing stones and stone circles fit in, both chronologically and culturally, are questions for future research to tackle; regarding individual standing stones, all that we can say for certain is that the example from Try, Cornwall, pre-dates a cist that has recently been dated to 3410±50 BP (GrA-30170, 1770-1630 cal BC at 1σ, 1880-1540 cal BC at 2σ using OxCal 4.1: Jones and Quinnell 2006). Henrietta Quinnell has long been an active researcher at the forefront of Peninsular archaeology, with an interest in topics such as this; long may this continue!

Bibliography

Allen, M. J. and Green, M. 1998. The Fir Tree Field shaft; the date and archaeological and palaeo-environmental potential of a chalk swallowhole feature. *Proceedings of the Dorset Natural History and Archaeological Society* 120, 25-37.

Anon. 1932. A greenstone celt from Dartmoor, *Proceedings of the Devon Archaeological Exploration Society* 1 (1929–32), 74.

Barclay, A. and Case, H. J. 2007. The Early Neolithic pottery and fired clay. In D. Benson and A. W. R. Whittle (eds.), *Building Memories. The Neolithic Cotswold Barrow at Ascott-under-Wychwood, Oxfordshire*, 263-281. Oxford, Oxbow.

Barton, N. and Roberts, A. 2004. The Mesolithic period in England: current perspectives and new research. In A. Saville (ed.), *Mesolithic Scotland and its Neighbours: the Early Holocene Prehistory of Scotland, its British and Irish Context and some North European Perspectives*, 339-358. Edinburgh, Society of Antiquaries of Scotland.

Bayliss, A. and Whittle, A. W. R. (eds.) 2007. *Histories of the Dead: Building Chronologies for Five Southern British Long Barrows. Cambridge Archaeological Journal* 17(1) (Supplement).

Bayliss, A., Benson, D., Galer, D., Humphrey, L., McFadyen, L. and Whittle, A. W. R. 2007. One thing after another: the date of the Ascott-under-Wychwood long barrow. In A. Bayliss and A. W. R. Whittle (eds.), *Histories of the Dead: Building Chronologies for Five Southern British Long Barrows*, 29-44. *Cambridge Archaeological Journal* 17(1) (Supplement).

Bayliss, A., Healy, F., Bronk Ramsey, C., McCormac, F. G. and Mercer, R. 2008 Interpreting chronology. In R. Mercer and F. Healy, *Hambledon Hill, Dorset, England. Excavation and Survey of a Neolithic Monument Complex and its Surrounding Landscape*, 378-411. Swindon, English Heritage.

Benson, D. and. Whittle, A. W. R (eds.), *Building Memories. The Neolithic Cotswold Barrow at Ascott-under-Wychwood, Oxfordshire*. Oxford, Oxbow.

Billard, C. 2007. Les pratiques funéraires au Néolithique moyen dans les abris-sous-roche de Mestreville à Saint-Pierre-d'Autils. In C. Marcigny, E. Ghesquière and J. Desloges (eds.), *La Hache et la meule:les premiers paysans du Néolithique en Normandie (6000–2000 avant notre ère)*, 138. Le Havre, Éditions du Muséum d'histoire naturelle de Havre.

Bishop, R. R., Church, M. J. and Rowley-Conwy, P. A. 2009. Cereals, fruits and nuts in the Scottish Neolithic. *Proceedings of the Society of Antiquaries of Scotland* 139, 47-103.

Bonsall, C., Anderson, D. E. and Macklin, M. G. 2002. The Mesolithic–Neolithic transition in western Scotland

and its European context. *Documenta Praehistorica* 29, 1-19.

Britnell, W. J. 1984. The Gwernvale long cairn, Crickhowell, Brecknock. In W. J. Britnell and H. N. Savory, *Gwernvale and Penywyrlod: Two Neolithic Long Cairns in the Black Mountains of Brecknock*, 43-154. Bangor, Cambrian Archaeological Association (Cambrian Archaeological Monographs 2).

Caseldine, C. J., Coles, B. J., Griffith, F. M. and Hatton, J. M. 2000 Conservation or change? Human influence on the Mid-Devon landscape. In R. A. Nicholson and T. P. O'Connor (eds), *People as an Agent of Environmental Change* 60-70. Oxford, Oxbow.

Cassen, S. and François, P. 2009. Classements et diagnoses de la production céramique à la Table des Marchands. In S. Cassen (ed.), *Autour de la Table: explorations archéologiques et discourse savants sur des architectures néolithiques à Locmariaquer, Morbihan (Table des Marchands et Grand Menhir)*, 491-567. Nantes, Laboratoire de recherches archéologiques, CNRS et Université de Nantes.

Cassen, S. Boujot C., Bella, S. D., Guiavarc'h, M., Le Pennec, C., Prieto Martinez, M. P., Querré, G., Santrot, M.-H. and Vigier, E. in press. Dépôts bretons, tumulus carnacéens et circulations à longue distance. (Breton hoards, Carnac tumuli and long-distance circulation.) In P. Pétrequin, S. Cassen, M. Errera, L. Klassen and J. A. Sheridan, (eds.), *Jade. Grandes haches alpines du Néolithique européen. V^e et IVe millénaires av. J.-C.* Besançon, Presses Universitaires de Franche-Comté (Cahiers de la MSHE C.N. Ledoux).

Chancerel, A. and Marcigny, C. 2006. Synthèse. In A. Chancerel, C. Marcigny and E. Ghesquière (eds.), *Le Plateau de Mondeville (Calvados) du Néolithique à l'âge du Bronze*, 181-189. Paris, Éditions de la Maison des sciences et de l'Homme.

Chancerel, A., Marcigny, C. and Ghesquière, E. 2006. L'occupation du Néolithique moyen II de la ZI sud (Mondeville, Grentheville). In A. Chancerel, C. Marcigny and E. Ghesquière (eds.), *Le Plateau de Mondeville (Calvados) du Néolithique à l'âge du Bronze*, 55-92. Paris, Éditions de la Maison des sciences et de l'Homme.

Cleal, R. 1990. The prehistoric pottery (Coneybury Anomaly). In J. C. Richards, *The Stonehenge Environs Project*, 45-57. London, English Heritage (Archaeological Report 16).

Cleal, R. 2004. The dating and diversity of the earliest ceramics of Wessex and south-west England. In R. Cleal and J. Pollard (eds.) *Monuments and Material Culture. Papers in Honour of an Avebury Archaeologist: Isobel Smith*, 164-192. East Knoyle, The Hobnob Press.

Cleal, R., Cooper, J., Freestone, I. and Williams, D. 1991. The earlier prehistoric pottery. In N. M. Sharples, *Maiden Castle. Excavations and Field Survey 1985–6*, 171-185. London, English Heritage (Archaeological Report 19

Clément-Sauleau, S., Ghesquière, E., Marcigny, C., Paez-Rezende, L. and Savary, X. 2003. Deux fosses du Néolithique moyen I/II à Fleury-sur-Orne « ZAC Parc d'Activités » (Calvados). *Révue archéologique de l'Ouest* 20, 87-97.

Clément-Sauleau, S., Ghesquière, E., Giazzon, D., Giazzon, S., Marcigny, C., Palluau and Vipard, L. 2010. L'enceinte Néolithique moyen de St-Martin-de-Fontenay « Le Diguet » (Calvados) : presentation liminaire. In M. Besse and I. Praud (eds.), *INTERNÉO 8* (Actes de la Journée d'information du 20 novembre 2010, Paris), 71-73. Paris, Association pour les Études interrégionales sur le Néolithique/Société Préhistorique Française.

Clough, T. H. McK. and Cummins, W. A. 1988. *Stone Axe Studies Volume 2*. London, Council for British Archaeology (Research Report 67).

Coles, J. M. and Orme, B. J. 1984. Ten excavations along the Sweet Track (3200 bc). In J. M. Coles, B. J. Orme and S. E. Rouillard (eds.), *Somerset Levels Papers 10*, 5-45. Cambridge and Exeter, Somerset Levels Project.

Coles, J. M., Orme, B. J., Bishop, A. C. and Woolley, A. R. 1974. A jade axe from the Somerset Levels. *Antiquity* 48, 216-220.

Coles J. M. and Coles, B. J. 1986. *Sweet Track to Glastonbury: the Somerset Levels in Prehistory*. London, Thames and Hudson.

Collard, M., Edinborough, K., Shennan, S. and Thomas, M. G. 2010. Radiocarbon evidence indicates that migrants introduced farming to Britain. *Journal of Archaeological Science* 37(4), 866-870.

Cooney, G. 1997. Images of settlement and the landscape in the Neolithic. In P. Topping (ed.), *Neolithic Landscapes*, 23-31. Oxford, Oxbow.

Cunliffe, B. 2008. *Europe Between the Oceans, 9000 BC to AD 1000*. New Haven (CT) and London, Yale university Press.

Darvill, T. 2010. Neolithic round barrows on the Cotswolds. In J. Leary, T. Darvill and D. Field (eds.), *Round Mounds and Monumentality in the British Neolithic and Beyond*, 130-138.

Davies, S. R. 2010. *The Early Neolithic Tor Enclosures of Southwest Britain*. PhD thesis, University of Birmingham. http://etheses.bham.ac.uk/1141/1/Davies_S_10_PhD.pdf

Evans, J. G. and Smith, I. F. 1983. Excavations at Cherhill, North Wiltshire 1967. *Proceedings of the Prehistoric Society* 49, 101-9.

Evans, E. D., Smith, I. F. and Wallis, F. S. 1972. The petrological identification of stone implements from South-Western England. *Proceedings of the Prehistoric Society* 38, 235-275.

Field, D., Matthews, C. L. and Smith, I. F. 1964. New Neolithic sites in Dorset and Bedfordshire, with a note on the distribution of Neolithic storage pits in Britain. *Proceedings of the Prehistoric Society* 30, 352-381.

Fitzpatrick, A. P. in press. *The Amesbury Archer and the Boscombe Bowmen: Early Bell Beaker burials at Boscombe Down, Amesbury, Wiltshire, Great Britain: Excavations at Boscombe Down, volume 1*. Oxford and Oakville, Oxbow Books.

Fyfe, R. M. and Greeves, T. 2010. The date and context of a stone row: Cut Hill, Dartmoor, south-west England. *Antiquity*. 84, 55-70.

Garrow, D. and Sturt, F. 2011. Grey waters bright with Neolithic Argonauts? Maritime connections and the Mesolithic-Neolithic transition within the 'western seaways' of Britain, c. 5000–3500 BC. *Antiquity* 85, 59-72.

Gent, T. H. and Quinnell, H. 1999. Excavations of a causewayed enclosure and hillfort on Raddon Hill, Stockleigh Pomeroy. *Proceedings of the Devon Archaeological Society* 57, 1-75.

Ghesquière, E. and Marcigny, C. 2011. *Cairon. Vivre et mourir au Néolithique*. Rennes, Presses Universitaires de Rennes.

Giligny, F. 2005. *Louviers "La Villette" (Eure) : Un site néolithique moyen en zone humide.* Rennes, Documents Archéologiques de l'Ouest.

Green, M. 2000. *A Landscape Revealed: 10,000 Years on a Chalkland Farm*. Stroud, Tempus.

Green, M. and Allen, M. 1997. An early prehistoric shaft on Cranbourne Chase. *Oxford Journal of Archaeology* 16(2), 121-132.

Jones, A. M. in preparation. CAS excavations at Carn Galva and Bosporthennis in 2009. *Cornish Archaeology*.

Jones, A. M. and Quinnell, H. 2006. Cornish Beakers: new discoveries and perspectives. *Cornish Archaeology* 45, 31-69.

Jones, A. M. and Reed, S. J. 2006. By land, sea and air: an Early Neolithic pit group at Portscatho, Cornwall, and consideration of coastal activity during the Neolithic. *Cornish Archaeology* 45, 1-30.

Jones, A. M. and Thomas, C. 2010. Bosiliack and a reconsideration of Entrance Graves. *Proceedings of the Prehistoric Society* 76, 271-296.

Kinnes, I. A. 1992. *Non-megalithic Long Barrows and Allied Structures in the British Neolithic*. London, British Museum Press (Occasional Paper 52).

Kirkham, G. 2011. Something different at the Land's End. In A. M. Jones and G. Kirkham (eds.), *Beyond the Core: Reflections on Regionality in Prehistory*, 101-111. Oxford, Oxbow.

Kytmannow, T. 2008. *Portal Tombs in the Landscape: the Chronology, Morphology and Landscape Setting of the Portal Tombs of Ireland, Wales and Cornwall*. (British Archaeological Reports, British Series 455). Oxford: Hadrian Books.

Laidlaw, M. 1999. Pottery. In A. P. Fitzpatrick, C. A. Butterworth and J. Grove, *Prehistoric and Roman Sites in East Devon: the A30 Honiton to Exeter Improvement DBFO, 1996–9. Volume I: Prehistoric Sites*, 148-151. Salisbury, Trust for Wessex Archaeology Ltd.

Lancaster, S., Davis, A., Hastie, M., McCulloch, R., Smith, C. Timpany, S. and Tipping, R. 2009. Palaeoenvironmental synthesis. In H. K. Murray, J. C. Murray and S. M. Fraser, *A Tale of the Unknown Unknowns. A Mesolithic Pit Alignmnent and a Neolithic Timber Hall at Warren Field, Crathes, Aberdeenshire*, 42-50. Oxford, Oxbow.

Lawson, A. J. 2007. *Chalkland: an Archaeology of Stonehenge and its Region*. East Knoyle, The Hobnob Press.

Le Roux, C.-T. 1979. Stone axes of Brittany and the Marches. In T. H. McK.Clough and W. A. Cummins (eds.), *Stone Axe Studies, Volume 1*, 49-56. London, Council for British Archaeology (Research Report 23).

Le Roux, C.-T. 1999. *L'outillage de Pierre polie en métadolérite du type A. Les ateliers de Plussulien (Côtes-D'Armor)*. Rennes, Université de Rennes I.

Liddell, D. M. 1935. Report on the excavations at Hembury Fort, Devon. Fourth and fifth seasons, 1934 and 1935. *Proceedings of the Devon Archaeological Exploration Society* 2, 135-175.

Louwe Kooijmans, L. P. 1976. Local developments in a border land. *Oudheidkundige Mededelingen uit het Rijksmuseum van oudheden te Leiden* 57, 227-297.

Marcigny, C., Ghesquière, E. and Desloges, J. (eds.) 2007. *La Hache et la meule:les premiers paysans du Néolithique en Normandie (6000–2000 avant notre ère)*. Le Havre, Éditions du Muséum d'histoire naturelle de Havre.

Markham, M. 2009. The Devil's in the detail:a review of Group I and Group III petrolographic thin sections. *Internet Archaeology* 26. http://intarch.ac.uk/journal/issue26/markham_toc.html

Mercer, R. 1981. Excavations at Carn Brea, Illogan, Cornwall, 1970–73 – A Neolithic fortified complex of the third millennium bc. *Cornish Archaeology* 20, 1-204.

Mercer, R. 1986. The Neolithic in Cornwall. *Cornish Archaeology* 25, 35-80.

Mercer, R. 1997. The excavation of a Neolithic enclosure complex at Helman Tor, Lostwithiel, Cornwall. *Cornish Archaeology* 36, 5-63.

Mercer, R. 2003. The early farming settlement of south western England in the Neolithic. In: I. Armit, E. Murphy, E. Nelis & D.D.A. Simpson (eds), *Neolithic settlement in Ireland and Western Britain*, 56-70. Oxford, Oxbow.

Monk, M. 2000. Seeds and soils of discontent: an environmental archaeological contribution to the nature of the early Neolithic. In A. Desmond, G. Johnson, M. McCarthy, J. Sheehan and E. Shee Twohig (eds.) *New Agendas in Irish Prehistory: Papers in Commemoration of Liz Anderson*, 67-87. Bray, Wordwell.

Nowakowski, J. A. and Johns, C. forthcoming. *Bypassing Indian Queens, Cornwall - Archaeological Excavations 1992-1994. Prehistoric and Romano-British landscapes and settlements*. Truro, Cornwall Council/ Highway Agency.

Pailler, Y. 2009. Neolithic fibrolite working in the west of France. In B. O'Connor, G. Cooney and J. C. Chapman (eds.), *Materialitas: Working Stone, carving Identity*, 113-126. Oxford, Oxbow Books and the Prehistoric Society (Prehistoric Society Research Papers 3).

Peacock, D. P. S. 1988. The gabbroic pottery of Cornwall. *Antiquity* 62, 302-4.

Peacock, D., Cutler, L. and Woodward, P. 2009. A Neolithic voyage. *International Journal of Nautical Archaeology* 39(1), 116-24.

Pétrequin, P., Sheridan, J. A., Cassen, S., Errera, M., Gauthier, E., Klassen, L., le Maux, N. and Pailler, Y. 2008. Neolithic Alpine axeheads, from the Continent to Great Britain, the Isle of Man and Ireland. In H. Fokkens, B. J. Coles, A. L. Van Gijn, J. P. Klejne, H. H. Ponjee and C. G. Slappendel (eds), *Between foraging and farming*, 262-279. Leiden, Leiden University (*Analecta Praehistorica Leidensia* 40).

Pétrequin, P., Sheridan, J. A., Cassen, S., Errera, M., Gauthier, E., Klassen, L., le Maux, N., Pailler, Y., Pétrequin, A.-M. and Rossy, M. 2011. Eclogite or jadeitite: the two colours involved in the transfer of of Alpine axeheads in western Europe. In R.V. Davis and M. Edmonds (eds.), *Stone Axe Studies III*, 55-82. Oxford and Oakville, Oxbow Books.

Pétrequin, P., Cassen, S., Klassen, L. and Fábregas Valcarce, R. in press a. La circulation des haches carnacéennes en Europe occidentale (The circulation of Carnac-type axeheads in western Europe). In P. Pétrequin, S. Cassen, M. Errera, L. Klassen and J. A. Sheridan (eds.), *Jade. Grandes haches alpines du Néolithique européen. V^e et IVe millénaires av. J.-C.* Besançon, Presses Universitaires de Franche-Comté (Cahiers de la MSHE C.N. Ledoux).

Pétrequin, P., Cassen, S., Errera, M., Klassen, L. and Sheridan, J. A. (eds.) in press b. *Jade. Grandes haches alpines du Néolithique européen. V^e et IVe millénaires av. J.-C.* Besançon, Presses Universitaires de Franche-Comté (Cahiers de la MSHE C.N. Ledoux).

Pétrequin, P., Cassen, S., Gauthier, E., Klassen, L., Pailler, Y. and Sheridan, J.A. in press c. Typologie, chronologie et répartition des grandes haches alpines en Europe occidentale (Typology, chronology and distribution of large Alpine axeheads in western Europe). In P. Pétrequin, S. Cassen, M. Errera, L. Klassen and J. A. Sheridan (eds.), *Jade. Grandes haches alpines du Néolithique européen. V^e et IVe millénaires av. J.-C.* Besançon, Presses Universitaires de Franche-Comté (Cahiers de la MSHE C.N. Ledoux).

Philippe, M., Rassart, V., Meurisse-Fort, M., Gosselin, G., March, R. J., Rassat, S., Guéret, C. and Caspar, J.-P. in press. Les horizons néolithiques du site des Sablins Étaples (Pas-de-Calais). Résultats preliminaries du programme 2003–2009. In F. Bostyn, E. Martial and I. Praud (eds.), *Le Néolithique du Nord de la France dans son contexte européen : habitat et économie aux 4e et 3e millénaires avant notre ère.* (Comptes rendus du 29e colloque interregional sur le Néolithique (INTERNÉO), 2–3 octobre 2009, Villeneuve d'Ascq). *Revue Archéologique de Picardie.*

Piggott, S. 1954. *Neolithic Cultures of the British Isles.* Cambridge, Cambridge University Press.

Pitts, M. 2009. Breton hoard of stone axeheads is first for UK. *British Archaeology* May/June 2009, 6.

Quinnell, H. 2006. Neolithic pottery. In A. M. Jones and S. J. Reed, 2006. By land, sea and air: an Early Neolithic pit group at Portscatho, Cornwall, and consideration of coastal activity during the Neolithic, 5-9. *Cornish Archaeology* 45, 1-30.

Quinnell, H. and Taylor, R. 1999. Pottery. In T. H. Gent and H. Quinnell, Excavations of a causewayed enclosure and hillfort on Raddon Hill, Stockleigh Pomeroy. *Proceedings of the Devon Archaeological Society* 57, 38-53.

Quinnell, H. 2003. The early Neolithic pottery. In D. Cole and A. M. Jones, Journeys to the Rock: archaeological investigations at Tregarrick Farm, Roche, 113-121. *Cornish Archaeology* 41-2 (2002/3), 107-143.

Richards, J. C. *The Stonehenge Environs Project.* London, English Heritage (Archaeological Report 16).

Rowley-Conwy, P. 2004. How the West was lost. A reconsideration of agricultural origins in Britain, Ireland, and southern Scandinavia. *Current Anthropology* 45, S83-S113.

Saville, A. 1990. *Hazleton North, Gloucestershire, 1979–82: The Excavation of a Neolithic Long Cairn of the Cotswold-Severn Group.* London, Historic Buildings and Monuments Commission for England.

Schulting, R. J. 2000. New AMS dates from the Lambourn long barrow and the question of the earliest Neolithic in southern England: repacking the Neolithic package? *Oxford Journal of Archaeology* 19(1), 25-35.

Schulting, R. J. 2004. An Irish sea change: some implications for the Mesolithic-Neolithic transition. In V. Cummings and C. Fowler (eds.), *The Neolithic of the Irish Sea: Materiality and Traditions of Practice*, 9-21. Oxford, Oxbow.

Schulting, R. J. 2007. Non-monumental burial in Neolithic Britain: a (largely) cavernous view. In L. Larsson, F. Lüth and T. Terberger (eds.), *Non-Megalithic Mortuary Practices in the Baltic – New Methods and Research into the Development of Stone Age Society*, 581-603. Schwerin, Römisch-Germanischen Kommission (*Bericht der Römisch-Germanischen Kommission* 88).

Sharples, N. M. 1991. *Maiden Castle. Excavations and Field Survey 1985–6.* London, English Heritage (Archaeological Report 19).

Shennan, S, J., Edinborough, K., 2007. Prehistoric population history: from the Late Glacial to the Late Neolithic in Central and Northern Europe. *Journal of Archaeological Science* 34, 1339-1345.

Sheridan, J. A. 2004. Neolithic connections along and across the Irish Sea. In V. Cummings and C. Fowler (eds.), *The Neolithic of the Irish Sea: Materiality and Traditions of Practice*, 9-21. Oxford, Oxbow.

Sheridan, J. A. 2007. From Picardie to Pickering and Pencraig Hill? New information on the 'Carinated Bowl Neolithic' in northern Britain. In A. W. R. Whittle and V. Cummings (eds.) *Going Over: the Mesolithic–Neolithic Transition in North-West Europe*, 441-492. Oxford, British Academy (*Proceedings of the British Academy 144).*

Sheridan, J. A. 2010. The Neolithization of Britain and Ireland : the 'Big Picture'. In B. Finlayson and G. Warren (eds.), *Landscapes in Transition*, 89-105.

Oxford and Oakville, Oxbow (Levant Supplementary Series 8).

Sheridan, J.A. and Pailler, Y. 2011. La néolithisation de la Grande-Bretagne et de l'Irlande : plusieurs processus, plusieurs modèles et des questions à l'attention de nos collègues français. In F. Bostyn, E. Martial and I. Praud (eds.), *Le Néolithique du Nord de la France dans son contexte européen : habitat et économie aux 4e et 3e millénaires avant notre ère*, 13-30. (Comptes rendus du 29e colloque interregional sur le Néolithique (INTERNÉO), 2–3 octobre 2009, Villeneuve d'Ascq). *Revue Archéologique de Picardie*.

Sheridan, J. A. Schulting, R., Quinnell, H. and Taylor, R. 2008. Revisiting a small passage tomb at Broadsands, Devon. *Proceedings of the Devon Archaeological Society* 66, 1-26.

Sheridan, J. A. Field, D., Pailler, Y., Pétrequin, P., Errera, M. and Cassen, S. 2010. The Breamore jadeitite axehead and other Neolithic axeheads of Alpine rock from central southern England. *Wiltshire Archaeological and Natural History Magazine* 103,16-34.

Sheridan, J. A., Pailler, Y., Pétrequin, P. and Errera, M. 2011. Old friends, new friends, a long-lost friend and false friends: tales from *Projet JADE*. In R.V. Davis and M. Edmonds (eds.), *Stone Axe Studies III*, 411-426. Oxford and Oakville, Oxbow Books.

Smith, I. F. 1956. *The Decorative Art of Neolithic Ceramics in South East England and its Relations*. Unpublished Ph.D. thesis, University College London Institute of Archaeology.

Smith, I.F. 1981. Neolithic pottery. In R. J. Mercer, Excavations at Carn Brea, Illogan, Cornwall, 1970-73 – a Neolithic fortified complex of the third millennium bc. *Cornish Archaeology* 20, 161-185.

Smith, I. F. and Darvill, T. 1990. The prehistoric pottery. In A. Saville, *Hazleton North, Gloucestershire, 1979–82: The Excavation of a Neolithic Long Cairn of the Cotswold-Severn Group*, 141-152. London, Historic Buildings and Monuments Commission for England.

Smith, G. 1990. A Neolithic long barrow at Uplowman Road, Tiverton. *Proceedings of the Devon Archaeological Society* 48, 15-26.

Smith, M. and Brickley, M. 2006. The date and sequence of use of Neolithic funerary monuments: new AMS dating evidence from the Cotswold-Severn region. *Oxford Journal of Archaeology* 25(4), 335-355.

Smith, M. and Brickley, M. 2009. *People of the Long Barrows: Life, Death and Burial in the Earlier Neolithic*. Stroud, The History Press.

Smith, W. C. 1963. Jade axes from sites in the British Isles. *Proceedings of the Prehistoric Society* 29, 133-172.

Thomas, J. S. 1991. *Rethinking the Neolithic*, Cambridge, Cambridge University Press.

Thomas, J. S. 1996. Neolithic houses in mainland Britain and Ireland – a sceptical view. In T. Darvill and J. Thomas (eds.) *Neolithic Houses in Northwest Europe and Beyond*, 1-12. Oxford, Oxbow.

Thomas, J. S. 1999. *Understanding the Neolithic*, London and New York, Routledge.

Thomas, J. S. 2003. Thoughts on the 'repacked' Neolithic revolution. *Antiquity* 77, 67-74.

Thomas, J. S. 2004. Recent debates on the Mesolithic-Neolithic transition in Britain and Ireland, *Documenta Praehistorica* 31, 117-130.

Thomas, J. S. 2007. Mesolithic-Neolithic transitions in Britain: from essence to inhabitation. In A. W. R. Whittle & V. Cummings (eds.) *Going Over: the Mesolithic–Neolithic Transition in North-West Europe*, 423-439. Oxford, British Academy (*Proceedings of the British Academy 144)*.

Thomas, J. S. 2008. The Mesolithic-Neolithic transition in Britain. In J. Pollard (ed.) *Prehistoric Britain*, 58-89. Oxford, Blackwell.

Vanmontfort, B. 2006. Can we attribute the Middle Neolithic in the Scheldt and Middle Meuse Basins to the Michelsberg cultre? In P.Duhamel (ed.), *Impacts Interculturels au Néolithique Moyen. Du Terroir au Territoire*, (Actes du 25ᵉ Colloque Interrégional sur le Néolithique, Dijon 20–21 octobre 2001), 109-116. Dijon, Société Archéologique de l'Est.

Whittle, A. W. R. 1977. *The Earlier Neolithic of Southern England and its Continental Background*. Oxford, British Archaeological Reports (International Series 35).

Whittle, A. W. R., Healy, F. and Bayliss, A. 2011. *Gathering Time: Dating the Early Neolithic Enclosures of Southern Britain and Ireland*. Oxford and Oakville, Oxbow Books.

Whittle, A. W. R., Pollard, J. and Grigson, C. 1999. *The Harmony of Symbols. The Windmill Hill Causewayed Enclosure, Wiltshire*. Oxford, Oxbow.

Whittle, A. W. R., Barclay, A., Bayliss, A., McFadyen, L., Schulting, R. and Wysocki, M. 2007. Building for the dead: events, processes and changing worldviews from the thirty-eighth to the thirty-fourth centuries cal. BC in southern Britain. In A. Bayliss and A. W. R. Whittle (eds.), *Histories of the Dead: Building Chronologies for Five Southern British Long Barrows*, 123-147. *Cambridge Archaeological Journal* 17(1) (Supplement).

Woodman, P. C., Anderson, E. and Finlay, N. 1999. *Excavations at Ferriter's Cove, 1983–1995: Last Foragers, First Farmers on the Dingle Peninsula*. Bray, Wordwell.

Woodman, P. C. and McCarthy, M. 2003. Contemplating some awful(ly interesting) vistas: importing cattle and red deer into prehistoric Ireland. In: I. Armit, E. Murphy, E. Nelis and D. D. A. Simpson (eds.) *Neolithic settlement in Ireland and Western Britain*, 31-9. Oxford, Oxbow.

Woodward, A. 2009. The pottery. In L. Ladle and A. Woodward, *Excavations at Bestwall Quarry, Wareham 1992–2005. Volume 1: the Prehistoric Landscape*, 200-271. Dorchester, Dorset County Museum.

Wysocki, M., Bayliss, A. and Whittle, A. 2007. Serious mortality: the date of the Fussell's Lodge long barrow. In A. Bayliss and A. W. R. Whittle (eds.), *Histories of the Dead: Building Chronologies for Five*

Southern British Long Barrows, 65-84. *Cambridge Archaeological Journal* 17(1) (Supplement).

Acknowledgements

Frances Griffith is thanked for having invited me to present the lecture from which this contribution has developed, and for providing information on long barrows in Devon; Cyril Marcigny is thanked for providing advice on the north-west French Middle Neolithic; Tim Darvill is thanked for permission to refer to the Hinckley Point monument; Alistair Barclay is thanked for information about early Neolithic pottery assemblages in Wessex; Andy Jones and Jacky Nowakoski are thanked for advice on sites in Cornwall; various authors and publishers are thanked for permitting the reproduction of pottery illustrations; and, above all, Sue Pearce is thanked for her patience as editor.

Pseudo-Quoit to Propped Stones

Tony Blackman

Abstract

This is an account of one strand of an archaeological journey on Bodmin Moor in Cornwall, and as such it is deliberately cast in the form of a story. Along the way, I have had the joy of working with my wife, and the involvement of friends, acquaintances and many members of the interested public. It has provided an archaeological richness, which I could not have conceived in 1993. For a Head Teacher, who was still to find his first prehistoric flint, retiring early to become more involved in archaeology was both a financial gamble and a steep learning curve. I confess to having had a secret ambition to discover previously unrecognised archaeology - but what hope had I of doing that in the light of the intensive research which had been carried out on Bodmin Moor by Nicholas Johnson, Peter Rose and Peter Herring since 1980, which has produced two major English Heritage publications. I decided that to further my skill in landscape study and to develop a keen, practiced eye I would go onto every landscape without consulting the SMR –for me all finds were to be 'first finds'. This approach, and the desire to learn from the farmers living on Bodmin Moor, some of whom were of the age and practice to inform me about sustaining a family in isolation, has served me well. I also wished to continue my work in education, opening up less obvious landscapes to both young and older eyes and giving opportunities to view and understand remains of the past which are not encountered in their everyday lives. Outreach is important in all my work.

Introduction

In 1995 Peter Herring and I were leading an archaeological walk on Leskernick Hill and the surrounding West Moor. When we arrived at the fairly insignificant Leskernick Tor, some way ahead of a slow moving group, we had time to ponder the rather strange top tor-stone supported at an angle by three much smaller stones obviously placed under it to elevate it (fig. 4.1). We discussed whether this might have been the work of home-guard farmers bored of continuous cold, lonely nights watching for Second World War German spies parachuting in prior to an invasion from the south-western beaches – this discussion stimulated by having just visited a Bronze Age cairn some 50 metres away where the stones had been re-arranged to provide shelter against the harsh weather of many watching nights.

Three weeks later we repeated the walk with a group of friends, having agreed to see the setting as a human construction in the light of the proposed the Home Guard theory. An immediate repost from a geologist condemned this because, he explained, under each of the three supporting stones was an erosion shadow meaning that the structure, however constructed, was very old. We knew nothing of erosion shadows, areas protected from erosion and thus still at the original height of the base stone upon which the supporting stones rested, and we were further informed that the technology was not yet available to age them. Some two hours later, we sat for lunch on a long 'sausage' mound about a kilometre away, and noticed that the mound pointed directly at the Tor construction previously under discussion, which now formed the only horizon feature on the western side of the gently curved Leskernick Hill. One member of the group suggested that we were looking in the direction of the mid-summer setting sun and compasses gave an approximate bearing of 313°, now known as an approximate bearing for this to happen. We decided to meet on the mound on 21st June to watch the sunset and see if this mound, the near hilltop construction and the theory that the sun might set behind it had any merit. The crowd that evening had swelled well beyond our initial small group. All my Young Archaeologists Club Cornwall Branch (YAC) members were present with their parents, as were curious members of the Cornwall Archaeological Society, some professional archaeologists and several moorland friends. Never before or since have I seen such a wonderful moorland sunset and never have we been as devastated as when we realised the setting sun was going to miss the monument. I had to sidestep eleven paces to the east to allow the setting we had so hoped for. We suddenly become aware of the concern in some of the group as they realised we had a mile to walk across open, featureless moorland in the dark.

Fig. 4.1

In the midst of reassuring the group came sudden words of comfort: 'if it had set behind the stone you would have been disappointed – you needed it not to do so to prove it an ancient erection'. Never had words been so welcome.

Peter had the landscape surveyed and the Greenwich scientists eventually produced a date when the sun would have set behind the monument, which by now Peter had named the Leskernick Pseudo-Quoit. When viewed from the mound, the date would have been approximately 3700 BC, but this date was determined for the 1.8m height of an average modern man. This may have produced a slightly skewed result, as we have no accurate information on the average height of prehistoric people on Bodmin Moor. The human height factor relating to prehistoric monuments when viewed, or viewing from, has come into more of our work since and I often carry a staff of inch-separated screws so that I can test monument and landscape effect against eye height.

The Next Steps

The attendance of my young archaeologists that evening was to have a profound effect on the future of the study – their unpolluted eyes which saw only what was on a landscape, not what was expected to be seen, gave the next few years a real fillip to our days out – they were finally convinced that there was still unrecognised archaeology and they set about discovery with a will. And what sharp eyes those young people developed – probably the keenest eyes of any belonged to Richard Hart who demonstrated this time and again but to embarrassing effect on one occasion. Listening to an archaeologist expounding about a well-known cairn he quietly asked about the several low, regularly spaced small cairns, which ringed it. Silence reigned during the assessment of the question before revealing that they had never before been noticed and were not on the SMR. Richard, with others, was to repeat this with me many times.

Many finds are attributable to our long periods of time exploring the moors and the now rampant enthusiasm of YAC to be involved. At this time we were building two replica upland roundhouses on Trewortha Farm, which serves as a residential centre for schools and youth groups, a place I took my school to in 1984 as the very first users and where the magic has never faded. Graham and Liz Lawrence, the owners, are now my very dear friends. This is important because in working with them and their farmer friends I was fulfilling that very important archaeological requisite – getting to know the landscape. I was also researching turf (peat) cutting on Wimalford Farm in the Fowey Valley with Jack Parkyn, whom I had found following a year of visiting farmhouses and catching the crumbs of a now redundant and environmentally restricted practices, essential for living on the moors before the Second World War. I learned to cut turf, dry it, rick it and thatch the rick with rushes. But Jack Parkyn taught me so much more about the moor. English Heritage's Bodmin Moor Volume 2 is dedicated to his memory.

Fig. 4.2

Peter and I realised that Leskernick may not be unique. We reassessed the 'Cannon Stone' on Carburrow Tor and also 'Elephant Rock' in the hedge line bordering West Moor. The Cannon Stone was given its name by Tor Keast, who farmed the tor, and this feature, assessed as natural in 1983, was reassessed and pronounced a human construction, and recognised as a wonderful picture frame, which frames the magnificence of Brown Willy and Roughtor. Elephant Rock was similarly reassessed. These two erections, together with one on Hawks Tor on the South East side of the moor, which I had found prior to Leskernick and which the farmer said was always thought to be some type of either shelter or altar, opened up the thought that there might just be more. It is interesting how powerful this thought became and on reflection how it directed much of my looking in the years to come. My desire to involve others in all our exploratory work can be seen in the following events.

A YAC national holiday I ran at Trewortha Farm allowed a sharp eyed group on top of Kilmar Tor to point out a stone which for them clearly stood out on the landscape below and for me cemented the fact that I needed glasses. An instant visit, revealing the erosion shadow, and further investigation, proved that this was an archaeological feature and is named the YAC Stone (fig. 4.2). The eyesight question is important for two reasons, firstly because the question we were soon to be asking ourselves was, why had we, and all others before us missed these constructions? Were we so driven by a known series of prescriptive monuments and landscapes, that we missed or saw and dismissed other remains of human activity? And secondly, what purpose did these constructions serve for their builders if they were apparently so discrete in the landscape? But were they so discrete when built? Much of the archaeology now displayed on the moors, both monuments and landscapes, has almost certainly developed after propped stone construction. An earlier good example of missing a monument type on Bodmin Moor is the recognition of stone rows. Only one was known in Cornwall before 1983 and now at least seven found on the moor since more intensive investigation; and they are still being found.

The problem that there may be no set type to our findings had arisen very quickly, but even more, we had to ask ourselves what absolute evidence had we that these different stone settings were indeed the work of human beings. It was time to call in the geologists. One well known to us, an experienced Bodmin Moor walker, was Dr Judith Bunbury, a Launceston girl, and a post-doctorate researcher in the geo-archaeology Department of Cambridge University. She visited several of the finds and pronounced some to be certain human structures, but recommended that three categories be defined, as Possible, Probable and Definite, and I still work with this categorisation today.

I was already personalising the stones. One on the summit of Kilmar Tor, I found on a Sunday evening whilst leading four young archaeologists to the top by a fairly torturous route because they were still not worn out after a weekend of round-house building. Ego allowed me to call it Tony's Stone (fig 4.3) and it still excites me on every visit, even after some fourteen years. It points directly at Stowe's Hill on the Minions landscape and initially I referred to it as a signpost stone, a title I soon dropped as I was constantly asked why 'they', the erectors, would have needed a signpost. However, the pointing is important, because for some time we had talked about the Roughtor Effect as it became recognised that several monuments were constructed to refer to Roughtor/ Showery Tor on the northern side of the moor, but Stowe's Hill on the southern side seems to have a similar reverence from some of the constructions.

James Mylod, then a Young Archaeologist of twelve years and just allowed some independence on the moors whilst roundhouse building at Trewortha Farm, reported that he had found another propped stone, the name now adopted, even though some of them were not, and it was three weeks before we took him seriously and visited his find. The structure was confirmed and is now known as James's Stone (fig. 4.4). Grahame Lawrence, who has grazed Trewortha Farm's sheep and beef cattle on Twelve Men's Moor under ancient right, questioned why he had never recognised it, for he knew every cist and round house on that part of the moor and also has an interest in archaeology. The discreteness of this monument type was becoming apparent; they were not going to be obvious, one had to look for them. James, in his excitement of making his find, had failed to do what he had been taught, to examine the surrounding landscape closely, and his disappointment was obvious when the three lesser propped stones close by were pointed out to him by Steve Hartgroves of HES who was helping in the building programme. This is the most concentrated collection of propped stones anywhere to date. James's Stone and the previously recognised low Neolithic long cairn on Twelve Men's Moor led me to visit Trewortha Tor on the other side of that moor to see if there was any feature which might form a linear link. Trewortha Tor had a rock structure I had long ago christened 'Impossible Rock' because it should have collapsed millennia ago! Close by that I found, partially collapsed, a structure not unlike James's Stone but constructed in the tor rocks which

Fig. 4.3

Fig. 4.4

Fig. 4.5

did indeed make that linking line. Later, I found a similar structure on Smallacombe Tor and since that time several more of similar type have appeared including the most prominent of them on Jacob's Tor (fig 4.5), a local name not found on maps, where a quite massive top tor stone has been propped by a large, reasonably spherical stone. Jacob's Tor, north of Golddiggings Quarry, is on private land and many a person on my walks has strained to look over the high medieval stone wall to get a glimpse! Indeed, this cluster demonstrates a monument type, which occurs when the tor outcrop is not on the top of the hill.

FIG. 4.6

A YAC investigative trip to Roughtor allowed Tansy Collins, then fifteen and now a practicing archaeologist, to gallop along the ridge with a loud and excited, 'Tone – come and see what I've found'. Another construction, now known as Tansy's Stone (fig 4.6), had been recognised. Later that year we found another and this caused us to pronounce on yet another, well known, nearby feature, also on the southern slopes of Roughtor as a human construction. The first construction is pointing to the summit of Brown Willy whilst the other's function, if any, is still hidden from us.

Further Discoveries

Running parallel to these early finds, so precious to me, were the finds that Dot and I were making on our investigative journeys, which brought further evidence of different types with obvious, possible or no perceived function.

In the early part of the third millennium Brian Williams, who had known nothing of our work, contacted me on advice from Henrietta Quinnell, questioning whether a setting on Pew Tor on the Western Edge of Dartmoor was a human construction. We visited, eventually found the construction and immediately pronounced that it was, and, indeed, was similar to Tansy's Stone on Roughtor. Soon after, I found the second largest propped stone to date on Feather Tor, close to Pew Tor. Soon after that and following a day out with Peter Clements, a doctorate student, who had asked me to introduce him to my own personal landscape investigative techniques – summed up as 'examine everything, think laterally and believe there's going to be something someone has missed-' reported one in the middle of his specialist study area further east and towards the centre of the moor. Dartmoor was revealing a similar monument type to Bodmin Moor. There is still much to investigate on Dartmoor, a fact recently agreed in conversation with Tim Gent the head of Exeter Archaeology.

We had long been aware that there was a requirement to examine the prehistoric relationship between Dartmoor and Bodmin Moor. When Cornwall YAC was helping Dr Andy Jones with work for his PhD study we were asked to find any remains of the barrows destroyed at the time of constructing the Second World War airfield on the Davidstow Moor landscape. The method used was to take Croft-Andrew's 1940 six figure grid references and to allow YAC members to develop navigating skills by using the moving ten figure grid references on GPS compasses, each identified spot being marked with a ranging pole. Two ranging poles were found to directly align with the only Dartmoor tor top visible on an otherwise totally flat and empty horizon.

Also, some nine years ago, whilst on a Wednesday evening minibus excursion to the Merrivale landscape on Dartmoor with the national YAC holiday members staying at Trewortha Farm, Dot pointed out (at no lesser time than when I was in full flow of explanation about Bronze Age landscapes) that the North and South pairs of stone rows pointed to the horizon landscape features from Caradon Hill to Stowe's Hill on eastern Bodmin Moor, The northern row of the southern pair has some unusually tall stones and at each of these the double row bends. A return visit and further investigation revealed that this was not the whole story :at each bend the new line pointed to a well known feature, Caradon Hill with its twenty-two barrows, the Hurlers Stone Circles and finally the Rillaton Barrow. The the Northern pair of rows, a simple straight line, pointed at Stowe's Hill tor enclosure. It has long been known that the single large stone at the end of each pair or rows form a line pointing to the 'prehistoric' midsummer sunset but a little later in the year, on the return visit, Dot recognised two stones, now both leaning, in the open Merrivale landscape, which point to midsummer sunrise and sunset and midwinter sunrise and sunset. We also proved that an especially large stone in the nearby reeve, surrounded by a ring of smaller stones, also points to the midsummer sunset, presumably when the stone rows were built. All three settings point to exactly the same horizon sunset point. We have led several archaeological days on the Merrivale landscape pointing out these 'new' features and I mention this and other significant finds/recognitions to show that we have not spent the past fifteen years purely locked into propped stones – indeed, just the opposite! It has surprised us, however, how little interest some professionals have paid to these recognitions. Is there a comfort in prescriptive landscapes?

Neil Burridge, the well-known 'prehistoric' bronze caster, contacted me about a propped stone on Carn Galva in Penwith. A photograph confirmed that this stone was very similar to the one on Hawks Tor at the edge of Twelve Men's Moor to which I referred earlier. Neil's identification was correct and it is now called Neil's Stone (fig. 4.7). This was a recognition that was to open up the Penwith landscape to investigation and confirm in my mind that a stone on Carn Kenidjack needed reinvestigation. I had spent ten years, three weeks a year, leading day circular walks on the Penwith Moors for two comprehensive schools, stopping at Carn Kenidjack to relate the story of the Demon Wrestlers. Leaving the Carn my eye was always drawn to

FIG. 4.7

FIG. 4.8

an ugly setting on its top, which I challenged children to say whether or not it was a human construction. Through the ten years, opinions seemed fairly equally divided but I have now placed it in the probable group.

We visited Carn Galva and Dot instantly recognised another setting which has become one of the iconic examples. This most spectacular setting, one large beautifully shaped stone, propped by what can only be another especially selected stone with a wide quartz vein running through it, sits mesmerizingly in the landscape challenging one to find a reason for its existence. This setting is now known as Dot's Stone (fig 4. 8). On our next visit we realised that we had missed a third, probably partially collapsed, setting. Soon after this Adrian Rodda sent a picture of another candidate on the Penwith coast. The distribution now spread over a hundred miles.

The Plot Widens

Now we had the proof of a monument spread over a wide area, but how wide, how far, from what time and with what significance?

We went to the Preseli Hills after Dr Vicky Cummings had informed us of a possible setting and on visiting this found another of similar type to the YAC Stone, an unpropped stone below the hills and close to a pedestrian entrance.

Dot is a Guernsey girl and we have spent exciting times visiting the prehistoric archaeology of her birth island. A visit to Herm in 2007 allowed us to forecast where a propped stone might be and we surprised ourselves by walking straight to it. Ugly it is, but there is no doubt about the propping. We have also visited a seemingly collapsed setting at the tower end of the Vale Churchyard, which is almost certain to be another candidate. The ground on which this stands would have been a significant rise on the western end of what was, until the channel was filled in, the northern of the two islands of Guernsey.

The study in Penwith came to an unintentional halt until in 2009, David Giddings, a well respected landscape archaeologist from Penzance, with knowledge of the study, informed me that he had cycled past a monument in Brittany, Dolmen du Marchais, and was certain that it was a propped stone. This stimulated David to begin a specific search on the Penwith landscape and following his first find, and as I write this report, I have received pictures of two more for examination. Now we have absolute proof that they are spread around the Penwith moors, I am hopeful that further investigation there will lead to a significant number being recognised. The variety of settings found and how they accord with those of Bodmin Moor and Dartmoor, will be of great interest.

Roger Farnworth has, in the last three years, found several examples on Bodmin Moor and concentrated on the idea that they are 'window stones', where the windows are formed by the propping stones and the views provided are of special places. This may be true for some but addresses only one of the possible reasons for the erections.

Following the discoveries on Carn Galva, a hill considered to have Neolithic archaeology, we decided to look at the known Neolithic hills. There is a propped stone on Helman Tor in mid Cornwall, probably the ugliest I know, and the only one to date where the two propping stones are clearly part of the separating erosion layer between two harder stones. However, there is obviously more of significance on Helman Tor; a huge stone, which has been swivelled, and may even have been moved to its position, points at Roughtor several miles away on North Bodmin Moor and is clearly visible as an horizon feature. There is a stone of cruder setting on Kilmar Tor, not recognised as a Neolithic hill, within metres of Tony's Stone, which also points at Roughtor. After three visits to Trencrom Hill, at the eastern end of the Penwith landscape, we have finally found the propped stone there, a testimony to the fact that even now some are far from obvious.

It is clear that much more work has to be done in studying the erection, movement, and significance of stones in prehistoric times and the motivation for it. I define a megalith as a stone which needs more than one person and a common accord to position it, and the vast majority of the propped stones and other constructions now being recognised fall into that category. Helman Tor also has a setting of three gigantic stones, for which the notion that they were naturally positioned defies reason to state, which point at Hensbarrow Downs and which require intense geological investigation. Unfortunately the Hensbarrow Downs, a known prehistoric landscape, have been severely disfigured by china clay extraction since the 1750s, a time before accurate archaeological recording was a consideration. On St Belermins Tor, on Bodmin Moor, is an insignificant propped stone which points at Burydown, a hill near Lanreath, which was excavated in the 1990s. This led to a proposal that it may have been the site of a causewayed camp. Several years after the recognition of Leskernick pseudo-quoit (it has never really lost its original title) a triangular stone set at an angle in the ground within metres of it was recognised as pointing at Showery Tor. These pointing stones are all directed from or at hills with Neolithic archaeology and associated with propped stones.

As more of these propped stones are found there is still the initial excitement of recognition. But because I have been involved with the study for so long, the identification of the method of discovery becomes blurred. To stand on a landscape and say that you feel there should be one there, to indicate where it might be and then be proven right can be eerie. I can only assume that we now have an inbuilt set of factors which inform that feeling. It does not lessen the feeling of disturbance, especially as I have always stated that I recognise no 'feelings' on archaeological sites and work from a purely rational set of criteria.

A chance conversation increased the likelihood of more of these monuments being found in other parts of the British Isles. I had contacted Professor Scarre, when I learned that he had an active archaeological programme on the island of Herm, to inform him of the propped stone there. In our conversation he told me of two connected points. At an archaeological conference in France he had heard two Irish archaeologists talking about similar monuments which geologists had assured them were natural; and also that there were examples of antiquarian writings describing such structures.

A rare visit to Megalithic.co.uk coincided with a posted photograph where information was being sought on a propped structure, immediately recognisable as a type encountered in our study. It had already been suggested that the poster of this photograph should read a back issue of Meyn Mamvro in which I had written an article some eight years ago. I believe this picture to have been taken somewhere in the northern half of the country.

Remaining Questions

At present I am left with a number of questions for which I am able to present few if any answers. What is the total geographical distribution of this monument and in what concentrations and types do they occur? Do the different types of similar monuments, appearing in this study, display variations of the same monument type, or are there several loosely or unrelated types? Were we too swift to give a general and perhaps undescriptive name to the possible set based simply on our first find and linked known and re-examined examples, and further, how sensible is it to design more descriptive names for possible sub-sets until such time as we have done more work and are more confident of our study parameters? Why are so many examples found on somewhat inhospitable areas of the landscape, or has historical use of land eradicated those on more favoured agricultural ground? The majority of the examples found so far are not significant landscape features, otherwise they should or would have been found and recognised very much earlier in archaeological landscape work. Does this indicate reasonably discrete special places? Does their occurrence on known Neolithic sites allow us to securely place them in a Neolithic context and do the erosion shadows apparent on some provide more security to this possible dating?

The general groupings for these erections can at present be classified as follows:

- A top stone with one prop to level it and secure it into its position
- A stone with more than one propping stone to secure it in position, placed in positions which do not form a viewing frame. A stone with more than one propping stone, placed to provide a viewing fram., even if in some cases unintentionally
- A large stone placed across two or more larger stones, which may or may not have been placed in position themselves.
- A stone placed on another stone, which has no propping stone, but forms a significant feature in the landscape.
- A stone, often of spherical form, placed under another much larger stone to enhance the top stone. This group includes, at present, the propped top stones of some Tors, especially where the tor outcrop is not at the top of the hill, the most significant of which so far is on Jacobs Tor.
- A stone placed under a much larger stone at ground or near ground level, which would otherwise have lain on the ground. Lest this group should create a comment about stone splitting requiring a propping stone to support it and create the best environment for the splitting, I must state that I have been studying stone splitting and dressing on the open moorland since 1983, own my own splitting tools and have an absolute ability to differentiate one from the other on the Cornish landscapes.

A number of propped stone positions on Bodmin Moor which have not been mentioned so far may be listed briefly. At Alex Tor, there is one in the 'false quarry' on the tor which points at Roughtor; at Brown Willy there are several, the main one being a spectacular mounting of a large stone bridging two under stones. Corner Quoit obviously takes its name from the small erection looking just like a miniature quoit. Tregarrick Tor has an insignificant mounting in view of Stowe's Hill but pointing in the opposite direction. Butters Tor, a very low tor with a deserted cottage nearby, has a top stone propping, which is a miniature version of that on Jacob's Tor. A Garrow field wall has a setting like the YAC Stone, set into a later field wall .Ridge Tor has a ground stone raised on one propped stone, and there is a construction on Temple Tor, long ago recognised but only confirmed in March 2010 when access was kindly granted to the landscape.

It is a certainty that there are many more to find. It is also a truth that Dot and I have never started a moorland investigation with the intent of finding a propped stone. Our work is all part of an investigation that is intended to find every possible human interference with a landscape. Granite moving drag trails, unfinished mill stones and cider presses, levelled areas probably associated with transhumance practices, unfinished domestic granite sinks and troughs, cairns which mirror landscape hills and much else all fascinate us and 'make our days' We are archaeological scavengers and from this the propped stones appeared in the landscape. We will, as always, design our holidays to involve archaeology and it would seem that several upland areas of England and an extended visit to Ireland are called for. But more importantly, if anyone reading this recognises similar structures in their own study landscapes we would love them to be in touch.

Between the Channel and the Chalk: A Regional Perspective on Grooved Ware and Beaker Pottery from the Mendip Hills, Somerset

Jodie Lewis and David Mullin

Abstract

Henrietta Quinnell has made an enormous contribution to our knowledge of both prehistoric ceramic studies and ritual and funerary monuments in South West Britain. In this paper, we wish to consider both of these topics in an area just outside that which has formed her main geographic focus, but which can still be counted as forming part of South West Britain: the Mendip Hills in Somerset. The focus of this paper is a reconsideration of Late Neolithic Grooved Ware and Early Bronze Age Beaker pottery from this distinctive geographic region, located between the Bristol Channel to the west and the chalklands of Wessex to the east. This upland limestone plateau has the most concentrated and diverse range of Late Neolithic and Early Bronze Age finds, sites and monuments in all of Somerset and these appear to exhibit a degree of regional cohesion (Lewis 2005; Mullin in press).

Introduction

The Mendip landscape is topographically distinct from those that neighbour it (the Cotswolds, the Wessex Chalk and the Somerset Levels), a distinction that must have been recognised in prehistory. It is predominantly a karst landscape with impressive features such as gorges, cliffs, combes and dry valleys, closed depressions, sinking streams and caves. The hills can be further divided into two landscape types: the high, steep-sided West Mendip plateau, dominated geologically by Carboniferous Limestone with a few rounded hills of Old Red Sandstone, and East Mendip where the limestone plateau is slightly lower and the geologies more diverse, with much more surface water in evidence. There is a denser concentration of prehistoric archaeology on West Mendip, suggesting that the difference between the two landscapes has been recognised and acknowledged for millennia. To the south of Mendip lie the Somerset Levels, a wetland landscape containing internationally important prehistoric sites that include the Sweet Track, whilst to the north of the hills are the North Somerset wetlands and Chew Valley, the latter the site of the impressive Late Neolithic monument complex at Stanton Drew.

The unusual features of Mendip engender a sense of difference to this place. The region is rich in mineral deposits such as lead and iron (with also occurs as ochre), which may be visible on the surface, exposed by animal or vegetation disturbance, and also in caves. Lewis (2007) has suggested that these and other minerals were recognised and viewed as attractive, useful or indeed magical at least by the Mesolithic period on Mendip. The large numbers of closed depressions known locally as swallets also play an important part in this sense of difference. These natural features exhibit peculiar traits: they can emit strange sounds due to water percolation; they fill with mist, which hovers just above them and they can even appear to "breathe", letting out exhalations of mist when the ambient temperature is lower than that inside the swallet. Many swallets started to open as a result of environmental changes in the earlier Holocene and prehistoric populations would have witnessed the ground around them being swallowed. That these features were significant in prehistory is unquestionable. Upon excavation, a number of sites have been found to contain an array of placed deposits, some of which are considered later in this paper. Other unusual landscape formations include caves, which show a long history of exploitation and veneration. Many of these caves occur in the side of the gorges and coombes that carve the sides of the plateau. These themselves offer a unique array of experiences, providing a route onto and off the plateau that may have been shared with wild animals. The large cliffs of the gorges at Cheddar, Ebbor and Burrington dwarf the body, creating a claustrophobic environment with a unique set of flora perhaps attractive to humans as well as other animals. Some of the caves are located high above the gorge floor, perhaps as difficult to access as the swallets, though this did not deter humans from using them for a wide range of activities.

The high points and edges of Mendip allow visual connectivity with other regions: Wales, Wessex, Exmoor, the Blackdown Hills and the Cotswolds. It is also island-like, rising dramatically from the lowlying North Somerset and Somerset Levels to the north and south. The western end of the plateau breaks up into a series of hills before ending at the Bristol Channel; these are considered part of Mendip because of their geological and topographical similarity. Brean Down, the most westerly of these hills, is the point where the broken Mendip ridge falls into the sea.

Mendip has one of the highest concentrations of round barrows in southern England, with nearly 400 examples cited in Grinsell (1971). Yet despite the large numbers of monuments, few have been found to contain Beaker burials. Instead, the Beaker burial tradition is more diverse in this region, occurring in contexts such as caves, swallets and as secondary deposits within earlier monuments. Whilst there are some impressive, rich "Wessex" graves from Mendip, there is no early metalwork from within barrows and very little early material from elsewhere in this region (Mullin in press), but there is evidence for the chronological overlap of the Grooved Ware and Beaker pottery traditions. Because of this, this paper will consider these two pottery traditions and their depositional contexts in order to address continuity and change between the later Neolithic and the earlier Bronze Age in this landscape (fig. 5.1). The lack of any modern study of Beaker pottery also means that this is the ideal opportunity to interpret the Beaker pottery in light of Needham's (2005) classificatory system, where possible, which should aid chronological resolution.

The Late Neolithic

The Early Neolithic period on Mendip is represented by long barrows, of which at least 23 have been identified (Grinsell 1971; Lewis 2005), lithic scatters and a possible "domestic" structure (Taylor 2001). Moreover, at least three caves appear to have been used as burial sites and others evidence limited, possibly expedient, use (Lewis 2005). The Late Neolithic period is, however, far richer in archaeological remains. There are six possible henges, including two small examples at Gorsey Bigbury and Hunter's Lodge, and the four Priddy Circles. There are also large lithic scatters over much of the plateau, which contain artefacts known to be associated with the use of Grooved Ware and Beaker pottery (see Lewis 1998; 2005 and in press). Pits are generally rare, with no known examples from the high Mendip plateau, although they have been found on the lower plateau and in the surrounding foothills. It is also at this time that we witness an intensification and diversification in the use of cave sites. Bridged Pot, Soldier's Hole and Outlook Cave, all on West Mendip, appear to show evidence for special deposition, containing axeheads and with fine flintwork that includes discoidal knives. Other caves in the area, such as Rowberrow Cavern and Sun Hole were seemingly used as settlements whilst some swallet sites have revealed important evidence for Late Neolithic mortuary practices. Taken together, the evidence appears to indicate intensification in the use of Mendip during the Late Neolithic, though whether this is linked to a growing number of inhabitants, a decline in mobility or a change in social practices is uncertain (Lewis in press).

Grooved Ware

Despite this increase in the number of Late Neolithic sites on Mendip, Grooved Ware pottery itself is still a rather rare find. The explanations for this are likely to be prosaic: Grooved Ware tends to be found during the excavation of monuments and there has been a lack of such excavations on Mendip. Moreover, the Mendip Hills are a designated Area of Outstanding Natural Beauty, which restricts commercial development and therefore there have been few large-scale, developer-funded archaeological interventions. Elsewhere in Britain it has been such work that has resulted in the discovery of large numbers of Grooved Ware pits. The absence of Grooved Ware from Mendip may, then, be more apparent that real, especially given the strong coincidence of Grooved Ware pits with round barrows: Ros Cleal (1999, 6) has noted that pits containing Grooved Ware are regularly found within close proximity to round barrows and, given the high numbers of barrows from Mendip, the likelihood is that more Grooved Ware pits await discovery.

The Grooved Ware that has been found occurs in two contexts: pits and caves. Only three pits containing Grooved Ware are known from the region, two from the same site at Abbey Quarry, Doulting, on East Mendip, where they were discovered during archaeological excavations carried out prior to the extension of the quarry (Hollinrake and Hollinrake 2002). The layout of a further six postholes suggests that they may have been connected with one of the pits, perhaps forming a screen or an approach to it (Lewis 2005). The pits were found to contain worked and unworked flint, a variety of burnt local and non-local stones, sherds of Grooved Ware pottery and a quantity of animal bone. One of the pits contained a very fine partially polished discoidal knife, which has parallels with those from some of the Mendip cave sites. A single date was obtained on a piece of cattle rib bone which calibrated to 2700-2250 cal BC (Wk 11579: Hollinrake and Hollinrake 2002).

To the north of Mendip, in the Chew Valley, excavations in advance of the flooding of the valley for a reservoir revealed a Grooved Ware pit at Ben Bridge. This was truncated by machine stripping but the surviving fill comprised burnt gravel and clay, charcoal, flint flakes and two large, and several smaller, sherds of Durrington Walls style Grooved Ware (Rahtz and Greenfield 1977). A single sherd of Grooved Ware was also found in the "Beaker pit" (Rahtz and Greenfield 1977, see below) at the same site.

Two caves contain Grooved Ware pottery, but interpretation is difficult due to problems of cave taphonomy and the early date of the excavations. For example, the excavations at Soldier's Hole in Cheddar Gorge were carried out between 1927 and 1929 and the post-Pleistocene deposits, encompassing the Neolithic to Romano-British periods, were described as being contained within the upper two feet (Balch 1928). The Grooved Ware pottery was first thought to be Globular Urn, but was later reinterpreted by Julian Thomas (Thomas 1988). Seemingly accompanying this were a partly polished flint axe, two fine oval flint implements, with bifacial working (probably discoidal knives), a large flint knife, a curved flint knife, a large flint scraper and a flint saw (Lewis 2005). On East Mendip, the cave site of Cockles Wood Lower (Hickling and Seaby 1951, 13) contained sherds of Grooved Ware and of Beaker pottery and a scraper. These 1947-50 excavations by the

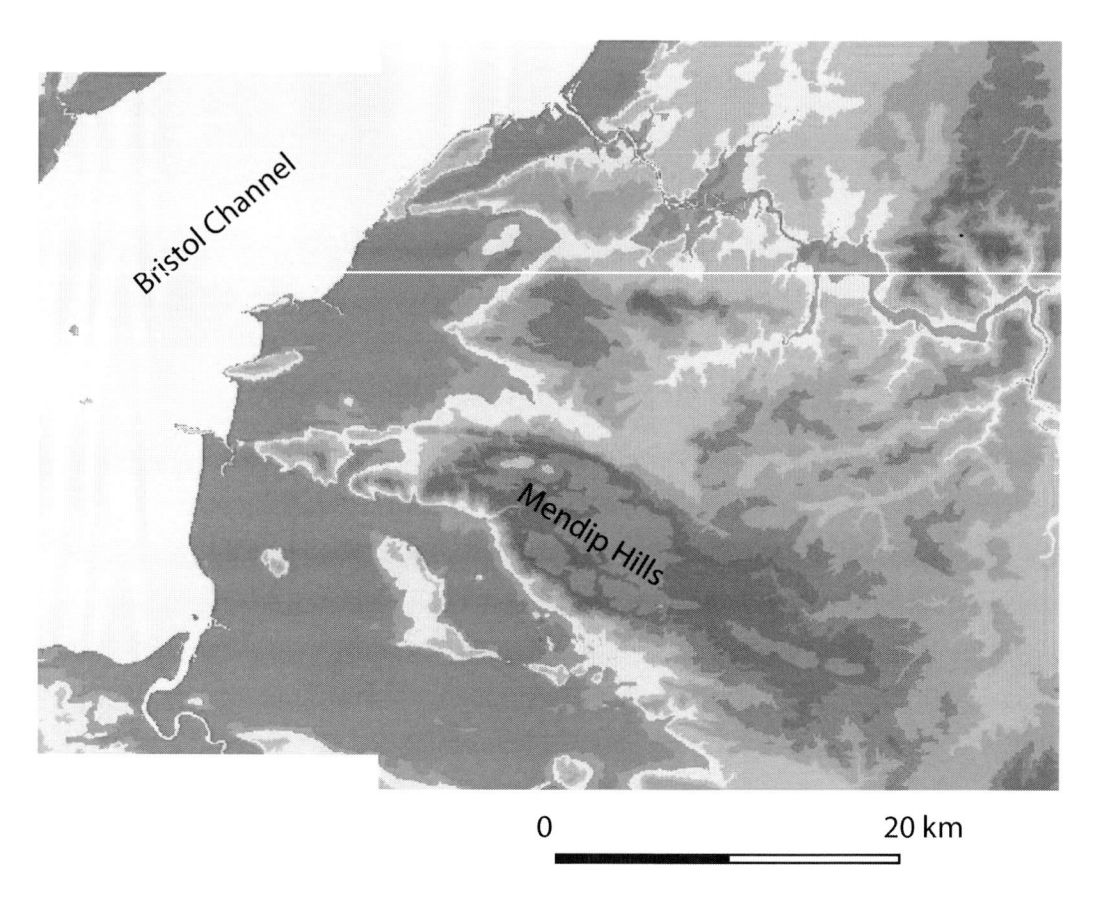

Fig.5. 1: Mendip location.

Downside Archaeological Society have never, however, been fully published.

Much better information exists for Brimble Pit Swallet. This site, on West Mendip, overlooks the Somerset Levels and forms part of a swallet system, with many other examples in the same field. Excavations were carried out not for archaeological reasons but to reinstate this natural feature which had been deliberately infilled in the modern period. The recovery of archaeological remains led the excavator, Dr William Stanton, to proceed with caution and separate the deposits removed and retrieve the artifacts they contained, noting their relative depth. The swallet was found to contain two separate shafts, both c.10m deep. From one shaft (previously explored) was a pristine stone axehead, probably of Continental European origin. The other shaft contained human and animal bone, lithics and 42 sherds of Grooved Ware, the largest collection of this type yet found in Somerset. An analysis of deposits from these and several other sites on Mendip suggests the deliberate placement of these items within the swallet shafts rather than their accidental accumulation (Lewis 2000).

Due to the small amounts of Grooved Ware recovered from Mendip, it is not possible to draw convincing conclusions from the form and fabric of this material. The examples from Brimble Pit Swallet exhibit a combination of the Clacton and Durrington Walls sub-styles, including spiral decoration, echoing the important example from Wyke Down henge, Dorset (Green 2000). At Ben Bridge, the pottery from the Grooved Ware pit was identified as belonging to the Durrington Walls sub-style, whereas the material from the Beaker pit was Woodlands sub-style. Fabrics have been poorly recorded but shell, quartz, limestone and grog were present within the pottery from Brimble Pit Swallet and shell, limestone and grog at Abbey Quarry. Generally, the fabrics appear to be relatively diverse and contrast to those of Beakers from the region.

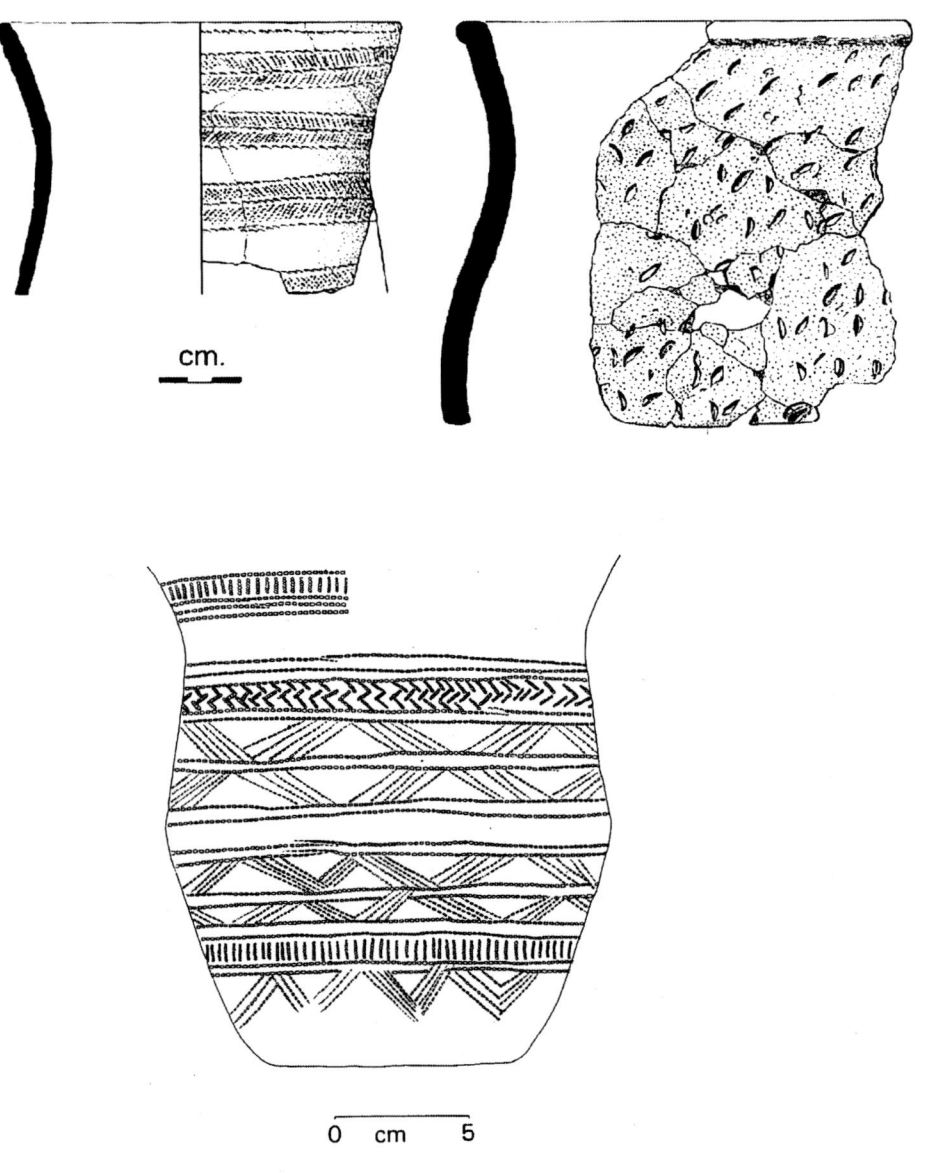

FIG. 5. 2: THE BEAKERS FROM BREAN (TOP) AND CHARTERHOUSE WARREN FARM SWALLET (BOTTOM). REPRODUCED WITH PERMISSION OF THE UNIVERSITY OF BRISTOL SPELAEOLOGICAL SOCIETY.

The Beaker Evidence

There are few excavated Beaker burials from Mendip, which is surprising given the high frequency of round barrows. Although many of the barrows were excavated in the 19th century by local antiquarians, very few have been excavated, or published, to a modern standard. Similarly, there are few pits containing Beaker material. The largest amount of material has instead been found within deposits associated with the "closure" of a henge and fragmentary Beakers have been found within caves and swallets.

Probably the earliest Beaker from Mendip is from the foreshore at Brean, where parts of at least two Beakers were recovered from a pit after a gale in 1936 (Taylor and Taylor 1949). Although no human bone was found, the fact that one of the Beakers appears to have been deposited complete led to the suggestion that this was a burial pit, although this has been contested (Bell 1990; see ApSimon 2000 for a fuller discussion). The more complete vessel (the upper half of which survived, the lower half postulated to have been swept away by the tide before discovery) had horizontal rows of twisted cord decoration separating diagonal "herringbone" lines made by a fine comb (ApSimon 2000). This Beaker (fig. 5.2, top left) has been described by Needham (2005) as belonging to the Cord-Zoned Maritime style, which should be early within the Beaker sequence. A radiocarbon date of 2010 to 1540 cal BC (3460 ± 80 BP, HAR 8547: Bell 1990) was obtained from charcoal associated with the burial, which seems rather late for this Beaker. It is, however, from unidentified charcoal which has probably suffered the "Marine Reservoir Effect" and cannot be considered to be reliable. The second Beaker at Brean (fig 5.2, top right) was decorated with rows of fingernail impressions and both Beakers were finely tempered with grog and probably locally made (ApSimon 2000).

The Maritime style Beaker from Brean is noteworthy as it fits within a pattern of other finds from Somerset of similar, early Beakers from near the coast. One example was recovered from the Wick Barrow (or Pixies Mound) at Stogursey (St George Grey 1908) and two other, very similar, examples came from excavations at Cannington Park Quarry (Rahtz et al 2000). The Wick Barrow example was fragmentary and accompanied an inhumation in a secondary context within a round barrow from which two other Beakers were also recovered, both also from secondary inhumations, one of which also contained a flint dagger. The two Beakers from Cannington Park Quarry, only 5km from the Wick Barrow, are both of similar form. One is decorated by discontinuous lines of horizontal comb impressions, the other by, roughly parallel, horizontal lines of fingernail impressions. The context of these Beakers is uncertain as they were recovered by workmen in a quarry without archaeological supervision, but it has been assumed that they belong to a disturbed burial. The Cannington Beakers may be paralleled by those from the foreshore at Brean, however, and it is equally likely that they may have also been recovered from a pit. Both Beakers contained grog in their fabrics with abundant quartz.

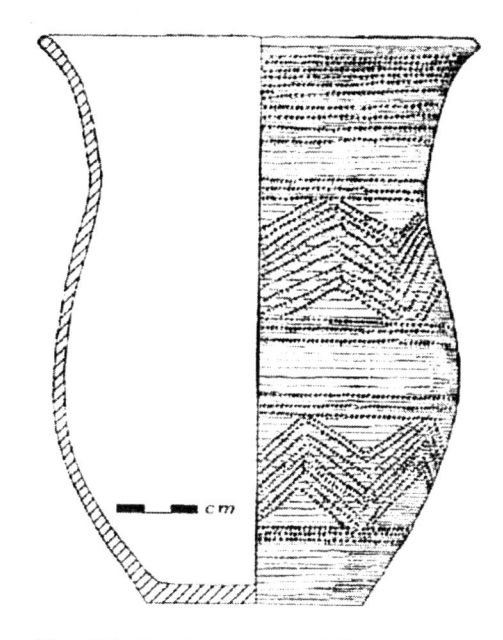

FIG. 5 3: THE BEAKER FROM T5, BURRINGTON. REPRODUCED WITH PERMISSION OF THE UNIVERSITY OF BRISTOL SPELAEOLOGICAL SOCIETY.

Beaker pottery from burial contexts is rare on Mendip, but has been excavated from the mound of a barrow at Piney Sleight Farm, near Tynings Farm, Cheddar (ApSimon 1968; Grinsell 1971: Cheddar 13). The best preserved material was, however, recovered from the, as yet still unpublished, excavations by the University of Bristol Spelaeological Society of a barrow on Blackdown in 1925 and between 1950 to 1956. The barrow, known as T5 (or Burrington 1 to Grinsell), covered a primary inhumation in a cist with a Beaker with "barbed wire" decoration (which is included in Clarke's (1970) corpus as number 784). The Beaker from T5 (fig. 5. 3) most likely fits into Needham's (2005) "Low bellied S-profile Beaker" class and the reconstructed vessel is on display in the University of Bristol Spelaeological Society Museum.

Whilst the burial from T5 appears to be the only definite example of a Beaker grave from a barrow, human remains were recovered from the henge at Gorsey Bigbury (Jones 1938, ApSimon et al 1976). Here, parts of an adult skeleton were found in a stone cist located on the ditch bottom in the north-west segment of the henge. The cist measured 1.07m long by 0.75m wide and contained the skull, mandible and fragments of limb bones of the crouched burial of an adult male. The remainder of the skeleton was found in the filling of the ditch in this area. Also, in the same area, were the remains (although no skull) of another individual, this time an adult female. Parts of a female skull were, however, found to the east of the henge entrance and it may be that this represents the missing part of the burial. It was suggested by the excavators that both of these skeletons originated within the cist but were subsequently disturbed. Cranial fragments of a child c 5 years old were also recovered to the east of the henge entrance, ApSimon et al (1976) suggesting that the bones could also derive from the cist. Artefacts were recovered from the cist and included a barbed and tanged arrowhead from by the knee of the male inhumation and a flint knife, a Beaker sherd, four bone needles and a bone scoop were found behind his skull.

The diversity of depositional locations for Beaker burials on Mendip is further illustrated by the swallet at Charterhouse Warren Farm (Levitan et al 1998), which contained a Beaker apparently deliberately placed 15 ½ m down a natural vertical shaft, probably by people descending into the swallet on ropes. The Beaker appears to have been deposited with disarticulated human bones which had cut marks at their articulation points, suggesting deliberate defleshing. The Beaker was described as difficult to classify, but probably belonging to the Developed Northern Beaker group and the published profile carries a low carination, which fits within Needham's "Low-Carinated" style (fig. 5. 2, bottom). Human bone from the same layer as the Beaker (Horizon 2) comprised the remains of at least seven individuals including adults, juveniles and infants, but was too fragmentary to assign sex. A single bone from this Horizon returned a radiocarbon date of 2470 to 1970 cal BC (3790 ± 60BP, Ox-A 1559: Levitan and Smart 1989). From a lower level in the swallet (Horizon 4) a total of five stone 'sponge finger stones', a bone pin, an antler spatula and a flint dagger were also recovered, the assemblage being unusually rich for Mendip and containing the largest number of 'sponge finger stones' found together in Britain (Levitan et al 1998, 208). A radiocarbon date of 2460 to 1960 cal BC (3760 ± 60 BP, Ox-A 1560) was returned from human bone in this deposit. A minimum of two individuals were represented here and were, in contrast to Horizon 2, all either perinatal or infant. The dates from the two Horizons can be considered to be contemporary and suggest that the intervening Horizon 3 was deposited rapidly, possibly as the result of deliberate backfilling (Levitan et al 1998). The date of the human remains with the Beaker from Horizon 2 fits well within the range of Low-Carinated Beakers within Britain (Needham 1995, 185).

A burial was also found at Chew Park in the Chew Valley, where a circular pit 1m in diameter and 0.30m deep contained cremated bone, worked flint, a fragment of a Langdale axe which appears to have been utilised as a hammer, and a total of 80 sherds of pottery, of which 31 represented at least eight Beakers (Rahtz and Greenfield 1977). Although no complete profiles can be reconstructed from this assemblage, it contains several interesting components. Whilst the majority of the material is fragmentary, it is dominated by comb impressed sherds from high on the vessel profile. The exceptions to this are large fragments of the base and wall of an undecorated Beaker; two sherds decorated by incised lines in a herringbone pattern and three sherds with a curved, fluted decoration, probably made by a fingertip.

This latter has more in common with decorative schemes found on pottery of the Grooved Ware and Peterborough Ware traditions. Also in the Chew Valley, at Ben Bridge, a circular Beaker pit measuring 1m in diameter was found to contain worked flint, a stone "wristguard" and 113 sherds from at least nine Beakers, alongside the single sherd of Grooved Ware already mentioned (ApSimon in Rahtz and Greenfield 1977). The material is weathered and worn but the Beakers have predominantly zoned decoration, mainly of comb impressions. The pit was interpreted as a grave, although no human bone was found and the dimensions of the pit seem rather small for this interpretation.

In common with the sparse burial record from Mendip, the evidence for "domestic" occupation is rare. On the sand cliff at Brean, above the location of the pit containing Beakers on the foreshore, a "Beaker sand" deposit has been excavated and may relate to occupation of the area to the south of Brean Down, although no archaeological features certainly associated with Beaker pottery were located during excavations in 1983-1987 (Bell 1990), or in subsequent work (Locock and Lawler 1995; Allen et al 1996; Allen et al 2000). It is currently thought that the main focus of Beaker activity was located to the seaward side of the present cliff, and has been subsequently eroded (Allen et al 2000, 47). The Beakers from Brean are fragmentary, but dominated by comb impressed decoration and were of a grog-tempered fabric.

Beaker pottery was also recovered from a purported occupation site at Bos Swallet, near Blackdown (Taylor 1964; ApSimon 1997). Here sherds representing 20 to 25 vessels were recovered and the assemblage interpreted as the result of episodic visits to the site by a small group, during which the pottery was deposited (ApSimon 1997). The fabric of the pottery was heavily grog tempered and has similarities to that recovered from Brean Down and Gorsey Bigbury (Russell and Williams 1998). Recent analysis of the material in the University of Bristol Spelaeological Society Museum (fig.5.4) suggests that, although it is highly fragmented, the forms and decoration are similar to the Long-Necked Beakers of Gorsey Bigbury. A further parallel with the Gorsey Bigbury material is that one of the Beakers from Bos Swallet appears to have been perforated. The material is more worn than that from Gorsey Bigbury and very abraded breaks are visible, suggesting that the pottery was deposited as sherds.

The greatest number of Beakers from Mendip has been recovered from the henge monument at Gorsey Bigbury, where fragments of at least 120 Beakers were recovered from the ditch of the monument during excavations in the 1930s. These occurred throughout the fill of the ditch and appeared to have been deliberately dumped into the monument, as pieces of the same vessels were found horizontally and vertically displaced throughout the ditch fill (ApSimon 1951; ApSimon et al 1976). None of this material appeared in Clarke's (1970) corpus and the site was not included in Needham's (2005) chrono-typological scheme as they were not from a funerary context.

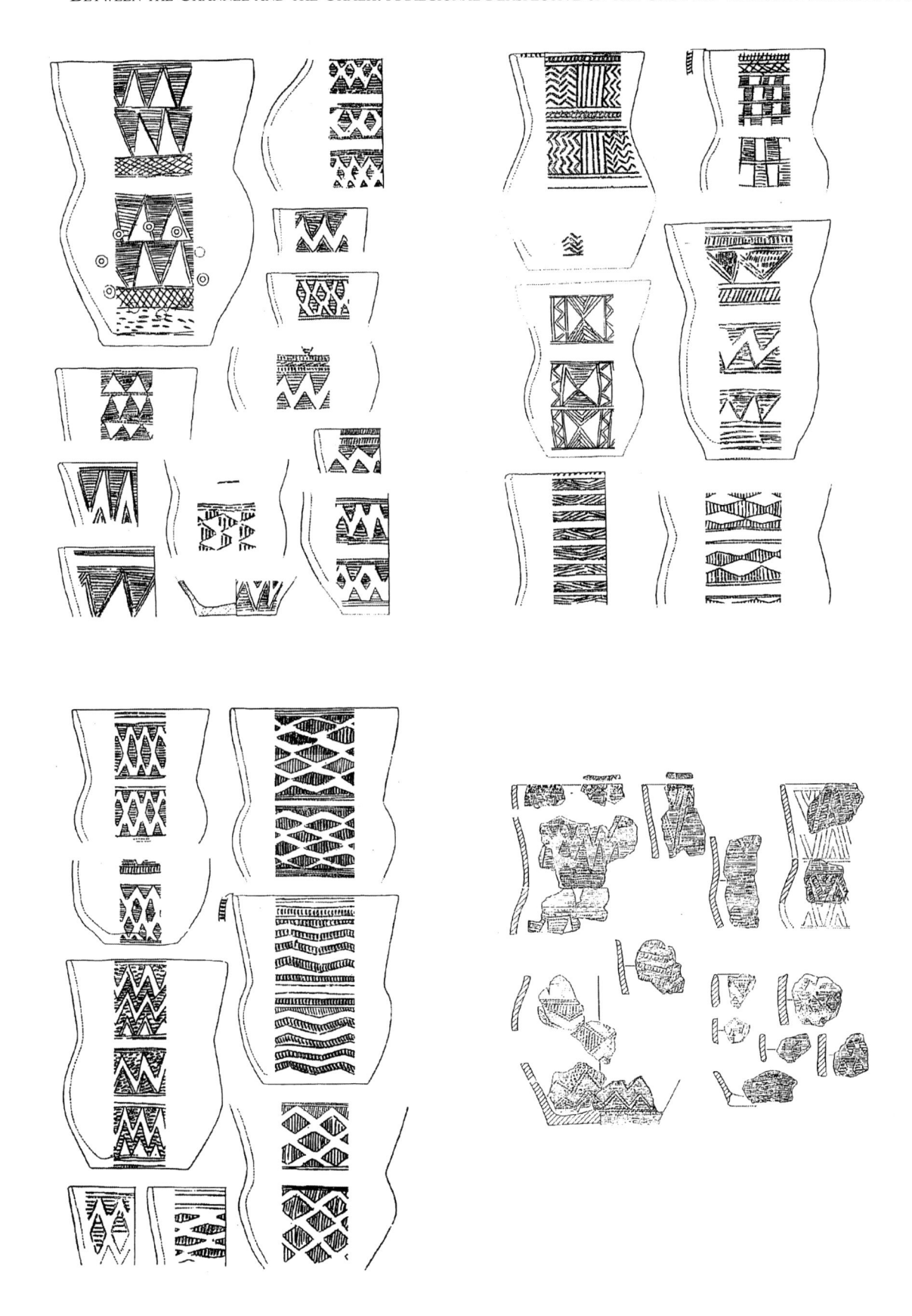

Fig. 5. 4: A selection of Beakers from Gorsey Bigbury henge and Bos Swallet (bottom right).
Reproduced with permission of the University of Bristol Spelaeological Society.

A total of 43 Beakers from Gorsey Bigbury are illustrated by ApSimon et al (1976) and a sample are reproduced here as fig 5.4. These appear to form a fairly homogenous group of Needham's Long-Necked style, although the reconstructions should be treated with caution, as the majority of the material was destroyed during World War II and cannot be fully reanalysed. Stylistically the Beakers are dominated by horizontally zoned zig-zag decoration, which also form closed lozenges and pendant triangles. One of the vessels (ApSimon et al 1976, reproduced here in Figure 4 top left) carries a series of countersunk perforations in an arc across the belly of the pot. An examination of the surviving material from Gorsey Bigbury held by the University of Bristol Spelaeological Society Museum suggests that, like the pottery from Bos Swallet, the material was already fragmentary when deposited as, although it is relatively unabraded, there are numerous old breaks and the average sherd size and weight is low.

Although a total of six radiocarbon dates were taken from samples from Gorsey Bigbury, providing a date range of 2500 to 1650 cal BC (ApSimon et al 1976), these dates are from unidentified (and probably bulked) charcoal and lack detailed stratigraphic information: one sample being merely described as "ditch, hearth on west side of causeway, outer side" and cannot be considered to be reliable. There does, however, appear to be a four phase sequence at the site (Lewis 2005) which involves the construction (and primary use) of the henge; the placement of the Beaker cist in the western ditch terminal; the subsequent manipulation of the bone from within this feature and the rapid backfilling of the ditches using "domestic" Beaker material. The origin of this deposit remains uncertain, but appears to have been rapidly incorporated into the ditch, possibly as a deliberate attempt to close down the monument (Lewis 2005). This continued interest in, and manipulation of, pre-existing monuments during the Beaker period is paralleled at a range of other sites in southern Britain, including Mount Pleasant, Dorset and the West Kennet long barrow, Wiltshire.

Beaker is the most common pottery type found in caves on Mendip, with sherds of at least 17 vessels having been recovered from eight caves (Lewis 2005, 122-3). Fragments of at least five Beakers were recovered from Rowberrow Cavern, where a flint knife and pieces of polished bone, interpreted as being the possible remains of a Beaker burial, were recovered from a "cemented floor" (Taylor 1921; 1922; 1923; 1924; 1925). Fragments of three Beakers were excavated from Chelm's Coombe Cave (Balch and Palmer 1927) and bone pins, worked flint and human remains were also recovered from the cave, although the stratigraphy had been badly disturbed by animal burrowing. At Cockles Wood Cave (Hickling and Seaby 1951) fragments of at least two Beakers were found in the same layer as sherds of Grooved Ware and the fragmentary remains of at least two individuals: a female and a male. The reconstruction published by Hickling and Seaby (1951) appears to be an S-profile Beaker with zoned chevrons and incised triangles and lozenges, but this does not appear to correspond to the material published by Hickling (n.d), which clearly illustrates sherds from the belly and base of a small S-profile Beaker and the belly of a slightly more globular S-profile Beaker, which have been combined to provide the single "vessel" in the 1951 illustration. Two sherds of rusticated Beaker were also found in the cave, although their relationship to the other Beaker material is uncertain.

Beaker was associated with human skulls and animal bone at Bone Hole (Cox 1976), although the excavations here were unsystematic and the context of the finds uncertain. The Beaker from the cave is on display in Wells Museum and appears to have been deposited in a fragmentary state, but has a low carination and is possibly early in the sequence. The decoration on the vessel comprises complex zones of cross-hatched triangles, incised dots, vertical lines and crosses which, although fitting within Clarke's (1970) Southern style, is difficult to parallel. Beaker pottery, again associated with human bone, was found at Beaker Shelter in Ebbor Gorge, although the exact details of the site are poorly recorded (Barrington and Stanton 1972). Sherds of at least three Beakers are also known from Sun Hole, where they were discovered in a deposit of charcoal alongside animal and human bone (Tratman and Henderson 1927). The deposit also contained fragments of Grooved Ware and worked flint including a barbed and tanged arrowhead and a flint knife.

Fabric and form

Petrological work by Russell and Williams (1998) on the Beakers from Gorsey Bigbury and Bos Swallet noted heavily grogged fabrics in nearly all of the Beakers examined from the sites, although different clay sources were probably used. Russell and Williams (1998, 136) suggest that the inclusion of so much grog within the fabric of the Beakers goes beyond the simple addition of material to alter the firing properties of the pottery and may instead relate to a long tradition of recycling pottery within the fabric of other pots. The overwhelming presence of "pure" grog tempers on Mendip is in contrast to fabrics from other regions, such as Wiltshire, where flint and sand are used in addition to grog (Cleal 1995), and may be suggestive of a local tradition of Beaker production in which grog is used as a tempering agent in preference to other materials.

The forms of the Beakers from Mendip, with the exception of the Maritime Beaker from Brean and the carinated Beakers from Charterhouse Warren Farm Swallet and Bone Hole, are generally Long-Necked in style. Needham (1995, 195) suggests that this style of Beaker is not particularly late in date, although late examples do exist. The lack of good radiocarbon dates for the Mendip Beakers is problematic in this regard and it is not possible to be certain how this material fits within the national framework which sees the style starting in at least the 22nd century BC (Needham 2005, 195).

Discussion

Despite relatively poor chronological resolution, there is reasonably good evidence for the overlap of Grooved Ware and Beaker on Mendip. One of the earliest of the Beakers, that from Charterhouse Warren Farm Swallet, has a radiocarbon date which overlaps with that from a pit containing Grooved Ware at Abbey Quarry. Beaker and Grooved Ware were also found together at Charterhouse Warren Farm Swallet as well as at Ben Bridge and within a number of caves. This may point to the late use of Grooved Ware on Mendip and, associated with the relative lateness of the majority of the Beakers and the lack of early metalwork, a fairly slow uptake of the Beaker "phenomenon". Unfortunately this interpretation is seriously hindered not only by the lack of dates for Beaker associated material from Somerset in general and Mendip specifically, but also a lack of Late Neolithic radiocarbon dates from the region. The treatment of the human remains at Charterhouse Warren Farm Swallet is, however, very reminiscent of Neolithic practices and has very little in common with the treatment of the body in Beaker burials. It is tempting to see the burial at Charterhouse as the continuation of an earlier tradition, but it is difficult to bridge the chronological gap between the burial traditions of the earlier Neolithic and this example, especially as formal burial in the later Neolithic is so uncommon. It is noteworthy, however, that disarticulated human remains associated with Grooved Ware have also been excavated from Brimble Pit Swallet on Mendip (Lewis 2000) and it may be that the provision of typical Beaker associated grave goods at Charterhouse may be better interpreted as a fusion of a localised, long-lived burial practice with a radically different and new one. This kind of fusion may also be seen in the use of caves. Although all of the Beakers from caves on Mendip are highly fragmented, the deposition of Beaker with human remains in caves appears to be a continuation, although in a different form, of the interest in caves shown in the Neolithic period (Lewis 2005, Chapter 7). This is especially interesting as there are few certain Beaker barrows recorded from the Mendip plateau and it is a possibility that the deposition of Beaker in caves may represent a distinctive local practise, where caves were used in preference to barrows for the disposal of the dead.

A number of themes can be identified in the treatment of Beakers from the Mendip region, perhaps the most striking of which is the deposition of fragmentary Beakers, rather than complete vessels. This may reflect a concern with fragmentation and the destruction of Beakers upon the end of their "lives", a concern which can also be seen in the recycling of sherds as grog within new Beakers. This use of grog may have been a way of extending a vessel's life, enhancing the life of old pots and imbuing new pots with ancestral power (Woodward 2008, 295). The widespread use of grog in Beakers (Cleal 1995) must be seen against the use of a variety of different materials which are added to the clay-and-grog mix and which mark out Beakers from different regions as different to each other, particularly when broken into sherds. This practice may represent cultural choices by individual communities as a way of making their own pots identifiable and different to those made by other people in other places: adding local materials to what may otherwise be seen as a stereotypical and widespread pottery style.

The distribution of Maritime style Beakers along the Somerset coast is also noteworthy, especially as most of the Beakers from Mendip itself seem to date to a later period. The connections across both sides of the Bristol Channel can be seen both in the early material, which includes a Beaker bowl from Tinkinswood long barrow, on the Welsh side of the Bristol Channel (Ward 1916) and in the later, Long-Necked Beakers from Gorsey Bigbury, which can be paralleled with examples elsewhere in south Wales (Savory 1980, 77). In particular the vessels from St Fagans, Riley's Tumulus and Llanmadoc have striking parallels with those from Gorsey Bigbury (Savory 1980, 201), whilst good parallels from the area immediately to the east of Mendip are more difficult to find. Clarke (1970, 83) saw the distribution of "European Bell Beakers" as reflecting the expansion of the Beaker phenomenon out of southern England along routes already established by groups using "All-Over-Cord" Beakers, but the distribution of early Beakers along the Somerset coast may suggest an alternative route, especially given the early dates for Beakers from the Iberian Peninsula and for metallurgy in southern Ireland. The Bristol Channel may have not so much been at the end of a route out of Wessex, or indeed a route into it, but rather it may have been the case that communities living in this region looked to the west, rather than to the east. Nevertheless, the predominantly later Beakers from Mendip itself may suggest that the people or ideas that initially brought the Beaker concept to these isles did not initially take root on Mendip. Why might this be the case, if early examples can be seen in coastal regions and further inland, in the Wessex landscape?

The answer might lie in the receptivity of communities living in the region to the ideas represented by the introduction of Beaker pottery, and the associated way of life. When Beakers are taken on board, there appears to be continued use of Grooved Ware pottery and the survival of Late Neolithic burial rites. Rather than replacing existing cultural traditions, then, Beakers may have been amalgamated into existing insular practices, such as the disposal of the dead in caves and swallets and the deposition of Beakers in places with pre-existing meanings. The nature of the Mendip landscape may itself have played a crucial role in the slow uptake of new practices. This landscape, full of mysterious – and indeed dangerous – features, was undoubtedly one full of myth and memory. Caves revealed evidence for the actions of earlier peoples, or fabled beings, revealed by human excavation or burrowing animals. Swallets could open overnight, swallowing the ground and anything upon it. This landscape, full of links and physical routes to the underworld, may have needed appeasement: the connotations were old and ancestral rather than new and innovative. The harsh weather conditions inflicted upon Mendip – rain, mist, snow, frost, winds – may have contributed to this feeling of otherness, the watery places that surround it on three sides adding to this sense of a place apart. To this landscape we must also add the wild animals, such as aurochs, which seem to have clung to their habitats here rather later than in Wessex, reflecting a more heavily treed, perhaps deliberately managed, "wildwood". This then may have been a landscape which was respected rather than challenged. It may be no coincidence then that the largest Beaker assemblage from the region comes from an (old) henge monument, where new materials and traditions could be introduced and their perceived danger diffused by the links to the past. The Beaker period on Mendip, then, appears as a period of slow negotiation, with ideas, people and things perhaps first avoided, then tentatively accepted, but in places made safe by their associations with existing people and with reference to existing (funerary; depositional) practices. That these, and other actions, were successful is undeniable: by the full Early Bronze Age, Mendip is transformed, round barrows are built in their hundreds and the similarity with the rest of central Southern England is tangible in both monument construction and the kinds of artefact encountered here.

This analysis of the Late Neolithic/Beaker age material from Mendip has demonstrated the presence of local practices within a wider framework of (inter)national traditions. The Mendip region is unusual and may have had more in common with areas to the west and south, rather than the east, populations being able to exploit their position between the "Atlantic" Bristol Channel and "Continental" Wessex. When seen in this light, the relatively late uptake of Beakers is not because of cultural "backwardness" and isolation, but the result of a prolonged period of negotiation and the assimilation of new, innovative practices with existing ones, deeply connected to a sense of place within a unique landscape.

Bibliography

ApSimon A.M., 1951. Gorsey Bigbury The Second Report. *Proceedings of the University of Bristol Spelaeological Society* 6, 186-199.

ApSimon, A.M., 1968. Archaeological Notes - Beaker sherd from Piney Sleight, Cheddar. *Proceedings of the University of Bristol Spelaeological Society* 11(3), 244-50.

ApSimon, A..M., 1997. Bos Swallet, Burrington, Somerset: Boiling site and Beaker occupation site. *Proceedings of the University of Bristol Spelaeological Society* 12(1), 41-82.

ApSimon, A.M., 2000. Brean Down Sand Cliff Revisited: Pleistocene Stratification, New Finds and the Date of the Maritime Bell Beaker. *Proceedings of the University of Bristol Spelaeological Society* 22(1), 53-80.

ApSimon, A.M, Musgrave, J.H, Sheldon J, Tratman E.K and van Wijngaarden, L.H., 1976. Gorsey Bigbury, Cheddar, Somerset: radiocarbon dating, human and animal bones, charcoals, archaeological reassessment. *Proceedings of the University of Bristol Spelaeological Society* 14(2), 155-183.

Allen, M.J, Crockett, A.D, Rawlings, M.N and Ritchie, K., 1996. Archaeological Fieldwork Along the Line of the Brean Down Sea Defences: new evidence for landscape change and human activity. *Archaeology in the Severn Estuary* 7, 31-38.

Allen, M.J and Ritchie, K., 2000. The Stratigraphy and Archaeology of Bronze Age and Romano-British Deposits Below the Beach Level at Brean Down, Somerset. *Proceedings of the University of Bristol Spelaeological Society* 22(1), 5-52.

Balch, H 1928. Soldiers Hole, Chedar Gorge. *40th Annual Report of Wells Natural History and Archaeological Society*, 36-40.

Balch, H and Palmer 1927. Excavations at Chelm's Combe, Cheddar. *Proceedings of the Somerset Archaeology and Natural History Society* LXXII, 93-124.

Barrington, N and Stanton, W 1976. *Mendip: The Complete Caves.* Bath: Dawson and Goodall.

Bell, M. 1990. *Brean Down. Excavations 1983-1987.* London: English Heritage.

Clark, D. 1970. *Beaker Pottery in Great Britain and Ireland.* Cambridge: Cambridge University Press.

Cleal, R.M.J 1992. Introduction: the what, where, when and why of Grooved Ware in Cleal, R and MacSween, A (eds) *Grooved Ware in Britain and Ireland.* Oxford: Oxbow Books, 1-8.

Cleal, R.M.J., 1995. Pottery Fabrics in Wessex in the Fourth to Second Millennia BC in Kinnes, I and Varndell, G (eds) *'Unbaked Urns of Rudely Shape' Essays on British and Irish Pottery for Ian Longworth.* Oxford: Oxbow Monograph 55, 185-194.

Cox, A 1976. An interim report...Bone Hole...from August 1967 to August 1976. *Mendip Caving Group Journal* 6, 17-30.

Green, M 2000. *A Landscape Revealed: 10,000 Years on a Chalkland Farm.* Stroud: Tempus.

Grinsell, L 1971. Somerset Barrows, Part 2. *Proceedings of the Somerset Archaeology and Natural History Society* 115, 44-137.

Hickling, M n.d. Pottery from Cockles Wood Caves at Nettlebridge. *Journal of the Downside Archaeological Society* 1(2), 1-5.

Hickling, M and Seaby, W 1951. Finds From Cockles Wood Cave, Nettlebridge, Somerset. *Proceedings of Somerset Archaeology and Natural History Society* XCVI, 193-202.

Hollinrake, C and Holinrake, N 2001. Doulting Abbey Quarry, Somerset. Archaeology 2001. *Proceedings of the Somerset Archaeology and Natural History Society* 145, 137.

Jones, S.J., 1938. The excavation of Gorsey Bigbury. *Proceedings of the University of Bristol Spelaeological Society* 5(1), 3-56.

Levitan, B, Audsley, A, Hawkes, C, Moody, A, Moody, P, Smart, P and Thomas, J. 1988. Charterhouse Warren Farm Swallet, Mendip, Somerset. *Proceedings of the*

University of Bristol Spelaeological Society 18(2), 171-239.

Levitan, B and Smart, P., 1989. Charterhouse Warren Farm Swallet, Mendip, Somerset. Radiocarbon Dating Evidence. *Proceedings of the University of Bristol Spelaeological Society* 18(3), 390-394.

Lewis, J.P 1998. The Everton Flint Collection in Wells Museum. *Proceedings of the University of Bristol Spelaeological Society* 21(2), 141-148.

Lewis, J.P 2000. *Upwards at 45 degrees: the use of vertical caves during the Neolithic and Early Bronze Age on Mendip, Somerset. Capra* 2 available at – http://www.shef.ac.uk/~capra/2/upwards.html.

Lewis, J.P 2005. *Monuments, Ritual and Regionality: The Neolithic of Northern Somerset*. Oxford: BAR British Series 401.

Lewis, J.P 2007. Experiencing the Prehistoric Landscape of Somerset in Costen, M (ed) *People and Places. Essays in Honour of Mick Aston*. Oxford: Oxbow Books, 1-22.

Lewis, J.P and Thompson, A (2007) Excavations East of Blackmoor, Charterhouse, Mendip Hills, Somerset. *Proceedings of the University of Bristol Spelaeological Society*, 24 (2). pp. 83-96.

Lewis, J.P in press. *On Top Of The World: Mesolithic And Neolithic Use Of The Mendip Hills Mendip in Lewis, J.P The Archaeology of Mendip: 500,000 Years of Continuity and Change*. Oxford: Oxbow Books and Heritage Marketing and Publications.

Locock, M and Lawler, M., 1995. Brean Down Sea Defences: Field Evaluation. *Archaeology in the Severn Estuary* 6, 23-28.

Mullin, D in press. Barrows and Bronzes: the Bronze Age of Mendip in Lewis, J.P T*he Archaeology of Mendip: 500,000 Years of Continuity and Change*. Oxford: Oxbow Books and Heritage Marketing and Publications.

Needham, S 2005. Transforming Beaker Culture in North-West Europe; processes of fusion and fission. *Proceedings of the Prehistoric Society* 71, 171-218.

Rahtz, P, Hirst, S and Wright, S.M 2000. *Cannington Cemetery. Excavations 1962-3 of prehistoric, Roman, post-Roman and later features at Cannington Park Quarry, near Bridgewater, Somerset*. London: Britannia Monograph Series No17.

Russell, M and Williams, D., 1998. Petrological Examination and Comparison of Beaker Pottery from Bos Swallet and Gorsey Bigbury. *Proceedings of the University of Bristol Spelaeological Society* 21(2), 133-140.

Rhatz, P and Greenfield, E 1977. *Excavations at Chew Valley Lake, Somerset*. Department of the Environment Archaeological Reports No.8. London: HMSO.

St George Grey, H 1908. Report on the Wick Barrow Excavations. *Proceedings of the Somersetshire Archaeological and Natural History Society* LIV(ii), 1-78.

Taylor, H 1921. Rowberrow Cavern. *Proceedings of the University of Bristol Spelaeological Society* 1(2), 83-86.

Taylor, H 1922. Second Report on Rowberrow Cavern. *Proceedings of the University of Bristol Spelaeological Society* 1(3), 130-134.

Taylor, H 1923. Third Report on Rowberrow Cavern. *Proceedings of the University of Bristol Spelaeological Society* 2(1), 40-50.

Taylor, H 1924. Fourth Report on the Excavation of Rowberrow Cavern. *Proceedings of the University of Bristol Spelaeological Society* 2(2), 122-124.

Taylor, H 1925. Percy Sladen Memorial Fund Excavation at Rowberrow Cavern, 1925. Being the Fifth Report on the Cave. *Proceedings of the University of Bristol Spelaeological Society* 2(3), 190-210.

Taylor, H, 1964. Bos Swallet, Mendip, Somerset. A disturbed Beaker Age deposit. *Proceedings of the University of Bristol Spelaeological Society* 10(2), 98-111.

Taylor, E.E. and Taylor, H., 1949. *An Early Beaker burial at Brean Down near Weston-super-Mare. Proceedings of the University of Bristol Spelaeological Society* **6(1)** 88-92.

Taylor, J.J 2001. A Burnt Mesolithic Hunting Camp on the Mendips: a preliminary report on structural traces excavated on Lower Pitts Farm, Priddy, Somerset in Milliken, S and Cook, J (eds) *A Very Remote Period Indeed. Papers on the Palaeolithic presented to Derek Roe*. Oxford: Oxbow Books, 260-270.

Thomas, J 1998. The Neolithic/Bronze Age Material in Levitan, B, Audsley, A, Hawkes, C, Moody, A, Moody, P, Smart, P and Thomas, J Charterhouse Warren Farm Swallet, Mendip, Somerset *Proceedings of the University of Bristol Spelaeological Society* 18 (2), 171-239.

Tratman, E and Henderson 1927. First Report on the Excavations at Sun Hole, Cheddar. Levels From Above The Pleistocene. *Proceedings of the University of Bristol Spelaeological Society* 3(2), 84-97.

Ward, J 1916. The St Nicholas Chambered tumulus, Glamorgan. *Archaeologia Cambrensis* 6 (Series 16), 239-94.

Woodward, A 2008. Ceramic Technologies and Social Relations in Pollard, J (ed) *Prehistoric Britain*. Oxford: Blackwell Publishing, 288-309.

Acknowledgements

Graham Mullan and Linda Wilson of the University of Bristol Spelaeological Society are thanked for granting access to the material from Gorsey Bigbury and Bos Swallet in the UBSS Museum and for permission to reproduce the published illustrations. Stuart Needham helped to verify the classifications of the Beakers from these sites, for which we are most appreciative.

Without Wessex:
the Local Character of the Early Bronze Age in the south west peninsula

Andy M Jones

Abstract

Ever since Colt Hoare's excavations in the nineteenth century the Early Bronze Age chalkland barrows of Wessex have become perceived as being 'typical' and have affected the way that barrows in other regions have become interpreted. This paper reviews the nature of the evidence from the Wessex chalkland before moving on to a more in depth consideration of the barrows and cairns which are found in the south west peninsula. The paper concludes that although there are points of similarity between the regions, the great range of site types and diversity of practices across the south west region means that they were much more that simple containers for the dead. It is argued that there is no such thing as a 'typical' barrow and archaeologists should in future take pains to consider their 'local character'.

Introduction

I first met Henrietta in the early 1990s, when I came to the south west to work on a two week excavation at Duckpool on the North Cornish Coast. I recall that we were both reading Julian Thomas's (1991) book *Rethinking the Neolithic,* and this began a long series of archaeological conversations and collaborations, which have continued to this day. Our subsequent joint projects have undoubtedly been greatly enriched by Henrietta's encyclopaedic knowledge of the south west peninsula's rich prehistoric record.

The distinctive character of Early Bronze Age barrows and cairns in the south west region is a subject in which Henrietta and I share a deep interest and in fact, much of the following paper is derived from a series of collaborative projects and discussions about the nature of the Early Bronze Age in the south west.

The name of this paper amalgamates those of two earlier papers. In the late 1960s Colin Renfrew (1979) used the then newly available radiocarbon dating evidence as a means of refuting a link between the societies of Early Bronze Age Wessex and those of Mycenae in southern Greece. This paper was significant because it encouraged British archaeologists to look closer to home and develop models, which were not entirely dependant on outside stimuli from the east. It is mentioned here because it balanced the local with more distant sources of evidence as a means of establishing difference, and it is this principle, which I wish to explore further.

However, the paper that forms the basis for much of the following discussion appeared in the *Proceedings of the Devon Archaeological Society.* In 1988 Henrietta wrote a paper entitled 'The local character of the Devon Bronze Age and its interpretation in the 1980s'. This paper outlined the sequence for the Early Bronze Age in Devon and in fact the broader south west region as a whole, and included Cornwall, Dorset and Somerset. Indeed, in addition to her ground breaking work on pottery, I would argue that one of the most important contributions which Henrietta has made to the study of prehistory has been the recognition of localised sequences and diversity, long before the recent increase in interest in doing so (Brophy and Barclay 2009; Gibson 2007; Hamilton 2003). In her paper, Henrietta adopted a non 'Wessex' centred approach to provide an overview of the Bronze Age. She considered artefacts, as well as the then small number of available radiocarbon determinations from the region's Early Bronze Age barrows and cairns.

Background

Henrietta's non-Wessex approach was significant because many of the major theories concerning the character of the British Early Bronze Age have been largely based on more than 100 years of archaeological fieldwork on the chalklands of southern England.

Particularly influential was Stuart Piggott's 1938 magisterial study of Early Bronze Age graves, which introduced the concept of the 'Wessex Culture' This model was based upon the evidence from a limited range of artefacts including goldwork and copper alloy daggers with midribs or lateral grooves, which had been recovered from a comparatively small number of richly furnished Early Bronze Age barrows on the chalkland (Piggott 1938). Piggott considered that these artefacts provided evidence of an aristocracy who represented an ethnic group of Breton origin who were distinct from the majority of the population. Although few archaeologists today would follow his concepts of ethnic identity, it is still the case that most of the theoretical models for Early Bronze Age Britain which have been put forward in the last few decades, whether they involve 'elites', shamans, the importance of 'ancestors', or even the changing sequence of burial rites from inhumation to cremation (Barrett 1994; Garwood 1991; Mitzoguchi 1992; Woodward et al 2005) have been developed from a quite restricted range of evidence from 'Wessex' barrows.

FIG 6.1: THE LINEAR BOWL BARROW CEMETERY, AT ALDBOURNE, WILTSHIRE (DISC BARROW IN FOREGROUND) (GRAEME KIRKHAM)

This dominance of the Wessex evidence is problematic, because such interpretations rely on an underlying assumption that everywhere beyond the chalk must have been the same during the Early Bronze Age. However, it is possible to turn this assumption on its head and ask the questions as to how typical are the chalkland barrows of Wessex in the wider British context and how applicable is the terminology, which has arisen from their study? Indeed, as Dave Field (forthcoming) has recently commented 'had the archaeology of Britain been written from a Yorkshire perspective, we might have a very different kind of prehistory'. Indeed, one might ask, just how typical are the few richly furnished chalkland graves of the broader Wessex region itself.

The domination of Wessex has been particularly difficult for the south west peninsula, and by this I mean Devon and Cornwall, because since the publication of the 'Wessex Culture' model, the finest objects and sites have often been 'cherry-picked' in order to demonstrate that the south west region was a Wessex 'extension area' (for example, Piggott 1938; 1973; Fox 1948; Grinsell 1983; 1994). This has hampered the development of more localised narratives, which are now needed to explain often quite complex data sets. Indeed, even recent interpretative models for sites in the south west have tended to use terminology from an understanding of monuments which is drawn from elsewhere, for example we have 'ancestral' monuments and landscapes, as well as, 'mourners' and grave goods for sites and barrow groups which are devoid of burials (for example, Owoc 2008; Tilley 1996, 172). To amplify this point further, I will briefly discuss the sequence in Wessex before considering the south west region in more depth.

Wessex

There are a very similar number of barrows in both Wessex and the south west peninsula. In the broader Wessex region there are somewhere in the region of 6000 (Webster 2008, 99, fig 4.2) barrows, with 2200 being found in Wiltshire of which more than 400 are found on the chalk around Stonehenge (Lawson 2007, 202). In fact several archaeologists have pointed out that many barrow groups are found in concentrations around the major Neolithic Wessex monument complexes, such as Stonehenge and Avebury (Bradley 1981; Woodward and Woodward 1996; Exon et al 2000). The importance of older monuments is further reinforced by the fact that both Beaker and subsequently Early Bronze Age artefacts and burials have been found inserted within earlier monuments, such as long barrows (Field 2007, 156-8), and by the alignment of round barrows onto earlier Neolithic long mounds, such as those at Winterbourne Stoke crossroads (Woodward 2000, fig 41).

In addition to there being a concentration of barrows around older ceremonial monuments, there is also (Field 2008, 84-5) an even more marked association between barrows and water. Springs, winterbournes, and meres all have associated groups of barrows. However, this connection is most notable along the river systems, with particularly dense concentrations of barrows alongside the River Avon and the Stour (Field ibid; Cleggett 1999). At the same time, and cross cutting this distribution is the degree of prominence given to barrows in the chalkland - with some being sited in Conspicuous places and others in Inconspicuous locales near to land which could have been cultivated. It is the former, Conspicuous sites which are associated with richer burials and 'fancy barrow types' and it is these which have become seen as being 'typical barrows'.

Although it has recently been pointed out that the variation of chalkland mound types has been underestimated (McOmish et al 2002, 33) and that there are large variations in mound sizes, there is, by comparison with the range of barrow types found in the south-west peninsula, a limited range - comprised of just eight types (Lawson 2007, 204). The simple bowl barrows are by far the most commonly found type of barrow (fig 6.1). In addition to these, there are smaller numbers of 'fancy types' such as bell, disc pond and saucer, which occur more frequently in the barrow groups in the vicinity of Stonehenge (Exon et al 2000, 79-81). A characteristic of the Wessex barrows is that in addition to being found in isolation they are frequently grouped into large linear cemeteries such as the Normanton Down group on Salisbury Plain, as well as nuclear and dispersed cemeteries (Fleming 1971; Woodward 2000, chapter 4).

Excavation has demonstrated that many chalkland barrow cemeteries had new sites added to them over time. At the same time, these events were often accompanied by the heightening of existing mounds, with primary interments often being followed by secondary or satellite burials as at Snail Down site 3, and Winterbourne Stoke G47 (Thomas 2005, 37-8; Gingell 1988). It has been argued that the development of the large Wessex cemeteries may have been linked with the development of lineages, whose ancestry was enshrined and mythologized and that competition may have existed between groups (Barrett 1990; 1994, 123-9). From the field evidence, Piggott created a post-Beaker sequence for the Early Bronze Age from the artefacts recovered from the barrows which was subsequently labelled 'Wessex I' and 'Wessex II' (ApSimon 1954; Annable and Simpson 1964). This division is still often cited, although the term Early and Late dagger graves has been employed more recently (for example, Lawson 2007, 219-32).

Broadly speaking, the sequence is currently understood to run as follows (Needham 1996):

Period 1 2500-2300 cal BC and Period 2 2300-2050 cal BC

From the period circa 2500 cal BC Beaker associated single inhumations occur in southern Britain. The earliest Beaker burials were not beneath large barrows but occur under low mounds or are found in flat graves. Within the Wessex region, Beaker burials are relatively commonplace and it is widely accepted by archaeologists that it is this form of burial which gave rise to the subsequent Early Bronze Age burial tradition (Needham 1996; Case 2003).

Beaker inhumations are found throughout the Wessex region. Examples have been recorded in the vicinity of Stonehenge (Cleal et al 1995, 487-91; Green and

FIG 6.2: WESSEX GOLDWORK –GOLD OBJECTS FROM THE BUSH BARROW GOLD (REPRODUCED WITH PERMISSION FROM WILTSHIRE HERITAGE MUSEUM, DEVIZES)

Rollo-Smith 1984), on Cranborne Chase (Green et al 1982) and around Avebury (Smith and Simpson 1966; Robertson-Mackay 1980). Occasionally metalwork finds are recovered, which include copper alloy daggers and as in the case of the recently discovered burial known as the 'Amesbury Archer', small amounts of goldwork, such as the basket earrings or more probably hair slides (Fitzpatrick 2003; 2009).

Period 3 2050-1750 cal BC

Around 2000 cal BC in the period roughly equating to Wessex I, there were changes in funerary behaviour. Large barrows appear and although there are a scattering of cremation burials (for example, Amesbury 39, Ashbee 1981) the predominant mode of burial is still inhumation during this period. From around 2000 cal BC the first Food Vessels and Collared Urns make their appearance in the archaeological record (for example, Christie 1967). However, large funerary vessels are comparatively rare in Wessex during this phase and where funerary vessels do occur they tend to be smaller accessory vessels (for example, Annable and Simpson 1964, 114-5). It is during this period that the "richest" grave deposits are found. Goldwork belonging to what has been termed the Wessex linear tradition by Stuart Needham (2000) is occasionally found accompanying burials, for example, the Bush Barrow lozenge, the gold covered cone and buttons from Upton Lovell G2 and the gold foil covered amber discs from Wilsford G8 (see Annable and Simpson 1964, 103, 100; Clarke et al 1985, 125; fig 6.2). Armorico-British daggers (Gerloff 1975, 69-73) and necklaces are found with burials dating to this period as for example, Shrewton barrows 5J and 5L (Green and Rollo-Smith 1984; Beck and Shennan 1991, 74).

Period 4 1750-1500 cal BC

From around 1750 to 1500 cal BC there was a further shift in burial practices as cremation became the dominant rite. There were also changes to the accompanying ceramic and metalwork assemblages. In particular, Camerton-Snowshill daggers are found with burials (Gerloff 1975, 99-100). Larger types of urn including Collared Urns come to the fore and are widely associated with cremation burials (for example, Amesbury 72, Ashbee 1984; or Shrewton barrow 5G, Green and Rollo-Smith 1984). However, there was a great deal of variation within the funerary record during this period (Barrett 1994, 119) and not all cremations were accompanied by ceramics: some were associated with daggers (for example, Amesbury 58, Ashbee 1984) and faience beads, etc. (see for example, Annable and Simpson 1964).

By around 1500 cal BC large-scale barrow construction was largely at an end and a new tradition of Deverel Rimbury associated burials beneath low mounds became established (Miles 1826; Ellison 1980). However, it should be pointed out that there are a surprisingly small number of radiocarbon dates from the Wessex barrows, and there are some archaeologists who have questioned this sequence and have suggested that rather than being a chronological sequence there may have been divergent contemporary traditions (Taylor 2005; Martin forthcoming).

Different traditions within Wessex might also be suggested by the differential siting of the 'Conspicuous' and 'Inconspicuous' barrow groups mentioned above (Peters 1999; Field 2008, 64-6), and the picture is further complicated by the large number of barrows in Wessex which were not richly furnished at all. Indeed, as Ann Woodward's recent study of Wessex grave associated artefacts has shown, at the time of burial, many of the objects such as the necklaces and daggers found in Wessex barrows were incomplete, repaired or worn implying that they were heirlooms, which had been handed down, rather than elite objects (Woodward et al 2006). Recent approaches to the Wessex burials have highlighted the fact that rather than being the graves of warrior chiefs they may have been more concerned with the establishment of other kinds of social identity (Barrett 1994; Woodward 2000; Woodward et al 2005). Artefacts such as amber, faience and jet beads, fossils or distinctive coloured stone objects (Oakley 1978; Beck and Shennan 1991; Sheridan and Shortland 2003; 2004) may have been included because of their perceived magical properties, and some objects may have been part of ceremonial costumes, such as those worn by shaman (Woodward et al 2006). In fact, it is likely that in addition to the act of burial, other forms of ritual were an important part of the activities undertaken at Wessex barrows (Thomas 2005, 305-6; Healy and Harding 2007). Nonetheless, however, we choose to interpret them it is clear that in Wessex, barrows were closely associated with the interment of the dead and with funerary rituals.

From the preceding discussion, it is possible to make the following points:

Firstly, there was an early tradition of Beaker-associated inhumation burials, which started in the middle of the third millennium cal BC, which sometimes involved the deposition of copper alloy daggers and very occasionally small gold objects in flat under low mounds or within flat graves – this tradition is likely to have given rise to the Early Bronze Age burial rites of the second millennium.

Secondly, Early Bronze Age barrow cemeteries have a strong focus around 'earlier' monuments and complexes, but particularly around river systems. Cemeteries grew over time with burials being added to existing mounds and new barrows added to existing clusters.

Thirdly, from around c. 2000 cal BC, inhumations are found within a fairly restricted range of sites, under chalk mounds with objects such as Armorico-British daggers, beads and very rarely thin sheet gold artefacts. After around circa 1750 cal BC evidence for cremation increases and cremations associated with Camerton-Snowshill daggers and large urns are found.

FIG 6.3: ONE OF THE CHAPMAN BARROWS, EXMOOR

Fourthly, and most perhaps importantly for the following discussion, regardless of whether barrows were associated with status, the defining of identities or lineages, it is clear that Wessex barrows were burial sites, firmly associated with the treatment of human remains.

The South West Peninsula

Moving now to the south west region, it is evident that there was a rather different situation. It would be churlish to deny that there are no earthen barrows, or burials, which resemble those in Wessex. There are also a number of artefacts which would not be out of place in Wessex type burials. At North Molton a faience, lignite and amber bead necklace was associated with a cremation (Fox and Stone 1951). The Upton Pyne 4 barrow covered a cremation deposit, accompanied by a small copper alloy dagger, a necklace of lignite beads, an accessory vessel and a copper alloy pin (Fox 1969; Grinsell 1983). At the Hameldown Down barrow an amber and gold studded dagger pommel was recovered (Beck and Shennan 1991, 159). Over the years, these objects, and perhaps most famously the Rillaton cup, have all been argued to be demonstrative of Wessex type burials (Fox 1948; Fox and Stone 1951; Grinsell 1983; Todd 1987, 144).

However, looking only at the final outward appearance of barrows or a small selected group of artefacts from isolated burials effectively decontextualises the evidence and masks the great variety of practices which are found in the Early Bronze Age across the south west region. In fact closer analyses reveal that many of the examples given above differ significantly from the classic Wessex burials. For example, the amber pommel from the Hameldown barrow was not found within the centre of the site, but instead had been placed under slabs on the southern side of the barrow with a cremation deposit (Grinsell 1978).

This diversity is highlighted by the fact that the seventy or so radiocarbon determinations which are currently available for the region (see for example, Jones 2005, 156; Jones and Quinnell 2008; Nowakowski 2007), reveal little evidence for a sequence comparable with that which has been described for the Wessex area.

There are around 5000 barrows in Devon and Cornwall (Griffith and Quinnell 1999; Webster 2008). In addition to apparently simple cairns, there is a wide variety of site types – indeed on Bodmin Moor alone nearly 50 different types of barrow were identified by the Bodmin Moor survey and studies of Dartmoor and Exmoor indicate a similar variety (Johnson and Rose 1994, 34-40; Turner 1990; Riley and Wilson-North 2001). These include ring-cairns, platform cairns, kerbed and tor cairns, as well as simpler bowl barrows (fig 6.3) and cairns.

FIG 6.4 : WHITE TOR CAIRN, DARTMOOR (GRAEME KIRKHAM)

In marked contrast to Wessex, the siting of barrows in the south west does not appear to have been strongly riverine or associated with ancient monuments. However, some barrow groups are not far from rivers, those at Upton Pyne being quite close to the River Exe (Pollard and Russell 1969); although even there, most of the mounds were not located in sight of the river. Likewise, there is some evidence for the reuse of older megalithic tombs, with, for example Bronze Age artefacts being recovered from Zennor Quoit, and barrows can, as at Craddock Moor in Cornwall or Bow in Devon (Tilley 1995; Jones 2005, chapters 2 and 4; Griffith 1985) be located near to stone circles, and henges, although they are not usually aligned upon 'older' monument complexes.

Interestingly, in addition to the construction of new cairns and barrows, the west of Cornwall may also have seen the reinvention of a megalithic tradition, possibly linked with other coastal sites around the Atlantic façade. Two entrance graves, Bosiliack and Tregiffian, have Early Bronze Age radiocarbon determinations and others are associated with Bronze Age Trevisker pottery (Jones and Thomas forthcoming).

However, the greatest number of barrows and cairns are found in the uplands, such as Dartmoor, Exmoor, Bodmin Moor and Penwith (Butler 1997; Johnson and Rose 1994, Riley and Wilson-North, 32-8; Russell 1971). There are also large numbers on most of the prominent hills and ridges, and in Cornwall along the coastal cliffs (Bonnington 1999). In addition, aerial photographic plotting of crop-marks across Cornwall by the National Mapping Programme would imply that although sites have undoubtedly been lost, this distribution is not simply the result of later agriculture destroying sites, but instead reflects a preference for high or liminal places for monument construction (fig 6.4), which may have had its roots in the Neolithic period - with the construction of tor enclosures and the digging of pits beside prominent rocky outcrops (Mercer 1981; Tilley 1995; Cole and Jones 2002-3). It could be argued to represent a continuing tradition of engagement with particular places which were deeply embedded in the social memory (Connerton 1984, chapter 1) of Bronze Age communities in Cornwall.

This process can be seen by the large number of ceremonial sites in the south west which are built in sight of, or near to distinctive hills and tors (Butler 1997 chapter 4; Jones 2005, chapter 4). However, it is most clearly demonstrated by a number of cairns in the uplands, which include in situ rocks and outcrops in their perimeters, for example as at Watch Hill (Jones and Quinnell 2006a), or within their centres, as can be seen on a massive scale at Showery Tor on Bodmin Moor, where a low rubble bank surrounds a massive, and visually very distinctive natural outcrop (Barnatt 1982, 212). The principle can be clearly seen at Watch Croft in Penwith, where not only is the barrow group aligned onto natural 'barrow-like' outcrops, but kerbing also encircles one of the outcrops. Indeed, when viewed in profile, the group has the appearance of a linear barrow cemetery. Within this one group there are sites, which are entirely cultural, natural or a fusion of the two

FIG 6.5: NATURAL OUTCROP WITH KERB AROUND BASE, WATCH CROFT, PENWITH

(fig 6.5). It may be the case that there was a desire to merge the 'natural' with the 'cultural' and link 'new' monuments with ancient places, which might have been considered to have been the work of supernatural beings or ancestors.

Cemetery organisation also differs somewhat from Wessex. Some south-western barrow groups do have linear components to them. However, as at Farway in Devon (Jones and Quinnell 2008), where there over 100 barrows and cairns, the linear aspect is just one element within a broader grouping and is likely to be associated with the underlying topography. Where multiple radiocarbon dates have been obtained, as at Farway, or Davidstow Moor and Stannon in Cornwall (Christie 1988; Jones 2004-5; Jones and Quinnell 2008), the results indicate that rather than developing sequentially as in Wessex, a range of monuments types were in use at the same time over several centuries – possibly associated with contrasting practices - which only sometimes involved the inclusion of burial-related deposits.

The external form of the mound can be misleading too. Many of the excavated cairns and barrows in Devon and Cornwall have revealed mounding to be a final stage, often after long periods of use as open enclosures. This can be seen at Farway in Devon, where several of the mounded sites were found to have cairn-rings or post-settings beneath them and at Caerloggas and Watch Hill in central Cornwall, where Henrietta's excavations revealed that mounds covered sites with complex histories. Unlike Wessex there is little evidence for mound heightening or satellite burials and at Watch Hill (Miles 1975; Jones and Quinnell 2006a) and other sites it may have been the act of burial, which finally triggered the site to become mounded. In other words, in the south west peninsula barrow mound construction frequently marks the ending for the use of an enclosed space and final closure.

In fact, in contrast to Wessex, many of the regions barrows and cairns do not contain burials at all (Wainwright et al 1979; Quinnell 1997; Jones 2005, chapter 3), or where human remains are present they comprise exceptionally small token quantities for example as at Upton Pyne 248b and Farway 28 in east Devon or Treligga 2 on the North Cornish coast (Pollard and Russell 1969; Jones and Quinnell 2008; Christie 1985). Conversely there are also multiple deposits, as at Chysauster, where the parts of several people being placed into the site a one time (Smith 1996) or being mixed together into one deposit. This latter practice can be seen at Stannon cairn 3, where two separate deposits of human bone were recovered from a Trevisker vessel (Harris et al 1984) and at Harlyn Bay where a burial, which was initially thought to be one person, has recently been found to be made up of several young people who were deposited with the burnt bones of a pig within a Trevisker urn (Jones et al in preparation). This variability within the burial record of course raises problems with some older interpretations of cremation burials – where larger amounts of human bone have been thought to represent individual persons.

It is therefore clear that human bone was used in a number of contrasting ways. Occasionally the individuality of the deceased may have been marked during funeral rituals, but at other times people may have been merged into a community of the dead. Perhaps more commonly still, the bone itself may have been considered to be a symbolic resource to be crushed and deposited with other deposits, such as quartz pebbles and charcoal within a sacred space. This is also suggested by the large number of barrows which do not contain primary burial deposits or burial associated artefacts. Instead artefacts were frequently taken apart and fragmented or deposited singly. Objects such as ceramics, beads and pebbles are found within pits and ditches (Miles 1975; Jones 2005, chapter 5; Jones and Quinnell 2008). In other words, many barrows in the south west may have been strongly associated with the performance of rituals and 'magic' rather than with burial.

In common with Wessex, and as Henrietta noted in her 1988 paper, most of the radiocarbon dating evidence for barrow building in the south west falls into the period between 2000 and 1500 cal BC. However, the diversity of traditions across the region and the comparatively low numbers of grave associated artefacts means that it is more difficult to present an orderly chronological sequence for the south west than in Wessex. Nonetheless, it can broadly be argued to run as follows.

Period 1 2500-2300 cal BC and Period 2 2300-2050 cal BC

The period before 2000 cal BC reveals comparatively little evidence for burial-related or monument building activity. Although Beakers are being found in increasing numbers across Devon and Cornwall, those that have been securely dated to the centuries before the turn of the second millennium have not been found with burials but instead are most commonly found in pits, as well as middens, cooking mounds and recently in association with a simple structure, near Sennen (Jones and Quinnell 2006b; Jones 2009).

It appears that is only from around c. 2000 cal BC that Beakers appear within burial-related sites (see Period 2 below), and then, although there are a few Beaker inhumations, as at Lousey in Cornwall and Burnt Common in Devon, they are deposited as part of rites which were typical of the south west region (see for example, Quinnell 2003; Jones and Quinnell 2008). For example, at Burnt Common (Sidmouth 9), a fragmented Beaker was deposited with an inhumation burial the centre of the ring cairn, which also contained pits and an area of burning (Pollard 1967; Jones and Quinnell 2008). Likewise, the Beaker from Lousey was fragmented and sprinkled around an inhumation burial. A cremation deposit was also found (Christie 1988). Other than the presence of Beaker vessels, the activity at these sites is absolutely characteristic of other barrows and cairns in the region.

Fig 6.6: Urn from Stannon Cairn 3 (Reproduced with permission of the Royal Institution of Cornwall)

Indeed, where Beakers are found in barrows or burial-related contexts in the south west, they are usually found with cremation deposits, as at Try, where a handled Beaker was found in cist along with sherds from a Trevisker vessel, Carvinack where the Beaker was found in site which also contained sherds from a Food vessel, and Farway 28, where a Beaker vessel was again found with a Food vessel (Dudley 1964; Russell and Pool 1964; Jones and Quinnell 2008).

Likewise, the goldwork from around the turn of the second millennium cal BC is rather different from both the Beaker trinkets and the Wessex linear goldwork tradition (Needham 2000). In Cornwall gold was probably obtained from Ireland and takes the form of gold crescentic shaped collars known as lunulae (Taylor 1980; Eogan 1994). To date four lunulae are recorded weight for weight a far larger quantity than all the gold in Wessex. It is worth noting, however, that the two lunulae with barrow associations from Harlyn Bay (fig 6.7) were not directly associated with the burial but were recovered from the mound (Mattingly et al 2009). So again, it is possible to argue that the defining of personality was not inherently strong in the south west.

Period 3 2050-1700 cal BC

From 2000 cal BC there is major change in the archaeological record for the south west, as it was during this period that most of the region's barrows were constructed. Recent radiocarbon determinations indicate that both inhumation burials and cremation deposits are found from an early date (Jones and Quinnell 2006a:

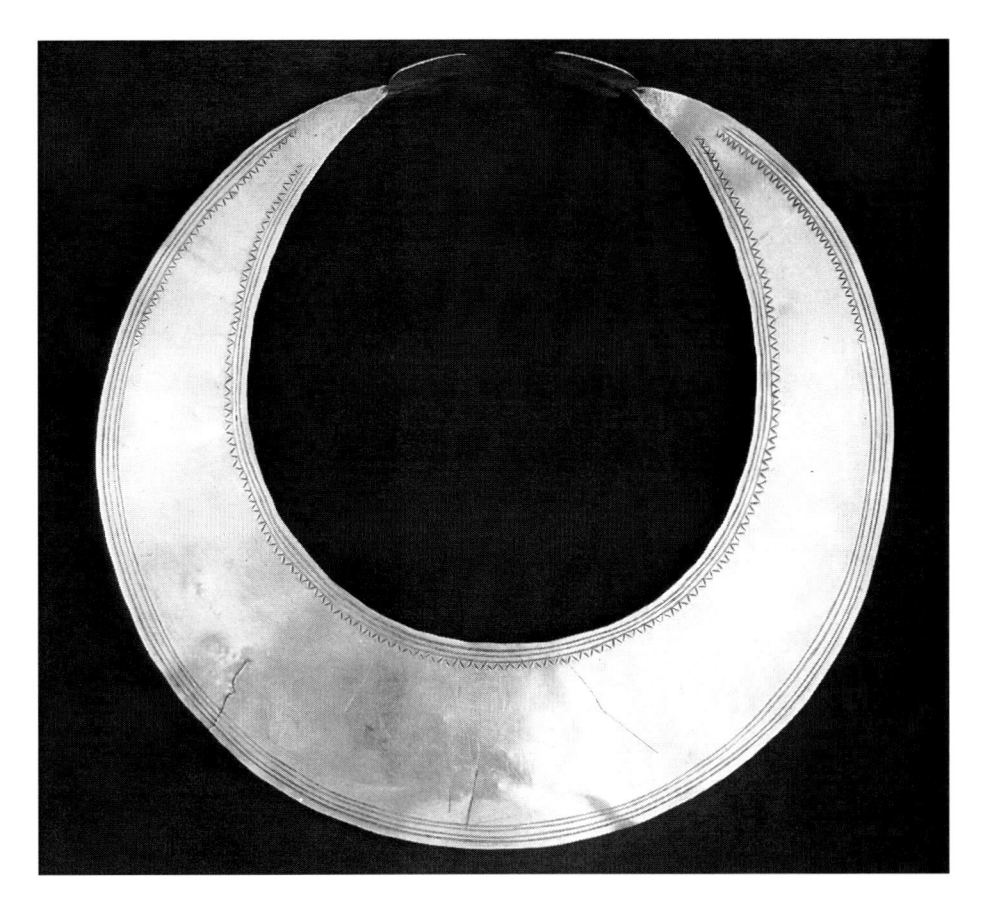

FIG 6.7: PROVINCIAL LUNULA FROM HARLYN BAY (REPRODUCED WITH PERMISSION OF THE ROYAL INSTITUTION OF CORNWALL)

Jones et al in preparation). However, despite being located in an area with the richest deposits of tin and copper in Britain there are very few early copper alloy objects from barrows in Cornwall and Devon. There are, for example no Armorico-British daggers, although the knife dagger accompanied by sherds of later Beaker and a V bored button from Fernworthy on Dartmoor is likely date to this period (Gerloff 1975, 165; Quinnell 2003). Likewise, there are no gold objects from the period between circa 2000 and 1750 cal BC and other objects such as amber beads are rare (see for example Beck and Shennan 1991, fig 6.1).

As Henrietta pointed out in 1988, ceramics are also uncommon in Devon but, in Cornwall the onset of barrow building is contemporary with the appearance of Trevisker ware pottery (fig 6.6). Early radiocarbon dates from Stannon cairn 3 and Harlyn Bay (Harris et al 1984; Jones et al forthcoming) support the emergence of the Trevisker ware series at the start of the second millennium. As with the Beakers, Trevisker vessels were sometimes deposited complete in barrows, as at Stannon Cairn 3, but usually as at Davidstow Moor site 16 or Stannon site 2 they were fragmented (Christie 1988; Jones 2004-5).

Although small numbers of Food Vessels, Collared Urns and Accessory Vessels have occasionally been recovered from sites in Devon and Cornwall (Griffith 1984; Watts and Quinnell 2001; Jones and Quinnell 2006a), it is Trevisker Ware pottery which dominates the ceramic record in Cornwall and, to a much lesser extent, Devon for the entirety of the second millennium cal BC.

This could be taken to imply that at the start of the second millennium cal BC communities in the south west suffered from cultural poverty – or that people simply chose not to bury their dead with ostentatious objects. This should not be an alien concept, for as Mike Parker Pearson (1982) pointed out in relation to the burial customs of contemporary British society, the dead do not bury themselves and social distinctions between people are not always expressed through the grave. In fact, the comparative lack of grave goods within barrows in the south west may again reflect older, established traditions of burying objects within pits rather than with people.

Period 4 1750-1500 cal BC

In the period after circa 1750 cal BC to circa 1500 cal BC there is evidence for an increasing number of objects being incorporated into barrow associated contexts. All but one of the identifiable daggers, such as those from Farway 32 (fig 6.8) and Fore Down (Gerloff 1975; Pearce 1983; Christie 1988), fall into this phase – as do the faience beads from Trelowthas and Stannon (Sheridan and Shortland 2004; Jones 2004-5). The shale cups from Farway and the gold cup from Rillaton also belong to this period, but again the relationship between artefacts and burials is not always a straightforward one. Many barrow-associated objects,

FIG 6.8.: FARWAY 32, BARROW AND ARTEFACTUAL ASSEMBLAGE (AFTER HUTCHINSON 1880)

such as the Farway cups, were deposited separately into the barrows, rather than with the burial deposit itself (Jones and Quinnell 2008), or as at Caerloggas were placed into the site in a broken state (Miles 1975).

As in the period prior to 1750 cal BC, cremation deposits are most commonly found within barrow sites, although it is of interest that Rillaton barrow, which belongs to this period contained a richly furnished single inhumation burial. Indeed, both the Farway barrow cups and the Rillaton burial with its gold cup and Camerton-Snowshill dagger show outside influences from beyond the south west region (Needham et al 2006). Stuart Needham (2009) has recently argued that such cups were linked with a wider European tradition of precious cup usage around what he has termed a 'maritory' which linked communities either side of the English Channel.

Nonetheless, aside from these exceptions, there are few apparent changes to barrow associated rites over the course of the first half of the second millennium cal BC. As in Wessex, it appears that barrow building ceased in most areas at around 1500 cal BC. However, again there are significant differences, as the Deverel-Rimbury ceramic tradition is absent and instead of cremation cemeteries there are smaller ceremonial-related structures that are found near to settlement areas (Gossip and Jones 2007; Jones 2008).

In summary, it is possible to make the following points:

Firstly, there was no early Beaker burial horizon in the south west region. Beaker associated burials are later in date and are usually associated with cremations. As a result there was no early established tradition of single inhumation burial or the construction of particular 'personas' at the graveside.

Secondly, although barrows appear at the same time as those in Wessex, circa 2000 cal BC), from the outset there are significant differences. Rivers and older monument foci seem to have been less important than tors and prominent hills. Barrows were set into a wider landscape of 'special' places and could be set in sight of, beside, or over such places.

Thirdly, there were a wide range of distinctive forms of barrows and cairns n the south west – which included open enclosures and sites with megalithic elements, such as large kerbs, cists, and orthostatic settings.

Fourthly, practices associated with Early Bronze Age barrows in the south west are less strongly connected with burial or with the establishment of 'identity' through the deposition of grave goods – instead barrows were involved with a variety of ritual practices, of which burial was just one feature. The undertaking of rituals at significant places may have been the most important aspect.

Conclusions

The scenario that has been outlined here is not intended to make a case for the isolation of the south west peninsula from the rest of Britain. Indeed, it is clear that the Early Bronze Age monuments and artefacts which are found across Devon and Cornwall were related to those found elsewhere in Britain – and there is good evidence for connections between places, both with communities to the east in Wessex, and at certain times with those around the Atlantic façade as well (Needham 2009). Nor am I arguing that there was any kind of greater independent south western identity or polity, which existed in direct opposition to what was happening on the Wessex chalk.

Rather, I would suggest that Bronze Age communities in the South West, Wessex and beyond interpreted new material culture in relation to traditions, practices, and local interactions which had gone before. In the chalklands of Wessex this led to marking of individual personalities beneath mounds, whereas in the south west it resulted in the referencing and embellishment of already important natural places in the landscape.

The archaeology of one region cannot therefore be seen as being 'typical' and I would suggest that when thinking about sites, archaeologists should remember Henrietta's wise words and consider their 'local character'.

Bibliography

Annable, F. and Simpson, D. 1964. *Guide catalogue of the Neolithic and Bronze Age collections in Devizes museum,* Devizes, The Wiltshire Archaeological and Natural History Society.

ApSimon, A. 1954. Dagger graves in the 'Wessex' Bronze Age, *University of London, Institute of Archaeology* 10, 37-61.

Ashbee, P. 1981. Amesbury Barrow 39: excavations 1960, *The Wiltshire Archaeological and Natural History Magazine* 74/75, 3-34.

Ashbee, P. 1984. The excavation of Amesbury barrows 58, 61a, 61, and 71, *The Wiltshire Archaeological and Natural History Magazine* 79, 39-91.

Barnatt, J. 1982. *Prehistoric Cornwall - the ceremonial monuments,* Wellinborough, Turnestone.

Barrett, J. 1990. The monumentality of death: the character of Early Bronze Age mortuary mounds in southern Britain, *World Archaeology* 22, 179-89.

Barrett, J. 1994. *Fragments from antiquity: an archaeology of social life in Britain, 2900-1200 BC*, Oxford, Blackwell.

Beck, C. and Shennan, S. 1991. *Amber in prehistoric Britain,* Oxford, Oxbow.

Bonnington, P. 1999. *Cemetery mounds in western Britain; with particular reference to Anglesey and West Penwith,* Unpublished BA Dissertation, University of Exeter.

Bradley, R. 1981. Various styles of urn – cemeteries and settlement in southern England, in R. Chapman, I. Kinnes, and K. Randsborg (eds.), *The archaeology of death,* Cambridge, Cambridge University Press, 93-104.

Brophy, K. and Barclay, A. 2009. *Defining a regional Neolithic: evidence from Britain and Ireland,* Oxford, Oxbow.

Butler, J. 1997. *Dartmoor atlas of antiquities, volume 5,* Tiverton, Devon Books.

Case, H. 2003. Beaker presence in Wilsford 7, *The Wiltshire Archaeological and Natural History Magazine* 96, 161-94.

Clarke, D. V., Cowie, T. G. and Foxon, A. 1985. *Symbols of power at the time of Stonehenge,* Edinburgh, National Museum of Scotland.

Christie, P. 1967. A barrow cemetery of the second millennium BC in Wiltshire, England, *Proceedings of the Prehistoric Society* 33, 336-66.

Christie, P. 1985. Barrows on the north Cornish coast: wartime excavations by C K Croft Andrew, *Cornish Archaeology* 24, 23-122.

Christie, P. 1988. A barrow cemetery on Davidstow Moor, Cornwall: wartime excavations by C K Croft Andrew, *Cornish Archaeology* 27, 27-169.

Cleal, R. M. J., Walker, K. E. and Montague, R. 1995. *Stonehenge in its landscape*, London, English Heritage.

Cleggett, S. 1999. The River Avon; real-time realm of the ancestors, *Proceedings of the Dorset Natural History and Archaeological Society* 121, 49-52.

Cole, R. and Jones, A. M. 2002-3. Journeys to the rock; archaeological investigations at Tregarrick Farm, Roche, Cornwall, *Cornish Archaeology* 41-42, 107-43.

Connerton, P. 1989. *How societies remember*, Cambridge, Cambridge, University Press.

Dudley, D. 1964. The excavation of the Carvinack barrow, Tregavethan, near Truro, Cornwall, *Journal of the Royal Institution of Cornwall* 4, 414-50.

Ellison, A. 1980. Deverel-Rimbury Urn cemeteries: the evidence for social organisation, in J. Barrett, and R. Bradley (eds.), *The later British Bronze Age Oxford*, British Archaeological Reports, British Series, 83, 115-26.

Eogan, G. 1994. *The accomplished art*, Oxford, Oxbow.

Exon, S., Gaffney, V., Woodward, A. and Yorston, R. 2000. *Stonehenge landscapes, journeys through real and imagined worlds*, Oxford, Archaeopress.

Field, D. 2007. *Earthen long barrow; the earliest monuments in the British Isles*, Stroud, Tempus.

Field, D. 2008. *Use of land in central southern England during the Neolithic and Early Bronze Age*, Oxford, British Archaeological Reports, British Series 394.

Field, D. forthcoming. Moving on in landscape studies: goodbye Wessex; hello German Bight?, in A. M. Jones and G. Kirkham (eds.), *Regionality in British prehistory*

Fleming, A. 1971. Territorial patterns in Bronze Age Wessex, *Proceedings of the Prehistoric Society* 37, 138-66.

Fitzpatrick, A. 2003. The Amesbury archer, *Current Archaeology* 184, 146-55.

Fitzpatrick, A. 2009. In his hands and in his head: the Amesbury archer as metalworker, in P. Clark (ed.), *Bronze Age connections, cultural contact in prehistoric Europe*, Oxford, Oxbow, 176-88.

Fox, A. 1948. The Broad Down (Farway) necropolis and the Wessex culture in Devon, *Proceedings of Devon Archaeological Exploration Society* 4.1, 1-19.

Fox, A. 1969. Appendix, the Upton Pyne cemetery, *Proceedings of the Devon Archaeological Society* 27, 75-8.

Fox, A. and Stone, J. F. S. 1951. A necklace from a barrow in North Molton parish, north Devon, *Antiquaries Journal* 31, 25-31.

Garwood, P. 1991. Ritual tradition and the reconstitution of society, in P. Garwood, D. Jennings, R. Skeates and J. Toms (eds.), *Sacred and profane*, Oxford, Oxford University Committee for Archaeology, 10-32.

Gerloff, S. 1975. *The Early Bronze Age daggers in Great Britain*, Munich, Prähistoric Bronzefunde.

Gibson, A. 2007. A Beaker Veneer, M. Larsson and M. Parker Pearson (eds.), *From Stonehenge to the Baltic, living with cultural diversity in the third millennium BC*, Oxford, British Archaeological Reports, International Series 1692, 47-64.

Gingell, C. 1988. Twelve Wiltshire round barrows, excavations in 1959 and 1961 by F de M and H L Vatcher, *The Wiltshire Archaeological and Natural History Magazine* 82, 19-76.

Gossip, J. and Jones, A. M. 2007. *Archaeological investigations of a later prehistoric and a Romano British landscape at Tremough, Penryn, Cornwall*, Oxford, British Archaeological Reports, British Series 443.

Green, C. and Rollo-Smith, S. 1984. The excavation of eighteen round barrows near Shrewton, Wiltshire, *Proceedings of the Prehistoric Society* 50, 255-319.

Green C., Lynch, F. and White, H. 1982. The Excavation of two round barrows on Launceston Down, Dorset Long Crichel 5 and 7, *Proceedings of the Dorset Natural History and Archaeological Society* 104, 39-58.

Griffith, F. M. 1984. Archaeological investigations at Colliford reservoir, Bodmin Moor 1977-78, *Cornish Archaeology* 23, 47-140.

Griffith, F. M. 1985. Some newly discovered ritual monuments in mid Devon, *Proceedings of the Prehistoric Society* 51, 310-15.

Griffith, F. M. and Quinnell, H. 1999. Barrows and ceremonial sites in the Neolithic and earlier Bronze Age, in R. Kain, and W. Ravenhill (eds.), *Historical atlas of Southwest Britain*, Exeter, University of Exeter Press, 55-61.

Grinsell, L. V. 1978. Dartmoor barrows, *Proceedings of the Devon Archaeology Society* 36, 85-180.

Grinsell, L. V. 1983. The barrows of south and east Devon, *Proceedings of the Devon Archaeology Society* 41, 5-46.

Grinsell, L. V. 1994. Round barrows and burials of the 'Wessex' earlier Bronze Age in Cornwall, *Cornish Archaeology* 33, 36-9.

Hamilton, S. 2003. Sussex not Wessex: a regional perspective on southern Britain c. 1200-200 BC, in D. Rudling (ed.), *The archaeology of Sussex to AD 2000*, Kings Lynn, Heritage Marketing, 69-88.

Harris, D., Hooper, S. and Trudgian, P. 1984. Excavation of three cairns on Stannon Down, St. Breward, *Cornish Archaeology* 23, 141-55.

Healy, F. and Harding, J. 2007. A thousand and one things to do with a round barrow, in J. Last (ed.), *Beyond the grave: new perspectives on barrows*, Oxford, Oxbow, 53-71.

Johnson, N. and Rose, P. 1994. *Bodmin Moor an archaeological survey, volume 1*, London, RCHME.

Jones, A. M, 2004-5. Settlement and ceremony; archaeological investigations at Stannon Down, St Breward, Cornwall, *Cornish Archaeology* 43-44, 1-141.

Jones, A. M. 2005. *Cornish Bronze Age ceremonial landscapes c.2500-1500 BC*, Oxford, British Archaeological Reports, British Series 394.

Jones, A. M. 2008. Houses for the dead and cairns for the living: a reconsideration of the Early to Middle Bronze Age transition in south-west England, *Oxford Journal of Archaeology* 27, 153–74

Jones, A. M. 2009. Beaker structure and other discoveries along the Sennen–Porthcurno pipeline 2007, *CBA Southwest Journal* 23, 30-3.

Jones, A. M., Hartgroves, S., Marley, J. and Quinnell, H. in preparation. *On the beach: new discoveries at Harlyn Bay.*

Jones, A. M. and Quinnell, H., 2006a. Redating the Watch Hill Barrow, *Archaeological Journal* 163, 42-66.

Jones, A. M. and Quinnell, H. 2006b. Cornish Beakers: new discoveries and perspectives, *Cornish Archaeology* 45, 31-70

Jones, A. M. and Quinnell, H. 2008. The Farway barrow complex in East Devon reassessed, *Proceedings of the Devon Archaeological Society* 66, 27-58.

Jones, A. M. and Thomas, A. C. forthcoming. Bosiliack Carn and a reconsideration of entrance graves, *Proceedings of the Prehistoric Society.*

Lawson, A. J. 2007. *Chalkland; an archaeology of Stonehenge and its region,* Salisbury, Hobnob Press.

Martin, A. forthcoming. The alien within: the forgotten sub-cultures of Early Bronze Age Wessex, in A. M. Jones and G. Kirkham (eds.), *Regionality in British prehistory.*

Mattingly, J., Marley. J. and Jones, A. M. 2009. Five gold rings? Early Bronze Age gold lunulae from Cornwall, *Journal of the Royal institution of Cornwall,* 95-114.

McOmish, D., Field, D. and Brown, G. 2002. *The field archaeology of the Salisbury Plain Training Area,* Swindon, English Heritage.

Mercer, R. 1981. Excavations at Carn Brea, Illogan Cornwall - a Neolithic fortified complex of the third millennium BC, *Cornish Archaeology* 20, 1-204.

Miles, A. 1826. *A description of the Deverel barrow, opened 1825,* London, Nichols and son.

Miles, H. 1975. Barrows on the St. Austell Granite, *Cornish Archaeology* 14, 5-81.

Mizoguchi, K. 1992. A historiography of a linear barrow cemetery: a structurationalist's point of view, *Archaeological Review from Cambridge* 11, 40-9.

Needham, S. 1996. Chronology and periodisation in the British Bronze Age, *Acta Archaeologia* 67, 121-40.

Needham, S. 2000. The development of embossed gold in Bronze Age Europe, *Antiquaries Journal* 80, 27-66.

Needham, S. 2009. Encompassing the sea: 'maritories' and Bronze Age interactions, in P. Clark (ed.), *Bronze Age connections, cultural contact in prehistoric Europe,* Oxford, Oxbow, 12-37.

Needham, S., Parfitt, K. and Vardell, G. 2006. *The Ringlemere cup, precious cups and the beginning of the Channel Bronze Age,* London, British Museum.

Nowakowski, J. 2007. Digging deeper into barrow ditches: investigating the making of early Bronze Age memories in Cornwall, in J. Last (ed.), *Beyond the grave; new perspectives on barrows,* Oxford, Oxbow, 91-112.

Oakley, K P, 1978. Animal fossils as charms, in J. R. Porter and W. M. S. Russell (eds.), *Animals in folklore,* Cambridge, Brewer, Rowman and Littlefield, 208-42.

Owoc, A. 2008. Monuments as landscape; place, perspective and performance practice, in P. Rainbird (ed.), *Monuments in the landscape,* Stroud, Tempus, 281-93.

Parker Pearson, M. 1982. Mortuary practices, society and ideology: an ethno-archaeological study, in I, Hodder (ed.), *Symbolic and structural archaeology,* Cambridge, Cambridge University Press, 89-98.

Pearce, S. 1983. *The Bronze Age metalwork of South Western Britain,* Oxford, British Archaeological Reports, British Series 120.

Peters, F. 1999. Farmers and their ancestral tombs: a study of the inconspicuous barrows and their relationship with the secular landscape, *Proceedings of the Dorset Natural History and Archaeological Society* 121, 37-48.

Piggott, S. 1938. The Early Bronze Age in Wessex, *Proceedings of the Prehistoric Society* 4, 52-106.

Piggott, S. 1973. The Wessex culture of the Early Bronze Age, in, E. Crittall, (ed.), *Victoria county history of Wiltshire,* volume 1 part 2, Oxford, Oxford University Press, 352-75.

Pollard, S. 1967. Seven prehistoric sites near Honiton, Devon, part I; a Beaker flint ring and three cairns, *Proceedings of the Devon Archaeology Society* 25, 19-39.

Pollard, S., and Russell, P. 1969. Excavation of round barrow 248b, Upton Pyne, *Proceedings of the Devon Archaeological Society* 27, 49-74.

Quinnell, H. 1988. The local character of the Devon Bronze Age and its interpretation in the 1980s, *Proceedings of the Devon Archaeological Society* 46, 1-12.

Quinnell, H. 1997. Excavations of an Exmoor barrow and ring cairn, *Proceedings of the Devon Archaeology Society* 55, 1-38.

Quinnell, H. 2003. Devon Beakers: new finds, new thoughts, *Proceedings of the Devon Archaeological Society* 61, 1-20.

Renfrew, C. 1979. Wessex without Mycenae, in C. Renfrew (ed.), *Problems in European prehistory,* Edinburgh, Edinburgh University Press, 281-93.

Riley, H. and Wilson-North, R. 2001. *The field archaeology of Exmoor,* London, English Heritage.

Robertson-Mackay, M. E. 1980. A 'head and hoofs' burial beneath a round barrow, with other Neolithic and Bronze Age sites, on Hemp Knoll, near Avebury, Wiltshire, *Proceedings of the Prehistoric Society* 46, 123-76.

Russell, V. 1971. *West Penwith survey, St Austell,* Cornwall Archaeological Society.

Russell, V. and Pool, P. A. S. 1964. Excavation of a menhir at Try, Gulval, *Cornish Archaeology* 3, 15-26.

Sheridan, J. A. and Shortland, A. 2003. Supernatural power dressing, *British Archaeology* 70, 18-23.

Sheridan, J. A. and Shortland, A. 2004. '. . . beads which have given rise to so much dogmatism, controversy and rash speculation': faience in Early Bronze Age Britain and Ireland, in I. A. G. Shepherd, and G. J. Barclay (eds.), *Scotland in ancient Europe,* Edinburgh, Society of Antiquaries of Scotland, 263-79.

Smith, G 1996. Archaeology and Environment of a Bronze Age Cairn and Prehistoric and Romano-British field system at Chysauster, Gulval, near Penzance,

Cornwall, *Proceedings of the Prehistoric Society* 62, 167-220.

Smith, I. F. and Simpson D. 1966. Excavation of a round barrow on Overton Hill, north Wiltshire, *Proceedings of the Prehistoric Society* 32, 122-55.

Taylor, J. 1980. *Bronze Age goldwork of the British Isles,* Cambridge, Cambridge University Press.

Taylor, J. 2005. The work of the Wessex master goldsmith: its implications, *Wiltshire Archaeological and Natural History Magazine* 98, 38-81.

Thomas, J. 1991. *Rethinking the Neolithic*, Cambridge, Cambridge University Press.

Thomas, N. 2005. *Snail Down Wiltshire, the Bronze Age barrow cemetery and related earthworks, in the parishes of Collingbourne Ducis and Collingbourne Kingston: excavations 1953, 1955 and 1957,* Devizes, Wilshire Archaeological and Natural History Society.

Tilley, C. 1995. Rocks as resources: landscapes and power, *Cornish Archaeology* 34, 5-57.

Tilley, C. 1996. The powers of rocks: topography and monument construction on Bodmin Moor, *World Archaeology* 28, 161-76.

Todd, M. 1987. *The Southwest to AD 1000*, Harlow, Longmans.

Turner, J. R., 1990. Ring cairns, stone circles and related monuments on Dartmoor, *Proceedings of the Devon Archaeology Society* 48, 27-86.

Wainwright, G., Fleming, A. and Smith, K. 1979. The Shaugh Moor project: first report, *Proceedings of the Prehistoric Society* 45, 1-34.

Watts, M. A. and Quinnell, H. 2001 A Bronze Age cemetery at Elburton, Plymouth, *Proceedings of the Devon Archaeological Society* 59, 11-43.

Webster, C. 2008. *South west archaeological research framework: the archaeology of South West England,* Taunton, Somerset County Council.

Woodward, A. 2000. *British barrows, a matter of life and death,* Stroud, Tempus.

Woodward, A., Hunter, J., Ixer, R., Maltby, M., Potts, P., Webb, P., Watson, J. and Jones, M. 2005. Ritual in some Early Bronze Age grave goods, *Archaeological Journal,* 163, 31-64.

Woodward, A. and Woodward, P. J. 1996. The topography of some barrow cemeteries in Bronze Age Wessex, *Proceedings of the Prehistoric Society* 62, 275-92.

Acknowledgements

I would like to thank Graeme Kirkham and Peter Rose for their comments on the text. Thanks are also due to Jane Marley and Laura Ratcliffe for providing and giving me permission to reproduce figs 6.6 and 6.7 and to Graeme Kirkham for figs 1 and 4

Earlier Bronze Age Cemetery Mounds and the Multiple Cremation Burial rite in Western Britain

Paul Bonnington

Abstract

Earlier Bronze Age barrows containing simultaneously deposited multiple cremation burials have long been recognised as important elements within the archaeological record of western Britain, where they are commonly known as cemetery mounds. This paper aims to examine these sites and the funerary rite which defined them in detail, by addressing a broad range of evidence from throughout the areas in which they occur, in particular Anglesey in North Wales and West Penwith in Cornwall, which both contain significant numbers of excavated sites. Regional and local factors are taken into account along with landscape context, artefactual evidence and the relationship between cemetery mounds and other contemporary and analogous sites, and evidence which suggests that the multiple cremation burial was a new rite which reflects possible changes in the organisational and ceremonial identities of earlier Bronze Age societies will be outlined and discussed.

Introduction

The traditional emphasis on the monuments of Wessex as the basis for studying Early Bronze Age round barrows in Britain has left several common misconceptions, chiefly that the main burial rite during this period was the internment of single primary deposits of human remains, usually at the centre of the monument, and very occasionally surrounded by lesser satellite deposits. This, however, was not universally the case, particularly in the barrows of western Britain and Ireland where multiple burial was commonly practiced alongside various expressions of the single-burial rite (Waddell, 1990). In some cases, the multiple burial rite could be interpreted as potential evidence for the continuity of earlier Neolithic rites and beliefs, and subsequently for the traditional and conservative nature of a significant number of Britain's inhabitants at this time (Peterson 1972, 25). Such sites would include the multiple burial barrows found in the Yorkshire Wolds, such as at Aldro 54 and Garton Slack 75 where deposits of inhumed and cremated bone were contemporaneously buried (Peterson 1972, 44, 54). Elsewhere, multiple burial sites became established over time via the piecemeal accrual of individual deposits, including at Barn's Farm near Dalgety in Fife (Watkins 1982, 137). However, a very different multiple burial rite was practiced in a significant number of western British barrows: the simultaneous deposition of multiple cremation burials in single definable episodes. Although this again could be taken as evidence for the continuity of older traditions, the obvious differences between this rite and the other models might equally be regarded as representative of a new practice that constituted a profound addition to the ritual activities undertaken by a significant proportion of earlier Bronze Age society.

The term coined to describe barrows which contained simultaneously buried multiple cremation deposits is cemetery mound (Lynch 1971), and the following paper will assess the character of these sites and the ritual activity which took place within them. It is of course impossible to ascertain their original geographical distribution due to the potential loss of sites or the lack of recognition. However, it is quite clear that they represent a particularly significant monument type within the archaeological record of western Britain and Ireland (although the latter are beyond the scope of this study), and were particularly abundant in Wales and Cornwall (fig.7.1). This study will therefore make particular reference to the latter areas, especially Anglesey in North Wales, and West Penwith in West Cornwall, both of which contain a significant number of

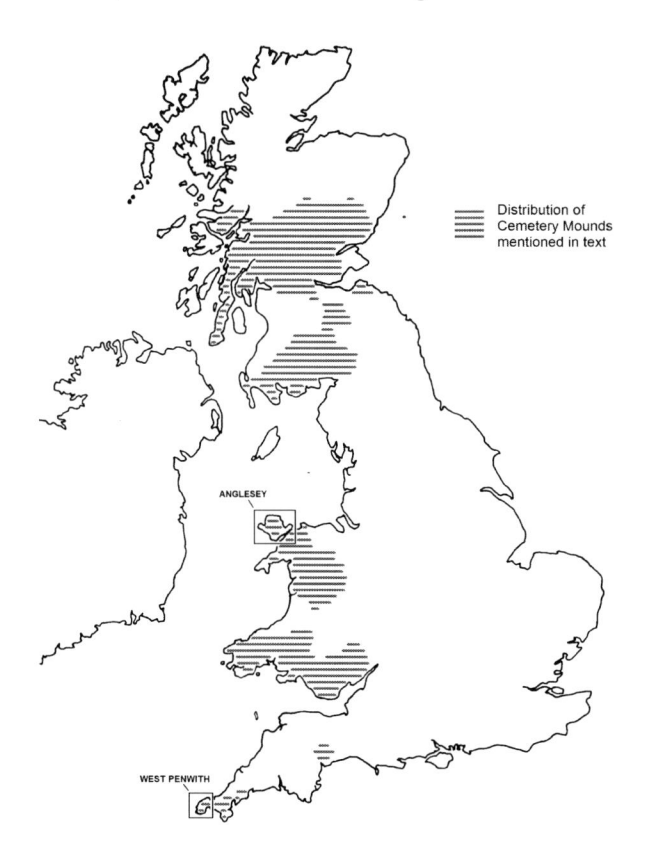

FIG 7.1: GENERAL DISTRIBUTION OF CEMETERY MOUNDS IN BRITAIN

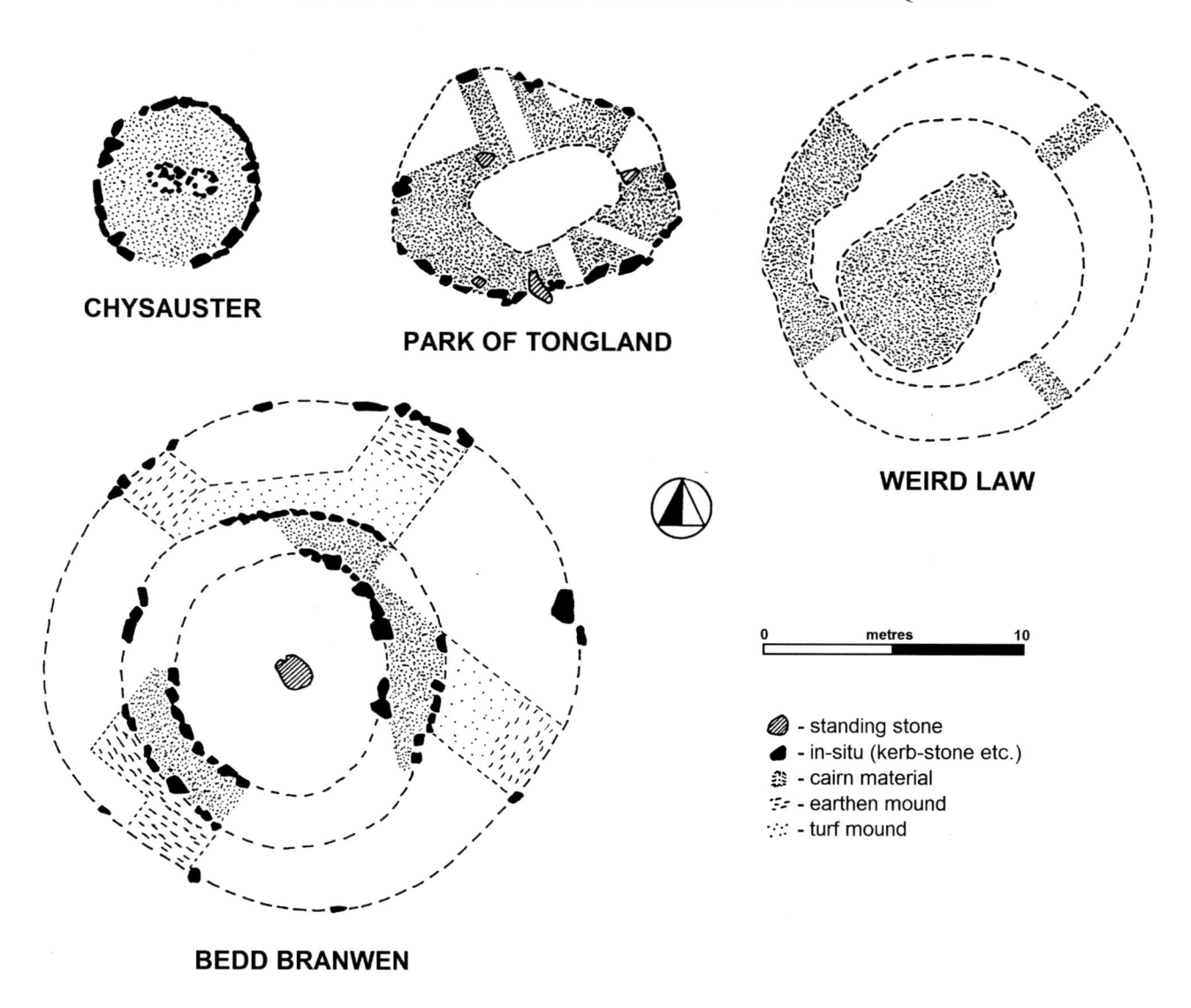

FIG. 7.2: SIMPLIFIED SITE MORPHOLOGY PLANS (ADAPTED FROM LYNCH 1971, FIG 41 & 46; BORLASE 1881, FIG 1 & 2; SMITH 1996, FIG 13; RUSSELL-WHITE ET AL. 1992, FIG 15; MACLAREN 1967, FIG 1)

cemetery mounds and are compact, well-defined zones in which inter-monument relationships are readily apparent.

Site Morphologies

The architecture of cemetery mounds was enormously diverse, with examples ranging from small simple mounds to large complex monuments (fig. 7.2). In some cases these had long complex histories characterised by multiple phases of construction and use, whilst others had much briefer lives resulted from a single ritual act.

The barrow at Bedd Branwen in north-western Anglesey is a classic multi-phase cemetery mound, and key to any discussion of the simultaneous multiple cremation rite in western Britain (fig. 7.3). Excavated by Frances Lynch between 1967 and 1968, it was found to contain twelve cremation burials which had been added in two distinct groups, both in association with specific structural episodes. The barrow's primary feature was a carefully constructed cairn ring, its inner and outer faces defined by contiguous kerbs of large flat boulders. This formed the focus for the burials, which were placed in and around it. It contained the disturbed remains of a stone cairn mound which encompassed the base of a small standing stone of pre-cairn origin (Lynch 1971, 19). This stone was located at the centre of the mound, and many of the cairn stones were carefully positioned so that they sloped towards it, thereby illustrating its role as the focal point of the monument (Lynch 1971, 57; Lynch 1991, 348). A kerbed mound of soil, clay and stacked turves of very local origin was then built to conceal the cairn. The excavator regarded this as a later addition as it was not concentric to the inner cairn ring, although she did consider them to be broadly contemporary based on the well-preserved condition of the internal cairn (Lynch 1971, 22)).

Elsewhere on Anglesey, two other cemetery mounds deserve particular attention for their architectural character. These are Treiorwerth, 3 miles SSW of Bedd Branwen, and Llanddyfnan in the east of the island. In contrast to Bedd Branwen, neither contained any internal structural

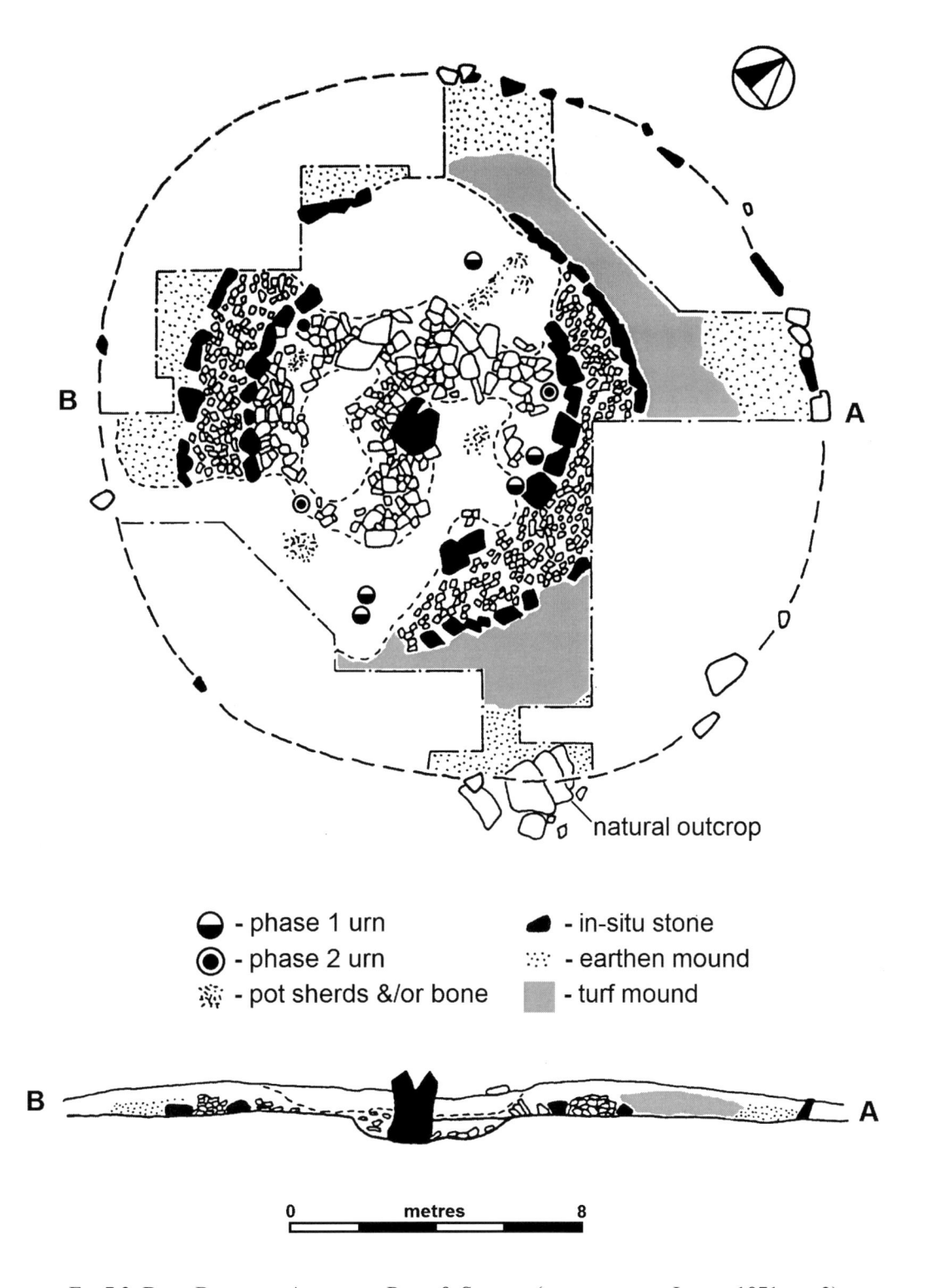

- phase 1 urn
- phase 2 urn
- pot sherds &/or bone
- in-situ stone
- earthen mound
- turf mound

FIG.7.3: BEDD BRANWEN, ANGLESEY: PLAN & SECTION (REDRAWN FROM LYNCH 1971, FIG 3)

features, the former being a roughly kerbed cairn of small glacial boulders capped by a thick layer of yellow/orange clay, and the latter a large mound of stone, gravel and sand (Lynch 1971, 99 and 1970, 137). Despite their apparent simplicity, both contained definable simultaneous multiple cremation burials: for example, Treiorwerth contained five cremations dating from two distinct episodes, the earlier associated with the structure of the mound and the later post-dating it (Lynch 1971, 44). Other Welsh cemetery mounds display the same structural diversity, including at Croesmihangel in Pembrokeshire where a simple kerbed mound of earth and stone was erected over a number of cremation burials sealed beneath a clay platform (Nye et al. 1983, 20-22), and at Newton, near Oystermouth in Glamorgan, where an existing barrow was transformed into a cemetery mound via the insertion of 3 cists designed to contain multiple cremation deposits (Savory 1972, 126).

The architecture of north-western British cemetery mounds was equally diverse. At Weird Law in Peebleshire, a number of pits with cremation burials were sealed beneath a layer of clean soil and a low 'pear-shaped' cairn, which had been erected inside a large circular stone bank that also contained the remains of a pyre site (MacLaren 1967, 95-96). The intimate spatial relationship between these burials and the structural features above them strongly implied that they both originated during a single episode, and this was also the case at Park of Tongland in Kirkudbright, where another distinctly contemporaneous group of cremation burials were deposited beneath a cairn ring which also incorporated a pair of existing standing stones before being concealed within a small kerbed cairn (McCullagh in Russell-White et al. 1992, 315). Although small, this would have been a visually impressive site, unlike the cemetery mound at Ratho near Edinburgh, which consisted only of a simple circular ditch with no internal mound (Smith 1995, 78).

In south west Britain, a significant number of cemetery mounds have been recognised, including at Upton Pyne near Exeter in Devon, which consisted of a large sand mound capped with turf and clay, which contained nine cremations placed in urned and un-urned deposits (fig 7.3, Pollard & Russell 1969). Further west, the large cemetery mound at Carvinack near Truro was significantly more complex, consisting of a cairn ring constructed largely from quartz and with an internal stake circle, which surrounded a group of features including a small quartz platform, a large free-standing cairn and four smaller versions, also predominantly built out of quartz (Dudley 1964, 423-426). Two of these smaller cairns, both of which were located within the north-eastern quadrant of the enclosure, contained cremation deposits, two in one example and one in the other, which along with the enclosed area generally had been sealed beneath a layer of pink clay before the overlying structures were built, thereby showing that they must have been deposited contemporaneously (Dudley 1964, 426). A final structural event, which based on the uniformity of the clay floor must have occurred soon afterwards, resulted in the addition of a large turf mound (Dudley 1964, 419). Other cemetery mounds in the region also used quartz in their construction, including at Treligga Common where two small cairns built mostly from slate were located on the cliffs at Start Point near Padstow, quartz being utilised as kerb-stones for Treligga 1 and within the mound at Treligga 2 (Christie 1985, 69 and 76).

Another significant Cornish site is Chysauster in West Penwith, located close to the famous Romano-British courtyard house settlement, and excavated by George Smith and the Cornwall Archaeological Unit (CAU) in 1984 (fig 7.4, Smith 1996). Despite its apparently simple construction, this small cairn proved to be a multi-phase monument which consisted originally of a circular kerb of large, carefully chosen granite blocks arranged with their best sides facing outwards. A two metre wide gap in the southern section, and a distinct charcoal spread within the enclosed area, suggested that its primary function was as a small ceremonial enclosure, perhaps for dedicatory activity (Smith 1996, 209-10). After an undetermined but probably short period of time, two cist-like stone settings were constructed at the centre of the enclosure and cremation burials were deposited inside them, and a kerb-high body of horizontally-laid granite blocks was established, effectively turning the site into a small platform cairn (Smith 1996, 184). Ultimately, three further cremations were deposited before a third and final construction phase effectively sealed the site beneath a further capping of stone (Smith 1996, 184 & 187).

Of the numerous other cemetery mounds in West Penwith, all were excavated and interpreted with antiquarian techniques, most notably by William Copeland Borlase who was the region's most prolific archaeologist during the later nineteenth century. For example, between 1878 and 1879, he investigated a group of small coastal cairns near Land's End which included several cemetery mounds on the cliffs at Boscregan (Borlase 1881,183-189). One of these consisted of a small kerbed cairn with an internal concentric wall, around which several cremation burials had carefully and almost certainly simultaneously been placed before the mound was erected (Borlase 1881, 183-84). Known as Carn Leskys, this site is apparently unique in Cornwall's archaeological record, due to its physical pairing with an identically sized ring cairn that contained no human remains, but rather enclosed a large centrally placed pile of fist-sized water-worn pebbles. A second cemetery mound at Boscregan also proved to be architecturally striking: Carn Creis, which consisted of a free-standing circular kerb arranged around a large natural boulder, next to which a multiple cremation deposit had been placed beneath a very discrete covering of stones (fig.7.4, Borlase 1881, 186-189). Known locally as tor cairns, several sites of this type have been recognised in west Cornwall, including at Tredinney, although no others were associated with the multiple burial rite (Borlase 1872, 123).

The architectural diversity seen at these and many other cemetery mounds is matched within contemporary tradition of round barrows used for different burial rites and traditions (e.g. Lynch 1993; Christie 1988). Kerbs, cairn-rings and internal walls are common features, and a significant number of non-cemetery mound types were built to incorporate pre-cairn structures, as at Kilpaison in Pembrokeshire and Try in West Penwith (Fox 1959, 12; Russell & Pool 1964). Excavation has even shown that within defined barrow cemeteries, cemetery mounds might be indistinguishable from those utilised for different purposes, as at Boscregan where Carn Leskys and a neighbouring barrow used for single-burial (Middle Carn) were practically identical in terms of their size and basic structure (Borlase 1881, figs 2 and 8). It can therefore be safely stated that in structural terms there were neither specific barrow types or of morphological features which distinguished cemetery mounds from their contemporaries, but rather that any architectural type could be created or utilised for whatever ritual function was deemed desirable or necessary.

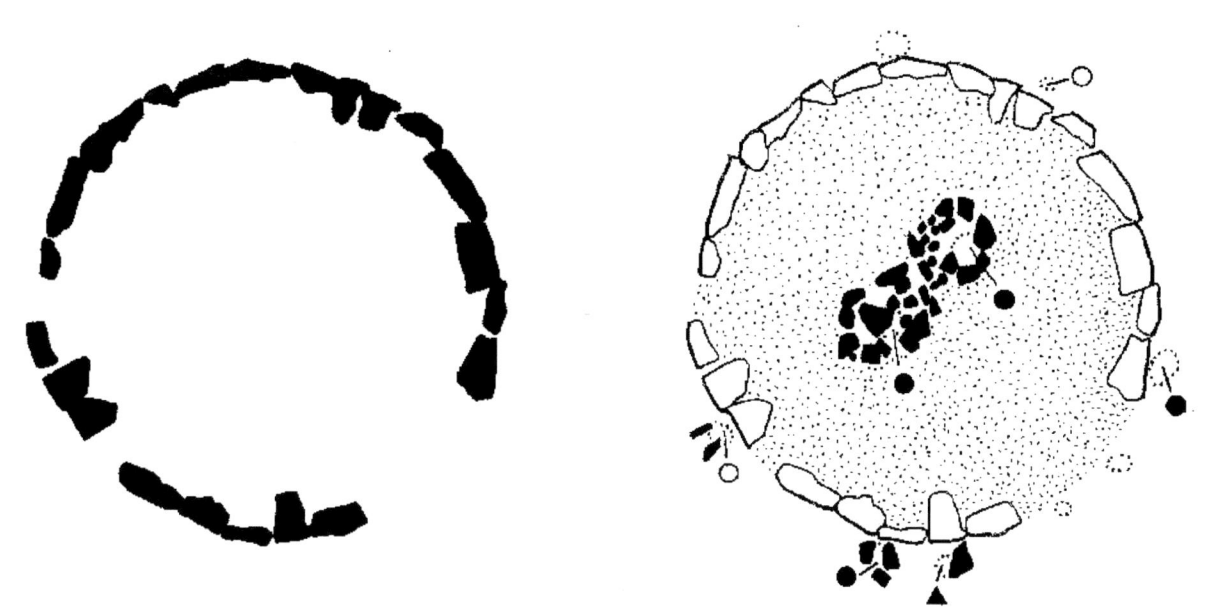

1: Free-standing 'ceremonial' kerb

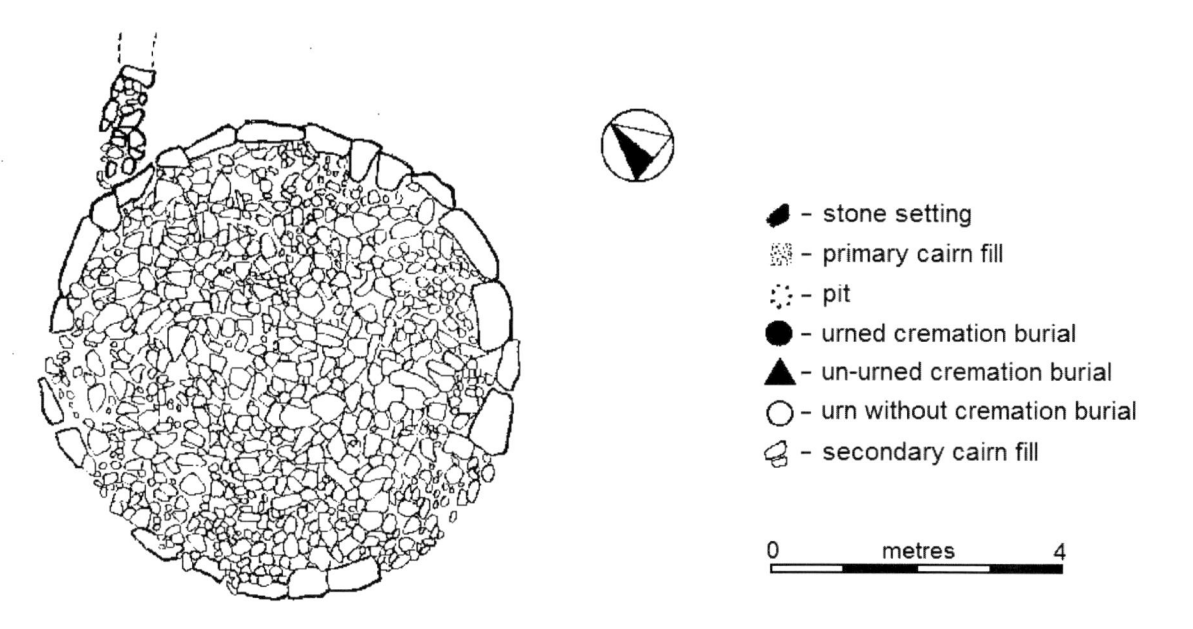

2: Cemetery Mound/Platform Cairn

3: Cairn with later boundary

- stone setting
- primary cairn fill
- pit
- urned cremation burial
- un-urned cremation burial
- urn without cremation burial
- secondary cairn fill

0 metres 4

FIG. 7. 4: CHYSAUSTER, WEST PENWITH: DEVELOPMENT PLAN (ADAPTED FROM SMITH 1996, FIG 10 & 13)

Burial Organisation

Although not specifically defined by any particular architectural features, the evidence from most cemetery mounds shows that the simultaneous multiple cremation rite generally related to the creation and/or physical adaptation of a monument. Furthermore, the organisation of the burials often reflected similar spatial concerns, which, though far from universal, need to be addressed in detail.

As we have seen, the multiple burials at some cemetery mounds were deposited in discrete groups that were concentrated in just one small part of the monument, as at Carn Creis where four cremations were placed in a single episode against the southern edge of the central boulder (fig.7.5, Borlase 1881, 186-189). Similar clustering also occurred at Carvinack and Treiorwerth where the north eastern part of the site was the focus for multiple cremation deposits, and at Chysauster where cremations were deposited in three of the five small pits arranged externally around the cairn, these being those closest to the kerb's southern entrance (Dudley 1964, fig 1; Lynch 1971, 44; Smith 1996, 209-210). In the case of the former, one deposit related to the construction of the site and the other to a post-structural event, whilst at the latter the chronological

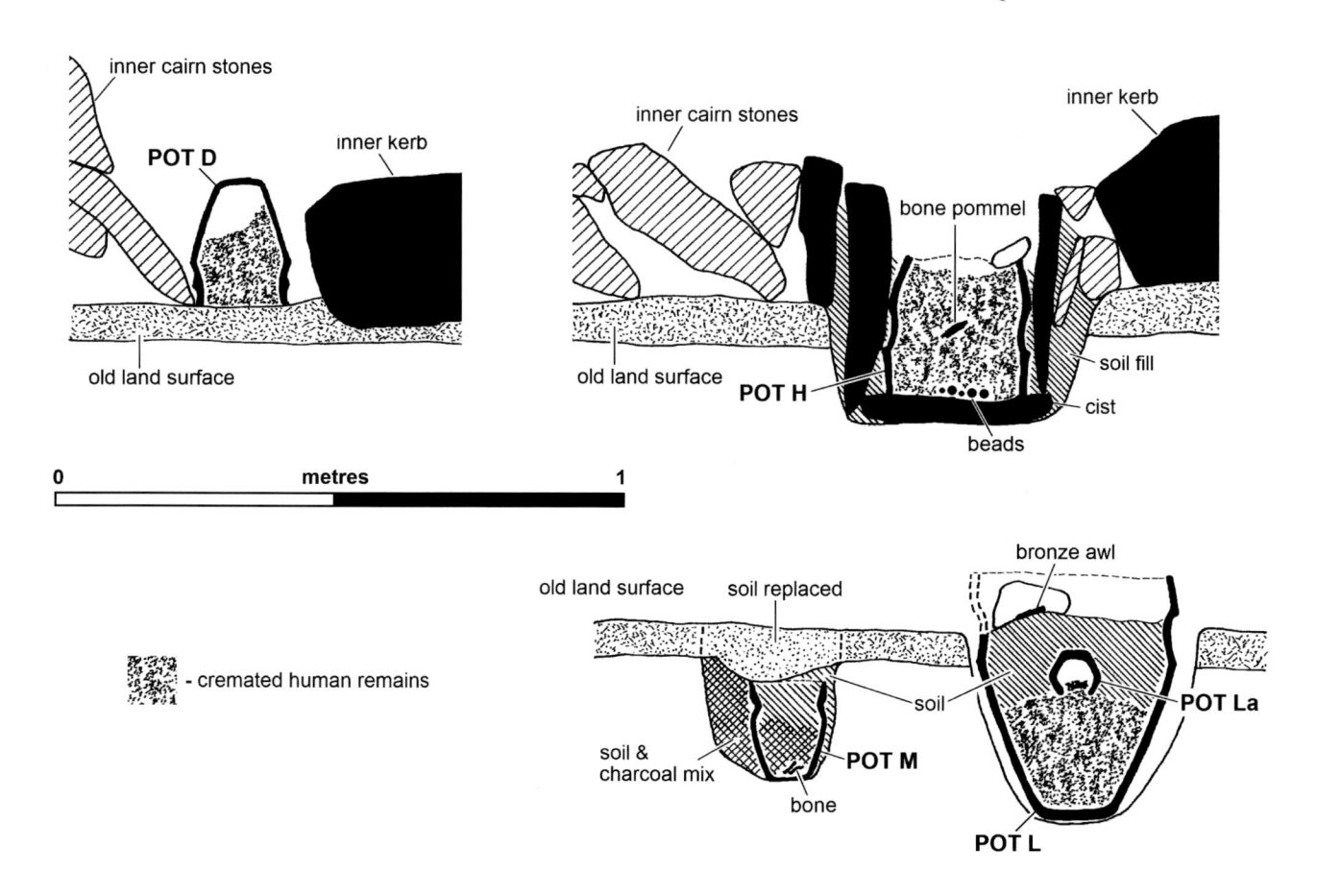

FIG. 7.5: BURIALS AT BEDD BRANWEN (REDRAWN FROM LYNCH 1971, FIG 6 & 7)

relationship was less clear, as the radiocarbon results were deemed unhelpful in this respect (Tomalin in Smith 1996, 193). Instead, the excavator relied on ceramic evidence to suggest that they belonged to a secondary burial phase, though subsequent studies of south-western ceramics have increasingly revealed the complexity of their chronological development, so we must view this interpretation with caution (Quinnell 1987; Parker Pearson 1990). In contrast, the two centrally placed cremations (pots 1 & 2) clearly related the transformation of the site from a free-standing kerb into a cemetery mound Smith 1996, 184).

At Bedd Branwen (fig. 7.5) the two distinct burial phases resulted in the deposition of a total of twelve cremations, all in conjunction with either the establishment of the cairn-ring or the later mound. Phase 1 consisted of five urned cremations, three in pits beneath the cairn-ring (pots C, L & M), one under a large inner kerbstone (pot J), and the other in a nearby cist inserted into the old land surface (OLS) (pot H) (Lynch 1971, 22). The spatial relationship between the first four deposits and the cairn-ring demonstrates their contemporaneity, as the site's architects must have had prior knowledge of their whereabouts to have been able to establish a feature which was so obviously in accordance with them (Lynch 1971, 22). In addition, the cist containing the fifth burial (pot H) was positioned so intimately with the inner kerb that their simultaneous construction was strongly implied. Another feature of the Phase 1 burials was that they seemed to have been arranged in pairs, although this was not definitely the case for pots E and F which had been disturbed prior to excavation (Lynch 1971, 22-24). After a period of time, seven more cremations were deposited, six in urns and one un-urned. In contrast to the Phase 1 examples, all were placed directly onto the OLS, and adjacent to the inner face of the cairn ring rather than beneath or within it (Lynch 1971, 26-27). All had been crushed by the weight of the subsequent mound, though their otherwise good survival combined with their originally unprotected status suggests that they must have been positioned immediately before or during its erection. Two of the Phase 2 burials might also have been paired (pot K and an un-urned deposit), thus potentially reflecting the continuity of tradition and indicating the close contemporaneity of both burial phases. A few other pieces of burnt skull and long bone were also recognised at the site, though these were sealed beneath the pre-cairn standing stone and therefore presumably predated the cemetery mound (Lynch 1971, 17 & 27).

The distribution of the Bedd Branwen cremations reflects a recognisable and oft-repeated concern for the placing of burials in arcs within or around cemetery mounds. Many similar examples occur in western Britain, including at Treiorwerth (Lynch 1971, 44), Querhow in Yorkshire, and Trelystan in Powys (Fox 1959, fig 43; Britnell 1982, fig 30). Several sites in West Penwith also displayed similar spatial concerns, as at Carn Leskys where at the remains of seven urns, two with cremation burials, were carefully

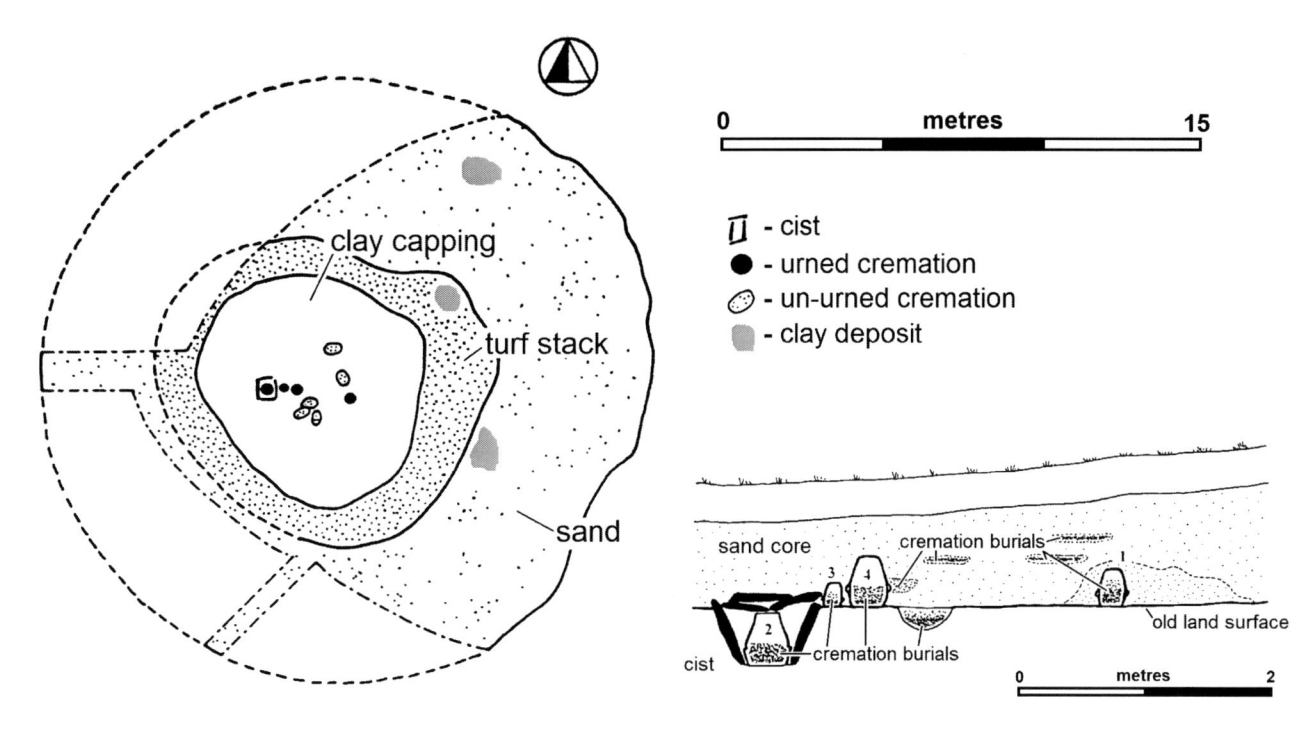

FIG. 7. 6: UPTON PYNE, DEVON: PLAN & BURIALS (ADAPTED FROM POLLARD & RUSSELL 1969, FIG 2 & 3)

spaced around the inner face of an internal concentric wall in ten separate deposits (Borlase 1881, 183-84). All were placed directly onto the OLS in a mixture of inverted and upright positions, their precise arrangement implying that they were simultaneously deposited just prior to the erection of the overlying mound. A potentially identical site on Higher Bositow Cliff near Nanjizal produced similar evidence, after being partly destroyed during the 1980's during an attempt to install a number of clay-pigeon traps into it. The resulting damage was recorded by members of the CAU who were able to recover several carefully spaced sherd deposits arranged around the inside of an internal concentric kerb (Nowakowski & Sharpe, pers comm).

Another West Penwith cemetery mound that contained multiple cremations was the now destroyed cairn at Chycarn, which originally stood at the foot of Chapel Carn Brea. The great Cornish antiquarian William Borlase reported that this small simple mound was opened by workmen in 1733, and was found to contain an urned cremation burial in a central cist which had been neatly surrounded by around fifty other urns, all containing cremated human remains (Borlase 1769, 234). Even if we allow for exaggeration and just ten or twenty cremation burials were actually present, this would reflect a large amount of bone, thereby implying perhaps the presence of a significant number of individuals. If this were the case, Chycarn would undoubtedly have been regarded as a very special monument, in spite of its humble appearance. What is significant here is that the careful distribution of so many urns around the central cremation strongly suggests that they were either all buried at the same time, or that the surrounding deposits were inserted in a single episode around an existing cist, thus absorbing it into the fabric of the new cemetery mound in the same way that the standing stones were incorporated at Bedd Branwen and Park Of Tongland.

Lynch has argued that sites with centrally placed burials such as Chysauster and Chycarn should not be classed as true cemetery mounds, as the centre of a barrow was its main focus and was therefore reserved for primary-status individuals (Lynch 1971, 54). However, the view that central burials were always the most significant, and that any associated 'satellite burials' were somehow of lesser importance, was developed for Wessex barrows where the overwhelming rite was clearly very different to that which predominated in the west. Indeed, the hypothesis is challenged by the evidence from a number of cemetery mounds, including Upton Pyne which contained nine cremations associated with two distinct structural phases, one of which was deposited near the middle of the barrow (fig.7.6, Pollard and Russell 1969, 49 & 66). This central deposit (pot 1) was regarded by the excavators as of primary importance, while the other eight, which were loosely arranged in an arc around it, were subsequently interpreted as lesser satellite cremations (Pollard & Russell 1969, 49). A reassessment of the evidence, however, shows that one of the non-central deposits been placed inside the barrow's only cist (pot 2), and might therefore just as easily be interpreted as the most significant. The implied higher status of particular cremations based on their location in unique but non-centrally placed structural features can also be seen elsewhere, as within the Phase 1 burials at Bedd Branwen, where pot H was also deposited inside the barrow's only cist. These and other examples which reveal that primacy could be represented within multiple cremation deposits show that the rite was therefore more variable than originally believed, probably due to subtle

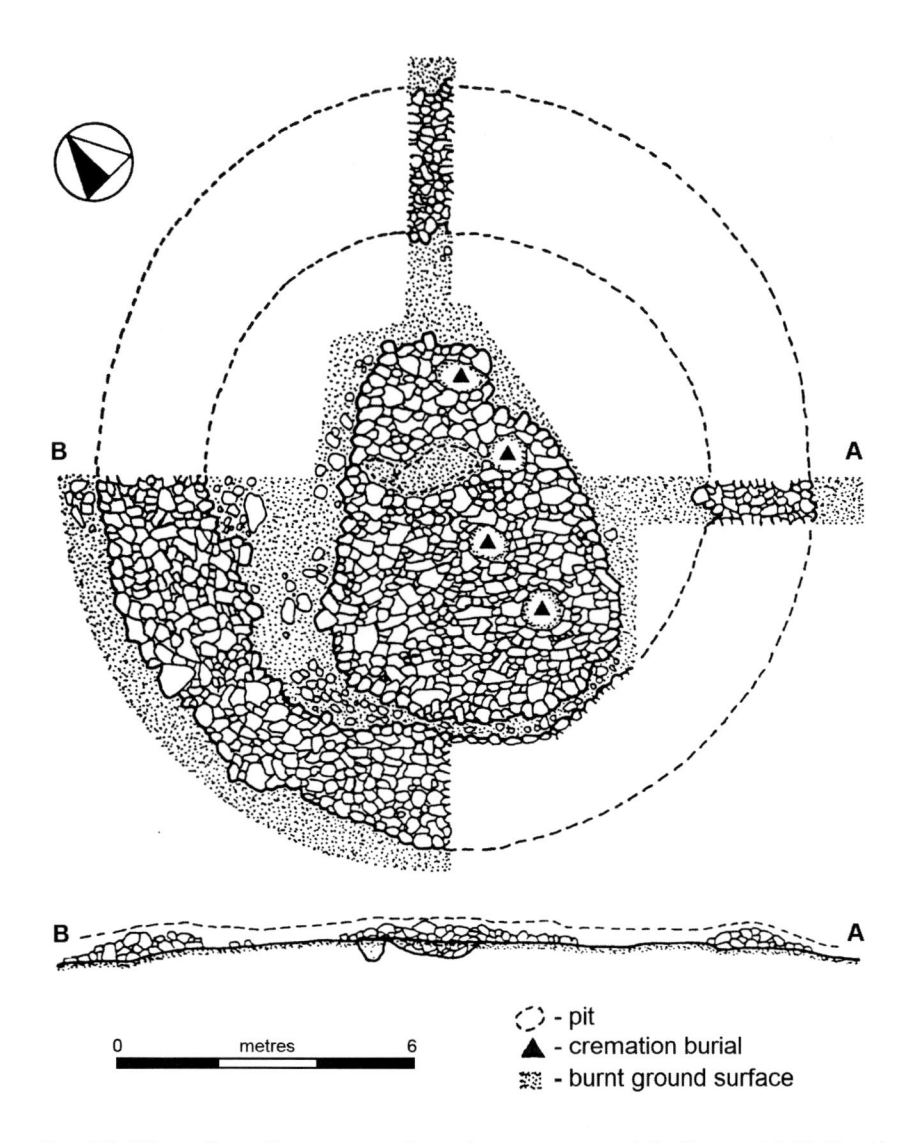

FIG.7.7: WEIRD LAW, PEEBLESHIRE: PLAN (REDRAWN FROM MACLAREN 1967, FIG 1)

regional or local differences, and possibly as a result of the merging of Wessex and western British barrow traditions, a phenomenon also seen, for example, at henges which were constructed or adapted to include western-type stone circles (Barrett 1988, 30-1; Burl 1991).

One final point which illustrates this argument is the fact that in some cases cemetery mounds were not even required for the ritual to take place. For example, the simultaneous cremation rite has been recognised at a number of pre-Early Bronze Age monuments, as in west Cornwall and the Isles of Scilly where multiple deposits were inserted into later Neolithic Scillonian Entrance Graves, thereby effectively turning them into cemetery mounds, as at Tregiffian near St. Buryan (Borlase 1872, 108-10), Port Hellick Down on St. Marys (Hencken 1932, 21-2 and 96) and Knackyboy on St. Martin (O'Neil 1952, 21 and 29). Similarly on Anglesey, a number of existing barrows which contained individual Beaker burials were adapted to contain secondary groups of simultaneously deposited cremation burials, as at Merddyn Gwyn and Porth Dafarch II (Lynch 1970, 150). Elsewhere, multiple cremations were even inserted into the fabric of natural places, as at Killeaba on the Isle of Man where a natural mound was utilised (Moffatt 1978, 208), and possibly within the rocky outcrops of Treryn Dinas in West Penwith (Sharpe 1992). It can therefore be safely stated that the multiple burial rite transcended any other factor in terms of it being the defining feature of cemetery mounds, or indeed of any other locations that were deemed appropriate.

Burial Deposits

Now we have seen something of the character of how and where multiple cremations were deposited, it is important to examine the physical nature of the burials themselves to determine whether there are any discernable reasons why they were specifically used in cemetery mounds. Again, the issue of status inevitably occurs, this time as a potentially determining factor for why certain individuals were selected for inclusion within a multiple cremation deposit.

In terms of the cremation process itself, the best evidence comes from Weird Law (fig. 7.7) where the burnt layer sealed by the cairn was interpreted as an actual pyre site

(MacLaren 1967, 95). Four cremation deposits were inserted into this scorched surface, combined with ash and gravel, and were then sealed by a further deposit of pyre residue and clean soil (MacLaren 1967, 95). Pyre debris has also been recorded at other cemetery mounds, including at Llanarmon yn Ial in Denbighshire where significant amounts of ash and charcoal were associated with a multiple cremations deposit, and at Chysauster where glass-like lumps of clinker were found, caused by the fusion of silica during the combustion process (Pennant 1810, 18-19; Mays in Smith 1996, 188). In some instances, cremation burials were clearly interred whilst still hot from the pyre, as at Carn Creis where one of the urns used to contain cremated bone was obviously still soft when the scorched remains were placed inside (Borlase 1881, 187). In contrast, human remains sometimes went through specific processes before being deposited, as at Quernhow in North Yorkshire where some cremated bones were apparently cleaned before deposition (Fox 1959, 74).

A respectable number of the deposits from cemetery mounds have contained enough bone to suggest the general age and, to a lesser extent, the sex, of some of the individuals buried inside them. However, as at contemporary barrows generally, there are no discernable trends that might illustrate how these factors determined an individual's higher importance in broad cultural terms. For example, the Phase 1 burials at Bedd Branwen consisted of one male and two unsexed adults (in Pots H, C and L respectively), as well as three infants represented by the cremated remains of their petrous temporal bones (inner-ear bones) (Lynch 1971, 22-34). In comparison with each other, the adult male in pot H stood out, due to his location in the barrow's only cist and the fact that he was significantly more complete than his neighbours, with an amount of bone almost consistent with that which would have survived the cremation process (Lynch 1971, 22-24). A very small number of similarly near-complete burials have been identified at other cemetery mounds, including Carn Creis, Ratho, and Simondston in Glamorgan (Borlase 1881, 187; Smith 1995, 83-92; Fox 1959, 82), and are all rare examples of an unusual phenomenon in western British Early Bronze Age barrows, where the deposition of much smaller amounts of cremated bone, known as token burials, was generally the norm (McKinley 1987). It might therefore be assumed that 'completeness' reflected specialness, and therefore that these individuals were of primary status within their group. This can certainly be argued for the larger burial at Bedd Branwen, where its greater significance is also reflected by its unique situation and by the artefacts associated with it. At Carn Creis, however, the opposite is apparent, as here the near-complete deposit was clearly secondary to the very token cremation of a child or young girl, who's higher status was implied by artefactual associations (Borlase 1881, 189). Age and gender was also apparent within the Phase 1 burials at Treiorwerth, which included the cremated remains of a young adult who may have originally been contained in a bag, and a six year old child represented again by just a pair of inner-ear bones (Lynch 1971, 44).

Treiorwerth also contained a male and probable female remains in a single urn, thereby demonstrating an apparent lack of importance based on gender, as well as the practice of multiple deposition within a single context, seen also at other cemetery mounds including Simondston, where three recognisable individuals were deposited between two urns (Fox 1959, 82).

In contrast to these examples, the gender and age of most of the individuals deposited in cemetery mounds, and in other earlier Bronze Age barrows and cist-graves generally, is impossible to ascertain, due to their token, and therefore anonymous, nature, as at Chysauster, Trelystan and Weird Law (Mays in Smith 1996, 189; Britnell 1982, 189; MacLaren 1967, 95). These token burials consisted of considerably less bone than would have normally have survived the cremation process, even in the case of infants, making the ear bones found at Bedd Branwen and Treiorwerth of particular interest as they must have been deliberately selected for inclusion from a greater volume of remains. Indeed, token burials can be seen as deliberate attempts to represent the deceased in a symbolic rather that wholly physical way, thereby signifying their wider cultural significance as a ritual resource, rather than just as the remains of specific people (see also Bruck 1995).

The anonymity of most token burials, and the lack of discernable patterns based on age or gender, means that we must examine the other objects and materials that were sometimes associated with multiple cremations for signs of individuality. In general terms the inclusion of artefacts in western British earlier Bronze Age barrows seems to have occurred less commonly than elsewhere, although cemetery mounds have produced numerous objects which might be regarded as evidence for personal status, and for broad cultural links with other areas. None however, or any of the means by which they were deposited, are unique to cemetery mounds, but rather reflect the same issues as seen within other British barrow types. The majority of artefacts recovered from cemetery mounds are ceramic urns, and although the typological characterisation of these is beyond the scope of this study, it is clear that they often conformed to wider contemporary styles whilst at the same time frequently reflecting the development of more locally focussed ceramic traditions. For example, finely made, regionally distinctive Collared Urns were deposited alongside more widely represented types at Bedd Branwen and Treiorwerth, these being known as Anglesey Necked Urns because of their internally decorated necks and their generally limited distribution elsewhere (Burgess 1986; Gibson & Woods 1997, 87). Similar local affinities are also reflected at other cemetery mounds, particularly in south west Britain where regionally distinctive Trevisker type urns were frequently used, as at Chysauster, Boscregan, and Clahar Gardens on the Lizard peninsular (Tomalin in Smith 1996, 189-95; Borlase 1881, 184-85; Patchett 1950, figs 3 & 4). In addition, other more widely distributed urns were sometimes utilised for the multiple cremation rite, as at Bedd Branwen and Treiorwerth where the deposition of a Food Vessel and a small Cordoned Urn respectively reflect broader cultural contacts with other parts of Britain (Lynch 1971, 34 & 50).

Urns such as these, which had distinctive origins and were more finely made than others, might easily be taken as representative of the primary or special status of their occupants, as at Bedd Branwen where the urn containing the near complete burial (pot H), was a very finely made Collared Urn of unique type within the larger group (Lynch 1971, 30-34). The single non-Collared Urn vessels at Bedd Branwen and Treiorwerth also contained distinctive deposits, these being the aforementioned burials of cremated children's ear bones, although at the former site the other two deposits of this type were placed in Collared Urns (Lynch 1971, 34 & 50). The use of such fine pots did not, however, always reflect special status, as seen where they were placed alongside much more basic containers that, in terms of the artefacts they contained, seemingly held more significant deposits. This was the case at Carn Cries, where the cremated remains of the child/young girl with its rich artefactual assemblage was originally contained either by a simpler urn than one its neighbours, or was un-urned and associated with a group of sherds (Borlase 1881, 188-189). Other cemetery mounds which contained un-urned cremation deposits include Weird Law, Upton Pyne, Chysauster, and Bedd Branwen (MacLaren 1967, 95; Pollard & Russell 1969, figs 2 & 3; Smith 210; Lynch 1971, 26-27). Elsewhere, other means were used, including organic containers such as the probable leather bag at Treiorwerth, and urns with no specific stylistic identity and/or of much poorer quality, as at Carn Lesky's and Carn Creis, where fine Trevisker pots were also used (Lynch 1971, 44; Borlase 1881, 183-189). An immediately local origin is suggested in some cases, as at Carn Cries where the previously mentioned unfired urn, which was poorly made and conformed to no specific typology, must have been manufactured just before the cremated deposit was added, and at Park of Tongland where the petrological analysis of two 'relatively unaccomplished' Collared Urns and an accessory vessel produced evidence for very local production (Borlase 1881, 187; McCullagh in Russell-White et al. 1992, 318-9).

A broad mixture of cultural associations and local traditions is also reflected by some of the non ceramic artefacts from cemetery mounds, some of which could be interpreted as personal or community-owned possessions, and others as more symbolic in nature. In terms of the former, these were often the result of fine craftsmanship, and were made from high quality materials, as at Bedd Branwen where pot H contained a number of apparently high status objects including a bone bead and a polished bone pommel, both of which had been burnt, presumably during the cremation process (Lynch 1971, 31). A similar burnt pommel was found in one of the Phase 2 burials (pot B) suggesting that it too may have been of special or primary status, although no other depositional factors supported this (Lynch 1971, 61). Similar pommels were found at cemetery mounds at Beech Hill House in Perthshire, and Hambledon in Devon, and it has been suggested that they were intended to symbolically represent complete daggers, thereby being in effect 'token' in character (Stevenson 1995, 212; Lynch 1971, 61). Occasionally, more complete daggers have been found, as at Llanddyfnan where a bronze Camerton-Snowhill type reflected clear affinities with parallels from Wessex barrows, including Winterbourne Monkton in Dorset (Lynch 1970, 143-44). Although rare, bronze was also used to manufacture a small awl found with one of the cremations in Treligga 1 (Christie 1985, 73).

In addition to the bone objects at Bedd Branwen, pot H also contained four decorated biconical jet beads, whilst another Phase 1 burial (pot C) contained a single specimen of the same type (Lynch 1971, 61) Analysis has shown that these might have derived from a relatively local lignite deposit rather than a true jet source, and there is evidence that they may have been specially created for the burial ritual as little or no wear had taken place before they were deposited (Lynch 1971, 158). Jet beads have also been found within other multiple cremation deposits, as at Balbirnie in Fife, Balneaves in Angus, and Treiorwerth where a grooved example found in 1870 is regarded to be from the same group as the Bedd Branwen finds (Ritchie 1975, 6; Russell-White in Russell-White et al. 1992, 300; Lynch 1971, 52). Significantly, some of these are stylistically linked to examples from Wessex, including from the Manton Barrow and Wilsford G.16 in Wiltshire (Sheridan & Davis 1998, 156). Beads made from other materials have also been found, including amber versions at Bedd Branwen (pot H again), and Chysauster, although the latter was in the cairn material rather with a cremation deposit (Lynch 1971, 31; Smith 1996, 197). Faience examples were also deposited, as at Carn Creis where twelve beads and a series of small shale 'spacer discs' which once formed a complete necklace were included with the child/young woman, two of biconical design and the others segmented (fig. 7.8) (Borlase 1881, 189). A single star-shaped faience bead was also found inside Knackyboy Entrance Grave, in association with one of two multiple burial episodes which resulted in the incorporation of 'three or four' tiers of urned deposits, some contained by Trevisker vessels (O'Neil 1952, 23-24). Faience beads of identical type have been in a number of Wessex barrows, suggesting cultural associations and potential importation (Annable & Simpson 1964, 115).

In contrast to these artefacts, all of which might be regarded as representative of wealth and status, other objects and materials which were deposited at cemetery mounds reflect very different concerns. As one might expect, flint tools were commonly included, these generally being scrapers and utilized flakes rather than the finely knapped knives and arrowheads seen elsewhere. In addition, quantities of waste flakes and raw materials have been identified at many sites, usually either on the OLS or within the structure itself, as at Chysauster, Upton Pyne, Bedd Branwen, and numerous others (Williams in Smith 1996, 196; Pollard & Russell 1969, 69-7; Lynch 1971, 35). Their frequent presence, both in cemetery mounds and other barrows, has usually been interpreted as accidental,

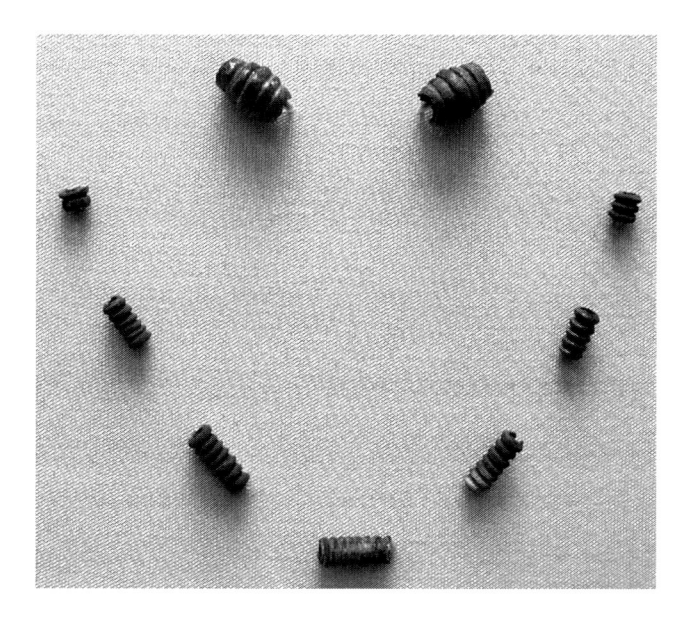

FIG.7.8: FAIENCE BEADS FROM CARN CREIS, WEST PENWITH (AUTHOR'S PHOTOGRAPH, TAKEN WITH THE KIND PERMISSION OF THE BRITISH MUSEUM)

relating either to pre or post-barrow knapping episodes, or their importation in building materials. The frequency in which they are found, however, and the volumes in which they sometimes occur, strongly implies that the locations chosen for these barrows or the materials used to construct them, might have been deliberately selected on the basis of their presence (Bonnington, forthcoming). The pre-barrow and importation models have also been used to account for the not uncommon existence of Mesolithic and/or Neolithic flints in western British barrows, including cemetery mounds such as Chysauster and Bedd Branwen (Williams in Smith 1996, 194; Lynch 1971, 34). Again, their repeated occurrence cannot be accidental, as they would no doubt have symbolised ancestral associations which would have made them highly significant resources in ritual contexts. Indeed, it is quite clear that other objects with the same associations were deliberately deposited at some cemetery mounds, potentially after a long period of curation, as at Carn Creis where a broken leaf-shaped arrowhead and a V shaped button of obvious late Neolithic origin accompanied the faience beads found with the cremated child/young woman, and at Carn Lesky's where one of the eight non-cremation deposits was a group of sherds from an incomplete Beaker Urn (Borlase 1881, 185-189).

The attribution of significance based on symbolic identity might also be used to explain the presence of other materials found in some cemetery mounds, all which again occur in many other western British barrows, but which have rarely been seriously addressed despite their obvious ritual importance. As we have seen, quartz was sometimes used within the structures of cemetery mounds, and it was also commonly deposited with and around multiple burial deposits, as at Upton Pyne where several similarly sized pebbles were found on the OLS, including a probable pot boiler which had been repeatedly heated,

and at Acharn in Argyll where a number of pebbles had been placed in a burial cist (Pollard & Russell 1969, 71; Ritchie & Thornber 1975, 18). Water-worn pebbles from beaches, rivers and streambeds were also used, their inclusion potentially due to their connection with these natural places, as at Carn Lesky's and Beech Hill House (Borlase 1881, 183; Stevenson 1995, 201). Similar associations might also explain the presence of the soil deposits found at some sites, including Chysauster where the external pits, including those with cremation burials, all contained a mixture of soil and gravel. Another common deposit was charcoal, as at Carvinack, and Chysauster, and at many other contemporary barrows, good examples being at ring cairns on Shaugh Moor on Dartmoor, and Shallowmead on Exmoor (Dudley 1964; Smith 1996; Wainwright et al. 1979; Quinnell 1997, 22-35). There are a number of explanations which might account for the obvious significance of this material, such as the special status of certain tree species in ritual terms (oak was most commonly used), or because it originated from a location with a defined symbolic identity (Gale in Quinnell 1997, 35). In addition, charcoal might have been considered to reflect the means by which bronze was produced, thereby linking it to the industrial process which defined the times that cemetery mounds were in use. A similarly symbolic role could also be applied to the flint debitage, especially if it resulted from the manufacture of tools for use within a ritual context.

Siting and Landscape Relationships

Traditional interpretations have often regarded the siting of barrows in utilitarian terms, based on the resources available at their chosen location. In this model, rocky outcrops were selected because of the plentiful supply of stone, and hillslope or valleys for their turf and soil. The proximity of some cemetery mounds near specific resources could be taken as supportive of this view, as at Bedd Branwen and Upton Pyne which were both situated close to the deposits of coloured clay used in their construction (Lynch 1971, 20; Pollard & Russell 1969, 57). However, as we shall see, it is clear that the locations chosen for cemetery mounds and barrows generally were determined by far more complex reasons, based on their cultural significance or symbolic identity.

In general terms, the physical siting of cemetery mounds reflects the same concerns that determined the positioning of other earlier Bronze Age barrow types in western Britain, such the use of ridges, hilltops and other natural watersheds (e.g. Fleming 1994, 66; Lynch 1993, 36) For example, at Boscregan Cliff the highest points were utilised for a group of five barrows which included the Carn Lesky's and Creis cemetery mounds, the former being built onto the peak of the rocky outcrop which gave it its name, and the latter on a natural crest so that, whilst visible from further away, it only became apparent from close by when approached from a particular direction. (fig.7.9) Many other cemetery mounds were established in similarly prominent locations, perhaps none more spectacularly than Croesmihangel in

FIG. 7.9: CARN CREIS (AUTHOR'S PHOTOGRAPH)

Pembrokeshire which was built on the southern slopes of Moel Trigarn (Nye et al. 1983, 20). In such cases, inter-site visibility was obviously an important issue, as at Boscregan where the group was positioned so that it was visible from several of the other clusters of small cairns which formed the greater Land's End cemetery (Bonnington, forthcoming). In some cases, the proximity of the sea seems to have been a defining factor, as was clearly the case at Boscregan, and at Treligga Common and other cliff edge sites. The significance of other watercourses can also be seen, as on Anglesey where Bedd Branwen was built on a slight natural rise on the valley floor close to the bend of the River Alaw, and at Llanndyfnan which was sited on the summit of a nearby gravel ridge (Lynch 1970, 123 & 136). A similar relationships occurred at Upton Pyne where a deliberate terrace was constructed on sloping ground close to the River Exe, and at Acharn and Seafield in Argyll which were both situated at the end of lochs (Arienas and Sween respectively) (Pollard & Russell 1969, 49; Ritchie & Thornber 1975, 18; Childe 1936, 84).

Another factor which influenced the siting of some cemetery mounds was their inclusion within larger barrow groups, including at Quandale on Rousay in Orkney, and Acharn in the far north, and, in many instances in south-west England, as at Upton Pyne, Treligga Common, Chycarn, Bosporthennis and Boscregan (Grant 1937; Ritchie & Thornber 1975; Pollard & Russell 1969; Christie 1985, 61-93; Hencken 1932, 96; Borlase 1872, 165 & 283, & 1881, 183-189). Site intervisibility was again an important factor in some cases, as at Boscregan where all five barrows were carefully placed so that they were visible from each other (Bonnington, forthcoming). The location of these and other cemetery mounds within larger barrow groups might be the result of the adoption of multiple burial rites within communities which had previously used single burial monuments, as has been suggested at Trelystan, although the architectural similarities noted at Boscregan shows that this was not always the case (Britnell 1982, 188; Borlase 1881, 183-186). Llanddyfnan on Anglesey was also built within a larger group, although the other cemetery mounds which were established on the island seem to have been built in relative isolation, including Bedd Branwen (Lynch 1993, 144). Indeed, the same can be said for Wales generally, where few obvious barrow cemeteries have been identified, especially in areas which contained significant numbers of cemetery mounds, such as Caernarvonshire and Merioneth (Lynch 1993, 39) Furthermore, where such groups do occur, cemetery mounds seem to be absent, as within the Brenig Valley barrow cemetery in Denbighshire (Lynch 1993, 39). Similarly isolated sites occur in other areas as well, as at Weird Law and elsewhere in Scotland, leading to the suggestion these may have served the community in the same way as groups of single focus mounds did elsewhere (MacLaren 1967, 93; Lynch 1993, 144).

In addition, some cemetery mounds were sited in relation to earlier monuments, a phenomenon which can most clearly be seen in West Penwith. For example, the issue of intervisibility identified between the Boscregan barrows and the other coastal groups can be extended to many other cemetery mounds and barrows in the wider landscape, most if not all of which were apparently positioned so that they had a visual relationship with Chapel Carn Brea, the site of Britain's most westerly Neolithic long cairn as well as, subsequently, the area's largest Early Bronze Age barrow (fig. 7.10) (Bonnington, forthcoming: Thomas

FIG.7.10: CHAPEL CARN BREA IN WEST PENWITH, THE FIRST HILL IN BRITAIN
(AUTHOR'S PHOTOGRAPH)

1990; Borlase 1881, 195-197). Numerous cemetery mounds were also built in close physical association with earlier sites, including Chycarn and a multi-cist mound at Carn Gloose located respectively near the massive Early Bronze Age barrows at Ballowall and Chapel Carn Brea, both of which had started life as later Neolithic Scillonian Entrance Graves before being transformed into immense cairns during the Early Bronze Age (Borlase 1881, 189-197). Cemetery mounds were also built close to the stone circles at Tregaseal, Boscawen-Un and Rosemoddress, the latter being another Scillonian Entrance Grave which was physically adapted and used for multiple cremation rite (Russell 1971, 13 & 17; Borlase 1879, 194). Although few in number, examples from other areas demonstrate similar concerns, including Merddyn Gwyn and Porth Dafarch 2 which related to Beaker sites, and Bedd Branwen and Park of Tongland which incorporated earlier standing stones. The incorporation of the large natural boulder at Carn Creis might also have been determined by its prior significance, as it is not unlikely that it would have been an important marker within the landscape for a considerable period of time before the cemetery mound was constructed (Borlase 1881, 186; Tilley 1996, 172). This suggestion is supported by the occurrence of large amounts of Mesolithic and Neolithic flint in the thin soils located along the cliffs and adjacent farmland at Boscregan, and in many of the other locations used for barrows in West Penwith (Sharpe 1996, 32).

Different ancestral associations might also have determined the locations of some cemetery mounds, as suggested by the environmental evidence from a few sites. For example, pollen samples from Bronze Age contexts at Bedd Branwen, including from the OLS and the mound, shows that, although a degree of cereal cultivation was taking place nearby, the site itself was constructed in a meadow surrounded by light woodland (Dimbleby in Lynch 1971, 73). Similarly, pollen from Chysauster showed that it was built in a previously established clearing which had subsequently been abandoned, possibly as a result of pre-cairn soil erosion caused by over exploitation (MacPhail in Smith 1996, 200). The use of such locations has been identified at a number of other barrow types, especially in Cornwall, as at Colliford Reservoir and Trelan 2 (Balaam in Smith 1984, 30; Maltby & Caseldine in Griffith 1984), and could be seen as evidence that they were utilised because they had been established by previous communities. It is also possible that the construction of cemetery mounds and other barrows on apparently exhausted land reflects an attempt to replenish fertility via ritual action. Environmental evidence from elsewhere, however, shows that not all cemetery mounds were established in marginal locations, as at Upton Pyne which was built on a relatively mature area of grassland overlying an undisturbed podsol, thereby suggesting contemporary grazing around the site (Pollard & Russell 1969, 49).

Chronology Although described throughout this paper as of earlier Bronze Age origin, the exact dating of cemetery mounds is generally problematic, due largely to the fact that many were excavated before the introduction of radiocarbon dating. In addition, where radiocarbon dates do exist they often consist of single examples, or are sometimes regarded as unsound, forcing their excavators to rely on stratigraphy and typological frameworks in an attempt to place their sites within a defined chronological context. However, despite these constraints it is possible to make some general comments about the creation and use of cemetery mounds based on the radiocarbon evidence, including via the reassessment of some formerly discarded results.

At Weird Law, charcoal from one of the pits containing cremated human remains produced a radiocarbon date range which placed the single burial phase and the overlying cairn firmly within the second quarter of the 2nd Millennium BC (MacLaren 1967, 98). Similar dates also came from Park of Tongland, where the site's two distinct multiple burial episodes were proven to be closely linked in terms of contemporaneity (McCullagh in Russell-White et al. 1992, 313-14). In contrast, the radiocarbon results from multiple contexts at Chysauster produced a much wider chronological range than expected, from 2580 cal BC for external pit 548 to 1220 cal BC for external pit 536 (Smith 1996, fig 24). Of even more concern was the variation between the two central deposits, whose contents produced dates of 1950-1530 cal BC for the cremation in pot 1 and 2460-1910 cal BC for that in pot 2 (Smith 1996, figure 24). These dates all came from mature oak charcoal which may have already been several centuries old when used, a common problem when dating archaeological sites (Smith 1996, table 1; Coles 1975, 123-5). Indeed, the charcoal used at Park of Tongland all came from fast-grown species (hazel, ash and young oak) and produced a much tighter date range (McCullagh in Russell-White et al. 1992, 313-4). As a result, an adjusted chronology of c.1750-1450 cal BC was suggested for the construction and use of the Chysauster cemetery mound, placing it in a slightly later period than other radiocarbon dated Cornish barrows, which ranged from 2180-1640 cal BC (Christie 1988, 164-5). (Tomalin in Smith 1996, 212). In the case of the central cremations, however, the disparate dates also raise the intriguing possibility that the older cremation came from another site which had been established many years before, and was perhaps judged to have been particularly successful in terms of achieving its ritual function and therefore of considerable symbolic significance. This idea of 'borrowing' resources from one barrow and using them for another has already been established for building materials (Miles 1975, 26; Quinnell, pers comm.), and might equally have occurred in the case of cremation burials and other symbolic resources, as possibly reflected by the undated and therefore potentially ancient disturbance of some sites.

Although apparently later than most other Cornish barrows, Chysauster did broadly relate to the same period as the other dated cemetery mounds discussed so far, all of which were in use during the later part of the Early Bronze Age, and in some cases extended into the following period. The radiocarbon dates from Bedd Branwen told a similar story, with charcoal from the site producing a date-range of 1871-1400 cal BC, including a terminus post quem for its construction of 1871-1520 cal BC from samples taken from beneath the cairn ring (Lynch 1991, 395). In addition, charcoal from a selection of the cremations produced date-ranges of 1690-1321 cal BC for the Phase 1 burials, and 1740-1400 cal BC for those deposited in Phase 2, which although seemingly contradictory, do strongly support the aforementioned stratigraphic evidence that the two events were not greatly separated in time (Lynch 1991, 395). Evidence for the continued use of these cemetery mounds in the Middle Bronze Age may seem surprising, as it contradicts with the commonly held perception that round barrows were only used during the preceding period. This, however, was clearly not the case, as in many parts of Britain barrows continued to be constructed or were used for secondary burials (Woodward 2000, 43). This has recently been proven for Cornwall, based on the excavation of a small coastal cairn on Constantine Island near Padstow which was found to contain a multiple burial deposit consisting of as many as five individuals, including a cremation burial and a complete crouched inhumation. Although yet to be published, the radiocarbon results show that these burials date to the Middle Bronze Age (Jones, pers comm.), thereby perhaps implying the continuation of the multiple burial rite, albeit in a different form.

Discussion

The absence of definable morphological traits at cemetery mounds, or the use of specific locations, shows that the rite of simultaneous multiple cremation burial was the single factor which determined the cultural and symbolic identity of these sites. This is mirrored by the utilisation of other contexts for multiple burials, such as ancestral monuments and natural places, and by the lack of discernable features which differentiate between the general character of single burials and those placed in simultaneous multiple deposits.

As we have seen, the single defining aspect of the simultaneous burial rite was the deposition of cremated human remains, as opposed to unburnt bones. It has been established that the latter rite gained increasing and near-universal importance during the 2nd Millennium BC, and distinctions have been made between inhumation and cremation burials based on their physical differences, the inclusion of burnt objects ('pyre goods') with cremations, such as the bone pommels from Bedd Branwen, and the burial of associated pyre debris with cremated human remains, as at Weird Law and Balneaves in Scotland (McKinley 1997, 130; Russell-White in Russell-White et al. 1992, 293). In addition, another more symbolic distinction has been formulated, based on the work of early 20th Century Parisian scholar Arnold Van Gennep who, via the study of anthropological evidence, pointed out that many of the rituals carried out by the people of the world included a distinctly important phase, which he called the liminal period, that related to the passage from one state of being to another (Huntington & Metcalfe 1979, 8). Archaeologists have increasingly embraced this idea, especially for funerary beliefs and rituals where the application of liminality to the period between death and the perceived moment when the soul of the deceased joined the ancestors in the afterlife seems particularly appropriate. For inhumation burials, therefore, it has been suggested that the liminal period ended when the corpse was placed within a grave, and that any subsequent monument or marker thereby fixed that event in space and time (Barrett 1988, 32). However, in the case of cremation burial it might seem more appropriate to regard the burning of the corpse as the signal that this period had ended, the cremated remains therefore being in themselves symbolic of this final act (Barrett 1988, 32). In addition, the pyre site and its resultant debris might also have attained a similar symbolic identity, making Weird Law and similar sites especially impressive in ritual terms.

Another key distinction is the contrast between the deposition of generally complete unburnt skeletons in some barrows, and the anonymity of the individuals represented by most cremation burials which, in cemetery mounds and other barrows and graves, were token in nature. Although it is fair to say that all cremation burials are token to some degree, the small amounts under discussion represented far less than would have survived the normal cremation process, or indeed the acidic soils of Cornwall and elsewhere (McKinley 1997, 130; Mays in Smith 1996, 188). As the petrous temporal bones from Bedd Branwen and Treiorwerth most ably demonstrate, this must illustrate deliberate selection, and therefore that only small amounts of surviving material were deemed necessary to represent an individual within a barrow or other structured burial context. This concept is supported by evidence from the ethnographic record, including from Bali where, in certain areas, mortuary practices included the collection of token deposits of previously inhumed bone from the ground for secondary cremation, as part of the funeral ritual employed for high status individuals such as priests and community leaders (Huntington & Metcalfe 1979, 86). In addition, soil from the burial ground could also be utilised in place of human remains, thereby potentially throwing an interesting light on the symbolic identity of the soil deposited at Bedd Branwen, Chysauster and numerous other cemetery mounds and barrows (Huntington & Metcalfe 1979, 86). As such, we can see that in earlier Bronze Age ritual contexts the identity of a cremated individual could have been equally insignificant when regarded in broad cultural terms, and that their true role was as anonymous or generic representatives of the wider society to which they had once belonged.

As we have seen, there is some evidence from cemetery mounds which might seem to challenge the importance of the anonymity model, demonstrated by the greater complexity of the structural contexts used for certain burials, the presence of artefacts or their greater richness in comparison to others, and the very occasional deposition of practically complete sets of cremated bone. As we saw, for example, at Bedd Branwen, one cremation (pot H) stood out from the others based on its location in the barrow's only cist, and the rich artefactual assemblage associated with it. These and similar objects, such as the faience beads from Carn Creis and the bronze dagger from Llanddyfnan reflect manufacture of considerable skill and specialisation, thereby implying the enhanced status of their owners and,

in some cases, broad links with contemporary communities elsewhere. However, the commonly-held assumption that grave or pyre goods were personal possessions has been challenged, both by ethnographic evidence and by the work of some archaeologists. For example, Barrett has suggested that certain artefacts associated with the funeral process might have been symbolic in nature, and could have been added at specific times during the ritual by people who were closely associated with the deceased (1990, 184-6). This is supported by ethnographic examples which shows that some societies regarded the deposition of prestige objects during funeral rites as act which enhanced the status of those who sacrificed them, including sometimes an entire community rather than just the deceased individual (Huntington & Metcalfe 1979, 15). On the other hand, if we reject this evidence and view the issue of potential status in more traditional ways, we can still interpret certain cremation deposits as more significant than others without abandoning the idea that they would have been simultaneously regarded as anonymous in wider cultural terms. This argument is based on the fact that the deceased were members of the community who built and used cemetery mounds and other barrows, and therefore would have been known by those who participated in their funeral rites. As such, one might actually expect reflections of individuality within some burials, particularly those simultaneously deposited in multiple groups where such issues would clearly be most recognisable.

Although separated by upwards of two thousand years, the anonymity of token burials and their multiple deposition in cemetery mounds does reflect one very significant quality also seen within Early Neolithic tombs, that being the deliberate creation of a generic ancestral body consisting of the collective remains of the dead. During the earlier 4th millennium BC this was achieved by the establishment of deposits of human bone within long barrows and other megalithic tombs which had been deliberately mixed together, an act clearly designed to deprive skeletal remains of their individuality (Lynch 1997, 11). This rite has been interpreted as representative of the communal aspects of Neolithic society, the mixed bones of numerous individuals designed to reflect the presence of a wider ancestral power within the landscape (Bradley 1984, 16 & 19; Lynch 1971, 55). Ethnographic evidence supports the idea that ancestor veneration was a crucial aspect of the belief systems of our early farming communities, and that their burial monuments and rituals would have served to legitimise territorial claims and help ensure the continued fertility of resources (Bradley 1984, 15-16; Lynch 1997, 59). Tombs would also have been the most important foci for ceremonies designed to reproduce social and authoritarian structures, in the latter case potentially by controlling access to the community's most important symbolic resource, the bodies of the ancestors (Bradley 1984, 10; Clarke et al. 1985, 15).

A similar role can equally be suggested for the burials found in earlier Bronze Age barrows, particularly when they were part of a multiple deposit as these would similarly have represented larger generic ancestral body. Indeed, the concept that, in wider cultural terms, human remains were primarily regarded as resources is demonstrated by the fact that many Early Bronze Age barrows were never used to house human remains (Miles 1975, 74). In western Britain this is a common phenomenon, as in Cornwall where around 40% of the barrows excavated between 1939 and the later 1990's were interpreted as empty in terms of human burial (Bonnington, forthcoming). Another important point is the association between the deposition of burials and defined structural episodes relating to the creation and/or subsequent adaptation of a monument. This implies that the human remains gave symbolic significance to such events, and challenges the idea that barrows were constructed primarily as graves, an argument also supported by evidence from Cornwall where over 80% of barrows excavated between 1939 and the late 1990's did not include human remains in their primary structural phase (Bonnington, forthcoming).

Returning to the communal aspect of the simultaneous multiple burial rite, it is interesting that cemetery mounds were still in use at broadly the same time that the landscape was starting to be partitioned via the construction of permanent field boundaries, as has been identified in many parts of western Britain (Fleming in Todd 1987, 115). This fact might be significant, as the construction of these field systems has been regarded as the result of communal activity and co-operation between different local groups (Fleming 1994, 65). Unfortunately, the relationship between cemetery mounds and contemporary settlement is unclear, largely because so few sites can be dated specifically to the Early bronze Age. Two examples from Cornwall, however, consisted of little more than temporary tent-like structures, which implies that in this area at least, Early Bronze Age communities may have been largely mobile within the areas defined by their barrows and other monuments (Sturgess in Nowakowski et al. 2007, 25-26; Jones, pers comm).

The intensively farmed landscapes, which characterises Anglesey and other areas where cemetery mounds were built, means that their relationship with settlements will probably never be known. However, in the granite uplands of West Penwith the landscape has remained largely unchanged, due to the fossilization of its prehistoric field systems which include elements thought to date from the earlier Middle Bronze Age, as at Chysauster and Bosigran near Zennor (Herring 1987). Cemetery mounds and other barrows tend to define the edges of these areas, being located on adjacent moorland or cliffs, as at Boscregan, reflecting their significance prior to the adoption of the sedentary farming lifestyle. This is demonstrated by the physical locations chosen for many cemetery mounds, in relation to watercourses, ridge-tops, hill-slopes and other watersheds in the landscape, and via their association with monuments and natural places with clear, long-term symbolic importance based on ancestral associations.

Conclusion

To conclude, the traditional consensus that the practice of multiple burial during the earlier Bronze Age reflected the continuation of older traditions, as apparently supported by the dense distribution of megalithic tombs in some parts of western Britain, might indeed be applicable for sites where multiple burials consisted of a mixture of inhumed and cremated bone, or accrued piecemeal over time (Lynch 1997). Based on the radiocarbon dates available, these monuments were generally established during the later 3rd and earlier 2nd Millennium BC, thereby not being greatly divorced from the preceding Neolithic era. In contrast however, for much of western Britain this period was defined by the burial of single individuals in round barrows or cists, often in association with Beakers and contemporary material culture, thereby demonstrating the initial impact and influence of this apparently intrusive rite (Lynch 1971, 54). It then seems that, after an intervening gap of some significance the deposition of sequential multiple cremation burials was established as a new rite during the later Early Bronze Age, as is indicated by the available radiocarbon results from cemetery mounds. The arrival of this ritual can clearly be seen in some cases, as at Trelystan where the cemetery mound was constructed within an existing group of single foci barrows. Elsewhere the rite was contemporaneously employed alongside other burial traditions within larger barrow groups, as at Boscregan, thereby implying that it wasn't in completion with existing burial rituals, but rather reflected an additional ritual possibility (Bonnington, forthcoming). Furthermore, its continued use during the earlier Middle Bronze Age shows that it remained a significant act for many generations of Bronze Age Britain's inhabitants.

Bibliography

Annable, F.K & Simpson, D.D.A. 1964. *Neolithic and Bronze Age Antiquities at Devizes Museum*. Wiltshire Archaeological & Natural History Society

Barrett, J.C. 1988. The Living and the Dead: Neolithic and Early Bronze Age Mortuary Practices. In Barrett, J.C. & Kinnes, I.A. (Eds) *The Archaeology of Context in the Neolithic and Early Bronze Age: Recent Trends*. 30-41

Barrett, J.C. 1990. The Monumentality of Death: The Character of Early Bronze Age Mortuary Mounds in Southern Britain, *World archaeology* 22 (2), 179-189

Bonnington, P. forthcoming, *West Penwith Coastal Cairn Survey*.

Borlase, W. 1769. *Antiquities, Historic and Monumental, of the County of Cornwall* (2nd edn). London

Borlase, W.C. 1872. Naenia Cornubiae. Truro & London.

Borlase, W.C. 1879. Archaeological Discoveries in St. Just and Sennen, *Journal of the Royal Institute of Cornwall* VI, 190-213

Borlase, W.C. 1881. Typical Specimens of Cornish Barrows, *Archaeologia* 49, 181-98

Bradley, R. 1984. *The Social Foundations of Prehistoric Britain.* London

Britnell, W.J. 1982. The Excavation of Two Round Barrows at Trelystan, Powys, *Proceedings of the Prehistoric Society* 48, 133-201

Bruck, J. 1995. A Place for the Dead: The Role of Human Remains in Late Bronze Age Britain, *Proceedings of the Prehistoric Society* 61, 245-77

Burl, A. 1991. Prehistoric Henges. Princes Risboorough

Burgess, C. 1986. 'Urnes of no small variety': Collared Urns Reviewed, *Proceedings of the Prehistoric Society* 52, 339-51

Childe, V.G. 1936. A Round Cairn Near Achnamara, Loch Sween, Argyll, *Proceedings of the Society of Antiquaries in Scotland* LXXI, 84-9

Christie, P.M. 1985. Barrows on the North Cornish Coast: Wartime Excavations by C.K. Croft Andrew 1939-1944, *Cornish Archaeology* 24, 23-122

Christie, P.M. 1988. A Barrow Cemetery on Davidstow Moor, Cornwall: Wartime Excavations by C.K. Croft Andrew, *Cornish Archaeology* 27, 27-169

Clarke, D.V., Cowie, T.G. & Foxton, A. 1985. *Symbols of Power at the Time of Stonehenge.* Edinburgh

Coles, J. 1975. Timber and Radiocarbon Dates, *Antiquity* 49, 123-5

Dudley, D. 1964. The Excavation of the Carvinack Barrow, Tregavethan, near Truro, J*ournal of the Royal Institution of Cornwall* 4 (4), 414-451

Fleming, A. 1994. The Reaves Reviewed, *Devon Archaeological Society Proceedings* 52, 63-74

Fox, C. 1959. *Life and Death in the Bronze Age: An Archaeologist's Field-Work*. London

Gibson, A. & Woods, A. 1997. *Prehistoric Pottery for the Archaeologist* (2nd edn). London

Grant, W.G. 1937. Excavation of Bronze Age Burial Mounds on Quandale, Rousay, Orkney, *Proceedings of the Society of Antiquaries of Scotland* 71, 72-84

Griffith, F.M. 1984. Archaeological Investigations at Colliford Reservoir, Bodmin Moor, 1977-78. *Cornish Archaeology* 23: 49-140.

Hencken, H. O'Neill. 1932. *The Archaeology of Cornwall and Scilly.* London

Herring, P. 1987. *Bosigran Archaeological Survey.* Truro

Huntington, R. & Metcalfe, P. 1979. Celebrations of Death. Cambridge

Lynch, F.M. 1970. *Prehistoric Anglesey.* Llangefni

Lynch, F.M. 1971. Report on the Re-excavation of two Bronze Age Cairns in Anglesey: Bedd Branwen and Treiorwerth, *Archaeologia Cambrensis* CXX, 11-83

Lynch, F.M. 1991. *Prehistoric Anglesey* (2nd edn). Llangefni

Lynch, F.M. 1993. *Excavations in the Brenig Valley: A Mesolithic and Bronze Age Landscape in North Wales.* Bangor

Lynch, F.M. 1997. *Megalithic Tombs and Long Barrows in Britain.* Princes Risborough

MacLaren, A. 1967. Recent Excavations in Peebleshire, *Proceedings of the Society of Antiquaries in Scotland* XCIX, 93-103

McKinley, J.I. 1997. Bronze Age 'Barrows' and Funerary Rites and Rites of Cremation, *Proceedings of the Prehistoric Society* 63, 129-45

Miles, H. 1975. Barrows on the St. Austell Granite, Cornwall, *Cornish Archaeology* 14, 5-81

Moffatt, P.J. 1978. The Ronaldsway Culture: A Review. In Davey, P. (ed) *Man and Environment in the Isle Of Man.* 177-218

Nowakowski, J.A., Quinnell, H., Sturgess, J., Thomas, C. & Thorpe, C. 2007. Return to Gwithian: Shifting the Sands of Time, *Cornish Archaeology*, 46, 13-76

Nye, A.C., Harrison, W. & Savory, H.N. 1983. Excavations at the Croesmihangel Barrow, Pembrokeshire, 1958-59, *Archaeologia Cambrensis* CXXXII, 19-29

O'Neil, B.H. 1952. The Excavation of Knackyboy Cairn, St. Martins, Isles of Scilly 1948, *The Antiquities Journal* XXXII, 21-34

Parker Pearson, M. 1990. The Production and Distribution of Bronze Age Pottery in South-West Britain, *Cornish Archaeology* 29, 5-32

Patchett, F.M. 1950. Cornish Bronze Age Pottery (Part 2), *The Archaeological Journal* CVII, 44-65

Pennant, T. 1810. Tours in Wales (2). London

Peterson, F. 1972. Traditions of Multiple Burial in Late Neolithic and Early Bronze Age England, *The Archaeological Journal* 129, 22-55

Pollard, S.H.M. & Russell, P.M.G. 1969. Excavation of Round Barrow 248b, Upton Pyne, Exeter. *Proceedings of the Devon Archaeological Society* 27: 49-74.

Quinnell, H. 1987. Cornish Gabbroic Pottery: The Development of a Hypothesis, *Cornish Archaeology* 26, 7-12

Quinnell, H. 1997. Excavations of an Exmoor Barrow and Ring Cairn, *Devon Archaeological Society Proceedings*, 55, 5-42

Ritchie, J.N.G. 1975. The Excavation of a Stone Circle and Cairn at Balbirnie, Fife, *The Archaeological Journal* 131, 1-32

Ritchie, J.N.G. & Thornber, I. 1975. Cairns in the Aline Valley, Morvern, Argyll, *Proceedings of the Society of Antiquaries in Scotland* CVI, 15-30

Russell, V. 1971. *West Penwith Survey.* Truro

Russell, V. & Pool, P.A.S. 1964. Excavation of a Menhir Cairn at Try, Gulval, *Cornish Archaeology* 3, 15-25

Russell-White, C.J., Lowe, C.E., & McCullagh, R.P.J. 1992. Excavations at 3 Early Bronze Age Burial Monuments in Scotland, *Proceedings of the Prehistoric Society* 58, 285-323

Savory, H.N. 1972. Copper Age Cists and Cist-Cairns in Wales: with special reference to Newton, Swansea, and other 'Multiple-cist' Cairns. In Lynch, F.M., & Burgess, C. (eds) *Prehistoric Man in Wales and the West*, 117-140

Sharpe, A. 1992. Treryn Dinas: Cliff Castles Reconsidered, *Cornish Archaeology* 31, 65-68

Sharpe, A. 1996. *An Archaeological Assessment of Boscregan Farm, St. Just, Cornwall.* Truro

Sheridan, A. & Davis, M. 1998. The Welsh 'Jet Set' in Prehistory: A case of keeping up with the Joneses ? In

Gibson, A. & Simpson, D. (Eds) *Prehistoric Ritual and Religion*. 148-62

Smith, A.N. 1995. The Excavation of Neolithic, Bronze Age and Early Historic Features near Ratho, Edinburgh, *Proceedings of the Society of Antiquaries in Scotland* 125, 69-138

Smith, G. 1996. Archaeology and Environment of a Bronze Age Cairn and Prehistoric and Romano-British Field System at Chysauster, Gulval, near Penzance, Cornwall, *Proceedings of the Prehistoric Society* 62, 167-219

Stevenson, S. 1995. The Excavation of a Kerbed Cairn at Beech Hill House, Coupar Angus, Perthshire, *Proceedings of the Society of Antiquaries in Scotland* 125, 197-235

Thomas, N. 1990. *An Archaeological Evaluation of Chapel Carn Brea, St. Just, Penwith*. Truro

Tilley, C. 1996. The Power of Rocks: Topography and Monument Construction on Bodmin Moor, *World Archaeology* 28 (2), 161-76

Todd, M. 1987. *The South-West to AD 1000*. London

Waddell, J. 1990. *The Bronze Age Burials of Ireland*. Galway

Wainright, G.J., Fleming, A., & Smith, K. 1979. The Shaugh Moor Project: 1st Report, *Proceedings of the Prehistoric Society*, 1-33

Watkins, T. 1982. The excavation of an Early Bronze Age cemetery at Barns Farm, Dalgety, Fife, *Proceedings of the Society of Antiquaries of Scotland* 112, 48-141

Woodwood, A. 2000. *British Barrows, A Matter of Life and Death*. Stroud

Acknowledgements

I would like to thank the following people for the kind help and support they gave me during the research and writing of this study: Andrew Jones, Jacky Nowakowski, Adam Sharpe and other staff from the Cornwall Historic Environment Service (formerly the Cornwall Archaeological Unit), Anna Tyack from The Royal Cornwall Museum, Pat West from Bangor Museum, Gillian Varndell from the British Museum, Bryony Coles, Sean Goddard, Linda Hurcombe, and Mike and Sue Rouillard at Exeter University, and David Giddings from the Cornwall Archaeological Society. I would also like to particularly thank Henrietta Quinnell for pointing me in the direction of this fascinating subject.

Interpreting the Dartmoor Reaves

Andrew Fleming

Abstract

The Bronze Age date of the Dartmoor reaves (ruined walls) was recognized some forty years ago. They were interpreted (by the author) as forming land boundaries and field systems; the patterns made by the reaves were 'read' in terms of 'territories' and tiers in a sociopolitical hierarchy. Since then, archaeologists (including the author) have become more interested in cognitive interpretations of such 'organised landscapes'. Recent interpretations of the reaves, most notably by Helen Wickstead, have approached the Bronze Age 'tenure' of Dartmoor in terms of 'personhood'. This article outlines and discusses these developments.

The Dartmoor reaves: recognising coaxiality

Henrietta and I were in our late twenties when the Dartmoor reaves came in from the cold. In 1968 two local historians, Elizabeth Gawne and John Somers Cocks, published a paper which recognized parallel reave systems as prehistoric. And then in May 1972 John Collis and I almost literally stumbled across the single reaves of the Upper Plym valley, and deduced that these too were prehistoric (Fleming and Collis 1973).

In those days, when we thought of Bronze Age agriculture, we tended to think of Gwithian, and tiny 'fields'; and when we thought of Dartmoor, we thought 'marginal land'. So the entry of very large Dartmoor reave systems onto the stage of British prehistory was inevitably dramatic. But in the early 1970s the Dartmoor reaves were not the only play in town. Other prehistorians were becoming interested in 'organised landscapes'. Soon there was an excavated Bronze Age coaxial field system to think about, at Fengate, just outside Peterborough (for all references, see Evans 2009); and it wasn't long before landscape historians in East Anglia were recognizing what I call perpetuated field systems, where many field boundaries still in use follow a dominant axis apparently established in later prehistory, though perhaps not as far back as the Bronze Age (Williamson 1987). Systems of parallel ditches also show up from the air, as soil- or cropmarks, again often in eastern England. In the mid 1980s, I suggested that these complex and distinctive layouts might be termed coaxial field systems and treated as a category of field monument, like hillforts (Fleming 1987). The interpretation and understanding of prehistoric coaxiality is now on the national archaeological agenda.

As I have pointed out in the new edition of The Dartmoor Reaves (2008), the Dartmoor coaxial systems are still the very best in the country, in terms of conservation. They are mostly quite well preserved, and not much 're-used' in comparison with East Anglian examples. Furthermore, on Dartmoor we can still study large areas of them and have upstanding boundaries to look at, rather than excavated ditch-fills (however complex). Even the comparatively large rescue excavations in the lowlands of southern England only provide tiny windows into the much larger systems, which are visible as crop- or soil-marks. On Dartmoor, too, we may study relationships between reaves and contemporary or near-contemporary settlement sites, and a good deal of diversity within parallel reave systems. But we also have to ask how far were the reaves and associated settlement sites complemented by wooden fences and timber buildings, and by ditches - traces of which are firmly sealed below the peaty humus on the surface. My own limited excavation campaign on Holne Moor suggests that the answer to this question is: quite a lot. If only for this reason, to claim the reave systems as anything like 'complete Bronze Age landscapes' would be seriously misleading. That said, however, these reave systems are a superb archaeological resource even by the high standards set by Dartmoor's field monuments in general.

Early interpretation

But how to explain them? When I started my research, I looked for patterns, as archaeologists do. And it's not hard to pick out the pattern made by the watershed reaves of the South Moor, or certain repeated characteristics of the parallel reave systems, for instance. Of course in places there are reaves which don't conform to the simple dichotomy between parallel systems and individual land boundaries, for example, the 'block system' just north of the Warren House Inn (Fleming 2008, fig. 20); and there are parts of parallel systems which do not follow the prevailing axis, as near Foxworthy in the Dartmeet system (Butler 1991, map 15). But then that's what generalisations are all about.

I decided that the reaves were land boundaries. I suggested that the spacing and density of the reaves, and their relationship to the local terrain, indicated the existence of different zones of land use, and I envisaged a territorial hierarchy of boundaries, corresponding to claims on the land asserted by social groups operating at different geographical and demographic scales. As in the Middle Ages, there would have been intercommons on the high moors, with the territories of different 'communities' ranged around them. These territories were quite large and often based on major valleys; most had a zone of upland grazing and a zone of enclosed land - a parallel reave system displaying coaxial boundaries. The houses within these parallel systems were mostly found in clusters, which I labelled 'neighbourhood groups'; in these areas most of the smaller parcels of enclosed land, and hence the greatest 'complexity', were to be found. I suggested that land division within the parallel systems was concerned with management of land held by a 'community'.

The most obvious problem with this rather inductive interpretation was that I was unable to demonstrate how coaxiality worked as a system of allocating land within a community. Within the Dartmoor parallel systems, the locations of the houses in the neighbourhood groups are puzzling in relation to the 'behaviour' of the axial reaves. Chronological depth no doubt plays a role here; but I've also suggested that this awkward fit may reflect unconformity between local groups and whatever 'authority' was responsible for the land division involving parallel reave systems. And I also found it impossible to decide on the socio-political context of the decision-making, which created the observed patterning – was it, for instance, 'bottom up' or 'top down'?

These ideas and interpretations are presented in *The Dartmoor Reaves*, and elsewhere (Fleming 1984, 1988, 1996, 2007). However, not long after the book was first published, in 1988, archaeological theorists started to attack the notion of landscape history as a means of reconstructing past political geography, agrarian history, and socio-political structures. They urged landscape historians to jettison material understandings of the archaeological record, and to work with meaning and cognition. None of this critique was aimed explicitly at my work on Dartmoor, but one could hardly escape its general implications. In the second edition of my book, I have tried to discuss the meaning of coaxiality. But I have also pointed out that the choice between materialism and cognitive approaches is a false one; we should be working with both. For some postmodern theorists, however, Bronze Age cognition now matters less than the reworking of material from the past into narratives and performative formats which resonate with contemporary concerns (see e. g. Pearson and Shanks 2001).

Interpreting coaxial field systems: the wider context

Even from a more traditional perspective it has become clear that prehistoric land allotment, and its interpretation, is a complex topic. The concept of a 'field system', especially one containing numerous houses and 'domestic' zones, intersects with many different areas of prehistoric life. Should we take the field systems to reflect the improvement of agriculture in some sense? Were their creators, in Peter Fowler's phrase (1981, 30), simply 'trying to be better farmers'? And what does 'being a better farmer' imply? Is it about increasing productivity, or better management of common land? Or did reaves and reave systems promote the maintenance and defence of a community's territory, and the control of land? Might the reaves represent the strengthening and intensification of a previously relaxed territorial system, as the social order became increasingly hierarchical, competitive, and predatory?

Should we focus on the boundaries, or on the spaces between them – the so-called 'fields'? Is it the overall coaxiality of a 'field system' which should be the main focus of our interest, and what exactly is a 'field system' anyway ? Clearly, there are different spatial scales of analysis. We may study individual details around the houses, or consider how a coaxial system 'works' in the landscape. We can think about the Dartmoor-wide pattern, and the spatial relationships between neighbours. And we also have to take account of coaxiality as a widespread phenomenon in the Bronze Age of southern and eastern England (Yates 2006); we may need to understand our local systems as a reflection of social and economic trends, which were much more widely distributed. The combination of good preservation and the magnitude of the areas of well-preserved reaves makes the Dartmoor coaxials the best in Britain, by quite a long way (and makes it all the more remarkable that it took so long to recognize their significance); but this, ironically, makes it difficult to judge how representative they are of coaxiality in England and Wales as a whole. It is fascinating to read Chris Evans's recently-published overview of prehistoric field systems investigated in the Peterborough fenlands over more than thirty years (2009, Chapter 6); his interpretive preoccupations respond in part to those of Francis Pryor, the leading excavator of this material, who famously re-interpreted part of a 'field system' as a community stockyard (Pryor 1996). Evans's discussion is so different from that relating to the Dartmoor reaves that the two could almost be said to be complementary.

The understanding of field systems seems to be a topic for the long haul. England's medieval open field systems have been discussed for a hundred years or more. For half that time, their dating and origins were badly misunderstood, and simple explanatory models were often sought. Only in recent years have we come to see beyond superficial overall similarities, and started to tease apart the different origins and development of openfield systems in different regions (Williamson 2003, Rippon 2009). We have come to recognize equifinality (several origins producing field systems which now look identical) and indeterminacy (one cause resulting in more than one kind of field system) (Baker and Butlin 1973). Origin models are growing in sophistication and complexity, especially since they also have to take into account the development of different types of settlement (see e. g. Jones and Page 2006). In some regions, medieval field systems may have evolved in a convergent manner, becoming more similar to one another than they were at the outset. The same thing might have happened with reaves. As in the case of other complex archaeological entities, the dialogue between natural 'lumpers' and congenital 'splitters' has its own dynamic, and will doubtless continue to do so.

Then there's the question of the social context of decision-making behind these boundaries and boundary systems. In his book *The Past in Prehistoric Communities*, Richard Bradley (2002, 82-5) refers to an unpublished story by Franz Kafka about the construction of the Great Wall of China. In Kafka's vision, no one is quite sure why the wall was built; the explanations supplied are contradictory and confusing, and the perceptions of the Emperor and of the builders are totally at variance with each other. The passage of time complicates the situation, as does the possibility that the will of the gods is involved. Was the Wall really about keeping out the northern barbarians, or was it essentially an act of deference and respect on the part of loyal but uncomprehending subjects? In Kafka's presentation, the Wall never had a single 'meaning'; even when it was built, various interpretations were both current and possible.

If we are to interpret the Dartmoor reaves, we have to explain both main kinds. As well as the parallel or coaxial systems, we also have to explain the individual reaves - the long-running boundaries which may form terminal reaves for the coaxial systems but also have their own territorial logic, such as the Great Western Reave, a long 'contour reave' at least 13 km in length; Venford Reave, terminal of the Dartmeet system but also a long-running boundary of at least 7.5 km in its own right. And the terminal of the Wigford Down system happens to be the Eylesbarrow Reave, a watershed reave nearly 8 km long. The questions posed by individual long-running boundaries are not restricted to Dartmoor. These kinds of boundaries are well-known in eastern England (see papers by Knight and Elliott, Roberts, Fenton-Thomas, and Chadwick in Chadwick 2008). I have interpreted the Dartmoor linears as boundaries demarcating the 'territories' of people occupying valleys and river basins, though some of them may also have separated higher moorland from lower-lying pasture ground. To some extent the spacing and positioning of stone circles and stone rows (some of which were respected by the reave builders) suggest that these 'territories' may have been established a good deal earlier (Barnatt 1989); perhaps the construction of reaves simply represented their firmer re-definition, in an age where physical boundaries were being put up all over the country.

And then there are the parallel systems. In 1991, Stephen Rippon drew a distinction between 'planned' and 'regular' or 'organic' landscapes, in connection with Essex coaxials. Tom Williamson, writing in 1998, also recognized this distinction, but wondered whether a planned landscape might morph into a more 'organic' landscape, as later users of the land allowed themselves to be influenced by the prevailing direction of old-established boundaries. And then in 2005 Bob Johnston published an article entitled 'Pattern without a Plan' - a title which encapsulates his argument. As a matter of fact, although I have sometimes discussed the idea of an overall 'plan' for the Dartmoor reave systems – a discussion which I feel is unavoidable - in *The Dartmoor Reaves* I use the word 'pattern' much more frequently. On reflection, I'm prepared to concede that 'planned' is not necessarily a very helpful adjective. What do we mean by it? That putting a parallel reave system into a particular zone was a definite decision, an historical event? Did such a decision also encompass the locations of the main parallel reaves, or did it involve even closer attention to detail? Does 'planning' imply that the work of boundary-making was closely supervised? And in the absence of close local control, couldn't a 'planned' system end up looking like an 'organic' system? If the word 'planned' is to be of further use, perhaps it should be defined more closely, in general and in relation to the situations to which it is applied.

Towards the personhood model

Johnston has argued that the heterogeneity of the boundaries which preceded reaves, and the diversity of the reaves themselves, imply what he calls a reflexive tradition of boundary construction. He writes about 'the working of individual agencies within the material conditions of an existing socialized landscape', and although this argument depends on very limited evidence, I have no problem with the idea that the people who created these boundaries already knew these landscapes intimately, and had invested them with meaning. The reaves had 'long and complex biographies' and their axes 'developed piecemeal', though 'as they were built and the, in places, unwavering regularity of the pattern was formalised, so further boundaries were repeated, mimicked and fitted in'. So for Johnston, any apparent patterns made by reaves result from the convergence of numerous piecemeal actions.

The trouble with the fashionable preoccupation with 'the dwelling perspective', inhabitation, and so on, is that it focuses unwaveringly on local spirituality, on ancestral ties to land, on the freedom of individuals who seem never to have been oppressed by a coercive or exploitative social order, or involved in competitive or emulative activities. But the local 'dwelling perspective' will never entirely 'explain' such field systems. Coaxial field systems were a widespread phenomenon, like megalithic tombs or cursuses. I don't believe that coaxiality was something towards which constructors of boundaries drifted unconsciously; nor do I believe that the similarities between different coaxial systems 'emerged' by coincidence. For me, coaxiality must have been a striking concept with a strong initial impetus; after all, there are, they say, no straight lines in nature. The main lines of the pattern, although maybe not the reaves themselves in all their three-dimensionality, probably became established in quite a short space of time. At first the boundary lines now marked by reaves may have been indicated by standing posts, trees, small cairns, and so on. And if radiocarbon dates from reaves are spread over a long time period, it does not necessarily follow that the boundary lines which they fossilize were initiated over a period of comparable duration.

If they were to make sense as boundaries, many of the reave lines would have to be complemented by other boundaries. One watershed boundary implies the existence of another. If a rectangular 'field' is to be created, four boundaries need to be constructed simultaneously. Land enclosure may be a piecemeal matter, but land division isn't. Once you've decided on a land division system, you have to get on with constructing it, in order to integrate it with the maintenance of your crops and livestock. But what about the building of reaves, as opposed to the installation of main boundary lines? Helen Wickstead (2008, 80) has claimed that the Dartmoor population postulated by Jeremy Butler could have constructed the reaves in just two months. But actually she proposes spreading the period of construction over 500 years or more (2008, 150) – which is three thousand times longer. If we take Butler's figure of 407 km for the total length of surviving reaves (1997, 73), and round it up to 500, then about a thousand metres of reave would have been built every year, on average. If that effort was distributed among, say, fifteen areas of intensive reave-building around the fringe of the Moor, that would be 66 m of reave built in an average year in each of these areas. That is not very much. Were reave systems always works in progress? According to Wickstead (2008, 108), my own early interpretations 'stressed the synchronicity of the reaves in order to interpret them as an integrated system of land division'. Actually it's the other way round; it was the pattern they made, and their interdependence, that persuaded me that many of the boundary lines represented by reaves were essentially synchronous.

Tenure as personhood

In her recent book *Theorising Tenure: Land Division and Identity in later prehistoric Dartmoor*, Wickstead's interpretation is based on the concept of personhood, a concept currently fashionable among prehistorians. Indeed before tackling *Theorising Tenure* the reader would be well advised to read Chris Fowler's The archaeology of personhood, which explains some quite difficult concepts with great clarity.

In the theory of personhood (which is based on anthropological work in Melanesia and India), the word 'person' is not used ,as in common speech, to mean an individual human being defined by his or her body. Rather, personhood involves 'different understandings of the boundaries of and interpenetrations between people and things, and one person and another. Some artefacts might be features of one person, or persons in their own right. Animals and objects and even natural phenomena may be persons: not just like people, but actually persons in their own right sharing the same social and technological world' (Fowler 2004, 6). Furthermore, 'in communities where personhood is stressed…it may not be the individual that is the locus of the diversity, innovation or decision-making, but a collective person. Houses or clans may constitute the "moral person". Uniqueness and innovation are features of clans, expressed through its [sic] members…not all persons in the community are necessarily human, and an emphasis on the individual neglects the role of other social agents accorded personhood (like ghosts, spirits, houses, axes, standing stones)….' (Fowler 2004, 21). People are 'partible' or 'dividual'; that is to say, different 'components' of their personhood may be shared with, or transferred to others. They are also permeable, open to being imbued with other properties. The situation is not static; various life events or happenings may change the character of personhood. We say 'You can take the girl out of Swansea, but you can't take Swansea out of the girl' and this conveys something of the concept of personhood. But we should add that the girl, or part of her, might be deemed to be still in Swansea even when she is elsewhere, that both the girl and Swansea are perceived as permeable, divisible entities, and that aspects of 'Swansea' may be transferred to the people or places which the girl encounters on her travels. If she gives someone else her mother's recipe for Bara brith, for example, her friend might carry for ever some of her mother's spirit.

The concept of personhood may be directly useful to archaeologists, in that it may help us to 'interpret' discoveries which are not susceptible to the application of our own culturally-specific 'common sense' – unexpected associations, juxtapositions and absences in burials and ritual deposits, or on house floors, for example. In general, it may help us to apprehend the 'otherness' of people and cultures of the past. It may also provide archaeologists with a justification for highly imaginative interpretations, unfettered by evidence or argument, which derive not from the more familiar area of post-modern ideas about the nature of the historian's enterprise, but rather from a considered acceptance of the massive perceptual gulf, which separates us from the people of the past.

Personhood and the reaves: a response

Wickstead (2008) seeks to reinterpret the coaxial reave systems of Dartmoor in terms of personhood. She identifies two historical theories of land tenure prevalent in Western thought. One is concerned with territorialisation, the other with exclusive property rights and the labour theory of value. Both are ultimately products of post-Enlightenment thinking; so Wickstead therefore rejects them as frameworks for interpreting reave systems and seeks to replace them with a 'personhood' theory of tenure. It is hard not to applaud this serious approach to the otherness of the Dartmoor Bronze Age, although it is disconcerting to find that a central tenet of Wickstead's critique is that modern nationalism has been the main driving force behind prehistorians' reading of 'tenure' as 'territory' (2008, 91-2). Don't Anglo-Saxon charters and compilations like *The Book of Llandaff* remind us that in both England and Wales there have been 'territories', in the sense of bounded if permeable entities, subject to a series of claims, rights, and exclusions, for well over a thousand years? And if one recalls the important role of 'territories' and 'ranges' in the social ecologies of numerous other species, does that make one an irredeemable ethological determinist? Wickstead carries out an analysis of the locational preferences of parallel reave systems, discovering that there is enough unreaved land of appropriate quality to suggest that there was no land shortage in the Dartmoor Bronze Age (2008, 55-9). It is surprising, given her approach, that she does not also acknowledge that scarcity of land is often a cultural construct - a matter of perception within the contemporary sociopolitical context – and sometimes a consequence of the operation of those exclusive property rights, which she regards as irrelevant in a Bronze Age context.

Despite these cavils, I have to acknowledge that my own interpretations of the reave systems are based mostly on my perception of the issues involved in commons management, and especially its history in England over the last millennium or so. This is unlikely to be the best approach to the otherness of the Dartmoor Bronze Age, and, as I have always acknowledged, it is hard to 'read' the apparent relationship between 'houses' and 'land divisions' in reave systems in terms of a recognisable, recurrent form of land allocation; we are not exactly dealing with tofts and crofts here. So a new approach to 'tenure' is to be welcomed.

Arguably, however, where the Dartmoor reaves are concerned, Wickstead's interpretation has not succeeded in narrowing the gulf between interpretation and the known archaeological record. She is interested in the 'increasingly place-bound sense of being' identified by Barrett (1994) among others, as characteristic of the later British Bronze Age and marked by a horizon of coaxial field systems and numerous more visible 'settlement sites'. She reinterprets this transition in terms of a theory of tenure involving personhood rather than 'territorialisation'. For her, tenure 'allowed land and its reproductive capabilities to be distributed and circulated as parts of persons in exchange….loan and exchange of access to pastures allowed land to be used more flexibly, and coaxial landscapes may have increased this flexibility, allowing spare capacity to be shared productively. Landscapes of land division do not signal "fragmentation" into individual territories but instead, provide interconnections between groups' (2008, 152). For me, there is nothing particularly contentious here. My 'territories' may have acted like a red rag to the post-processual bull, but for the record, I have never thought of them as hard-edged, in social terms, nor regarded their boundaries as impermeable. Detailed similarities between the coaxial systems on the periphery of Dartmoor do indeed suggest a rich network of contacts between their 'inhabitants'. I have never regarded the reave systems as constituting 'territories' by themselves; I have always regarded the 'tenure' of individual 'fields' within such systems as a matter for discussion. Wickstead evades the nub of the 'territorial' issue by showing no interest in the reaves which behave most like 'territorial' boundaries – the long, cross-country single reaves mentioned above, including the 'watershed' reaves of the South Moor – which sometimes formed the 'terminal' boundaries of coaxial reave systems. As I have already noted, comparable long, cross-country boundaries exist elsewhere. As far as I can see, many of Wickstead's strategies of personhood, and the development of 'projects of value', could have been undertaken largely within such territories, which may have operated on a different geographical and perceptual scale.

The other major issue raised by Wickstead's work is that of 'pattern without a plan'. There are many fields, other than land division, within which strategies of personhood might have been conducted. However, the poverty of the local archaeological record, in terms of other kinds of evidence, means that if Wickstead (and Johnston before her) are to pursue the 'personhood' theory on Dartmoor, they need to place considerable emphasis on the heterogeneity of reaves within parallel systems, and to stress the likelihood that the construction of reaves involved numerous distinct actions, or 'projects of value', ideally performed over a long period of time. This would represent episodes in the 'construction of identity' - or perhaps its near-continuous performance. No doubt it is possible to make the case for regarding parallel reave systems as 'works in progress' in their day, and to read them as representing composites of many work episodes spread evenly across a period of five hundred years or so. However, the evidence is thin; not many reaves have been excavated, and there are not many relevant radiocarbon dates.

The heterogeneity of reaves expresses itself in various ways – for example, differences in constructional technique, the nature of underlying (excavated) boundaries, the diversity of 'farmyard' areas, the contrast between relatively straight, grid-like reaves and more straggly examples. But the boundary line may have been as important as the boundary fence. Might not the line have been there for centuries as a constant mental construct? Most of the potentially 'unfinished' reaves occur not within parallel systems, but outside them. One cannot help noting that a rectangular 'field' needs to have four 'sides' if it is to be effective in a farming sense. Isn't the 'gradualist' model constrained by the minimum number of completed 'fields' to which a group of farmers needed to have access, in order to operate effectively with the livestock under their control? Isn't a 'placebound sense of being', in John Barrett's phrase, closely contingent upon an environment quite rich in fences, walls and hedges, or at least notional boundary lines, used for practical purposes by groups of farmers in daily contact with one another? Do those who puzzle over apparent patterns have to choose between interpreting them as the result of 'planning' and thinking of them as the consequence of a myriad 'projects of value', or expressions of 'the distributed mind'? And are there cases known to anthropologists where the essential feature of the lines of division or boundaries marking off parcels of land within a system of pasture management is that they are a consequence of the 'personhood' model of tenure?

The subject of choice raises another set of questions. Do we have to choose between personhood and post-Enlightenment theories of property tenure? And is the

Papua New Guinea version of 'personhood', which seems extreme enough to be helpful to anthropologists and archaeologists who wish to explain the concept to others, likely to be the one most likely to apply to Bronze Age Dartmoor? Only thirty or forty generations before they appeared in the writings of classical authors, did the peoples of north-west Europe really think rather like twentieth century Melanesians? Have archaeological theorists allowed enough time, or envisaged enough 'social process', for the spiritually sensitive, touchy-feely people of the Neolithic and Bronze Age to develop into the predatory, aggressive, hierarchical societies, which we know from later, text-aided contexts? Are many miles of walls, laid out in recognizable patterns, more likely to be closer to the former state of mind, or to the latter? How did the 'distributed mind' of personhood intersect with other mindsets which placed more practical emphasis on the integrity of the individual, corporeal human being, acting persistently in the pursuit of his/her interests (or those of the social group) - which surely did not wait until the Early Modern period before they got going? What of past mindsets which seem more closely concerned with personal, group, or class advantage, in a more Darwinian or Marxian sense?

In any case, is an area like Dartmoor the best place to explore and develop these issues? There is a certain irony here. Although Dartmoor could be said to contain one of the best 'prehistoric landscapes' in north-west Europe, and definitely the 'best' coaxial landscape known in Britain, we need to exercise due diffidence in our interpretive discussions. Our perception of the nature and history of these coaxial field systems would certainly change massively if we undertook large-scale area excavations within them. And for someone attempting to work through the concept of personhood in a real archaeological situation, the Dartmoor Bronze Age record, as it exists at present, is virtually uni-dimensional, providing a data set which must be difficult to use for this purpose.

How far in any case is it a priority for prehistorians to reconstruct the mindsets of prehistoric peoples, in preference to developing materialist narratives of their history? The promotion of this project was certainly most important in Cambridge some thirty years ago, in a world of archaeological theory in which the materialist, scientific perspectives of Colin Renfrew and Lewis Binford seemed about to reduce prehistory to a cybernetic wasteland, in Julian Thomas's memorable phrase. But the world has surely moved on since then, beyond the single-minded pursuit of this objective; it is no longer necessary to present archaeologists with such stark choices.

Over the last forty years or so, interpretations of the Dartmoor reaves, at first dependent mostly on inductive reasoning and contemporary 'common sense', became more sensitive to cognitive insights before embracing the personhood perspective. Interpretations will always be contested – and rightly so. It will be for prehistorians of the future to judge the insights of the present time, and distribute bouquets or brickbats as they see fit. But as the long debate about the origins and nature of medieval field systems has demonstrated, interpretation isn't just a matter of changing fashions in archaeological theory. We do make progress. And we should remember that interpretations are not there just to be critiqued; it is also permissible to build on them.

Bibliography

Baker, A. and Butlin, R. 1973. *Studies of field systems in the British Isles.* Cambridge: Cambridge University Press.

Barnatt, J. 1989. *Stone circles of Britain.* British Archaeological Reports, British Series 215.

Barrett, J. 1994. *Fragments from antiquity: an archaeology of social life in Britain.* Oxford: Blackwell.

Butler, J. 1991. *Dartmoor Atlas of antiquities. Vol 1: The East.* Exeter: Devon Books.

Butler, J. 1997. *Dartmoor Atlas of antiquities. Vol V: The East.* Exeter: Devon Books.

Bradley, 2002. *The past in prehistoric societies.* London: Routledge.

Chadwick, A. (ed) 2008. *Recent approaches to the archaeology of land allotment.* British Archaeological Reports International Series 1875.

Evans, C. 2009. *Fengate revisited.* Cambridge: Cambridge Archaeological Unit.

Fleming, A. 1984. The prehistoric landscape of Dartmoor: wider implications. *Landscape History* 6: 5-19.

Fleming, A. 1987. Coaxial field systems: some questions of time and space. *Antiquity* 61: 188-202.

Fleming, A. 1988. *The Dartmoor reaves: investigating prehistoric land divisions.* London: Batsford.

Fleming, A. 1996. The reaves reviewed. Pp. 63-74 In Griffiths, D. (ed) *The archaeology of Dartmoor: perspectives from the 1990s* (also published as volume 52 of the Proceedings of the Devon Archaeological Society).

Fleming, A. 2007. *The Dartmoor reaves: investigating prehistoric land divisions.* (second edition) Oxford: Windgather.

Fleming, A. and Collis, J. 1973. A late prehistoric reave system near Cholwich Town, Dartmoor. *Proceedings of the Devon Archaeological Society* 31: 1-21.

Fowler, C. 2004. *The archaeology of personhood.* London, Routledge.

Fowler, P. 1981. Wildscape to landscape: 'enclosure' in prehistoric Britain, in Mercer, R. (ed) *Farming practice in British prehistory.* Edinburgh: Edinburgh University Press.

Gawne, E. and Somers Cocks, J. 1968. Parallel reaves on Dartmoor. *Transactions of the Devonshire Association* 100: 277-91.

Johnston, R. 2005. Pattern without a plan: rethinking the Bronze Age coaxial field systems on Dartmoor, south-west England. *Oxford Journal of Archaeology* 24 (1), 1-21.

Jones, R. and Page, M. 2006. *Medieval villages in an English landscape: beginnings and ends.* Bollington, Windgather Press.

Pearson, M. and Shanks, M. 2001. *Theatre/Archaeology.* London: Routledge.

Pryor, F. 1996. Sheep, stockyards and field systems: Bronze Age livestock populations in the Fenlands of eastern England. *Antiquity* 70: 331-9.

Rippon, S. 1991. Early planned landscapes in south-east Essex. *Essex Archaeology and History*, 22: 46-60.

Rippon, S. 2009. *Beyond the medieval village: the diversification of landscape character in southern Britain.* Oxford: Oxford University Press.

Wickstead, H. 2008. *Theorising tenure: land division and identity in later prehistoric Dartmoor.* British Archaeological Reports, British Series 465. Oxford: Hadrian Books.

Williamson, T. 1987. Early coaxial field systems on the East Anglian boulder clays. *Proceedings of the Prehistoric Society* 53: 419-31.

Williamson, T. 1998. The 'Scole-Dickleburgh field system' re-visited. *Landscape History* 20: 19-28.

Williamson, T. 2003. *Shaping medieval landscapes: settlement, society, environment.* Bollington, Windgather Press.

Yates, D. 2006. *Land, power and prestige: Bronze Age field systems in southern England.* Oxford: Oxbow.

Telling Tales from the Roundhouse.
Researching Bronze Age Buildings in Cornwall

Jacqueline Nowakowski

Our house, in the middle of our street
Our house, in the middle of our street……

Our house it has a crowd
There's always something happening
And it's usually quite loud
Our mum she's so house-proud
Nothing ever slows her down
And a mess is not allowed

Our house, in the middle of our street
Our house, in the middle of our ..

(Instrumental interlude)

Our house, in the middle of our street
Our house, in the middle of our ..

I remember way back then when everything was true and when
We would have such a very good time such a fine time
Such a happy time
And I remember how we'd play simply waste the day away
Then we'd say nothing would come between us two dreamers

Our house, in the middle of our street
Our house, in the middle of our street

Madness, Extracts from 'Our House', Rise and Fall album 1982

All memory of the old house, its needs, conditions, and duties is cancelled, and the new communal identity proceeds to embark on the adventure of life without delay. Even the situation of their late home is effaced from memory.

Lucy Ellman, *Man or Mango*, 1998

Abstract

Roundhouses lie at the heart of prehistoric settlements and are a principal dataset providing insights into the daily lives of Bronze Age communities. Understanding how they were built and what they were used for are key in revealing the significance and importance of settlement and place during the second millennium BC (Brück and Goodman 1999). This paper reviews advances in the investigations of Bronze Age buildings in Cornwall over the past twenty-five years. Detailed studies of individual buildings have revealed tremendous variety particularly across the lowland scene. This growing area of research sheds light on differences in architectural styles alongside the potential varied uses and life histories of these buildings. The dominant homogeneous picture of, and the generalised traditional study of the British Bronze Age roundhouse, is changing.

Introduction

Over the past twenty-five or so years, there have been considerable advances in our understanding of the prehistoric roundhouse – particularly so for the Bronze Age in Cornwall (Christie 1986). In this paper I wish to explore some of the main themes and emergent results of this research and suggest how these may be taken forwards. Roofed round and oval buildings are a key innovation of Bronze Age landscapes across prehistoric Britain and their detailed study has much potential in revealing the complex relationships between people, their lives, histories and land.

In Cornwall the principal advances for our understanding Bronze Age roundhouses may be summarised as follows:

- A clearer chronology through modern scientific dating
- Understanding the types of resources and processes of roundhouse construction
- Appraising the variety of different building styles
- Examining how buildings may have been used

Alongside these has been a growing awareness of the significance of the individual stories of buildings; their genesis, use-lives and in particular, their potential treatment on abandonment, and what these varied processes might reveal about wider social and cultural practices (Nowakowski 2001). In this, recent work on Bronze Age Cornish roundhouses has been informed by wider theoretical approaches which have emphasised cultural needs and symbolic systems and shown how these are deeply embedded within prehistoric traditions and are at the core of how past societies perceived and used built roofed spaces in their daily lives (Parker Pearson and Richards 1994; Brück 1999a; Brück 1999b and see Townend 2007).

Buildings are the outcomes of a whole suite of possibilities, and woven into their fabric and the mechanics of their construction, that is why a building may be built and how it may be used, is a shared system of expectations: meanings and values understood by its builders and users. These underpin societal needs, which are not seen, but may be inferred, as vernacular styles become emergent and dominant traditions. It is the archaeologist's challenge to tease out and interpret these meanings in the archaeological footprints they leave behind.

In recent study there has also been a welcome change in terminology. The traditional term the 'hut circle', may no longer seem appropriate, for it could be argued, that with its humble connotations, the term has to some degree perpetuated a simplistic appreciation of the potentially pluralistic approach that could be adopted in the study of the prehistoric 'domestic' building. The term 'roundhouse' has gained new currency and has ensured that these buildings occupy centre stage in settlement research as they offer fruitful opportunities as analytical units of study in their own right. These changes have arisen from opportunities to fully investigate individual buildings as well as groups of buildings. For although extensive field surveys of upstanding ruins have emphasised the morphological variety in the plans and patterns of roundhouse settlements across upland Cornwall (e.g., Johnson 1980; Johnson and Rose 1994), excavations have sharpened our ideas and urged us to look more closely at the tales of individual sites and how these may relate to the once living and lived in spaces. In recent years more and more roundhouses are being discovered. Many have been found unexpectedly during the construction of pipelines, house building schemes and road-building projects, and a marked increase in opportunities to fully excavate these sites, means that we are becoming better acquainted with their potential variety. This is particularly so for those discovered off the upland areas of south western Britain. Recent advances in roundhouse research in Cornwall, as elsewhere, owes much to the opportunities offered by the rise of developer-funded archaeological fieldwork.

A Brief History of Bronze Age Roundhouse Research in Cornwall

Round house research really started with the excavation of number of 'hut circles' at Trewey Downs in Zennor, West Penwith during the 1930s (Dudley 1941). In 1936 and 1937, on the slopes of this upland valley to the southeast of Zennor churchtown in West Cornwall, F. C. Hirst, helped by Mr Cave Day and Dorothy Dudley, investigated three well-preserved stone-walled roundhouses. The site at Trewey was chosen because the buildings were intact upstanding ruins, which lay within a contemporary field system with linked roadways. At this time the principal aim was to date the buildings and to determine how they differed from the archetypal (later) prehistoric structure: the West Penwith courtyard house. The courtyard house, a feature of later prehistoric and Romano-British landscapes in West Cornwall and the Isles of Scilly, was considered a 'domestic' building which comprised multiple-rooms or cells arranged around an open courtyard and formed a unified probable 'household' unit (Hencken 1933, 278; Hirst 1937a). It is completely different in size, form and design to the single-roomed roundhouse. Early in the 1930s, Hirst had initiated a series of yearly excavations of a number of courtyard houses at Porthmeor, also in Zennor (Hirst 1937b). The courtyard houses and the hut circles all lay in upland zones and the main strategies of these pre-war excavations was to strip out the interiors of these upstanding stone-walled buildings in the anticipation that occupation and floors surfaces could be found to date the buildings.

The interiors of a handful of roundhouses were also excavated on the cliff castle at Gurnard's Head (also in Zennor) in the late 1930s (Gordon 1941). At all these sites intact and clearly defined floor surfaces invariably proved to be elusive and were not easy to identify. Limited attempts were made to section house walls or to look deeper into the foundations of these buildings to reveal how they were constructed, or to fully reveal their potential long histories of use. Few closely datable finds were made: a mere handful of pot sherds, quartz pieces, some flints and the odd granite muller were, for example, found at Trewey and on the basis of one pot sherd alone, the Trewey huts were considered to date to the Later Bronze Age (Dudley 1941). The few sherds recovered from the three huts investigated at Gurnard's Head were considered Iron Age in date and although some of the buildings were indeed probably in use then, it is only through a recent examination of the archive, that some sherds have been identified dating to the Bronze Age (by Henrietta Quinnell in Nowakowski and Quinnell in press). This throws into question their potential long uses.

During the 1950s, Cornish Bronze Age settlement began to receive more focussed attention. Then three key excavations took place: Gwithian, east of Hayle (Thomas 1958), Kynance Gate, on the Lizard (Thomas 1960) and Trevisker, St Eval (ApSimon and Greenfield 1972). These excavations differed in scope and scale and kick-started research about the character of settlements situated off the moors. Gwithian and Kynance Gate were both coastal sites while Trevisker lay within a lowland (inland) setting. Investigations at Gwithian and Kynance were research projects, while the work at Trevisker was an early rescue excavation (ApSimon and Greenfield 1972), and all contributed new information. At all of these sites groups of buildings were examined and emergent results began to demonstrate the potential for architectural variety within the wider Bronze Age settlement scene beyond the ubiquitous upstanding but ruined stone walled roundhouses so characteristic of the moors. At all three sites, large quantities of finds, particularly pottery, were discovered. The impressive assemblage of cord-impressed and incised decorated pots discovered and first published at Trevisker, ensured that this became a site type for this period and consequently gave its name as a cultural marker for the entire south-western Bronze Age (ApSimon and Greenfield 1972). The Bronze Age settlement excavated at Trevisker to date still remains the only fully published site from this decade although the work at Gwithian has recently been revisited (Nowakowski et al. 2007 and see below). A full report on the work at Kynance Gate, unfortunately, never materialised (Thomas 1960). In the early 1960s a sizeable collection of Trevisker pottery, bronzes and stonework was found at Tredarvah on the outskirts of Penzance (Pearce and Padley 1977). This material was discovered during the construction of a bungalow with no opportunity for full investigation of the site, but it was clearly settlement debris and was a significant discovery highlighting the potential good survival for Bronze Age settlement within the lowland scene.

In the following two decades and the early 1980s, excavations at settlements such as Stannon Down, on

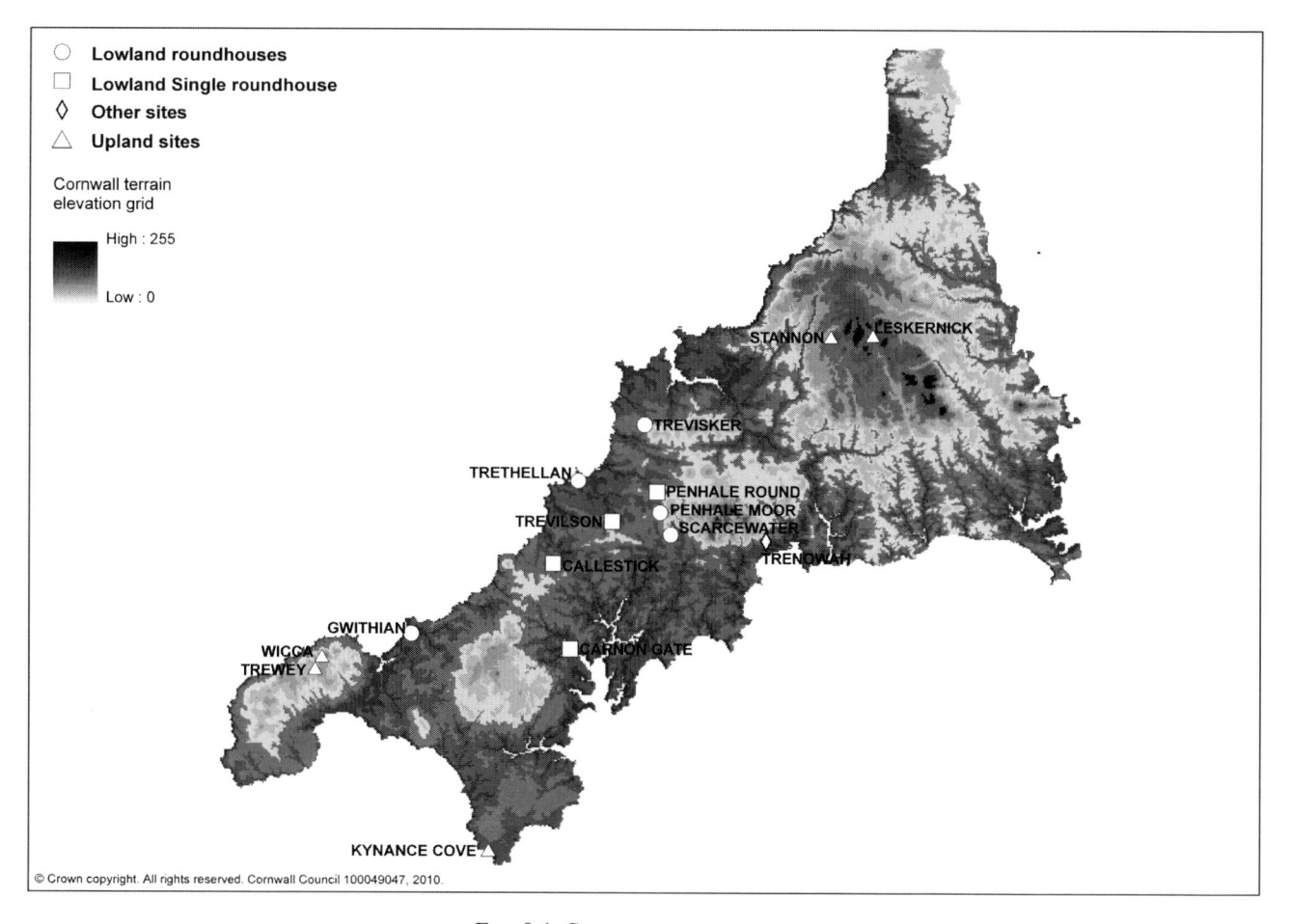

Fig. 9.1 Sites discussed in text.

north west Bodmin Moor (Mercer 1970) and Poldowrian, St Kerverne (Smith and Harris 1982) added further information. Here moorland houses were found to comprise substantial buildings with stone walls often up to 2 metres wide which upheld wooden superstructures usually represented by single post-rings, some with central posts. Stone floors, stone-lined drains and threshold stones were found to be common interior features. Yet overall absences of central hearths and the general lack of finds suggested that many of these buildings were only in occasional, probable seasonal use. Their histories of use seemingly limited, a picture now addressed with more recent work (e.g., at Stannon, Jones 2004-5)

Recent advances in dating

Since the mid 1980s over a dozen or so sites with Bronze Age roundhouses have now been excavated in Cornwall giving a boost to settlement research. In 1987 the major excavation of a Bronze Age village at Trethellan Farm, Newquay, offered the opportunity to comprehensively examine an entire settlement when seven roundhouses were discovered (Nowakowski 1991). Since then other sites have been investigated through developer-funded projects such as Penhale Moor, St Enoder (Nowakowski 1998), Scarcewater, St Stephen in Brannell (Jones and Taylor in press), and Pawton Farm, St Breock (Wardle 2004). At these sites groups of buildings have been examined and now fuller pictures of the character of settlement are beginning to emerge. To this we must add investigations of individual roundhouses (fig. 9.1) such as at Penhale Round, Fraddon (Nowakowski 1998), Callestick, Perranzabuloe (Jones 1998-99), Trevilson, Newlyn East (Jones and Taylor 2004), Trenowah, St Austell (Johns in prep), Boden Vean, St Anthony-in-Meneage (Gossip and Johns in press) and Carnon Gate, Feock (Gossip and Jones in prep). All, with the exception of Scarcewater, are sites located off the moors (Scarcewater is not on the moors but the group of three roundhouses lie on higher ground, Jones and Taylor in press).

Some of these buildings discovered at these sites have been fully excavated and more importantly, the majority have produced radiocarbon determinations. There are now over sixty scientific dates from eleven sites and it is apparent that for the latter half of the second millennium say, from 1500 to 1000 BC, the tradition of building roundhouses in wood and, in stone and wood, was very much a feature of the general lowland scene. These dates confirm the emergent national picture where settlements (that is groups of buildings), some accompanied by extensive field systems, were widespread across the landscapes of southern Britain (Bradley 2007; Yates 2007 and see Brean Down, Somerset, Bell 1990; Bestwall Quarry, Wareham, Ladle and Woodward 2009). Some, but by no means all, of the individual roundhouses and buildings dating to this period in Cornwall, and those which have been fully excavated, were constructed in purpose-dug hollows. Some have been interpreted as dwelling houses, that is, primarily residential, although it is apparent, that not all roundhouses even those found at the same sites, were used in the same way.

Building Resources

Recent excavations have shown that prehistoric buildings were built of natural resources: wood, mud, daub (clay) and stone. Evidence of varying combinations of wood (as charcoal), hardened/fired clay and a variety of different types of stone found in many of the excavated Cornish roundhouses would suggest that form and style were not solely dictated by resources only locally to hand and/or by geology alone. Although locally available resources would clearly have been important, it is also apparent that Bronze Age communities cast much wider nets. Access to locally managed woodland resources would clearly have been a priority for new build, but the use of stone is not solely a feature of upland houses and so access to suitable and appropriate building stone would also have been a consideration in the lowland zone. Over the past thirty or so years experimental archaeology in Britain has shown that the construction of a prehistoric roundhouse (fig.9.2) does not necessarily require a great deal of engineering skill but more a pragmatic approach combined with an awareness of how the superstructure holds itself together with optimisation and effectiveness (e.g., Reynolds 1982; Wood 1999).

Knowledge of the inherent properties of the building materials would also have been important and we can be certain that the Bronze Age builders understood the functional properties of the resources they employed, as, for example, in the types of wood used for construction. Mature oak and hazel (charcoal) is a common find on many excavations (e.g., Trethellan Farm, Trevisker and Gwithian: Nowakowski 1991; ApSimon and Greenfield 1972; Gale 2007). Oak is eminently suitable as a structural medium and provides sturdy upright posts for the main framework of a wooden superstructure, as well as for the main load-bearing wood, the rafters. Coppiced hazel provides a flexible medium for use in stakes, purlins and the withies suited for interior screens and fixtures and outer wattle walls. In a few examples, favourable preservation has ensured the actual survival of structural wood: during the excavation of a Bronze Age house [358] at Penhale Round in 1993, the physical charred timbers of a (once suspended) wooden (oak) planked floor was found (Earwood 1994).

There is now increasing evidence that not all new buildings were necessarily constructed of new materials. For example the stone wall which lined the deep hollow of the well-made roundhouse found at Callestick, Perranzabuloe (excavated in 1996), contained fragments of worked stones. Some have been identified as mullers and rubbing stones. These objects, originally derived from elsewhere, had been reused as walling material and petrographic analyses of the Callestick stones have shown that many of the items were not local but had come from a wide catchment area (Quinnell and Taylor in Jones 1998-99, 27-36). A cup-

FIG 9.2 WOODEN ROUNDHOUSES IN PROCESS OF RECONSTRUCTION AT SAVEOCK CELTIC VILLAGE IN CORNWALL IN 1992. THE TEMPLATES FOR THE BUILDINGS WERE BASED ON THE EXCAVATION PLANS OF ROUNDHOUSES EXCAVATED AT TRETHELLAN FARM, NEWQUAY IN 1987 (© STEVE HARTGROVES).

marked stone, presumably reused, was found built into the stone wall of a Bronze Age House [1079] at Gwithian, West Cornwall (Sturgess in Nowakowski et al. 2007, 31). Cup-marked stones were also found in association with structures at Trethellan Farm (Nowakowski 1991, fig 65). Conjoining fragments from the same large chunky Trevisker-decorated vessel were used as packing material for wooden posts within two neighbouring Bronze Age buildings found at Penhale Moor, St Enoder in 1994 (Nowakowski 1998; Nowakowski and Johns in prep). And at Trethellan Farm, Newquay, the outer wall of House 2222 (see below) was lined with distinctive large (non-local) spa quartz blocks: whether they were structural props or decorative, remains unresolved. Reycling resources which potentially once belonged to the distant ancestors (e.g. structural parts of former houses, objects etc) for reuse and build into new projects, would have harnessed latent power and promoted familial and group identity (Chapman 1994; Chapman 1999).

All these examples demonstrate that the materiality of the roundhouse was much more than the total sum of all its apparently efficient parts. In the drive to understand the mechanics of a roundhouse build, there remains the danger that historical processes and cultural traditions, part and parcel of an architectural build, may be overlooked. In a recent critique of the value of modern reconstructions of prehistoric roundhouses in Britain, Stephen Townend has made this point quite forcibly (2007). He has suggested that the 'raw' materials brought together in a single house build may have operated on many levels:

the actual building materials may have been meaningful (that is beyond straight efficiency and not necessarily because they were functionally 'ideal'), the places from where house building resources derived may have been culturally (and historically) significant, and their inclusion and placement in the building was likely to have been informed by a shared culture and ideology (2007, 103). The hand of the individual house builder may be invisible and any architect's 'signature' may be subsumed, but it would have been all too clear to those who participated in the house-building project (Townend 2007, 100).

Over time natural (organic and worked or refashioned) resources transform and decay and this must have implications for the intended use lives of buildings when they are brought together in a single build. Martin Bell has recently suggested that experimental archaeology, especially roundhouse reconstruction, has a great deal to offer in attempts to estimate the life histories of individual buildings (Bell 2009). Bell highlights the lessons to be learnt from the collapse of reconstructed prehistoric buildings such as Longbridge Deverill Cow Down House (built at Butser Ancient Farm, Hampshire) which was built in 1992, and which only after eighteen years has shown signs of serious decay. The roundhouse built at the Somerset Levels and Moors Centre outside Glastonbury, Somerset, started to collapse just after fourteen years when its wattle and daub walls no longer had the strength to support the roof. The roundhouses built at Saveock Celtic village, all based on the ground plans of Bronze Age buildings excavated at Trethellan Farm in Cornwall, started to fall to ruin, despite maintenance, within the last eighteen years (Jacqui Wood pers. comm. and see fig 9. 2.)

If, as Bell has suggested, the average life of a wooden roundhouse should perhaps be considered as ten to twenty years, then this clearly has implications for the expectations of the builders and users. How did Bronze Age communities regard their buildings? Were they built to last? When we survey the archaeological evidence looking for clues of the use-lives of roundhouses, how many show evidence for made-up occupation layers and floors? When they do how should we interpret this? When they do not does this mean that the interiors of houses were regularly cleaned out and then new floors relaid? How do we detect household or even genealogical timelines? Were these built into the templates for buildings, particularly for those we interpret as residential, that is the principal dwellings (Cleary 2006)? Such considerations would clearly have affected the length of time a building may appropriately be used and consequently how it may have been treated on its demise (see below). Woodward has recently noted that many post-built roundhouses excavated in southern Britain show little evidence for rebuild perhaps indicating that the occupants moved on only after one or two generations of use, and that life history of a building may be closely related to a particular family or individual (Ladle and Woodward 2009, 364). And if we detect evidence for major rebuild, what may this mean?

There is clear research potential in the detailed studies of roundhouses to contribute to the complex study of the relationships of people, building and place.

Tales from the south west

In this brief review, I would like to illustrate the variety of information now at our disposal by focussing on groups of buildings investigated at Gwithian (Nowakowski et al. 2007), Trevisker (ApSimon and Greenfield 1972) and Trethellan Farm (Nowakowski 1991). I will contrast these with the stories of buildings investigated at Callestick, Penhale Round and Penhale Moor (Jones 1998-9; Nowakowski 1998; Nowakowski and Johns in prep). The sites at Trevisker, Trethellan and Callestick are fully published (ApSimon and Greenfield 1972; Nowakowski 1991; Jones 1998-99). Detailed analyses of the histories of buildings investigated at Gwithian, Penhale Round and Penhale Moor are currently in hand but our observations to date allows us to set out current working interpretations (Nowakowski et al., 2007, Nowakowski 1998; Nowakowski and Johns forthcoming). It is clear that there is such a range of information now available for settlement found in the lowlands that any general picture will doubtless continue to change with future work. The stories from these sites do however provide a foundation upon which to build working models for settlement archaeology. I will show how their individual tales reveal insights into the evolution and character of settlements, and how these may fit into wider roles about how different landscape zones may have been regarded and used, revealing the importance of settlement and the concepts of place in the lives of Bronze Age communities in the south-west.

Gwithian

The discovery of a Bronze Age settlement by Charles Thomas at Gwithian in West Cornwall in the 1950s was a major advance in settlement research (Thomas 1958). The excavations were never fully written up but have recently been revisited and this has offered the opportunity to situate the results within current knowledge of buildings dating to this period (Nowakowski et al. 2007). The unique sequence of intact former land surfaces, which were later sealed beneath the sand dunes at Gwithian, and which recent scientific dating has confirmed spans the entire Bronze Age period (the best part of a 1,000 years), still remains unmatched in the south-west. Well-preserved ground plans of freestanding buildings lying within fields and enclosures (alongside direct evidence for ancient agricultural practices) were found. The following summary highlights some of the key features of the Bronze Age buildings found at Gwithian.

The earliest building [1642] found at Gwithian was a sub-circular wooden single-celled building which measured 7.5m in diameter, contained a single hearth and sported a porch which fronted its south-east facing doorway (site GMXV - Phase 1, fig. 9.3). The building was partly built into a levelled terrace but had not been erected in a purpose-dug hollow. Deep foundation gullies were found along the front of the building and these may well have held split posts or planked timbers: this wooden panelling would have made up the front wall of the house while to the side and rear, evidence for double-stake lined walls, with earth and/or mud cores, revealed a rather eclectic and varied build. This building of unusual design contained a shallow central unlined hearth and many finds, but there was very little indication of floor surfaces as the 'floor' was just worn-down bedrock (Nowakowski et al. 2007). Recent re-assessment has suggested that the building may well have had a single-phase use-life and only underwent piecemeal repair (contra Megaw 1976). The building lay within a wooden fenced enclosure. This enclosed and separated 'space' is also unusual when compared with other wooden buildings. The place may be interpreted as a 'homestead' and its position on an upper valley slope sets it apart. We presume it overlooked fields (Nowakowski 2009).

Currently there are two scientific dates (AMS dates) from finds associated with building [1642]. Both are from carbonised residues on fragments of 2 different vessels found on the house floor. One (OxA-14568) gave a determination of 3430 + 50 BP with a calibrated date range of 1890-1610 cal BC, and the other (OxA-14490), 2961 + 36 BP, calibrates to 1310-1040 cal BC (Hamilton, Marshall, Roberts, Ramsey and Cook in Nowakowski et al. 2007). Although these dates provide a cultural marker for the building they do not precisely date its construction and clearly further scientific dates are required. Its

FIG 9.3. GWITHIAN, CORNWALL. HOUSE 1642 (SITE GMXV). RECONSTRUCTING THE OUTLINES OF THE EARLIEST BRONZE AGE BUILDING WHICH LAY WITHIN A FENCED ENCLOSURE. THE DEEP GULLIES ARE AT THE FRONT OF THE BUILDING © MURRAY, GWITHIAN ARCHIVE.

remarkable preservation however must have been the result of its purposeful wholesale abandonment at the end of its use-life. It was sealed and its ground plan was protected when another other probable stone and wooden building [1503] was later built at this location (Nowakowski et al. 2007). This example of a building being replaced by another is a recurrent theme throughout the Gwithian Bronze Age story.

At the latter end of the Bronze Age sequence discovered at Gwithian a number of buildings were uncovered. These are assigned to the upper part of the sequence, phase 5, and which, on current scientific dating, is c 1300-900 BC (Hamilton, Marshall, Roberts, Ramsey and Cook in Nowakowski et al. 2007). During phase 5 there were a number of stone and wooden buildings of different architectural styles. The buildings formed a group and collectively can best be described as representing a farming hamlet, which perhaps served several related households (Nowakowski et al. 2007, fig 5). Some of the buildings were made of wood and some were made of stone and wood: their different styles show case varied aspects of vernacular architecture for this period.

This latest phase of settlement at Gwithian comprised five circular wooden buildings: each with distinctive individual histories. The earliest buildings were of wood and at some point in time, at least three were replaced with buildings made of wood and stone. All lay within an area between two north-south field walls, an area 30 sq metres in extent, and so would have been surrounded by fields and enclosures: some fields were under arable cultivation and some used for stock (Nowakowski 2009). At least three of these buildings could be described as 'houses', that is primarily residential. All were essentially timber post-built structures, each with central pebble-lined hearths, all had made-up floors and each showed some evidence of minor repair. Two of the buildings may have been workshops.

At site GMX 'House 1' two buildings [724] and [725] were found. The latest [724] was a circular wooden building: 6m in diameter. Fragments of daub and hardened clay discovered along its circumference suggest that it originally had an outer wall of wattle and daub. A number of floor surfaces survived within [724] alongside many finds of worked stone and bone tools. At its centre lay a pebble-lined hearth: a feature very typical of the Gwithian buildings for this period (fig.9.4). Building [724] had been built upon the site of an earlier wooden building [725]. This was also 6m in diameter. In this earlier building, a remarkable wooden bowl (filled with unfired clay and granite chips) was found set into its floor (Nowakowski et al., 2007, pl 11). A stone saddle quern and a pit full of stone tools were also found. Both were sealed by layers of unfired clay. Two long bones of a human infant and a second wooden bowl, again with human baby long bones,

FIG 9.4 GWITHIAN, CORNWALL. SITE GMX "HOUSE 1" 724/725 PHASE 5B. A PEBBLE-LINED HEARTH LAY IN THE CENTRE OF THE BUILDING. RANGING POLE IMPERIAL SCALE (©JVS MEGAW, GWITHIAN ARCHIVE).

were also found in the earlier building. On the south side of the building were a couple of clay-lined pits and at the rear of the building, a complete infant skeleton was found in a small pit. When the later building [724] was built over this area, all these earlier deposits were buried intact and undisturbed.

Both buildings, one built upon the other, were probable dwelling houses and the discovery of human remains within the earlier building gives it a marked personal story. At some stage the later building [724] appears to have been burnt down and across the area where it, and its earlier predecessor had once stood, broken pots and scatters of pot sherds were dumped. Sometime later a small stone enclosure was built over the area and this was subsequently partly buried by a midden.

The complex sequence of linked events revealed at site 'House 1' with its two buildings, one built upon the other, reveals time-depth and some interesting trends, which we see repeated elsewhere during this phase of settlement. Here an earlier building is replaced with another of the same size and apparently similar build. At Gwithian it is apparent that the wholesale make-over or rebuild of buildings is not uncommon. Parts of human bodies were deposited and secreted away into the earlier building. The new building is therefore built upon the tradition of the old respecting the earlier layers and history of the former building. This may signify how deeply personal and rooted the histories of some houses for this period may have been. How buildings are potentially re-fashioned, or not, and how they are treated at the end of their use-lives reveals something about people and their relationship to particular places in the wider landscape. Further analysis of the finds associated with both buildings is desirable (Sturgess and Lawson-Jones 2006).

To the south, two other buildings 'House 4' [1134/730] and 'House 5' [1085] were found (site GMIX). These too were probably dwelling houses. One, 'House 4', ([1134/730]), was oval (measured 7.5m N-S x 4.5m E-W). Compared to its immediate neighbour ('House 5', see below) it was quite spacious at least 33.75 sq m in size. It was built of wood and had wattle and daub outer walls. The fragment of a single stone axe mould was found in this building and this links to a fragment of the same piece found in House 1 [724] (see above and Quinnell in Nowakowski et al. 2007, 35-36). 'House 4' also contained wooden (and clay) basins (again filled with clay) and three pebble-lined hearths. A reddened diffused burnt clay layer recorded across the entire floor area suggests that on its abandonment, this building had been burnt down. A large number of (animal) bone pins, were found in House 4 as well as human skull fragments. Here again there is a close link between people and building signifying a personalised history. The fact that the building was burnt down may have been a deliberate act of closure cementing this relationship (see below).

The full extent of its immediate neighbour 'House 5' (GMIX) - the site of two successive buildings [1085/1079] - was not fully defined. A clear ground plan of the earlier wooden building [1085] is limited but it appears to have had a darkened floor and evidence for wooden beam slots (Sturgess and Lawson-Jones 2006). How this darkened horizon formed is unknown although it could suggest that the building may have had a suspended wooden floor or that it too had been burnt down. Contemporary with [724] was building [1079]. This circular building was 9.0m in diameter and had been built on the exact spot where the earlier wooden building [1085] had once stood (Nowakowski et al. 2007, pl 9). The architectural build of [1079] was distinctive and it had survived remarkably well: its walls comprised well-made stone-faced coursed walls (0.9m wide, with an earth and rubble core with 4-5 courses of stonework extant). Inside, parts of a made-up clay floor had survived. A small clay oven was built into its rear inner wall face. On its demise, rubbish was thrown into the interior. No attempt was made to dismantle or salvage the building stone. When excavated, it emerged as a ruined shell from the sandy layers which, ultimately, concealed it from view. Both these buildings had probably been dwelling houses.

The remains of a small post-built sub-circular building [1023], which had been interpreted by the excavators as a 'granary', were also found (site GMIX). This building was only 2.5m in diameter. Caches of pottery were found close by. Originally it may have had a raised floor (Sturgess and Lawson-Jones 2006). It is evidence that within these settlements some buildings were specially built to serve specific uses.

Gwithian: The Changing face of Village Life

During this phase at Gwithian the histories of the buildings portray a complex series of linked events that reveals the changing faces of a living village revealing something about settlement dynamics, fig.9.5). At Gwithian there is clear evidence for the co-existence of different types of buildings. On present evidence we may assume that at least two or three buildings during this phase were dwelling houses, that is places where people gathered together, prepared and ate food and slept. At least one building with its possible raised floor, appears to have served a special function. There was a large quantity and wide range of finds (pottery, worked stone, bone and flint tools, shale, Nowakowski et al. 2007, 32-37) associated with this phase and it is clear that other less substantial buildings may also have existed alongside working hollows, that is, open 'unroofed' spaces. These may have been the foci for activities such as bone and leather-working, metalworking and making pots. The picture is busy, suggestive of a vibrant thriving hamlet with lots going on.

In contrast to roundhouses found on some other sites in Cornwall, none of the buildings at Gwithian were erected in deep hollows. However with evidence for buildings being rebuilt on the same spot there is a sense of strong

Gwithian - the changing faces of village life

DWELLING HOUSE 1
Wooden roundhouse 725
Rebuilt as 724
Burnt down
Buried by stone enclosure and midden

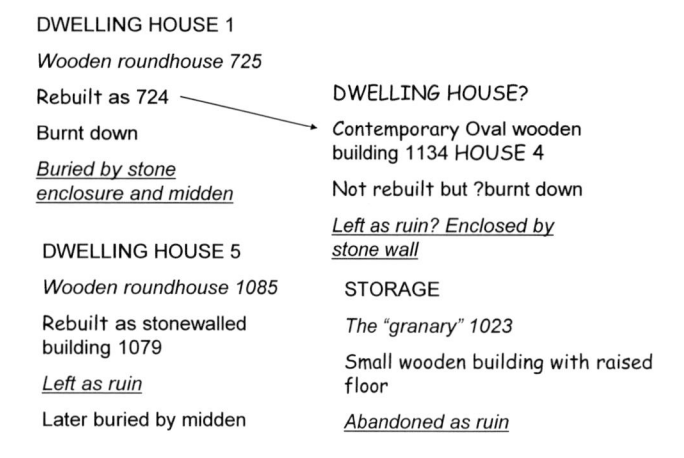

DWELLING HOUSE?
Contemporary Oval wooden building 1134 HOUSE 4
Not rebuilt but ?burnt down
Left as ruin? Enclosed by stone wall

DWELLING HOUSE 5
Wooden roundhouse 1085
Rebuilt as stonewalled building 1079
Left as ruin
Later buried by midden

STORAGE
The "granary" 1023
Small wooden building with raised floor
Abandoned as ruin

FIG 9.5 GWITHIAN, CORNWALL – PHASE 5 - CHARTING THE INDIVIDUAL BUILDING HISTORIES (THE SHARED FONTS INDICATE CONTEMPORARY EVENTS)

attachment to place. Such a bond to a particular tract of land is also evident throughout the long history of enclosure at Gwithian where it is clear that field walls are maintained and even remade.

Another significant result from Gwithian was evidence for field and enclosure boundaries. Our most comprehensive picture for the layout and pattern of enclosure dates to c. 1500 - 1200 cal BC during phase 3. By this time the physical map of the domesticated landscape appears well developed and this was maintained into subsequent phase 5. During phase 5 the houses lay surrounded by a network of enclosures: a large terraced field system (Nowakowski et al. 2007, figs 5-6 and Nowakowski 2009).

During the excavations two major boundaries were found: both survived as stone walls and both were aligned N-S up and down slope. Remarkably they were fixed very early in the sequence of enclosure at Gwithian (that is during phase 1: the earlier Bronze Age, see below). The eastern boundary in particular was a major fixture (Nowakowski et al. 2007, pl 5). No obvious local source of stone is available in the immediate vicinity, so the material for this wall (as indeed the houses) would have been brought to the site and could have been sourced at least one kilometre up the river valley. Such large quantities (hundreds of hand-sized stones), either carried, carted or barrowed to the site, revealed considerable resource gathering and investment. In its earlier manifestation this principal boundary had developed as an earth bank or lynchet, which had been created by ploughing. In one area of the site, within the shadow of the wall, four large pits were found. These were arranged in a line and were dug into the lynchet. At least two of the pits were sealed by slates and small pebble mounds. The pits contained quantities of burnt bone, shell, snails and charcoal. Some of the bone was animal and some was human. The quantities of human bone varied (each averaged about 300-400g). Recent identification has shown that these represent the partial remains of at

FIG 9.6 FIXING THE LAND AT BRONZE AGE GWITHIAN SITE GMX20. LAYER 3 LYNCHET BUILD UP OVER EARLIER PLOUGHMARKS AND LATER FIELD WALL – CREMATION PITS WERE DUG ALONG THE LINE OF THE EARLIER (PHASE 1) BOUNDARY. POSITION OF ONE PIT IS MARKED BY B/W SCALE. IMPERIAL RANGING POLE (© JVS MEGAW, GWITHIAN ARCHIVE)

least four adults (McKinley 2004). Later two pits had been ploughed over (during phases 4-3) and then they became sealed under the stone wall during phase 5. This boundary had a demonstrably long history and its ongoing maintenance was marked. On a practical level these boundaries served as field and enclosure walls, their stone build would trap moisture in the thin soils of this coastal sandy landscape.

Given their long histories of continuous investment, like the houses, it would suggest that the fixing of boundaries was considered important (fig.9.6). As we have seen with the buildings, this behaviour appears to signal strong attachment to land. At Gwithian it would therefore seem that at least some of the dead were used as a poignant resource in the fixing of boundaries in a land that is already deeply rooted, personalised and owned. The locations of these pits containing human bone do not appear random. They have been deliberately sited along an important boundary which already has a significant history and the acts of deposition here would seem to accentuate this by legitimising the boundary and committing it to long-term memory, and by doing so building up a community history.

We could interpret these human remains as representative parts of individuals from different generations linked by the same kinship community, whose relationship with this tract of land had long deep familial ties. Their remains deposited and mixed up with other settlement debris, may be read as token symbols taken from the life of the settlement which are deposited into land owned and controlled by their dead ancestors. In this they are truly bonded with and to the land. One can only guess at the rites that may well have accompanied such events. The historical tradition of 'beating the parish bounds' practised widely throughout medieval Christian England (Hutton 1996, 285-287), but known to have derived from Roman fertility customs, were regarded as key fertility ceremonies which not only blessed the fields, the crops, but reinforced the power of tenure, ownership, and exorcised the land to drive out potential evil spirits.

As we have seen, this is not the only context in which the dead appear at Gwithian. The discovery of human bones within the buildings, the boundaries, and in the middens at Gwithian, reveals a practice now widely recorded for Bronze Age settlement across Britain and Ireland (e.g. Brück 1995; Parker Pearson et al. 2004; Cleary 2005). The physical presence of the dead in the landscape of the living sheds considerable light on the many different levels that living spaces may have operated during the Bronze Age. Ethnography and anthropology has shown that the presence of the 'token' dead in living spaces are likely to be varied and complex (e.g. Barley 1997). Jo Brück has suggested that the deposition of the bones of the dead within a settlement within particular places (for example under the threshold stone) may mark significant events in a community's history as well as the history of occupation within particular buildings. The curation of human bones may for example link the occupants of a particular building directly with their past as the bones of former family members are carefully curated to ensure, for example, the good fortune and future health of surviving kin (Brück 2001). The curation of human bones into buildings could also denote ownership and affirmation of a claim to land. In doing so, the building may acquire or even have been built with a familial personality that is tied to individual people and households. Deposition of bones may also be part and parcel of the life-cycle of a building perhaps pre-empting closure and abandonment .

The latest phase of Bronze Age settlement at Gwithian is marked by such a huge amount of settlement debris: tons of pottery, worked stone, animal and human bone, flints, daub, burnt clay, shells, seeds and animal bone (Quinnnell and Thorpe in Nowakowski et al. 2007, 33-37). Finds were found in pits and hollows within the buildings and surrounding areas around the buildings. Parts of the settlement space may well have been zoned for particular activities. Assessment of the bone assemblage has identified on-site bone working as unfinished bone tools were found alongside bone waste (Riddler 2007). We also know that throughout its history, attempts were made at Gwithian made to bulk up the soils within the fields by adding organic and settlement waste (Guttmann 2006). It is apparent that the Gwithian Bronze Age communities were active composters with piles of settlement debris were stock-piled up against field walls to decompose before being added to the soils. When this final phase of settlement at Gwithian declined, the buildings appeared to have been surrounded by smouldering piles of rubbish and were then ultimately buried by the rubbish. This abandoned landscape would have been marked by a series of undulating mounds which many centuries later were buried by sand (Nowakowski et al. 2007, 13). While ensuring the intact survival of what lay beneath, the settlement rubbish created at Bronze Age Gwithian clearly played a central role in wider cultural practice related to systematic protection and concealment, a trait which has now been increasingly documented at other settlements (see below).

Trevisker – Burning Down the House!

At the same time these extraordinary discoveries were being made at Gwithian, Arthur ApSimon and Ernest Greenfield were excavating a small Bronze Age farmstead at Trevisker at St Eval in mid Cornwall (ApSimon and Greenfield 1972). Two circular timber wooden roundhouses A and D were found at Trevisker and these lay alongside each other and were contemporary with other slighter buildings. There was evidence that buildings at Trevisker underwent repair and rebuild.

The largest house, House A, was a wooden circular roundhouse 8m in diameter, which had been erected in a worn shallow hollow. Its conical roof was held up by a double post-ring, the eaves of which would have rested on an outer wattle and daub wall. It had a central stone-lined hearth and towards the rear wall, the settings for at least three upright weaving looms were found. A sump with stone capping suggests an internal drain. Stone-capped drains have not been found on many lowland roundhouses to date but were a feature of the roundhouses excavated at Stannon on Bodmin Moor (Mercer 1970). At Trevisker ApSimon suggested that repeated modification to the interior of House A (replacement posts and fittings) is an indication of piecemeal repair and maintenance. House A has been interpreted as a residential building which, on abandonment, was burnt down.

Neighbouring and contemporary house D was also a circular wooden building, but was slightly smaller at 7m diameter. It too appeared to have a double-post ring that upheld the roof and had a wattle and daub outer wall. Its uneven floor surface was worn away by wear and tear suggesting some history of use but unlike its neighbour A, House D did not appear to have been repaired or refurbished. On its demise, another building house B – this time a rectangular building of stone and wood – was built upon it. The detail of D is much obscured by the later building B but ApSimon does suggest that D was also a likely dwelling house. The later building B is difficult to distinguish in plan but because of its lack of a hearth, occupation debris and finds, ApSimon suggested it may have been a byre or storage place. Another building house C was also identified but this was difficult to interpret because so little remained.

The settlement at Trevisker can best be interpreted as a homestead, for one or perhaps two households. Here again is some evidence for different types of buildings serving different needs. House A is the likely dwelling space alongside House B a store. That D also a dwelling house, was replaced, again shows that buildings are subject to adaptation and change and were likely not to have been built for ever. The act of deliberately burning down the house, if interpreted correctly, is of interest. Deliberate house-burning has been documented as a feature of central and eastern European prehistory and would have been an awesome spectacle for any community to witness. John Chapman has reviewed the continuing debate on the many reasons why buildings burnt down and has suggested that if the fires were deliberate, then this could be interpreted as an act of transformation and closure as the 'natural' life-cycle of a house and its occupants comes full circle (Chapman 1999 and see Tringham 1991).

Different types of buildings in different landscapes

The Bronze Age sites at Gwithian and Trevisker highlight the variety of settlement that is likely to have existed across the entire lowland Cornwall and other regions of south west during the second Millennium BC. As more and more land was enclosed and 'domesticated' through enclosure, farmsteads, hamlets and larger settlements all probably, co-existed across all landscape zones (coastal, upland and lowland) practising arable and stock farming. Alongside this some settlements may have been specialised (see below) where buildings performed specific uses. At Penhale Moor and Penhale Round, Fraddon, a handful of unusual Bronze Age buildings indicate how certain places in the landscape may well have been specialised at this period (Nowakowski and Johns forthcoming and see below).

In early 1994 the remains of two wooden buildings were discovered at Penhale Moor, Fraddon (Nowakowski 1994; Nowakowski and Johns forthcoming). These lay alongside one another in an arrangement similar to the Trevisker homestead. Both structures were erected in shallow hollows and surrounded by a scatter of pits and smaller working hollows. The buildings appear to sit in an enclosure. The larger building [1013] may primarily have been a residential building although its interior is dominated by a number of very large pits and its build is of an unusual design: more sub-circular than strictly round, the main outer wall appears to have been a sturdy stake fence line but this did not to appear to have run full circuit, so that the main façade of the building (facing west) was open and unprotected. The roof was upheld by a single post-ring positioned less than 1 metre in from the house wall (Nowakowski and Johns forthcoming). Its neighbour, [1018], was sub-rectangular, of simple wooden build, and distinguished by a notable lack of interior features.

No formal midden deposits were found at Penhale Moor and the overall poor preservation and general absence of plant remains for cereal cultivation and food processing could suggest that these buildings performed specialist roles. Current analysis of the palaeoenvironmental data from this site as identified a variety of both wild and domesticated plants remains which may be indicative of a more or less rough and ready setting, with the suggestion that the immediate surrounding landscape was partly scrubby and not wholly improved. Plant macrofossils were scarce with grain, chaff fragments and weeds found in very low numbers. This may suggest small-scale daily processing of cereals prior to cooking (Wendy Carruthers pers comm; Nowakowski and Johns forthcoming).

The small oval building found during the excavations at Penhale Round in 1993 adds further evidence of the variety now being found across these landscapes. Here a wooden building [358], was replaced by one of wood and stone, and both were erected in a small worn hollow (6m x 5m in size). The earlier wooden building without any distinguishing interior features apart from a suspended wooden floor was burnt down. Its stone replacement was later systematically abandoned when the hollow was filled in with pottery and stonework so that all traces of the building were concealed from view (Nowakowski 1998; Nowakowski 2001; Nowakowski and Johns forthcoming). Given the absence of hearths and general lack of plant remains for both structures the Penhale Round Bronze Age building, found as a solitary structure, has not been interpreted as a dwelling house and like its nearby neighbours (Penhale Moor site lies less than ¼ mile to the west), may have played a specialised role.

The excavation of a single roundhouse found during pipeline work at Callestick in mid Cornwall is further evidence that points up anomalies within this growing repertoire of Bronze Age buildings now emerging from the wider excavation scene. Callestick was a well-made stone and wooden roundhouse without any distinguishing features such as a central hearth or floors although the building appeared to have had an unusually long and low porch. It was built in a deep hollow and its stone wall, which lined the inner face of the hollow, was well-made and contained fragments of worked stones, such as mullers and rubbing stones clearly reused as walling material. Little within the interior gives an indication of how the building may originally have been used since most of the finds (375 sherds from at least 5 vessels) relate to the building's abandonment. Callestick has been interpreted as a ritual building, perhaps for the storage of the dead, set aside from possible close by settlement. On its demise the building appears to have been systematically filled-in, with the walls kicked in and quartz stones set around its circumference (Jones 1998-9). Another anomalous building is a possible sub-rectangular building of probable Middle Bronze Age date which was found close to a landscape setting of timber post circles found at Tremough, Penryn (Gossip and Jones 2007, 21). There was limited direct evidence for a domestic settlement per se at Tremough, which may have been located close by, but Tremough adds further evidence of how different types of buildings may have operated in different places at this period.

In recent years Bronze Age circular wooden farm buildings and other less substantial structures have also been found in Devon, for example during the A30 Honiton road scheme in east Devon (Fitzpatrick et al. 1999). At Castle Hill a small wooden building was found lying within a co-axial field system alongside other 2 and 3 post wooden 'structures'. Given its lack of a hearth and few finds, this roundhouse has been interpreted as a temporary farm building perhaps used more for the storage of animal feed. At Castle Hill, excavation was limited but it is further indication of the varied roles of roundhouses. At Patteson's Cross, two more buildings were found. One, a simple wooden post-ring building, lay in a small compound, but another, again a simple wooden post-ring building, seems to have stood on its own out in the fields. No floors or hearths were found and finds were few. There was sparse evidence for cereal remains and the buildings have been interpreted as seasonally used and lying within in a pastoral zone (Fitzpatrick et al. 1999, 73-90).

At Hayne Lane, near Honiton, a small enclosed Bronze Age farmstead was also excavated. This comprised a large dwelling double-post ring roundhouse standing alongside a smaller roundhouse. One has been interpreted as a dwelling building, and the other (smaller) used for textile and food production, an arrangement not too dissimilar to the scale and character of Trevisker in Cornwall. A number of raised buildings have been interpreted as granaries (Fitzpatrick et al. 1999, 99-129). Interestingly, at the very few lowland sites of this period that have now been discovered in Devon, none of the roundhouses appeared to have been built in hollows.

Trethellan – A Model village?

My final case study is Trethellan Farm, a site excavated in 1987, and still to date, the most comprehensive excavation of a settlement for this period in the 2nd millennium BC (Nowakowski 1991). The site was found by accident during the construction of a housing estate on the edge of Newquay by the Gannel estuary. The key thing about Trethellan, like Gwithian, was exceptional preservation. There were two reasons for this. Firstly, the way the Bronze Age settlement was abandoned at the hands of its inhabitants, and secondly, the fact that the entire site was covered by a massive overburden of soil over two metres deep. The latter phenomenon is difficult to clearly explain because it looked as though at sometime at the end of the first millennium BC, a massive volume of soil had moved wholesale down slope obliterating all traces of the terrace. This movement of soil had not been caused solely by ploughing (Macphail in Nowakowski 1991, 156-160).

In plan the Bronze Age settlement at Trethellan Farm comprised at least seven roundhouses, each variously built of wood and stone and these all lay next to each other, respecting each others space, strung along a natural terrace on the south-facing slopes of the Gannel estuary. Each roundhouse, except for one, had been erected in a purpose-dug hollow. These hollows varied in size and depth. Radiocarbon dates showed a history of settlement for around 300 years 1200-900 BC (Nowakowski 1991). This village is therefore part of the contemporary lowland scene alongside Trevisker and the latest phase of settlement at Gwithian.

At Trethellan, the village appeared to have a formal arrangement with the three larger residential/dwelling houses located on the east and the four smaller buildings on the west (fig.9.7). All were roundhouses and all, with the exception of one, had evidence for minor repair and maintenance but none showed wholesale rebuild and there was no evidence that any of the buildings had been burnt down. The buildings appeared to have performed specific constant roles, with distinct activities were taking place in the different parts of the terrace and this overall plan presents a rather tidy arrangement: was Trethellan a model village? Those buildings that have been interpreted as dwelling houses were architecturally more robust and different from those whose uses may have been flexible and far more fluid. In addition, there were unroofed spaces

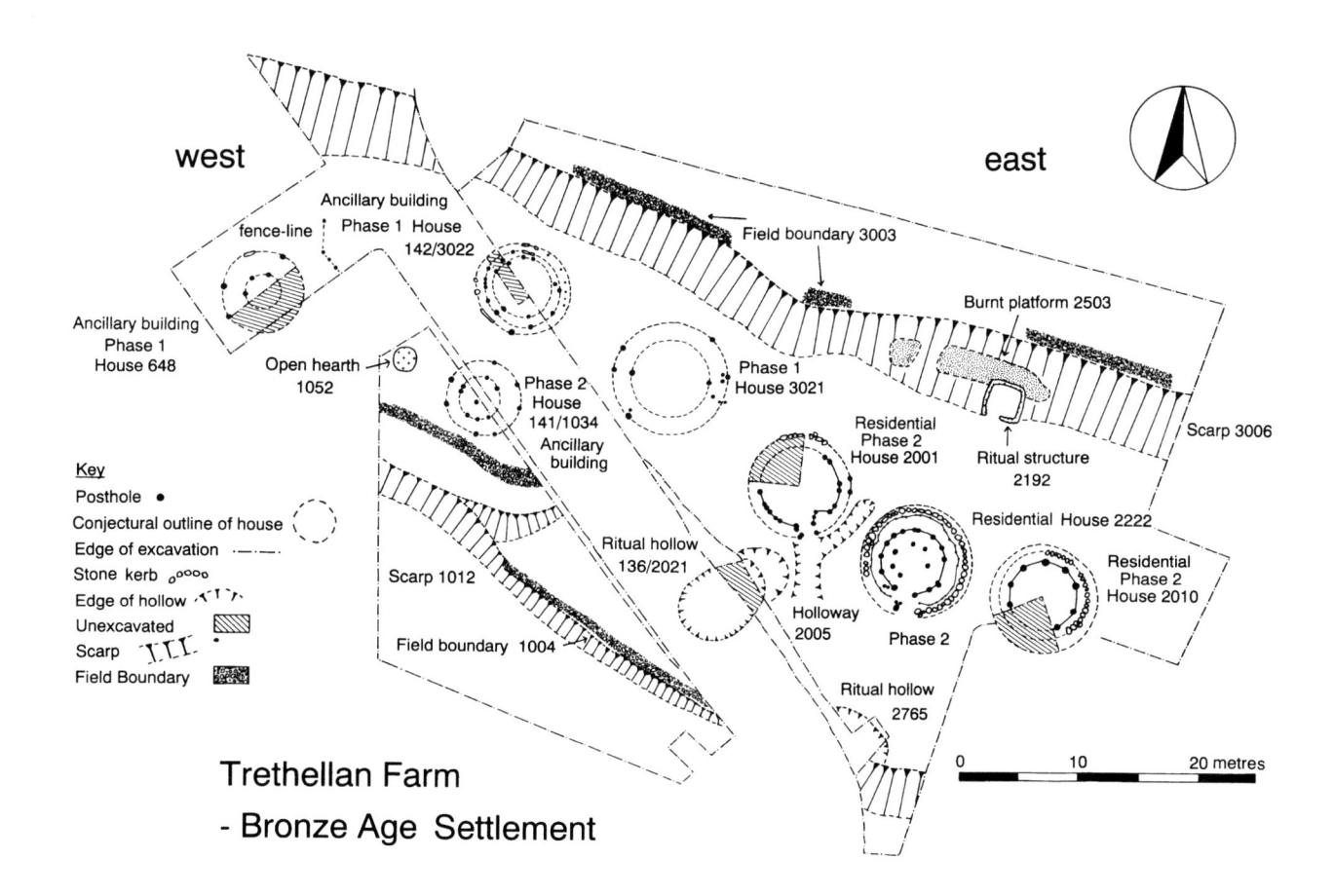

FIG. 9.7. TRETHELLAN FARM

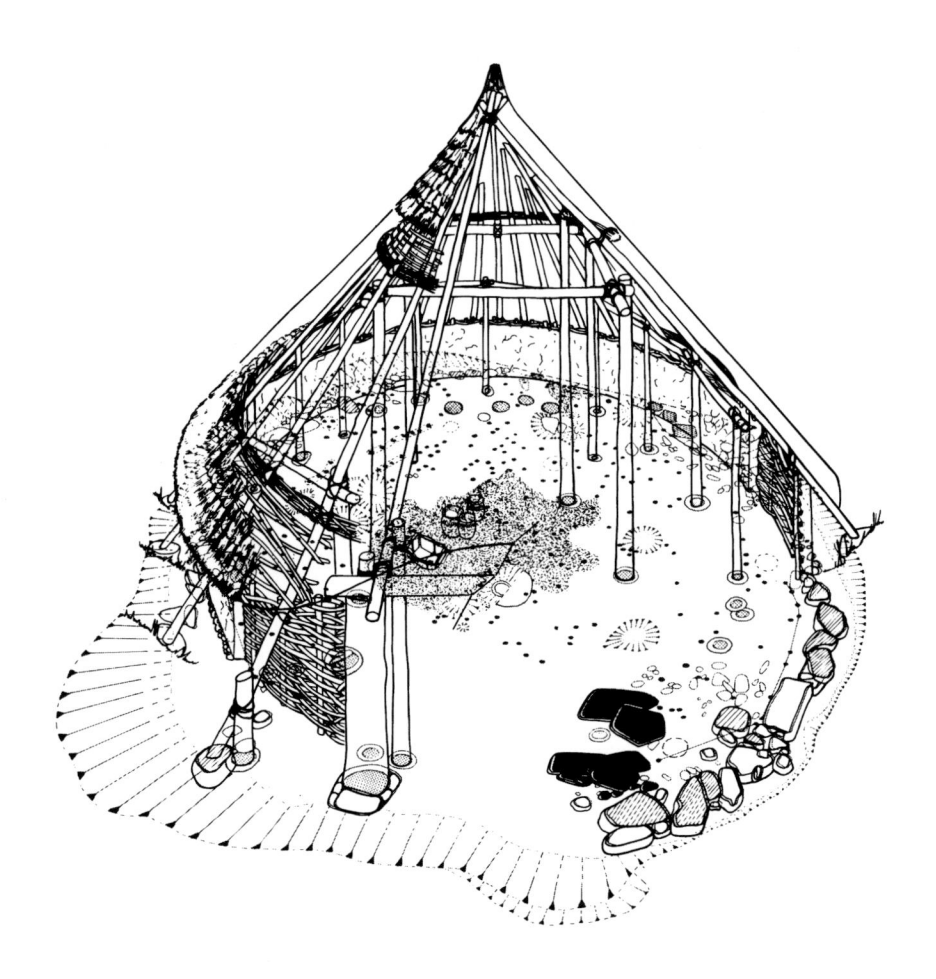

FIG. 9.8 RECONSTRUCION OF TRETHELLAN HOUSE

within the settlement, which were the foci for the activities that involved the frequent burning of small fires alongside the burial of odd deposits. At the back of the settlement, built into the foot of a slope, was an extraordinary square stone-built building with a slanting roof, which was flush with the angle of the slope, which would have blended the building into the slope. It seems to have been infrequently used (Nowakowski 1991, 96-100, fig. 9.9).

House 2001 has been interpreted as one of the residential houses at Trethellan. At 9m in diameter, this circular wooden building had been erected in an exceptionally deep partly lined hollow. It had a south east facing porched doorway with a paved threshold. A paved and kerbed pathway therefore lead up and in through the doorway and this was maintained and regularly relaid during the use-life of the building (Nowakowski 1991, fig 9.8). The roof was upheld by a double post-ring, with some evidence for repair and refurbishment. Within three successive floors built up on another suggested a long history of use. Central slated-lined hearths were found and each time a new floor was laid the new hearth was built upon the exact same spot as the previous one. A rather unusual square slate-lined box [2304] lay close to the central hearth during phase 3 (Nowakowski 1991, fig 6). This was filled with charcoal, some seeds and a few finds. Perhaps it was a small closed oven or an ash box, which worked rather like a cloam oven.

Cloam ovens were, and they a feature of south-western Britain in historical times were very efficient.

Dug into the successive floors in House 2001 were pits. Some contained finds: a perfect complete fine-grained saddle quern had been concealed in one large early pit ([2527], Nowakowski 1991, fig 5). Under this lay two rubbing stones, one of fine biotite granite and the other of sandstone, apparently specially selected and hidden away (Nowakowski 1991, 21). Throughout this building's history the way the interior was used appeared organised and formally arranged mirroring earlier arrangements. Towards the end of its occupancy, another very large and heavy granite saddle quern was placed into another very large pit ([2027] Nowakowski 1991, 25). Under this too a collection of 7 rubbing stones or mullers lay concealed. Here there are clear similarities with the kinds of behaviour discovered in the Gwithian houses where wooden bowls were found set into floor surfaces and then sealed from view (see above). At Trethellan and Gwithian, objects which were likely to have been closely linked to the individuals who lived in the houses had been deliberately buried at key moments in the buildings' histories.

Standing next to house 2001 was roundhouse 2222. Interpreted as a dwelling house it appeared to have a simpler history than its western neighbour. At 9.5m

FIG 9.9 TRETHELLAN FARM, NEWQUAY. THE UNUSUAL STONE BUILT RITUAL STRUCTURE 2192 DISCOVERED AT THE REAR OF THE BRONZE AGE VILLAGE IN 1987. IT HAD A SIDE ENTRANCE AND A PRISTINE FLOOR WHICH SUGGESTED THAT WAS INFREQUENTLY ENTERED. THE LOW SINGLE PITCH ROOF MIRRORED THE NATURAL SLOPE AND THE INTERIOR WOULD HAVE BEEN QUITE DARK AND COOL. ON ABANDONMENT THE ENTIRE BUILDING WAS FILLED IN WITH STONE RUBBLE AND COMPLETELY CONCEALED FROM VIEW (© TRETHELLAN FARM ARCHIVE, HE, CORNWALL COUNCIL).

diameter, this was the second largest building on the settlement (Nowakowski 1991, table 15). It had been erected in a fairly deep hollow that was deeper at the rear than at the front. The hollow was lined with distinctive large quartz blocks. The roof was held up by a double post-ring and the outer wall was made of wattle and daub (fig 9.8). In common with its neighbour 2001, some slate paving had been laid across the threshold area and fed into the house. Within only one clear intact floor surface was identified into which animal teeth, burnt clay, charcoal as well as bits of pot had been trodden. At the back of the house a very deep pit [2640] (Nowakowski 1991, fig 16c) had been cut through the floor and this was lined with a pot, perhaps some evidence for below-ground food storage. If so this was unusual, as storage pits have not been identified within other Cornish Bronze Age roundhouses to date, although some of the large jars identified within the Trevisker repertoire are considered for storage use. At just under 6,000 sherds (weighing 78.8 kg) the Bronze Age pottery assemblage from Trethellan is the largest yet found for this period in Cornwall. These fragments are from large and medium sized vessels, all are highly decorated with the familiar cord-impressions, incisions and fingernails motifs, characteristic of Trevisker ware. The majority of pots were used for storage, food preparation and consumption (Woodward and Cane 1991). Analysis of the animal fats found as residues on the insides of some vessels have shown that dairying was important at Trethellan so perhaps the storage of milk and diary products was important (Copley et al. 2003).

In the centre of house 2222, the partial remains of a male adult burial was found in an unusual shaped pit. This 'burial' pit had cut into two underlying hearths and was then, in turn, buried under ashy hearth spreads accompanied by a slate-lined ash box or oven [2292] (Nowakowski 1991, fig 16a). The body had been buried under the hearth during the routine occupation of the building. No other human bone was found at Trethellan. That any survived at all is quite remarkable but the occurrence of the body under the hearth is further evidence of how some roundhouses brought the world of the dead together with that of the living.

Alongside the three dwelling houses were other roofed spaces at Trethellan; all other types of wooden buildings and (with the exception of one), all built in hollows although these were much shallower than the residential houses. These all contained huge quantities of finds. In these buildings distinct floor surfaces were less easy to identify and indeed in one, the floor surface was worn bedrock. They all were in use at the same time but they did not display the formally arranged interiors so marked in eth residential buildings. Indeed these inner spaces were rather messy indicating flexible uses. They have been interpreted as ancillary buildings, perhaps stores and workshops, where a whole range of activities: the storage and preparation of food, leather and bone working, drying and smoking meat and fish, butchering animals, and even perhaps small-scale metalworking took place. Hearths in these buildings tended to be more haphazard, diffuse and not necessarily centrally placed. Indeed a variety of different types of hearths were found in these buildings at Trethellan that contrast with the central slate-lined affairs in the residential buildings. Some comprised no more than unlined pits (eg [70] in 142/30220), fired clay mounds studded with pebbles, or raised settings of flat slates over which hardened fired clay had baked to form a hot plate (eg [605] in 648 and [1053] in 141/1034). In one building 142/3022 a collapsed domed furnace [3035] was found (Nowakowski 1991, fig 21).

At Trethellan there was evidence for all aspects of domestic life covering food preparation and storage, craft activities and communal living. An integral part of this was clear evidence of many aspects of ritualised behaviour expressed in a number of ways: the structured deposition of unusual deposits within the buildings and hollows, the quiet dark space offered by ritual structure 2192 (fig. 9.9) which lay at the back of the village, the careful curation of human bone in one of the buildings alongside the frequent deposition, and the concealment of selected deposits, like crushed muscle shell and animal bone such as a cut red deer antler. The site was marked by the way all traces of the village were systematically concealed on abandonment when quantities of settlement debris were dumped into the hollows where the buildings had once stood (Nowakowski 1991; 2001). The spaces between the buildings were markedly clean and more-or-less find-free and intriguingly there were no conjoins between the finds associated with individual buildings despite a thorough examination of the large pottery collection during analysis (Woodward and Cane 1991). In this the treatment of the roundhouses, on their demise, appears key and it could be suggested that the time for abandonment was predetermined. In some respects this is in contrast to the way the settlement at Gwithian evolves with its evidence for buildings being remade with the new built on the old, but it also shares some similarities on the way settlement debris was dumped in and over the buildings on their demise.

Emerging themes

The individual tales from buildings investigated at Gwithian, Trevisker and Trethellan present fairly full pictures of how varied some Bronze Age settlements may have developed. The detailed excavations of individual roundhouses shows that even within the same setting there maybe major differences between what is going on in and around individual buildings, major differences in their use as well as treatment on abandonment. It is apparent that not all buildings were obvious dwelling houses and that this was a period when specialist buildings emerged clearly as part of the wider vernacular scene (e.g., Callestick, Penhale Moor and Penhale Round). Within the settlements, buildings are likely to have played a variety of roles. There is also increasing evidence now for special treatment on the abandonment for some buildings. That this was not wholesale practice is clear as many of the upland roundhouses appear to have been left to ruin. Some of these seem to have been adapted for reuse such as those excavated at Bodrifty, Madron (Dudley 1956) and Kynance Gate, the Lizard (Thomas 1960). At both sites, Bronze Age finds indicated that some earlier buildings had survived and were adapted for reuse in the Iron Age. When Ivor Thomas excavated some stone roundhouses at Kynance Gate on the Lizard in the 1950s, he suggested that the buildings were probably built in the Middle Bronze Age and that these were later reoccupied in the Iron Age when people just moved into the empty ruins and laid down new floors. The sites were later abandoned and left to nature to survive today as hut circles.

The deliberate and systematic abandonment of houses (death by burial) may be an indication that some roundhouses were constructed with a built in time-code in mind. This is alongside other forms of behaviour such as the evidence for the wholesale rebuild of buildings (new build on old) and the intriguing evidence that some houses may have been deliberately burnt down. Elsewhere I have suggested that one of the buildings at Penhale Moor may indeed have been 'ritually killed', as a poorly preserved copper alloy side-looped spearhead was found piercing the upper layers at a 70% angle and looked as if it had been thrust into the ground (Nowakowski 2001, 145; Nowakowski and Johns forthcoming). More detailed analysis of these emergent traits is clearly required as more roundhouses are fully excavated in the future. Other sites in lowland Cornwall have produced varied evidence suggestive too of the deliberate abandonment of some buildings such as Callestick (Jones 1998-9), Boden, St Anthony in Meneage (Gossip and Johns in press) and at Scarcewater, Pennance (Jones and Taylor in press). Andy Jones has recently suggested that the kinds of ritualized practices of abandonment documented at some Cornish Bronze Age roundhouses may have drawn upon Early Bronze Age traditions associated with the performance rituals played out at barrows (Jones 2008). On the abandonment of the building at Callestick and one of the largest of three roundhouses found at Scarcewater, Jones suggests that the buildings took on the appearances of cairns (Jones 1998-9; Jones and Taylor in press).

Looking Forward

The traditional view of the Bronze Age roundhouse is changing. These buildings were clearly more than just architectural constructs and recent studies have heightened their potential variety as living and lived in spaces. Over the past twenty-five years the detailed investigations of individual buildings in Cornwall have brought alive their stories allowing the living histories of the people who built and used them to be told. There is clearly more investment in some buildings than in others and signs of specialised treatment, perhaps through such processes as planned abandonment and rebuilding, may be linked to personalised histories and community identities. These studies elevate the previously overlooked cultural weight of the roundhouse. It is now clear it may reveal something deeply symptomatic about the roles of buildings and communities' relationships with and to place, not least through historical ties and bonds with particular tracts of land (e.g., Gwithian: Nowakowski 2001 and Nowakowski 2006; 2009). After all, the body under the hearth at Trethellan, and the young peoples' bones buried in the house at Gwithian, were hardly accidental deposits.

The results of recent work on roundhouses in the lowlands also clearly has an impact on past ideas about sizes of populations at such settlements and the ways different types of settlement may have evolved and operated in different landscape zones. The uplands of the south west are characterised by the survival of large numbers of groups of roundhouses (cf., Bodmin Moor, Johnson and Rose 1994) where past studies have tended to assume large settled communities (for example Stannon, Mercer 1970 and Leskernick, Bender et al 2008). Evidence from the excavated sites discovered in the lowlands make it clear that not all buildings within a group may have been used in the same ways and therefore calculating settlement size on the basis of numbers of buildings is a crude exercise. The general paucity of finds seemingly characteristic of those few wholly excavated upland buildings, is of interest as such sparseness could reflect multiple and sporadic use over longer periods of time and this may have been part and parcel of their build for many appeared to have been left to ruin as empty shells when finely abandoned.

Themes for the Future.

Future research on the Bronze Age roundhouse has much to gain by study of a number of emergent themes. Work on roundhouses has much to offer and these buildings should not be perceived as a uniform architectural phenomenon. Their clear variety is likely to reveal varied functions and meanings. That buildings can be adapted and serve multiple uses is all too clear. Increasing evidence for repair and maintenance has significance for ideas about permanence and the idea of what constitutes a settlement. What does it mean if a building is refashioned? Is this affirmation of tenure and ownership alongside familial and community attachment to particular places? Or something else? It is also apparent that deliberate abandonment of buildings may not be wholesale cultural practice during the Bronze Age and that special treatment for some buildings may point to how these once roofed structures were regarded by their builders and users. The contrasting stories, apparent in the histories and treatment of buildings in upland zones, requires further scrutiny. Were they all just left to ruin and random reuse? And finally the materiality of the roundhouse is an area ripe for further research although such research can only be advanced by the comprehensive excavations of individual roundhouses. It is clear that when opportunities arise we need to broaden our interpretative approaches to the study of buildings to animate their remains and bring their stories alive!

Bibliography

ApSimon, A. M. and Greenfield, E. 1972. The excavation of the Bronze Age and Iron Age settlement at Trevisker Round, St Eval, Cornwall. *Proceedings of Prehistoric Society* 38, 302-381.

Barley, N. 1997. *Dancing on the Grave. Encounters with Death.* London, Abacus.

Bell, M. 1990. Brean Down Excavations 1983-1987. English Heritage Archaeology Reports 15. London.

Bell, M. 2009. Experimental Archaeology: changing science agendas and perceptual perspectives, in M. Allen, N. Sharples and T O'Conner (eds.), *Land and People, Papers in memory of John G. Evans*, 31-45, Prehistoric Society Research Paper 2. Oxford, Oxbow.

Bender, B. Hamilton, J. and Tilley, C. 2008. *Stone Worlds. Narrative and Reflexivity in Landscape Archaeology*, Left Coast Press.

Bradley, R. 2007. *The Prehistory of Britain and Ireland*, Cambridge World Archaeology, Cambridge University Press.

Brück, J. 1995. A place for the dead: the role of human remains in Late Bronze Age Britain, *Proceedings of Prehistoric Society* 61, 245-277.

Brück, J. 1999a. What's in a settlement? Domestic practice and residential mobility in early Bronze Age southern England, in J. Brück and M. Goodman (eds.), *Making Places in the Prehistoric World*, 52-75. London, University College Press.

Brück, J. 1999b. Ritual and Rationality: some problems of interpretation in European archaeology, *European Journal of Archaeology* 2, no 3, 313-344

Brück, J. 2001. Body metaphors and technologies of transformation in the English Middle and Late Bronze Age, in J. Brück (ed.), *Bronze Age Landscapes Tradition and Transformation*, 149-160. Oxford, Oxbow.

Brück, J. and Goodman, M. (eds.) 1999. *Making Places in the Prehistoric World.* London, University College Press.

Burgess, C. 1976. The Gwithian mould and the forerunners if South Welsh axees, in Megaw 1976, 69-75 (appendix II).

Chapman, J. 1994. The Living, the Dead and the Ancestors, in J. Davis, (ed.), *Ritual and Rembrance. Responses to Death in Human Societies*, 40-85. Sheffield Academic Press.

Chapman, J. 1999. Deliberate house-burning in the prehistory of central and eastern Europe, in *Glyfer och arkeologiska run: En vänbok till Jarl Nordbladh*, 113-116. Gotarc Series A. (3). Göteborg: University of Göteborg Press

Christie, P. 1986. Cornwall in the Bronze Age. *Cornish Archaeology.* 25, 81-110.

Cleary, K. 2005. Skeletons in the closet: the dead among the living on Irish Bronze Age settlements, *The Journal of Irish Archaeology*, Vol XIV, 23-37.

Cleary, K. 2006. Irish Bronze Age Settlements: more than meets the eye? *Archaeology Ireland*, Vol 20, no 2, 18-21.

Copley, M.S. Berstan, R. Dudd, S.N. Doherty, G. Mukherjee, A.J. Straker, V. Payne, S. and Evershed, R.P. 2003. Direct chemical evidence for widespread dairying in prehistoric Britain, *Proceedings of the National Academy of Sciences*, Vol 100, No 4, 1524-1529

Dudley, D. 1941. A Late Bronze Age Settlement on Trewey Downs, Zennor, Cornwall. *Archaeological Journal* 98, 103-130.

Dudley, D. 1956. An Excavation at Bodrifty, Mulfra Hill, near Penzance, Cornwall, *Archaeological Journal*, 113, 1-32.

Earwood, C. 1994. Report on wood from Excavation of Bronze Age Structure [358] at Penhale Round, Fraddon, Cornwall in E. Davis, J. Grove, J. Heathcote, C Johns and J Nowakowski, *Archive Report on the Archaeological Excavations at Penhale Round, Fraddon*, Cornwall 1993, Cornwall Archaeological Unit report number 1999R045.

Ellman, L. 1998. *Man or Mango*, Review

Fitzpatrick, A.P. Butterworth, C.A. and Grove, J. 1999. *Prehistoric & Roman sites in East Devon: the A30 Honiton to Exeter Improvement DBFO Scheme, 1996-9 Vol 1.* Wessex Archaeology and Highways Agency. Wessex Archaeology Report no: 16

Gale, R. 2007. Gwithian Archive: Charcoal Assessment in J. Nowakowski, *Excavations of a Bronze Age landscape and post-Roman industrial settlement 1953-1961, Cornwall. Assessment of individual key datasets 2003-2006. Vol. II,* Historic Environment Service report 2007R017, Truro. Cornwall.

Gordon, A.S.R, 1941. The Excavation of Gurnard's Head, an Iron Age Cliff Castle in

Western Cornwall. *Archaeological Journal* 97, 96-111

Gossip, J. and Johns, C. in press. The evaluation of a multi-period prehistoric site at Boden Vean, St Anthony in Meneage, Cornwall 2003. *Cornish Archaeology.*

Gossip, J. and Jones, A. M. in prep. A Bronze Age roundhouse at Carnon Gate, Feock. *Cornish Archaeology.*

Guttmann, E. 2006. Gwithian 2005: Soil Assessment in J. Nowakowski, J. Sturgess and A Lawson Jones, *Gwithian, Cornwall. Report on Palaeoenvironmental sampling fieldwork June 2005,* Historic Environment Service report 2006R042, Truro. Cornwall.

Hencken, H. O'Neil, 1933. An Excavation by H.M. Office of Works at Chysauster, Cornwall, 1931, *Archaeologia*, 83, 237-284

Hirst, Lieut-Col. F. C. 1937a. Courtyard house sites in W. Cornwall, *Journal British Archaeological Association.* Series 3, 2, 71-98

Hirst, Lieut-Col. F. C. 1937b. Excavations at Porthmeor, Cornwall, 1933, 1934 and 1935, *Journal of the Royal Institution of Cornwall* Vol XXIV, Appendix II, 1-81.

Hutton, R. 1996. Stations of the Sun. Oxford, Oxford University Press.

Johns, C. J. in prep. The excavation of a multi-period archaeological landscape at Trenowah, St Austell, Cornwall, 1997. *Cornish Archaeology.*

Johnson, N. 1980. Later Bronze Age settlement in the south-west, in J.Barrett and R. Bradley (eds.), *The British Later Bronze Age*, 141-180. British Archaeological Reports, British Series 83. Oxford.

Johnson, N, and Rose, P, 1994. Bodmin Moor An Archaeological Survey Volume 1.

The Human landscape to c 1800, English Heritage and Royal Commission Historic Monuments England

Jones, A. M. 1998-9. The excavation of a later Bronze Age structure at Callestick. *Cornish Archaeology* 37-8, 5-55.

Jones, A.M. 2004-5. Settlement and Ceremony: archaeological investigations at Stannon Down, St Breward, Cornwall, *Cornish Archaeology* 43-44, 1-140.

Jones, A.M. 2008. Houses for the dead and cairns for the living: a reconsideration of the Early to Middle Bronze Age transition in south-west England, *Oxford Journal of Archaeology,* 27, 153-174.

Jones, A.M. and Taylor, S.R. 2004 *What Lies Beneath... St Newlyn East & Mitchell. Archaeological Investigations Summer 2001.* Historic Environment Service, Truro, Cornwall.

Jones, A.M. and Taylor, S.R., in press. *Scarcewater, Pennance, Cornwall. Archaeological excavation of a Bronze Age and Roman landscape*, British Archaeological Report, British Series, Oxford.

Ladle, L. and Woodward, A. 2009. Excavations at Bestwall Quarry, Wareham 1992-2005. Volume 1: The Prehistoric Landscape. *Dorset Natural History and Archaeological Society Monograph Series*: 19.

Macphail, R.I. 1991. Soil Report, in J. A. Nowakowski 1991, 156-160

McKinley, J. 2004. Human bone assessment in J. Nowakowski, Archaeology beneath the Towans. Excavations at Gwithian, Cornwall 1949-1969, *Updated project Design, Historic Environment Service report 2004R071*, Truro. Cornwall

Mercer, R. J. 1970. The excavation of a Bronze Age hut-circle settlement, Stannon Down, St Breward, Cornwall, 1968. *Cornish Archaeology* 9, 17-46.

Megaw, J.V.S. 1976. Gwithian. Cornwall: some notes on the evidence for Neolithic and Bronze Age settlement, in C. Burgess and R, Miket (eds), *Settlement and economy in the third and second millennia B.C., 51-79.* British Archaeological Report, British Series 33. Oxford.

Nowakowski, J.A. 1991. Trethellan Farm, Newquay: the excavation of a lowland Bronze Age settlement and Iron Age cemetery, *Cornish Archaeology*, 30, 5-242

Nowakowski, J.A. 1994. Finally bypassing Indian Queens – The A30 Project, *Cornish Archaeology*, 33, 224-225.

Nowakowski, J.A. 1998. *A30 project, Cornwall – Archaeological Investigations along the route of the Indian Queens Bypass 1992-1994, Assessment and Updated Project Design.* Cornwall Archaeological Unit reports 1998R023-26, Truro. Cornwall

Nowakowski, J. A. 2001. Leaving Home in the Cornish Bronze Age: insights into planned abandonment processes, in J. Brück (ed.), *Bronze Age Landscapes Tradition and Transformation*, 139-148. Oxford, Oxbow.

Nowakowski, J.A. 2004. *Archaeology beneath the Towans. Excavations at Gwithian, Cornwall 1949-1969, Updated project Design,* Historic Environment Service report 2004R071, Truro. Cornwall

Nowakowski, J. A. 2006. Life and Death in a Cornish Valley. *British Archaeology*, 89, 12-17.

Nowakowski, J.A. 2009. Living in the Sands – Bronze Age Gwithian, Cornwall, Revisited, in M. Allen, N. Sharples and T O'Conner (eds.), *Land and People, Papers in memory of John G. Evans*, 115-125, Prehistoric Society Research Paper 2. Oxford, Oxbow.

Nowakowski, J. A., Quinnell, H., Sturgess, J., Thomas, C. and Thorpe, C. 2007. Return to Gwithian: shifting the sands of time, *Cornish Archaeology* 46, 13-76.

Nowakowski, J.A. and C. Johns forthcoming *Bypassing Indian Queens, Cornwall, - Archaeological Excavations 1992-1994. Prehistoric and Romano-British settlements and landscapes,* Cornwall Council and The Highways Agency.

Nowakowski, J.A. and H. Quinnell in press. *Trevelgue Head, Cornwall: the importance of Croft Andrew's 1939 excavations for prehistoric and Roman Cornwall*, Cornwall Council and English Heritage.

Quinnell, H, and Taylor, R. 1998-99. Stone Artefacts, in Jones 1998-99, 27-36

Parker Pearson, M. and Richards, C. 1994 *Architecture and Order. Approaches to Social Space.* London, Routledge.

Parker Pearson, M., Sharples N., and J. Symonds. 2004. *South Uist. Archaeology and History of a Hebridean Island.* Stroud, Tempus.

Pearce, S. M. and Padley, T. 1977. The Bronze Age find from Tredarvah, Penzance, *Cornish Archaeology* 16, 25-41.

Reynolds, P. 1982. Substructure to Superstructure, in P.J. Dury (ed.), *Structural Reconstruction: approaches to the interpretation of the excavated remains of buildings,* 173-198. British Archaeological Report 110. Oxford.

Riddler, I. 2007. *Gwithian:Bone Age Objects and waste of bone and antler in J. Nowakowski, Excavations of a Bronze Age landscape and post-Roman industrial settlement 1953-1961, Cornwall.* Assessment of individual key datasets 2003-2006. Vol. II, Historic Environment Service report 2007R017, Truro. Cornwall.

Smith, G. and Harris, D. 1982. The excavation of Mesolithic, Neolithic and Bronze Age settlements at Poldowrian, St Keverne, 1980. *Cornish Archaeology* 21, 23-66.

Sturgess, J. and Lawson-Jones, A. 2006. *Bronze Age Gwithian, revisited. Archaeological excavations between 1956 and 1961 in Cornwall.* Truro. Cornwall County Council Historic Environment Service report 2006R067. 2 vols.

Thomas, A. C. 1958 *Gwithian. Ten Years' work (1949-1958),* Gwithian (excavation staff and West Cornwall Field Club). Camborne, Cornwall.

Thomas, I. 1960. The excavations at Kynance Gate 1953-60. *The Lizard* 1:4, 5-16.

Tringham, R. 1991. Households with Faces: the challenge of Gender in Prehistoric Architectural Remains in J. Gero and M Conkey, *Engendering Archaeology. Women and Prehistory,* 93-130. Oxford, Routledge.

Townend, S. 2007. What have reconstructed roundhouses ever done for us? *Proceedings Prehistoric Society*, 73, 97-111.

Yates, D. 2007. *Land, Power and Prestige. Bronze Age field systems in southern England,* Oxford, Oxbow.

Wardle, P. 2004. *Interim report – archaeological excavations at Pawton Store, Pawton, St Breock, Wadebridge, Cornwall*, Goring-on-Thames.

Wood, J. 1999. *Discovering Archaeology Magazine,* October.

Woodward, A. and Cane, C. 1991. The Bronze Age Pottery in Nowakowski, J.A., 103-133.

Acknowledgements

A much shortened version of this paper was given at Tavistock, Devon, in October 2009. I am very grateful to Francis Griffith, Eileen Wilkes, Susan Pearce and the Devon and Cornwall Archaeological Societies for the opportunity to participate and join in the celebration of Henrietta Quinnell's lifetime work in the south west. I have been very lucky to have had the privilege and opportunity of working with Henrietta my entire working life as a professional archaeologist in Cornwall and I offer this paper as a gift to her inexhaustible enthusiasm, engagement and support she has brought to our many collaborations. I have also been lucky to work alongside many supportive colleagues and thanks are also extended to Emeritus Professor Charles Thomas, Carl Thorpe, Peter Herring, Adam Sharpe, Peter Rose, Nicholas Johnson, Andy Jones, Anna Lawson-Jones, Jo Sturgess, James Gossip and Charlie Johns – all at Historic Environment, Cornwall Council. Beyond Cornwall my work has been informed and inspired by many people active in Bronze Age research and I would particularly like to thank Professor Richard Bradley, Joanna Brück, John Chapman, the late Professor J G Evans, Emeritus Professor Andrew Fleming, Stuart Needham, Rachel Pope, Kate Waddington and Ann Woodward. But most of all, thank you Henrietta, long may our collaborations continue!

In the Footsteps of Pioneering Women: Some Recent Work on Devon Hillforts

F. M. Griffith and E. M. Wilkes

Abstract

This paper reviews the use of the term 'hillfort' and the possible functions of the monuments known by this term. It discusses new evidence, and emphasises the quantity of available evidence with a bearing on these issues, both known and potential.

Introduction

It is a great pleasure for both of us to offer this paper to celebrate the work of our friend Henrietta Quinnell. Our title refers to the fact that a high proportion of past work on Devon hillforts has been carried out by a succession of remarkable women, amongst them of course Henrietta. Our objective here is not to offer a comprehensive reinterpretation of Devon hillforts, but to review them in the context of some recent work in a field with which Henrietta continues to be closely involved. Henrietta's excavation at Woodbury Castle was one of the first modern rescue excavations in the county, necessitated by a road widening scheme. Although she felt at the time (Miles 1975) that her results were limited, we can now see they show that Woodbury is in company with many other Devon hillforts in having a more complex life story than had previously been thought. The post holes of a palisaded enclosure of unknown date were found beneath the inner rampart, while the evidence of changes to the northern entrance indicates a fairly long-lived occupation. (Woodbury, incidentally, remains the only Devon site to have produced clear evidence for a breastwork on top of the rampart, in both phases of use.)

'Hillfort' is a term that has meant different things to different people at different times. As with most archaeological terms it has always reflected contemporary concerns: thus hillforts have at various times been described as military (complete with such anachronistic elements as barbicans, glacis and covered ways), as commercial, as centres of power in hierarchical societies, as gathering places in egalitarian communities, and many more. While we shall not be essaying any new overall theory of hillforts it will be necessary to touch upon some of these alternative (or parallel) explanations for hillforts in the course of this paper, and we would remark at the outset that we are pretty sure that the monuments lumped together under this term have no single function.

For hillfort studies in England the shadow of Wheeler still looms large in our subconscious thinking. In the South West one of our remarkable women, Lady (Aileen) Fox, contributed greatly to the study of hillforts – and also to their recognition and protection. Much of the recent work in England has concentrated on the area of Wessex, where these monuments dominate the landscape with their imposing physical presence. Key analyses of these sites in the 1970s and 1980s drew heavily on the work of Professor Barry Cunliffe who interpreted hillforts as focal points (e.g. Cunliffe 1984), central places in landscape and society that were the residences of the elite, for defence, the control of stock, storage of surplus and centres of production and exchange. Later writers such as J. D. Hill have re-examined the evidence to suggest that hillforts complemented rather than dominated the settlement pattern (Hill 1995).

Hill's critique of hillforts as central places put forward the alternative model of them as 'not farmsteads': places where diverse activities took place, apart from hamlets and spatially distinct from them. Such activities include exchange, communal rituals and festivities, while hillforts in this model were seen as 'by and for the people' rather than necessarily as evidence for a highly stratified chiefly society. These wider roles have recently been re-emphasised by Lock (2007), who has examined a number of Oxfordshire hillforts and proposes that White Horse Hill, Uffington, was predominantly social or religious in its function, with 'deeply rooted historical connections', whereas nearby Segsbury, built 'in a landscape without deep historical connections', related to the economic aspects of sheep farming.

At Maiden Castle - a site which in both its structure and in its demonstrable history quite clearly was at least partly defensive in its role - Sharples (1991, 260) has identified evidence of repeated episodes of refurbishment of the ramparts which has led him to suggest that it was the iterative action of carrying out the work as much as the finished result that may have been important. The collaborative, or possibly coercive, nature of the construction may have in itself have been part of the role of the hillfort in drawing groups together and establishing

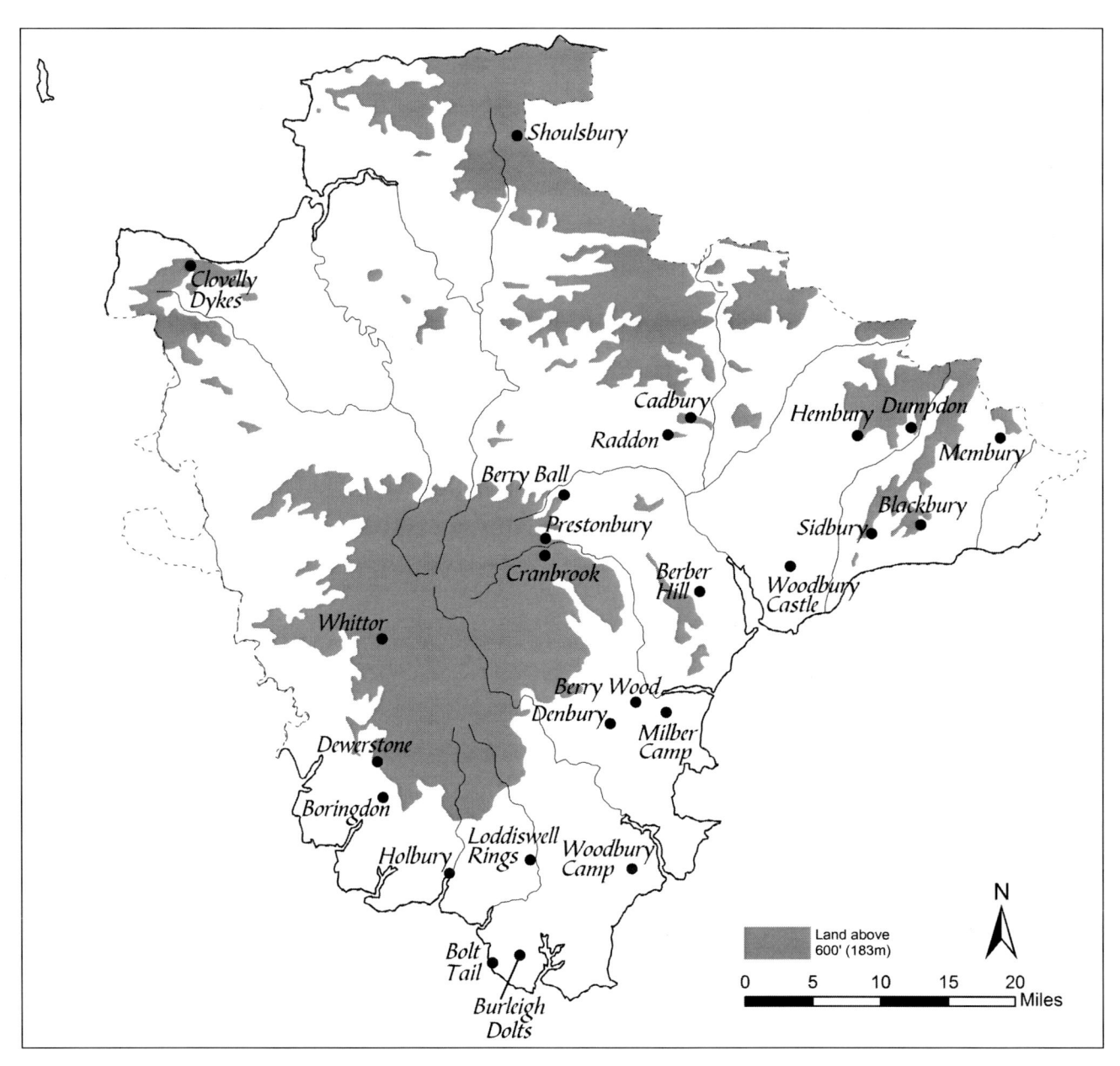

Fig.10.1 Sites mentioned in the text. Plan by E. M. Wilkes.

social cohesion – in much the same way as we now envisage the creation of structures of earlier periods, such as causewayed enclosures, as having been important in its own right as an act or series of acts, as well as in creating a 'monument'. How far these Wessex models can be applied more widely has been considered by various writers for different areas of the country. At the European scale Ralston (2006) has recently examined hillforts and restated his belief in their primary defensive role.

Much of the work on Devon hillforts in the twentieth century was carried out by Lady (Aileen) Fox, a founder member of the national Hillfort Study Group. Her publication (1996) is the only summary produced of these monuments in the county: she provided detail on forty-eight hillforts in what was intended not as a comprehensive review but rather a useful small guide. The Devon Historic Environment Service (HER) records almost a hundred monuments classified as 'hillfort' or 'cliff castle', and includes examples of most of the different forms within the wide-ranging monument class. There are large, multivallate examples that would not look out of place on the chalk of Wessex or in Wales: these are mainly found east of the Exe (Fox 1977, 35), including Hembury (see below), Sidbury, Membury and Dumpdon. But there are also many monuments that are either smaller, less massive, or occupying less precipitous locations: these are the sites that Fox (1952a) characterised as 'hillslope enclosures', but which we are including in our consideration here. Such less complex monuments include Loddiswell Rings (Wilson-North and Dunn 1990) and Holbury (see Fox 1955 for description, and below), both in the South Hams. Among these are examples of the special type classified by Fox (1952a; 1977) as 'Multiple Enclosure Forts', which she regarded as a phenomenon peculiar to South West England and Wales, and which are discussed below.

While a couple of rescue excavations have been conducted, most of the work we report here in Devon in recent years (fig.10.1) has been carried out under the general heading of 'site management', with non-destructive geophysical surveys carried out for the purposes of future management decisions. This technique has proved extremely useful not only in the production of data on the survival of internal features, for example (which can support proposals for the removal of hillfort interiors from cultivation), but also, as in the case of the much larger (and better-funded) Wessex Hillforts project (Payne et al 2006), in providing some insight into the possible nature of activity in the interiors. Since the campaigns of Devon Archaeological Society at Hembury in the 1920s-30s, at Milber 1937-8, and at Blackbury in 1952-4, Devon has seen almost no hillfort excavations of any scale, and thus we have very little modern archaeological information about the activities that would have taken place in them. This presents a second serious problem (not confined to hillfort studies in the county), namely that there are very few hard dates available for these sites in Devon, either for their construction and original use or for their subsequent re-use. On the whole, suggestions of phasing and chronology have relied on stratigraphic information, on artefacts retrieved during excavation, and on typological comparisons with sites elsewhere, particularly with the form and style of ramparts. As the pattern and form of hillforts in Devon may not be entirely comparable with those in other areas, this is less than ideal. The paucity of modern excavations of hillforts in Devon means that the number of radiocarbon dates for hillforts in the county is only very slowly increasing.

New sites

In common with those in other areas of the country, despite the substantial nature of their original defences, many Devon hillforts have suffered attrition over the years (e.g. Woodbury Camp, fig.10.2). Fox (1964, Fig 37) produced what was thought to be the full distribution of multivallate hillforts in the South West, but remarkably we can still add to that distribution, particularly following the work of the Devon Aerial Reconnaissance Project over the past twenty-five years or so (Griffith 1984; 1988; 1990; 2009).

In the excellent cropmark conditions of 1984, FMG identified an oval hilltop enclosure measuring c. 150m x 80m on Berber Hill in the parish of Kenn (fig.10.3;

FIG.10.2 WOODBURY CAMP, STOKE FLEMING, VISIBLE AS AN EARTHWORK UNDER THE HEDGEBANK, AS A SOILMARK IN THE FIELD TO THE RIGHT OF THE HEDGEBANK, AND A CROPMARK IN THE LOWER FIELD. PHOTO F. M. GRIFFITH, DEVON CC, 18 JULY 1989.

FIG. 10.3 BERBER HILL, KENN. THE CURVING HILLTOP BANK SHOWS THE SURVIVING RAMPART, AND CROPMARKS SHOW THE REMAINDER OF THE CIRCUIT AND OUTWORKS ON TWO SIDES. PHOTO F. M. GRIFFITH, DEVON CC, 29 JUNE 1984.

Griffith 1984). The main enclosure has annexes to the north and south (on the more gentle slopes). The entrance is in the west and has a curious short outwork ditch just beyond. On the ground the western rampart still survives under the modern hedge, with the ditch still visible, and this, together with the place name Berberry on the Kenn Tithe Apportionment (1841),[1] could perhaps have led to the identification of this site without the need for an aircraft! At present this site is identified as a hillfort solely on its form, and no more detailed investigation has yet been carried out.

Another hillfort discovered, or rather rediscovered,[2] in the Devon Aerial Reconnaissance programme was at Raddon, on the top of an east-west ridge of Permian rocks lying to the west of the Exe Valley. This was the site of excavation shortly after its discovery, as the construction of a road by South West Water necessitated rescue recording of a strip through the centre of the monument (Gent and Quinnell 1999). The results of this work are discussed below. Another site of hillfort proportions and siting was recorded by Bill Horner near Staverton, South Devon in 1996 (fig. 10.4). It is a surprise and a delight that we are still able to add to the record of Devon's hillforts in this way.

Survey

Other techniques are also proving to be of much benefit where sites are already known. Geophysical surveys in recent years, principally using magnetometry, have served to enhance our understanding and provide further detail on the known hillforts in the county. Much of this work has been carried out by EMW to inform management practices at the monuments, most of which lie in agricultural land. One such survey at Holbury in the South Hams provided evidence for the survival of internal features despite heavy ploughing across the monument in modern times (fig.10.5; Wilkes 2007). An ovoid enclosure with antennae ditches leading from its west-facing entrance is clearly evident within the interior and is located on an area of flatter ground within the gently sloping hillfort.

Holbury itself is a rather odd shape. The single bank circuit runs around the rounded top of a hill overlooking the river Erme to the south with the trace of a second external bank beyond the northern rampart (Devon HER SX65SW/8/1), possibly an outwork connected with the entrance in that area. The main bank circuit includes a 'bulge' in the southwest corner, which gave rise to a question of whether an earlier monument had been extended at that point, but

---

[1] For a discussion of 'berry' names as indicators for hillforts and other enclosures, see Griffith 1986.
[2] In 1630 Thomas Westcote (1845, 131-2) had recorded 'On the height of the hill, which we call Raddon Top, was some time a large kind of fortification, now well near made even by the plough with the ground', but the site had not been known to archaeologists in more recent years.

Fig.10.4 A large hilltop enclosure near Staverton, partly surviving in the present field boundary and partly visible as the cropmark of its ditch. Photo Bill Horner, Devon CC, 31 July 1996.

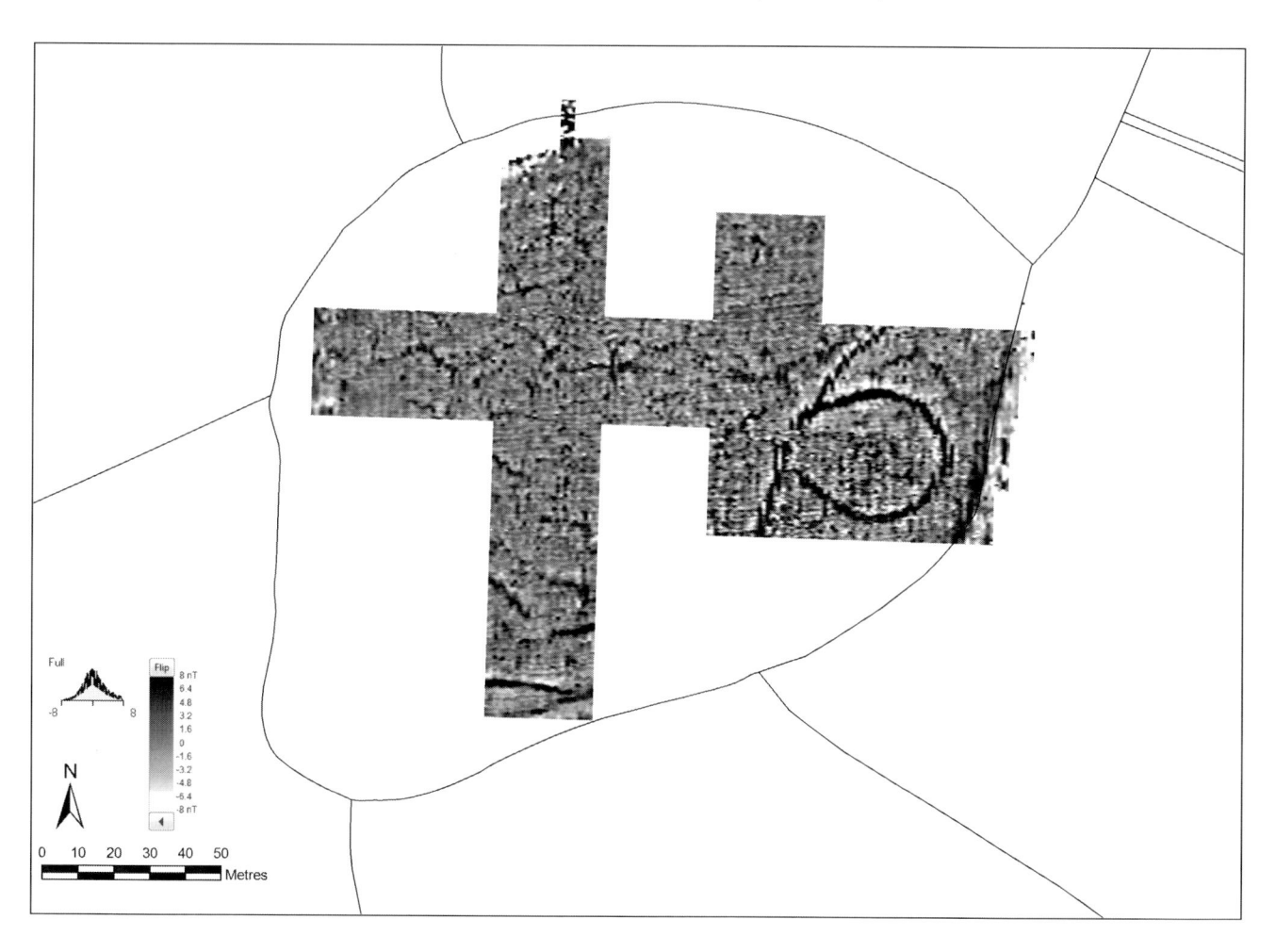

Fig.10.5 Magnetic gradiometry greyscale plot of evaluation survey at Holbury Camp, E. M. Wilkes, January 2007.

geophysical survey has not confirmed this. The original entrance to the monument is in the north-east (Fox 1955) whereas the three other entrances around the monument are considered to be modern, and that in the north has been enlarged in recent years (Wilkes 2007).[3]

Dating and phasing

Of the large hillfort sites in the county it is perhaps the multi-phase site at Hembury, Payhembury, that is best known, described by Fox as "the most impressive and important of Devon hillforts" (1996, 36). Hembury occupies the tip of one of the Greensand spurs running south from the Blackdown Hills. Excavation was conducted here in the 1930s by another pioneering woman, Dorothy Liddell (1930; 1931; 1932; 1935; for a convenient summary, see Fox 1996, 36-7) and in the early 1980s by Malcolm Todd (1984). The early excavations revealed a Neolithic origin to the site, and new radiocarbon analysis of charcoal fragments and residues from the old excavations has recently given a series of dates in the thirty-seventh century BC (Whittle, Bayliss and Healy 2011, 479-93). The Neolithic causewayed enclosure at Hembury (fig 10.6) was a very important discovery in its time, and provided the name for the distinctive style of Early Neolithic ceramics (including the round-based bowls with 'trumpet lug' handles) found in southwest England.

The site was re-used in the first millennium BC when the surviving earthworks were enhanced and expanded. A single timber-faced box rampart and ditch were constructed, for which Lady Fox (1996, 30) suggests a date around 400BC. This was subsequently developed into a much stronger dump rampart, with two further ramparts downslope with deep ditches. These ran around the contour and made a formidable defence, while the two inturned entrances, on the western and eastern sides of the monument, were expanded with raised causeways running through the series of ditches. Massive post holes within the western entrance were interpreted by the excavator as having contained upright supports for a bridge across the entrance for the use of defenders of the hillfort (Liddell 1932, 163; Fox 1996, 9). Hembury shows definite Middle Iron Age occupation, with South-western Decorated ceramic finds, and may have continued into the Late Iron Age, but the site fell into disuse well before the end of the Iron Age. In the first century AD the still strong defences were exploited by the incoming Roman army to provide a temporary base, complete with timber barrack blocks and *fabrica* (Todd 1984). While we do not know when the hillfort was abandoned, an interesting suggestion of its state at the time of the arrival of the Romans is provided by its possible identification with the Moridunum of Roman toponymic sources (Rivet and Smith 1979, 420-1). When Todd's excavations reminded the world of the Roman presence at Hembury, the suggestion was made by the late

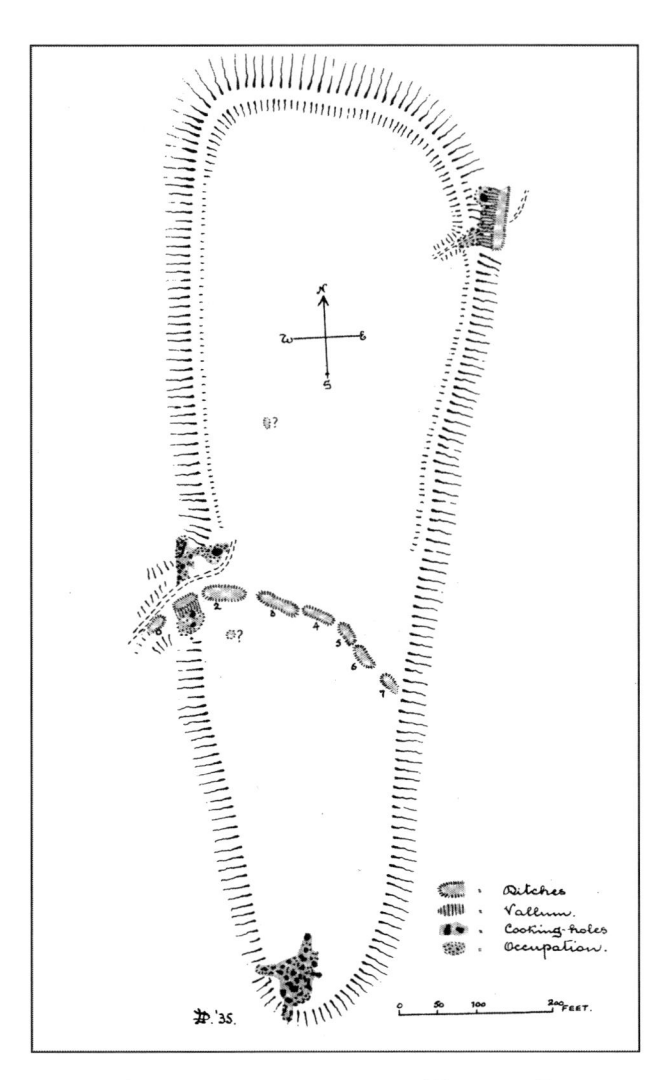

Fig.10.6 The Neolithic features at Hembury (Liddell 1935, Fig. 15). Reproduced by courtesy of Devon Archaeological Society.

Leo Rivet that the name could derive from Latin *morum*, 'blackberry', with *dunum*, a fortified hill, which might describe the abandoned bramble-covered state in which the Romans found the site (Todd 1984, 266).

As mentioned above, Raddon, a hillfort in central Devon west of the river Exe, is a site that benefited from the Devon aerial reconnaissance programme (fig.10.7), as its first modern record came from observations by the project's pilot, the late Dickie Dougan. As part of the Devon Post-Reconnaissance Fieldwork Project (a Devon County Council-sponsored programme of field visits to all newly-discovered sites and their farmers), once the aerial identification had been made, a field inspection by the late Rosemary Robinson reported that upstanding elements of the monument survived around the hilltop. The recognition of the site came none too soon, as the hilltop had been selected as the location for an access road for a reservoir by South West Water, and the photographic and field record ensured an evaluation and subsequent excavation recorded the archaeology along the line of the road.

---

[3] Excavation of the bank terminal in advance of enlargement of the entrance unfortunately did not produce any datable material (Wilkes 2007).

FIG.10.7 RADDON HILL FROM THE SOUTH, SHOWING THE COMPLEXITY OF DITCHES.
PHOTO F. M. GRIFFITH, DEVON CC, 7 JUNE 1990.

The excavation at Raddon was carried out by Exeter Archaeology in 1994 with a geophysical survey completed by Oxford ArcheoTechnics (Gent and Quinnell 1999, Fig. 2). Although the restricted spatial scope of the excavation (along the line of the new access road) made detailed interpretation difficult, a clear phase plan was produced based on excavation evidence, aerial photographs and field observations (fig. 10.8). As at Hembury, multiple phases of use were identified. The earliest activity on the hill was the construction in the thirty-seventh century BC (Whittle, Bayliss and Healy 2011, 493-7), and thus broadly contemporary with Hembury, of a Neolithic causewayed enclosure with an annex or enlargement to the south west. During the Early Iron Age the site was redefended, initially by the erection of a palisade roughly around the area of the Neolithic enclosure. This was later enhanced with a single bank and ditch circuit along the same line, broken by a single entrance in the west. The enclosed area was greatly increased, still within the Early Iron Age period, by extending the bank circuit to the east to provide a second, conjoined enclosure, as large as the first and with its entrance facing to the northeast. All the enclosure activity appears to relate to the early Iron Age but features within the monument provided dates of Middle and Late Iron Age phases, suggesting that the site continued to be occupied through the first millennium BC. As at Hembury, the apparent diminution in the use of ceramics in the Late Iron Age in the South West as a whole (H. Quinnell pers. comm.) makes dating in this period very difficult. A post-Roman phase of occupation was also identified.

The excavation at Raddon provided samples from which sixteen radiocarbon dates were obtained. These begin in the earliest phase in the Neolithic, show a break until the first millennium BC and, after another break, further activity in the post-Roman period, which is of course also virtually aceramic in Devon (Gent and Quinnell 1999, Table 16; Whittle, Bayliss and Healy 2011, 493-7). The dates from Raddon are also one of the very few sequences of dates yet determined for a hillfort in Devon. Mention must also be made here of High Peak, on the east Devon coast, where once again a Neolithic - Iron Age - post-Roman sequence was suggested (Pollard 1966; 1967), and of the ramparted hilltop sites at Dewerstone and Whittor on south-west Dartmoor, which although never excavated have been suggested to be Neolithic defended enclosures rather than hillforts at all (Silvester 1979, 187-8; Griffith 2001, 70-1). Certainly in other parts of the country it is not unusual for hillforts to have been found to have their origins in the Bronze Age, as for example at Rams Hill, Berkshire. However, none from this period has yet been identified in Devon, perhaps solely due to the paucity of excavation.

One of the few other hillforts with firm dates from modern excavation is Berry Ball, south west of Crediton (Manning and Quinnell 2009). This site too was excavated in advance of work by South West Water. One side of the hillfort of 'Leathern Castle' had long been known in upstanding form, and therefore survey and excavation were undertaken in advance of the pipeline. Geophysical survey within the interior of the monument in 2007 detected a track running from a presumed ancient entrance, but identified no internal features (Stephens in Manning and Quinnell 2009, 103-6). However, excavation demonstrated two possible phases of rampart construction, the curvilinear ditches of roundhouses, and post holes and pits. The number of round houses - at least nine - within the 6.5m wide excavated strip across the monument makes this in fact the most densely occupied Devon hillfort yet known (which however merely emphasises the lack of area excavation within most of them). Three radiocarbon determinations derived from

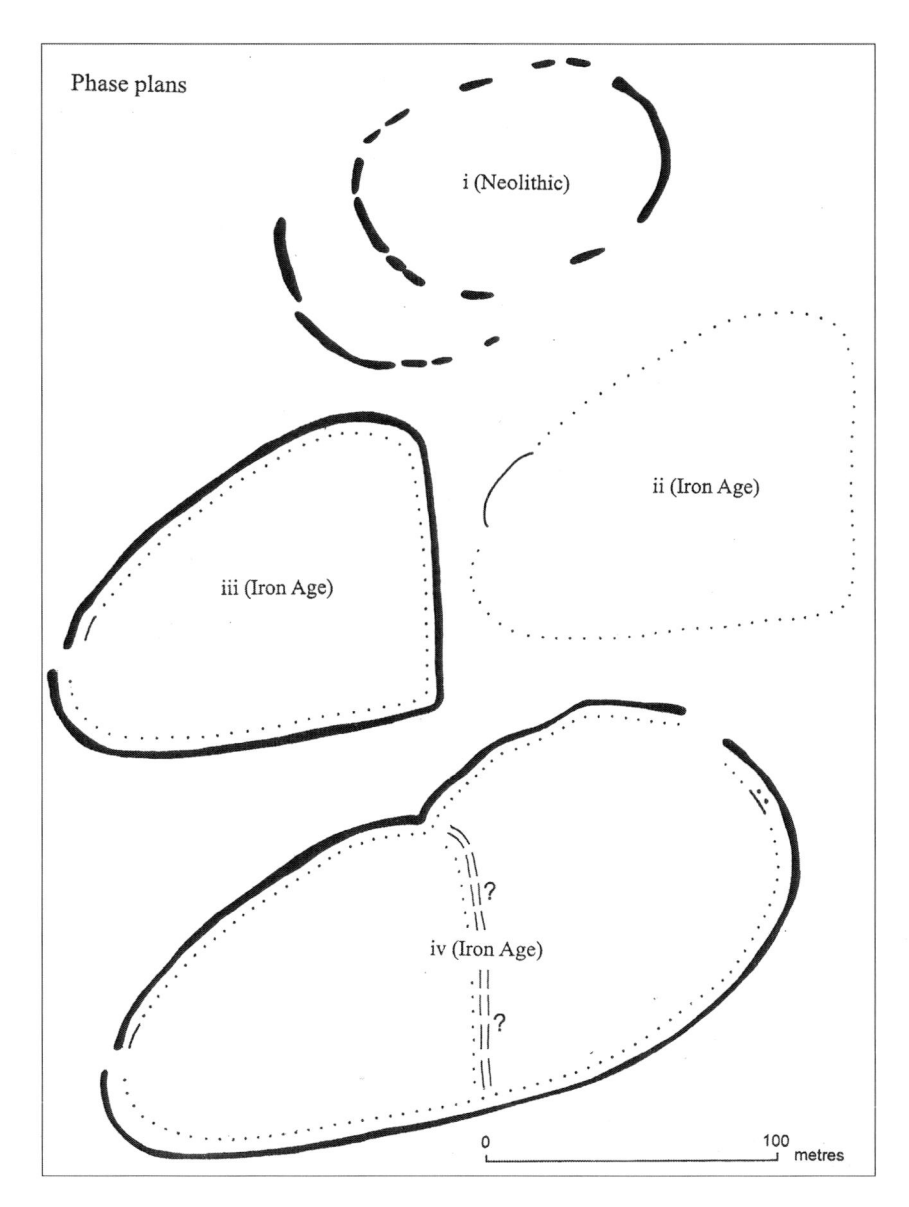

FIG.10.8 RADDON: PRINCIPAL PHASES (GENT AND QUINNELL 1999, FIG. 8).
REPRODUCED BY COURTESY OF DEVON ARCHAEOLOGICAL SOCIETY.

wood charcoal indicate that the site was occupied between 400 and 200 BC – the Middle Iron Age. One pit contained a pale turquoise glass bead with brown, white and blue decoration. It has been identified as Guido's Garrow Tor type (Henderson in Manning and Quinnell 2009, 116-20) characteristic of the Middle Iron Age (c. 300 – 200 BC) and a relatively unusual type to find in Britain. The date range accords with the radiocarbon determinations from three samples (two of which were obtained from material from the same pit as the bead).

So few hillforts in Devon have been excavated that we can ask how many others may occupy hilltops that have seen pre-Iron Age activity and even fortification. In fact, the sites of Berry Ball, Blackbury and Milber are currently the only Devon hillforts that have seen any significant excavation yet have not produced material dating from before the first millennium BC.

Multiple Enclosure Forts

As discussed above, Aileen Fox considered hillforts to be very much concerned with defence, designed as strongholds to protect people, things and animals against attack. Her interpretations of the hillforts she visited and recorded were based largely on that consideration. However, following Morgan (1920, 204-5), she also drew attention to a puzzling group of 'hillslope forts' which seemed almost perversely oblivious to the optimal defensive topographical siting available to them (Fox 1952a; 1977). Fox identifies four varieties within this classification but interprets all of them as mainly concerned with the protection of cattle and people, located with proximity to water and grazing, and with multiple enclosures to segregate the herds for milking, mating, selection for slaughter and other activities. Although there may be some continental parallels, she considered these sites to be 'insular developments' (1964, 125), due to the adoption of a pastoral economy suited to the southwestern and south Welsh environment. The ramparts and often banked-up entrances provided 'positions from which the overseer could observe the herd without getting trampled' (Fox 1952a; 1977). In the later analysis, she used the term 'multiple enclosure fort' for her Class III to describe sites such as Milber and Clovelly Dykes – sites with substantial ramparts but which are still not optimised for defence. Fox interpreted both these sites as being of more than one phase, with the outer enclosures being added to the original inner enclosure (the defended occupation area for the chieftain and kin group), to create protected areas in which to keep stock (Fox 1964, 124). The final form of Clovelly Dykes, still a magnificent earthwork site today, comprises over three kilometres of banks, enclosing an area that totals eight hectares (Fox 1996, 27).

Milber Camp is perhaps the classic example of Fox's 'multiple enclosure' hillslope sites. Its location, south of the estuary of the river Teign, below the lowest crossing point of the river, is on a hillslope and not easily defensible (Fox 1996, 42). The entrance to Milber Camp (fig.10.9) runs as a funnel into the monument from the west where the closest source of water, the Aller Brook, lies. Fox (1987; 1996, 42) read this as an embanked droveway through the outer enclosure to channel stock without damaging any surrounding crop. However, Milber can be interpreted as much more than a simple pastoral settlement, as it shows a number of traces of some sophistication, notably the presence in the upper ditch fills of a unique and delightful assemblage of bronze animal figurines – a duck, a bird and a stag, dated approximately to the first century BC (Fox et al., 1949-50). It is a multivallate monument with widely spaced enclosures, and we could suggest that the entrance way may have a less utilitarian function than that proposed, and that that the long entranceway leading uphill from the west is an elaborate and grand way into the site for people rather than for animals, a key element in the design of the site.

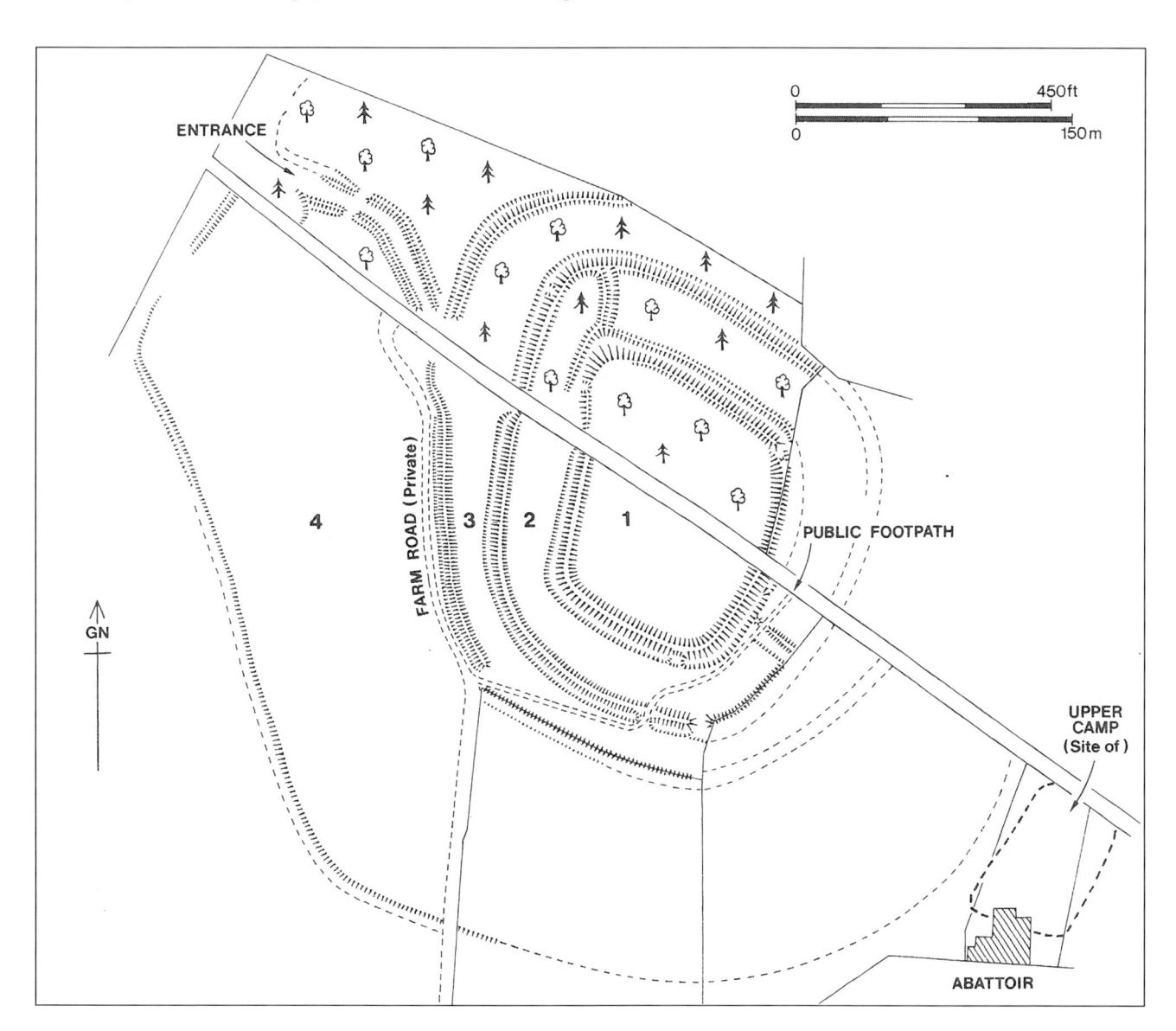

FIG.10.9 MILBER DOWN HILLFORT. PLAN BY NORMAN QUINNELL, FROM FOX 1987. REPRODUCED BY COURTESY OF DEVON ARCHAEOLOGICAL SOCIETY.

FIG. 10.10 BURLEIGH DOLTS AS RECORDED ON 10 DECEMBER 1946 IN RAF AIR PHOTOGRAPHY (RAF/CPE/UK 1890 40361).

FIG. 10.11 MAGNETIC GRADIOMETRY GREYSCALE PLOT OF EVALUATION SURVEY AT BURLEIGH DOLTS. E. M. WILKES 2006.

A similar multiple enclosure fort is that of Burleigh Dolts near Malborough in the South Hams. This monument, now all but levelled, lies on a high ridge with views to the coast both to the west and south. Until the 1940s it remained with multiple large, upstanding banks defining wide spaced enclosures, particularly to the south and west (fig. 10.10). The banks were then deliberately flattened to assist ploughing and now survive only for a short length in the north under a hedge line (Fox 1951, 35). Geophysical survey here (fig. 10.11) has identified the surviving ditches that accompanied the destroyed banks, and shown that there are interior features and divisions within the enclosed spaces. It also revealed a previously unknown round barrow immediately east of the monument (Wilkes 2006a). As at some of the other sites, the entrance runs uphill through the wide-spaced enclosures in a simple line with no apparent 'defensive' considerations, which again parallels the usual picture at multiple enclosure forts.

Fox considered that the multiple enclosure hillforts, as well as having a stock corralling role, might also have associations with maritime trade, suggesting a link with Strabo's comments that British exports in the later Iron Age were favoured for their cattle, hides and corn – exactly the sort of agricultural produce with which these sites would have been concerned (Fox 1952a, 17). They are often found near harbours or estuaries and Fox proposed a link between them and people using the western sea routes through the English Channel and Bristol Channel. Certainly the sites at Burleigh Dolts, Milber and Clovelly are well-placed to exploit maritime and riverine connections as well as providing good access to inland routes. Burleigh Dolts lies just inland from the Kingsbridge Estuary, Clovelly sits just a mile from the northern coast and is at a nodal point where three ridgeway routes meet, while Milber lies above the Teign Estuary on high sloping ground (see further Wilkes 2004 137; 450-1).

Annexes and entrances

Following the excavation of Blackbury Camp, east Devon, by the Devon Archaeological Society, the director, Kitty Richardson, suggested that the unusual annexe on the south of the monument was a 'barbican' (Young and Richardson 1954-55, 50-2). The additional ramparts defend the southern entrance and look out across the valley of the stream known locally as the Nanny Water, a tributary of the river Coly. However, according to the excavators, the interior of the monument had suggested very little in the way of permanent occupation (a series of trial trenches produced only the post-holes of what was identified as a hut) so the need for a barbican can be questioned, and a defensive function for this element must be doubtful, given that the additional banks add c. 30% to the line needing to be defended. The excavators themselves (Young and Richardson 1954-55, 57) describe the site as 'not defensive in a military sense'. Moreover, the approach from the south is not the obvious line of attack – the land here slopes steeply down to a small valley – whereas to the north of the monument the land is essentially flat, and apparently more convenient to attack. One might therefore anticipate enhancement of the ramparts on this side rather than in the south, if defence were the prime objective, but there is no evidence for elaboration or enhancement on the northern side. Perhaps an alternative suggestion can be made. Blackbury, well positioned on a ridge, may have served as a gathering place for markets or ceremonies along the lines of the 'not farmstead' model proposed by Hill (1995). The two sides of the 'barbican' would serve as stock enclosures – not necessarily for long-term defence, but for managing stock in connection with the market or feasting within the main monument. (A stock pen function is indeed later suggested by Fox herself (1977, 46) in a shift from her previous acceptance of 'barbican' interpretation.[4]) The additional ramparts could enhance the entrance here for prestige rather than serious defence (although why the entrance is on this side at all, rather than in the northern side, is unclear, and the presence of what are identified as hoards of sling stones by the main entrance still has to be remembered). Excavations revealed post holes of gate structures within the entrances of both the main enclosure and the 'barbican' that, as at Hembury, have been interpreted as supporting a bridge across the gated entrance (Young and Richardson, 1954-5, 56).

A comparable complex outwork has been recognised at Boringdon Camp in the Plym valley (Slater and Pearson 1985, Fig. 3), outside the point where earlier mapping had recorded an inward bulge in the single rampart. Again, this outwork elaborates an entrance on the downslope side of the monument. This does not seem much concerned with defence, but rather provides a degree of ostentation to the entrance into the monument. The monument itself survives in near circular univallate form. The interior has twice been surveyed by magnetic gradiometry, originally by the Ancient Monuments Laboratory (Bartlett 1979) and more recently as part of monument management work by EMW (Wilkes 2006b). The geophysical surveys have highlighted the high degree of cultivation damage suffered by the interior of this monument in the past: plough marks are clearly visible. However, the results (fig. 10.12) indicate that there is still some survival of internal cut features, including an internal ditch within the upstanding bank, the post-holes of possible four-post structures and a curvilinear inner partition ditch. Due to dense scrub cover it was not possible to survey the area of the annexe but, based on the upstanding form and plan of this area, it is suggested here that the elaborated southern entrance parallels that at Blackbury and may be considered more for prestige and flamboyance rather than purely, if at all, for defence. The internal ditch within a circular monument may of course give us some cause to suspect that the site may have its origins in a pre-hillfort form, perhaps even a henge, but invasive work would be necessary before this idea can be more than kite-flying.

---

[4] Fox suggests a similar interpretation for the annexe at Castle Dore (Cornwall) where excavation revealed numerous small post holes suggestive of "supports for hurdling used for penning beasts from time to time" (Fox 1977, 46).

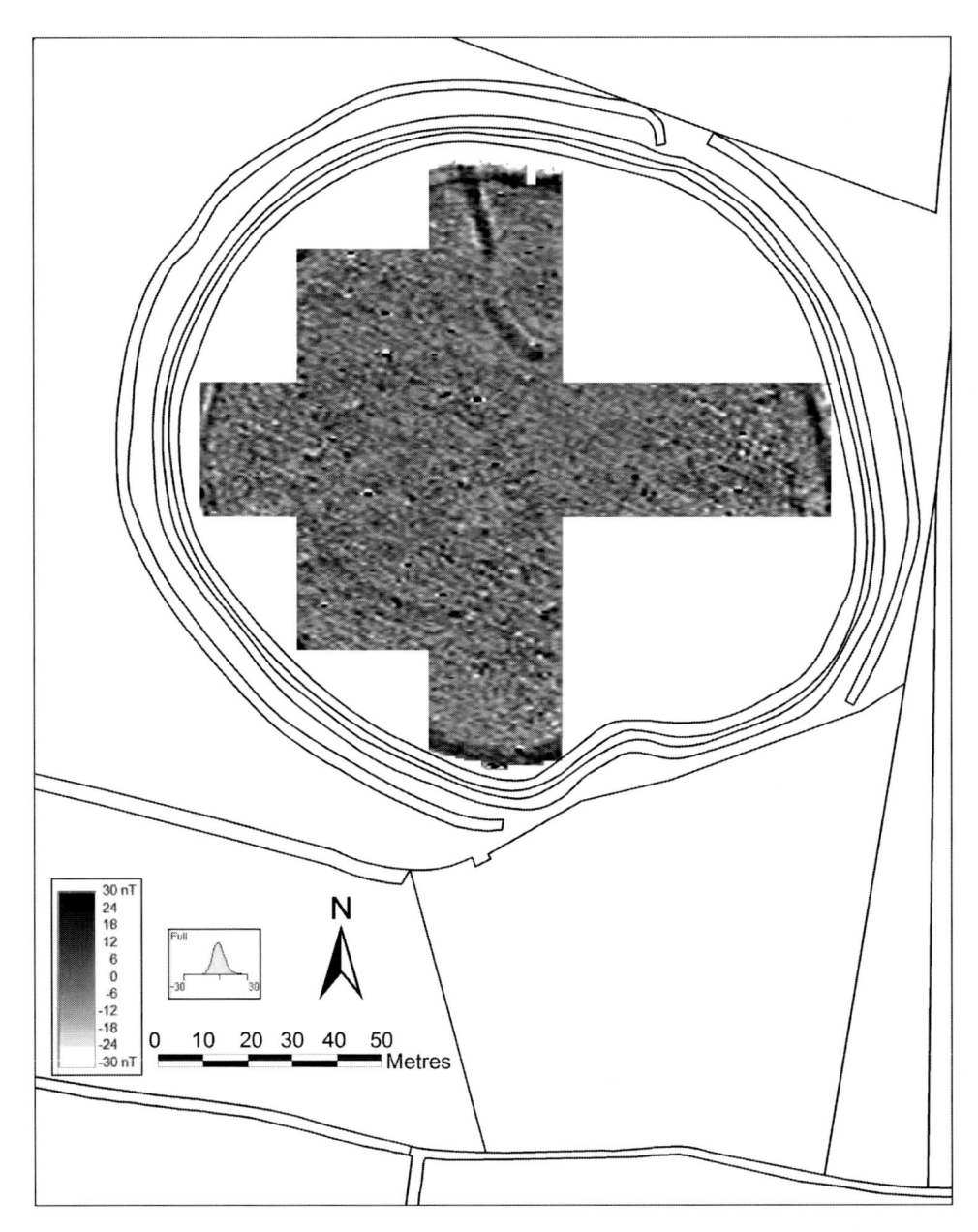

FIG. 10.12 MAGNETIC GRADIOMETRY GREYSCALE PLOT OF EVALUATION SURVEY AT BORINGDON CAMP. E. M. WILKES 2006.

Pairing

In her discussion of hillslope forts, Lady Fox recognised a recurrent pattern of pairing between the hillslope fort and a more typical hilltop-sited 'contour fort' in the same area - in Milber's case, the hillfort of Denbury in Berry Wood (Fox 1952a, 17). We would like to suggest another possible pairing higher up the Teign where Prestonbury and Cranbrook lie opposite each other across the upper Teign on Dartmoor. The close siting and obvious intervisibility of these two hillforts across the Teign valley has often been remarked upon. Fox (1952a,10) initially dismissed Prestonbury as being a multiple enclosure fort but later (1964, 123) describes it as one. The relationship between these two sites is interesting (fig.10. 13). Neither seems to have a complete suite of defences, and those that they do have are most complex on the sides that face away from the other: in other words, unlike some of the forts along the Tamar, they do not seem to be glaring at one another, with their fiercest facades facing. Rather, the bank and ditch defences of both monuments are 'guarding their backs', and presenting a facade to landward approaches up the gentler slopes whilst between them they overlook the Teign valley. Cranbrook is unusual in a Devon context in being a stone-built monument, and indeed Fox (1996, 29) refers to it as "the best example of a stone-built hillfort in Devon". The faced stone rampart is two metres high and encloses 2.8 ha. The southern circuit has a parallel bank and ditch but this does not extend to the north. It has been described as an 'unfinished hillfort' (Silvester and Quinnell 1993; Fox 1996, 29) but it is perhaps the case that large banks were simply not required on the ground

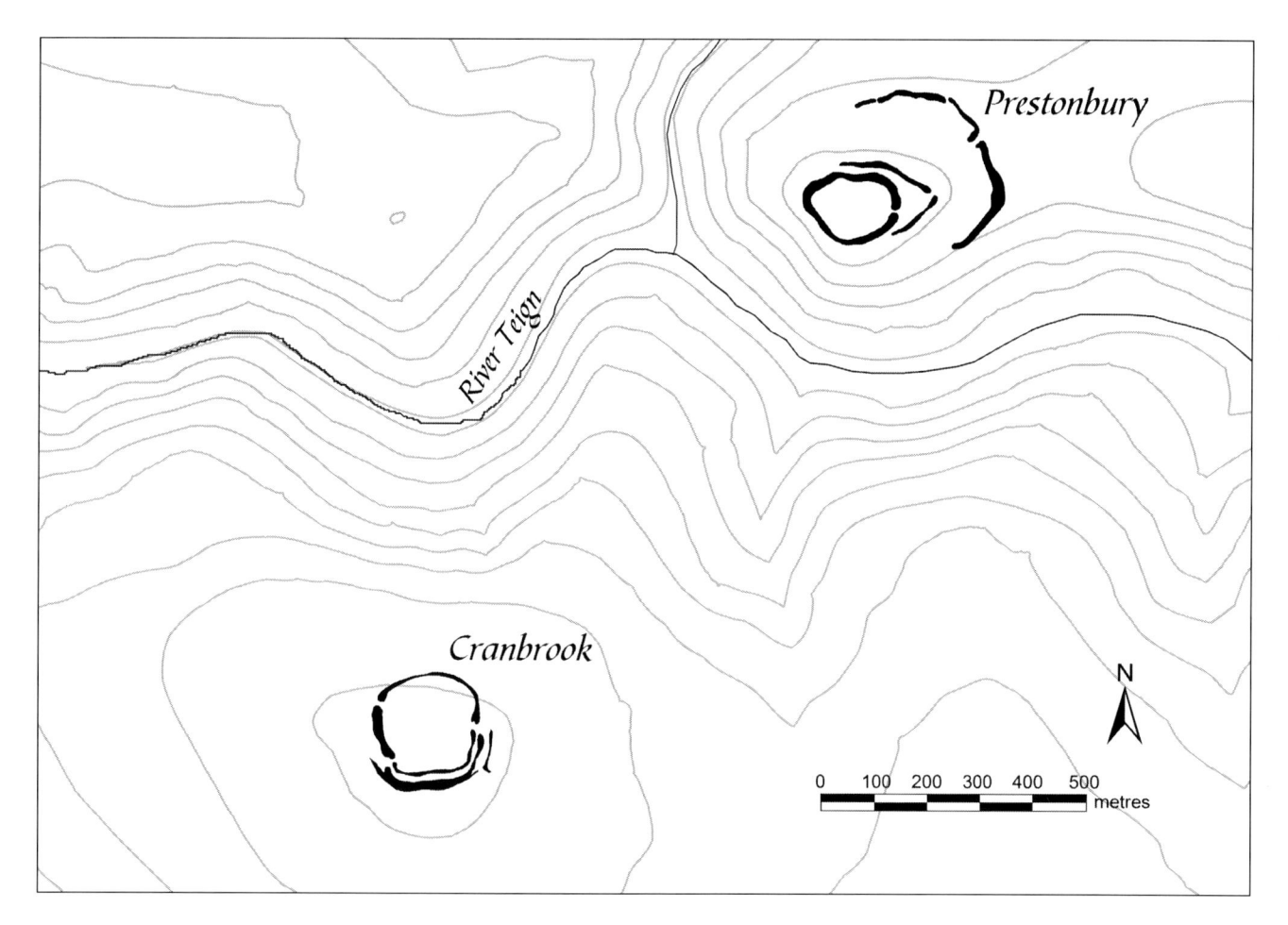

FIG. 10.13 THE SITING OF PRESTONBURY AND CRANBROOK CASTLE HILLFORTS, OVERLOOKING THE RIVER TEIGN. PLAN BY E. M. WILKES. CONTOURS AT 25M INTERVALS.

facing across the Teign to Prestonbury.[5] The northern side of Cranbrook is marked only by a low bank, and the south and west of Prestonbury is marked by a single line of bank whereas the rest of the monument has been enhanced with two further bank and ditch arcs lower down the slope, with again, as at Milber, an apparent emphasis on the entrance from the more gentle slope. At the foot of the valley, directly between the two monuments, is the crossing place of the Teign at what is now Fingle Bridge. It is possible to suggest that the two monuments were working in tandem to oversee the Teign route that lay between them, and that they present a strong face to the exterior but a more friendly view toward each other.

Cadbury

Some of the most recent work on a Devon hillfort has taken place at Cadbury Castle in Cadbury parish, west of the Exe Valley (fig. 10.14). In conjunction with monument management work for an Environmental Stewardship Scheme, a geophysical and topographic survey conducted by EMW has revealed interesting features of the monument that were previously unsuspected. Cadbury first came to public notice when a well or shaft feature within the monument was 'excavated' by George Fursdon in 1848 (Tucker 1848). The excavation recorded a depth of 58 feet for the shaft. Within the shaft were found Roman pot sherds and various items of Roman bronzework, mainly bracelets and rings (Tucker 1848; Fox 1952b). It is interesting that a folk tale, recorded from at least the seventeenth century, tells of a dragon that flies between Cadbury and nearby Dolbury to protect its treasure (Westcote 1845, 10-11). Most Devon hillforts do not have dragons, so the association of such a legend with one of the few Devon sites to yield 'treasure' is interesting, suggesting perhaps a folk memory of other finds from the site (cf. Bloody Pool, South Brent, which had this name before the nineteenth century discovery of a group of Bronze Age spears in the pool (Tucker 1867, 121-2)).

The entrance to Cadbury is from the gently sloping southern direction (the break in the northern side is a modern intrusion) and, as at Hembury, Milber and other hillforts, the entrance runs to a causeway through the inner ditch. Cadbury lies only 3.5km north east of Raddon. The monuments are intervisible, though interestingly neither

---

[5] We see the same feature at Shoulsbury, on Exmoor, which has also been suggested (Silvester and Quinnell 1993, 27-8; Jamieson 2005) to be an unfinished monument, but where again the site sits in a dominant position overlooking a steep drop, and where the purpose of the 'unfinished' outer rampart may also be to present a finer appearance on its most approachable side.

FIG.10.14 CADBURY CASTLE FROM THE NORTH. THE INNER, EARLIER ENCLOSURE CAN BE CLEARLY SEEN, WITH ITS INTURNED ENTRANCE. PHOTO F. M. GRIFFITH, DEVON CC, 26 MARCH 1986.

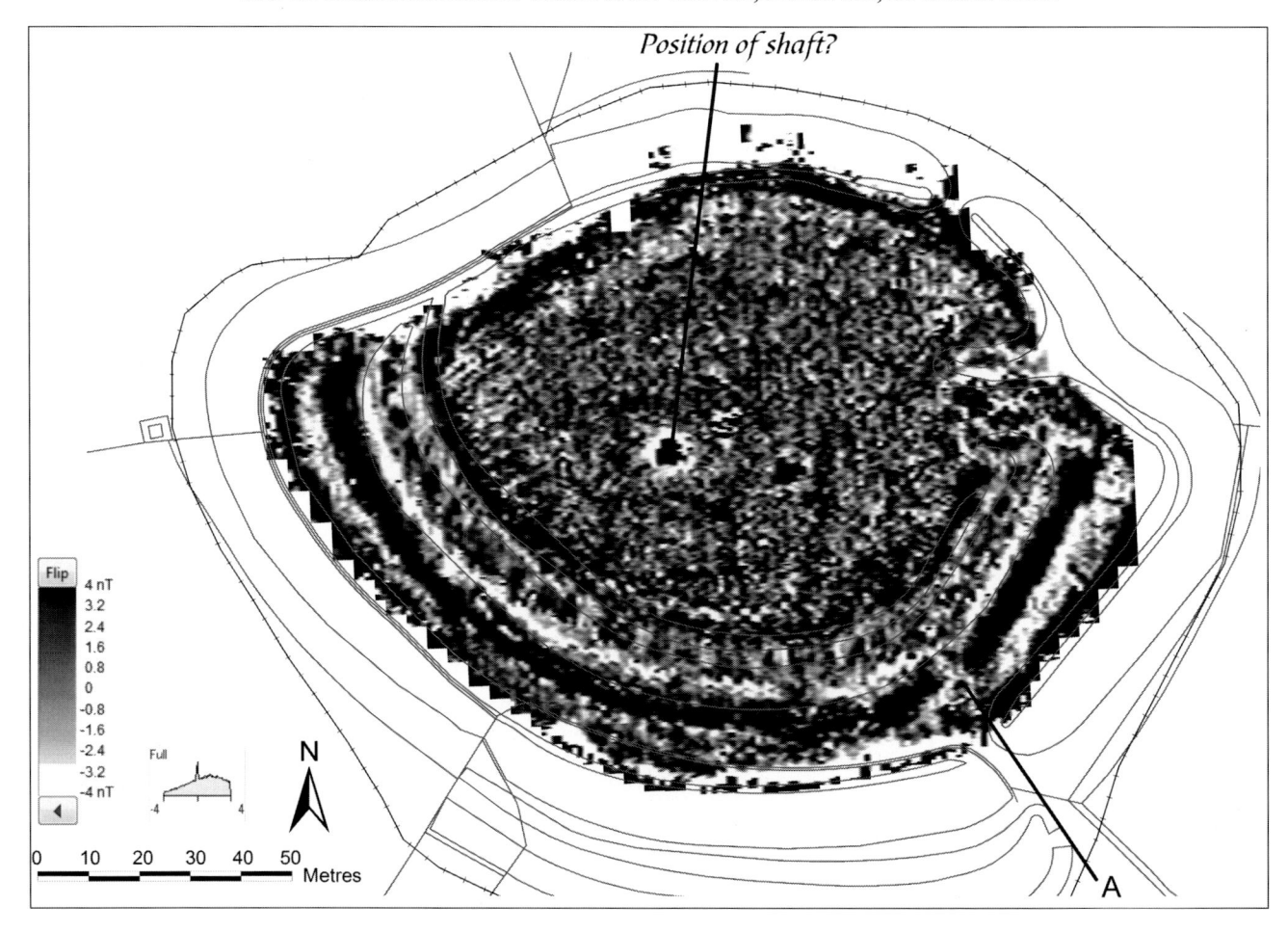

FIG.10.15 MAGNETIC GRADIOMETRY GREYSCALE PLOT OF EVALUATION SURVEY AT CADBURY CASTLE. E. M. WILKES, 2009.

hilltop looks particularly striking or dominant from the other, although subjectively when one stands on either of them one has a strong sense of overlooking all the surrounding country. These two sites do not seem to fall very conveniently into Lady Fox's 'pairing' of hillforts, but it is noteworthy that Raddon contains the only other known potentially deep shaft in the county (Gent and Quinnell 1999, 16).

Lady Fox (1952b) produced a plan of Cadbury Castle suggesting there were two phases to the monument. Phase I consisted of a simple ovoid enclosure with an inturned entrance facing east. Phase II added a second rampart around the south with a new entrance from the gently sloping southern approach. She later elaborated this to include a counterscarp bank as part of the Phase II development (Fox 1996, 25). Geophysical survey at the site by EMW in 2009 and 2010 has confirmed and fleshed out this (fig. 10.15). It has also confirmed the presence of a bank for the inner enclosure, now almost wholly eroded by ploughing, and shows some evidence of the nature of the construction of that bank, internal segmentation being clearly visible on the magnetometer plot. The presence of a bank blocking the Phase 1 ditch and turning the person entering through the Phase 2 entrance to the right, up to the existing Phase 1 entrance in the original enclosure, can be clearly seen (marked 'A' on fig. 10.15). It is possible that the geophysical survey has identified the site of the shaft, whose exact location was not recorded at the time of its excavation, but since Cadbury has always been seen as a natural site for Millennium and Jubilee bonfires, Armada beacons and the like, the various areas of high magnetic response in the interior have more than one possible explanation. At the time of writing, further survey work both within and outside Cadbury is shedding further light on the construction and development of the monument, and it is intended to publish this in more detail elsewhere (Wilkes, Quinnell and Griffith forthcoming).

The offset entrance in Phase 2 at Cadbury has a possible parallel at Cranbrook, where an outer entrance in the outer (partial) bank in the SE quarter of the monument runs along within the bank before entering the inner enclosure in the middle of its eastern side (Collis 1972, Fig 2).[6] John Collis suggests that here again we may be looking at a two-phase monument. The exact positioning of the entrance is also an interesting feature in ongoing research at Bolt Tail, a promontory fort at the south of Bigbury Bay (Quinnell 1992). Although there has been no excavation recorded at this site, it is generally assumed to be Iron Age in date due to its form, which is similar to many other such monuments in the South West. A single bank and ditch

---

[6] John Collis later (1979) published a revision of his suggested phasing of Cranbrook, but we find the earlier one more persuasive, and it is to that that we refer here. The present overgrown state of the monument makes detailed recording of the outer entrance almost impossible.

FIG.10.16 THE VIEW TO BURGH ISLAND FROM THE ENTRANCE TO BOLT TAIL. PHOTO E. M. WILKES, 2006.

runs approximately north – south to isolate the promontory at the neck. The ramparts are not strongly visible from the sea – either when approaching or running out of Bigbury Bay, although they appear massive from some viewpoints on the land (Griffith and Wilkes 2006, 82-3). The oddly-placed single entrance through the rampart is of interest due to its peculiar alignment. The rampart is sited so that anyone approaching enters through a rising gap that, when the crest of the rise is reached, presents a direct view across the water to Burgh Island, 4 km away (fig.10.16). It seems more than likely that the entrance was aligned specifically to set up that view. The concept of 'designed views' is one with which we are now familiar in relation to the Neolithic and Bronze Ages: are we looking at a later example of the same thing here, or have we perhaps got the date of Bolt Tail quite wrong? The relationship between Bolt Tail and Burgh Island is being considered as part of wider investigations into the late prehistoric use of Bigbury Bay, and it is intended to carry out geophysical survey here in the future.

Conclusion

In this paper we have not tried to offer a new scheme for looking at Devon hillforts, nor radically to change the reading of them. However, we hope we have shed light on the growing picture of them as monuments that have long and complex histories that are capable of some disentanglement even without excavation. The majority of those that we have looked at show clear evidence of recurrent episodes of use of their sites, which in many cases had begun long before the hillfort phase of occupation. Those few excavations that have taken place in recent years, notably at Berry Ball, (a site which might formerly have been thought of as one of Devon's least distinguished hillforts), demonstrate the scale of information that may still be available to us. Both the presence of closely-set round houses here and the external relationships suggested by the presence of the exotic bead at a site so far from obvious trade routes remind us how very little we really know about what went on in most of these monuments. The opportunities for non-destructive survey that have been made and taken have helped us to take our picture of some of these sites further, and this must be an avenue we continue to exploit, while hoping at the same time that the range of real dates available to us will be expanded in future years.

It is striking that while we began this paper with a reference to Henrietta's excavation at the hillfort of Woodbury Castle in 1971, her most recent publication on the subject is the report on the hillfort of Berry Ball in 2009, and a quick look at our Bibliography shows that we hope that she will soon be publishing more. Her contribution to this subject rivals that of Lady Fox, and it is with respect and affection that we offer our own small contribution.

Bibliography

Bartlett, A. 1979. *Magnetometer Survey of Boringdon Camp* (Ancient Mons. Lab. Report G14/79).

Collis, J. 1972. 'Cranbrook Castle, Moretonhampstead. A New Survey' *Proc. Devon Archaeol. Soc.* 30, 216-21.

Collis, J. 1979. 'Cranbrook Castle Revisited' *Proc. Devon Archaeol. Soc.* 37, 191-4.

Cunliffe, B. 1984. *Danebury, an Iron Age Hillfort in Hampshire* (London, CBA).

Fox, A. 1951. Twentieth report on ancient monuments. *Trans. Devonshire Assoc.* 83, 34-35.

Fox, A. 1952a. 'Hill-Slope forts and related earthworks in South-West England and South Wales'. *Archaeol. J.* 109, 1-22.

Fox, A. 1952b. 'Roman objects from Cadbury Castle'. *Rep. Trans. Devonshire Assoc.* 84, 105-114.

Fox, A. 1955. 'Archaeology and early history, 22nd report'. *Rep. Trans. Devonshire Assoc.* 87, 319-26.

Fox, A. 1964. *South West England.* (London, Thames and Hudson).

Fox, A. 1977. 'South-western hill-forts'. In: (ed. S.S. Frere) *Problems of the Iron Age in Southern Britain.* (London, Institute of Archaeology, UCL), 35-60.

Fox, A. 1987. *Milber Down* (Devon Archaeol. Soc. Field Guide 1).

Fox A, 1996. *Prehistoric Hillforts in Devon* (Tiverton, Devon Books).

Fox, A. and Ralegh Radford, C.A., Rogers, E.H. and Shorter, A.H. 1949-50. 'Report on the Excavations at Milber Down, 1937-8', *Proc. Devon Archaeol. Soc.* 4 (2 and 3), 27-66.

Gent, T. and Quinnell, H. 1999. 'Excavation of a causewayed enclosure and hillfort on Raddon Hill, Stockleigh Pomeroy'. *Proc. Devon Archaeol. Soc* 57, 1-75.

Griffith, F. M. 1984. 'Aerial Reconnaissance in Devon in 1984: A preliminary Report and the Discovery of a Hillfort', *Proc. Devon Archaeol. Soc.* 42, 7-10.

Griffith, F. M. 1986. '*Burh* and *Beorg* in Devon', *Nomina* 10, 93-103.

Griffith, F. M. 1988. *Devon's Past, an Aerial View* (Exeter, Devon Books).

Griffith, F. M. 1990. 'Aerial Reconnaissance in Mainland Britain in 1989', *Antiquity* 64, 14-33.

Griffith, F. M. 2001. 'Recent work on Neolithic Enclosures in Devon' in (eds. Darvill, T. and Thomas, J.) *Neolithic Enclosures in Atlantic Northwest Europe* (Oxford, Oxbow), 66-77.

Griffith, F. M. 2009. 'The Joys of Enclosures' in (eds. James, H. and Moore, P.) *Carmarthenshire and Beyond: Studies in History and Archaeology in Memory of Terry James* (=Carm. Antiq. Soc. Monograph 8), 107-22.

Griffith, F. M. and Wilkes, E.M. 2006. 'The Land Named from the Sea? Coastal Archaeology and Place-Names of Bigbury Bay, Devon', *Archaeol. J.* 163, 67-91.

Hill J D, 1995. 'How should we understand Iron Age societies and hillforts? A contextual study from southern Britain'. In (eds. C G Cumberbatch and J D Hill) *Different Iron Ages: Studies on the Iron Age in temperate Europe*. (Brit. Archaeol. Rep. Int, Ser, 602, Oxford, Tempus Reparatum), 45-66.

Jamieson, E. 2005. *Shoulsbury Castle, Exmoor, Devon*. (Swindon, English Heritage Arch. Investigation Rep. Ser. AI/13/2005).

Liddell, D. 1930. 'Report on the Excavations at Hembury Fort.' *Proc. Devon Archaeol. Soc.* 1(2), 40-73.

Liddell, D. 1931. 'Report on the Excavations at Hembury Fort, Devon'. *Proc. Devon Archaeol. Soc.* 1(3), 90-120.

Liddell, D. 1932. 'Report on the Excavations at Hembury Fort'. *Proc. Devon Archaeol. Soc.* 1(4), 162-90.

Liddell, D. 1935. 'Report on the Excavations at Hembury Fort (1934 and 1935)'. *Proc. Devon Archaeol. Soc.* 2(3), 134-75.

Lock, G. 2007. 'Wessex Hillforts after Danebury: Exploring Boundaries', in (eds. Gosden, C., Hamerow, H., de Jersey, P., and Lock, G.) *Communities and Connections: Essays in honour of Barry Cunliffe*, 341-56.

Manning, P. and Quinnell, H. 2009. 'Excavation and field survey at the Iron Age hillfort of Berry Ball, Crediton Hamlets'. *Proc. Devon Archaeol. Soc.* 67, 99-132.

Morgan, W. L. 1920. 'The Classification of Camps and Earthworks', *Arch. Cambr.* 20, 201-23.

Miles, H. 1975. 'Excavations at Woodbury Castle, East Devon, 1971', *Proc. Devon Archaeol. Soc.* 33, 183-208.

Payne, A., Corney, M. and Cunliffe, B. 2006. *The Wessex Hillforts Project : extensive survey of hillfort interiors in central southern England*. (London, English Heritage).

Quinnell, N. 1992. *Bolt Tail* (Exeter, Devon Archaeol. Soc. Field Guide 8).

Ralston, I. 2006. *Celtic Fortifications* (Stroud, Tempus).

Rivet, A.L.F. and Smith, C. 1979. *The Place-Names of Roman Britain* (London, Batsford).

Sharples, N. M. 1991. *Maiden Castle: Excavations and Field Survey 1985-6* (London, English Heritage).

Silvester, R. 1979. 'The Relationship of First Millennium Settlement to the Upland Areas of the South-West', *Proc. Devon Archaeol. Soc.* 37, 176-90.

Silvester, R. and Quinnell, N. 1993. 'Unfinished hillforts on the Devon moors'. *Proc. Devon Archaeol. Soc.* 51, 17-32.

Slater, W. and Pearson, T. 1985. 'A survey of Boringdon Camp'. *Proc. Devon Archaeol. Soc.* 43, 112-15.

Todd, M. 1984. 'Excavations at Hembury Hillfort (Devon): a Summary Report', *Antiq. J.* 64, 251-68.

Tucker, C. 1848. 'An account of the discovery of Roman remains in the British hill-fortress called "Cadbury Castle" near Tiverton, Devon'. *Archaeol. J.* 5, 193-198.

Tucker, C. 1867. 'Antiquities of Bronze found in Devonshire', *Archaeol. J.* 24, 110-22.

Westcote, T. 1845. (eds. Oliver, G. and Jones, P.) *A View of Devonshire in MDCXXX, with a Pedigree of most of its Gentry*. (Exeter, William Roberts).

Whittle, A., Bayliss, A. and Healy, F. 2011. *Gathering Time: Dating the Early Neolithic Enclosures of Southern Britain and Ireland* (Oxford, Oxbow).

Wilkes, E.M. 2004. *Iron Age Maritime Nodes on the English Channel Coast. An investigation into the location, nature and context of early ports and harbours*. PhD thesis, Bournemouth University.

Wilkes, E.M. 2006a. *Report on geophysical survey at Burleigh Dolts, south Devon*. Unpublished client report (SHDC) available at Devon HER.

Wilkes, E.M. 2006b. *Report on geophysical survey at Boringdon Camp, south Devon*. Unpublished client report (SHDC) available at Devon HER.

Wilkes, E.M. 2007. *Report on geophysical survey and targeted excavation at Holbury Camp, south Devon*. Unpublished client report (SHDC) available at Devon HER.

Wilkes, E.M. 2010. *Report on geophysical survey at Cadbury Camp, Devon*. Unpublished client report (Natural England and Fursdon Estate) available at Devon HER.

Wilkes, E.M. Quinnell, H. and Griffith, F. M. forthcoming. 'Cadbury Castle, Devon, Reconsidered'.

Wilson-North, R. and Dunn, C. 1990. ' "The Rings", Loddiswell: a new survey by the Royal Commission on the Historical Monuments of England'. *Proc. Devon. Archaeol. Soc.* 48, 87-100.

Young, A. and Richardson, K. 1954-55. 'Report on the excavations at Blackbury Castle'. *Proc. Devon. Archaeol. Soc.* 5 (2&3), 43-67.

Acknowledgments

We have prepared this paper discussing the work both of the various pioneering women and of many other colleagues, to all of whom we are grateful. Some of the work was undertaken while FMG was the holder of a Leverhulme Research Fellowship and EMW the Hogg Research Fellowship of the University of Wales, Lampeter, and we are very grateful to both these bodies, as well as to our employing institutions, for their support. The programme of aerial reconnaissance mentioned in this paper has been carried out by FMG since 1983, and more recently also by Bill Horner, for Devon County Council, funded by the County Council, English Heritage and private supporters, while the bulk of the post-reconnaissance work was carried out by the late Rosemary Robinson. The geophysical surveys by EMW were commissioned by Devon County Council, South Hams District Council, and Natural England, and we are very grateful to the landowners and farmers of all the sites surveyed for their help. We have drawn upon Devon County Council's Historic Environment Record for much information, and we are grateful to the County for permission to publish the aerial photographs, to Devon Archaeological Society for permission to reproduce figures 10.6, 10.8 and 10.9, and to Sue Pearce for her work as Editor. Finally, we wish to acknowledge all the fruitful discussions we have both enjoyed on many topics with Henrietta over the years, and to thank her for her continuing inputs to our work and that of many others.

Romano-British brooches – of Cornish origin?

Anna Tyacke, Justine Bayley and Sarnia Butcher

Abstract

The recent discovery in Cornwall of a cluster of seven brooches of a type previously only known from a very few examples has raised the exciting possibility that they may have been made in the far south-west. The brooches are described and illustrated and parallels drawn with types to which they may be related. Scientific study has identified both the copper alloys used to make them and the ways in which they were decorated.

Introduction

In March 2009, a well-preserved copper alloy Romano-British brooch was discovered in Sennen parish by David Edwards, using a metal detector. It was reported to one of us (Tyacke 2009a) as Finds Liaison Officer for the Portable Antiquities Scheme (PAS, see www.finds.org.uk), along with other Roman finds from the same field. The brooch (fig.11.1,1) has a most unusual cruciform-shaped bow and a fantail foot, features which are not normally found in combination. The bow has expanded arms that terminate in cylindrical settings, which are now empty. The remains of rivets show it originally had further decoration attached. The form of these attachments can be visualised because of a more recent find of a pair of similar brooches in even better condition. These were found about 10 metres apart by Robin Tidball, while using a metal detector, in St. Hilary parish in July 2009 (Tyacke 2009b; Tyacke 2009c). Pairs of later 1st and 2nd AD Roman brooches like these are a western British phenomenon so are to be expected in Cornwall (Dr J. D. Hill pers comm).

Since discovering this unique Cornish type of brooch, two other brooches previously recorded on the PAS database as too unusual or too worn to classify, have been identified as further examples of this type. The first, from Constantine, was found by Harry Manson in March 2008 (Tyacke 2008) and the second, from Marazion, by Roy Powell in June 2003 (Tyacke 2004); both found while using a metal detector. Three further examples of similar brooches were noted by M. R. Hull in his corpus of brooches from Roman Britain (forthcoming) and were recalled (by SB) from notes she made in the late 1960s. These were two published brooches, from St. Mawgan-in-Pydar (Murray Threipland 1956, 71-2) and from Old Man, Isles of Scilly (Tebbutt 1934), and an unpublished one from Charterhouse, in the Mendips, held in City Museum, Bristol. Since writing this paper fragments of three further related brooches have been identified in the PAS database. Two are from Ludgvan in Cornwall, one found by David Edwards (Tyacke 2005) and the other by Roy Powell (Tyacke 2007), and one from Kingsdon, just south of the Mendips, found by Roger Evans (Booth 2009).

Descriptions of the brooches

This group of brooches share many features, though no two are quite the same. To avoid too much repetition in the individual descriptions, details of construction and decoration are summarised in Tables 11.1 and 11.2; this allows easy comparison of their similarities and differences. All the brooches were cast in something very close to their final form, though some details would have been added or embellished after they were removed from the moulds. The features common to all the brooches are a head with a long crossbar that holds an axis bar on which the hinged pin swung, a strongly-arched cruciform bow with riveted-on bosses, and a fantail foot covering a relatively large catchplate. Hull classified them as his Type 31 and described the shape of the bow as double peltate (Bayley and Butcher 2004, 231), which emphasises its expanded, rounded ends where it joins both the head and fantailed foot. In the better-preserved examples the curved edges of the bow are emphasised by a slight ridge, seen most clearly in Figures 11.1,3 and 11.1,6. Most of the brooches have some traces of tinning, and in three cases there is more or less definite evidence that parts of the surface were covered by decorative metal foils or wires that were soldered on (see below). Most of the brooches were also decorated with enamel on the head or, less often, on the foot.

Sennen (PAS ref: CORN-8FDAD6; fig 11.1,1)

The crossbar of this bronze brooch is decorated with four sunken triangular fields, which still contain some of the original enamel, separated by oblique engraved lines. The decoration near the ends is more elaborate than on the other brooches; a pair of engraved lines bordering a rib that has been punched to produce a zigzag. The iron corrosion on the head is from the axis bar. The bow has side arms that terminate in hollow settings that would almost certainly have been filled, perhaps with knobs or bosses of metal or glass. There is also evidence for applied decoration on the bow as the remains of an iron rivet runs through the centre of it. The fantail foot is badly pitted by corrosion, giving the appearance of five sunken triangles

		Sennen 8FDAD6	St Hilary 1 DE55F7	St Hilary 2 DEC722	Constantine 3A58B3	Marazion 82B305	Ludgvan 1 459FB7	Ludgvan 2 51A8A7
Head					mostly missing			mostly missing
	Tinning	no	no	no	-	yes	no	-
	Enamel	traces in 3 of 4 fields; 2 triangular 2 sub-triangular	red in 3 of 4 triangular fields	none survives in 4 triangular fields	-	slight traces of 4 triangular fields	no	-
	Relief	bands at ends	angled parallel grooves on top	?groove at fracture	-	no	3 or 4 grooves at ends	-
Pin								
	Hinged/sprung	hinged	hinged	hinged	hinged	hinged	hinged	hinged
	Pin	-	-	-	copper alloy	-	-	-
	Axis bar	iron	copper alloy	iron	copper alloy	iron	iron	-
Bow								
	Studs (copper alloy)	one near head lost; remains of iron ?rivet in centre	4 (of 5) survive	2 (of 4) survive	3 (of 5) with 'washers' survive	one in centre (?2 lost from sides)	none	blind hole in centre may have held stud
	Tinning	yes	none survives	none survives	yes	yes	yes (?solder/ overlay)	none survives
	Enamel	no	no	no	no	no	no	no
Foot		fantail	fantail	fantail	fantail	fantail	missing	mostly missing
	Tinning	yes	none survives	none survives	yes	yes	-	none survives
	Enamel	no	no	none survives in at least 3 fields	? slight traces of fields	no	-	no
	Solder/overlay	yes	no	no	yes	yes	-	no
Alloy								
	Main casting	bronze	leaded bronze/gunmetal	leaded bronze	leaded bronze	(leaded) bronze	(leaded)? bronze	leaded bronze
	Studs	copper ??	leaded bronze/gunmetal ?	leaded bronze ?	leaded bronze ?	(leaded) bronze ?	-	-
	Washer	-	-	-	? tinned	-	-	-

Key: - = area missing so no information. ? denotes uncertainty

TABLE 11.1: FEATURES OF THE NEWLY-DISCOVERED CORNISH BROOCHES.

	St Mawgan 1956.64	Charterhouse Fb 8973	Kingsdon SOM-183E93	Old Man, Scilly
Head			missing	part missing
Tinning	-	yes	-	-
Enamel	no	no	-	no
Relief	groove(s) at ends	grooves at ends	-	-
Pin			missing	missing
Hinged/sprung	hinged	hinged	-	hinged
Pin	copper alloy	copper alloy	-	-
Axis bar	copper alloy	copper alloy	-	-
Bow			mostly missing	
Studs (copper alloy)	one lost from centre	blind hole in centre probably held stud	One, cast in one with bow, survives near foot; surface cross-hatched	central perforation
Tinning	yes	yes	?	-
Enamel	no	no	-	no
Foot	fantail	missing	fantail	Missing
Tinning	yes	-	yes	-
Enamel	no	-	traces survive in at least 3 (of 6) fields	-
Solder/overlay	none survives	-	?	-
Alloy				not analysed
Main casting	bronze	leaded bronze	leaded bronze	-
Studs	-	-	leaded bronze	-
Washer	-	-	-	-
Key: - = area missing so no information. ? denotes uncertainty				

Note: The brooch from Old Man has not been seen so details were determined from a drawing

TABLE 11. 2: FEATURES OF THE OTHER BROOCHES DISCUSSED.

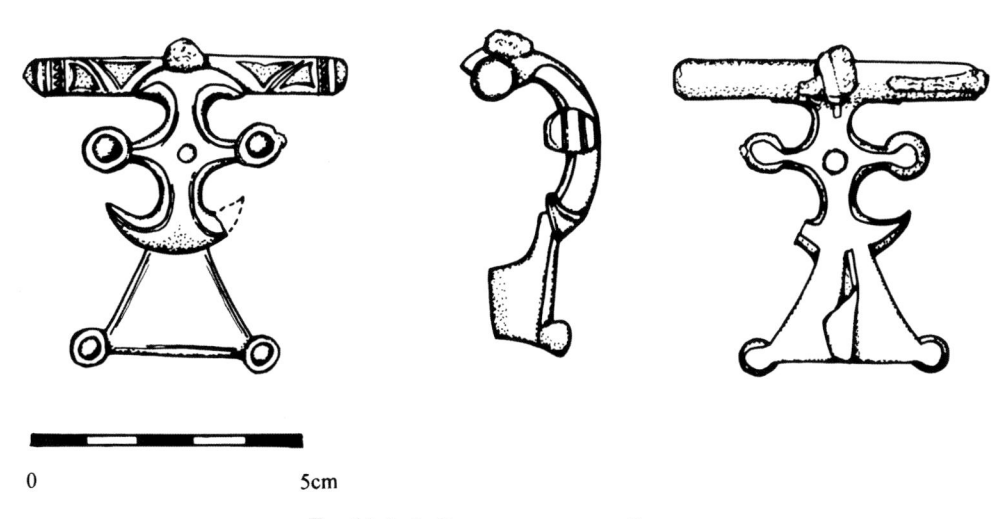

FIG 11.1, 1: THE BROOCH FROM SENNEN.

around a central circle in a wheel formation, though the depressions are far shallower than the triangular fields on the head so it is unlikely that they originally held enamel. Scientific examination and analysis suggest instead that the foot was originally smooth metal that was tinned all over and probably covered, in part at least, with repoussé-decorated metal foils or beaded wires. By comparison with other Romano-British brooches, these metal overlays are most likely to have been brass or silver (Bayley and Butcher 2004, 44). The two bottom corners of the foot have settings like those on the arms of the bow and the whole of the catchplate survives on the back of the foot.

St. Hilary 1 (PAS ref: CORN-DE55F7; Fig 11.1, 2)

Leaded bronze/gunmetal brooch with crossbar decorated with oblique engraved lines on the top, and on the front four sunken triangular fields which still contain some of the original red enamel. The bow was decorated with riveted-on hemispherical knobs or bosses; four of the original five survive. There is one at the end of each arm and three in a line down the centre of the bow. As on the brooch from Sennen, the fantail foot appears to have four incised triangles around a central triangle in a wheel formation, but again these pits are probably the result of corrosion. The two bottom corners of the foot have been broken off, suggesting that they may originally have had perforated lugs to take knobs like those on the bow, or decorative settings like those on the brooch from Sennen. Nearly the whole of the catchplate remains on the back of the foot.

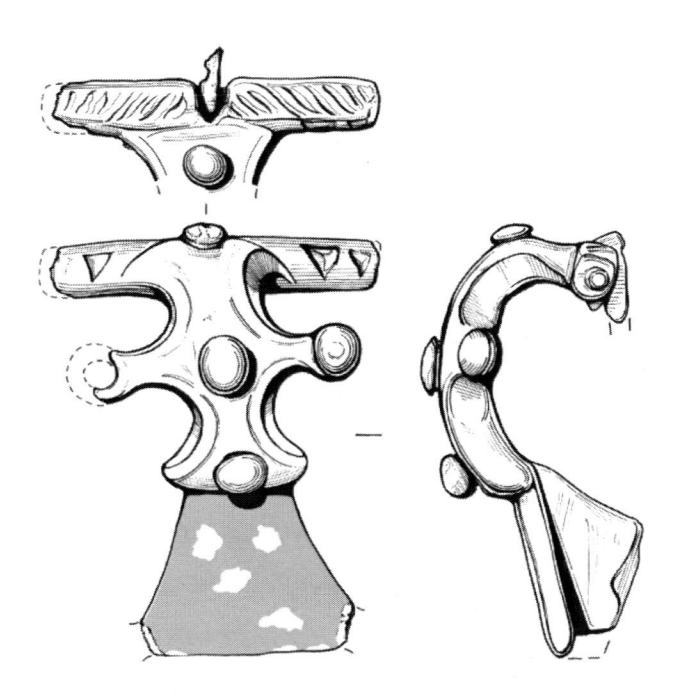

Fig 11.1, 2: The first brooch from St. Hilary. The grey tone indicates areas on the foot where the tinned surface survives.

St. Hilary 2 (PAS ref: CORN-DEC722; Fig 11.1, 3)

Leaded bronze brooch. There are slight losses from the ends of the crossbar which was decorated with four sunken triangular fields, though none of the original enamel survives. The marginal ridges on the bow show clearly. Like the other brooch from St. Hilary, the bow was decorated with riveted-on hemispherical knobs or bosses. Two survive on the centre line but those at the ends of the arms are lost. The area around them appeared black, but this was probably just a corrosion phenomenon. There was no boss near the fantail foot but a circular depression at the top of the foot may have been an aborted attempt to attach one here. Substantial parts of the foot have been lost, and only half the catchplate survives on the back. The foot was decorated with fields that would most probably have held enamel. The pattern is not clear due to erosion of the surface but appears to be an incised double-trumpet pattern, defining a palmette shape in reserved metal. Traces of a third field for enamel survive on the bottom edge of the foot so the design was probably the same as on the fragment from Kingsdon (fig 11.1, 8).

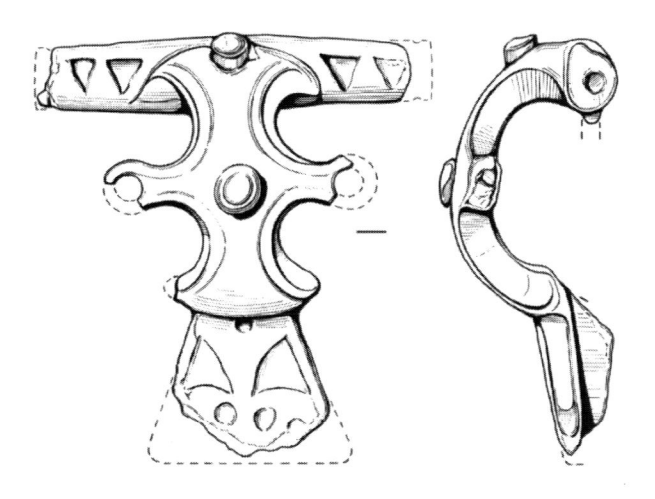

Fig 11.1, 3: The second brooch from St. Hilary.

Constantine (PAS ref: CORN-3A58B3; Fig 11.1, 4)

Leaded bronze brooch, originally with three riveted knobs in a line down the centre of the bow. The upper two have a truncated conical form and sit on a 'washer' but of the third, only the rivet survives on the back of the bow. Both the arms at the centre of the bow are broken, but sufficient survives to show that their form was very similar to those on the two brooches from St. Hilary, including a perforation to take a riveted knob. There is further loss of metal from the sides of the lowest portion of the arched bow, and also from the foot, so its original form is not known; it was probably similar to that of the second brooch from St. Hilary as there are the shallow remains of fields to take enamel. These are two triangular and two circular indentations, evenly spaced and forming a double-trumpet pattern, which would have been enamelled; the pattern again is the same as on the fragment from Kingsdon (Fig 11.1, 8). The foot also has traces of tinning and solder which most likely originally attached silver strips or wires that are found surrounding enamel on other types of Romano-British brooches (e.g. Bayley and Butcher 2004, plate 8). Only traces of the catchplate survive, and much of the crossbar is also lost, but the surviving portion shows it would have been similar to those described above.

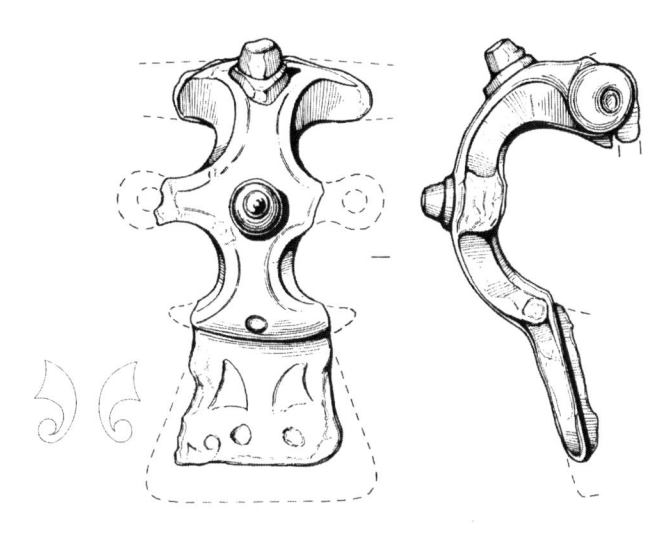

FIG 11.1, 4: THE BROOCH FROM CONSTANTINE.

Marazion (PAS ref: CORN-82B305; Fig 11.1, 5)

Lightly-leaded bronze brooch, similar to those described above, but distorted and the corroded surface rather badly eroded. Details of the decorative moulding is unclear, though traces of four triangular fields for enamel on the head and a central hemispherical knob on the bow are present, as are stubs of the side arms. The fantail foot is pitted and, like the brooch from Sennen, has traces of both tinning and of applied metal overlay. The catchplate appears almost intact.

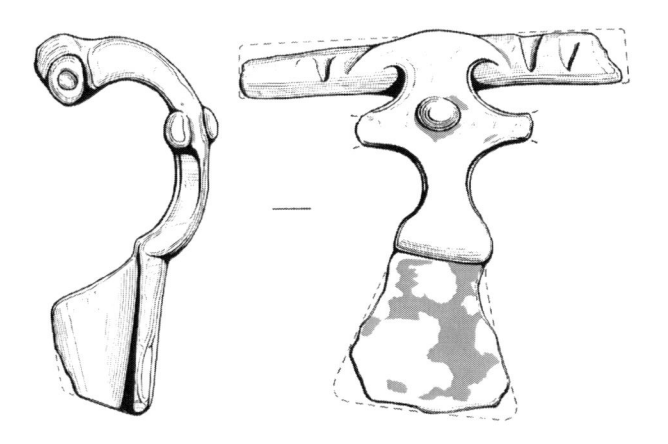

FIG 11.1, 5: THE BROOCH FROM MARAZION. THE GREY TONE INDICATES AREAS WHERE THE TINNED SURFACE SURVIVES.

St. Mawgan-in-Pydar (TRURI 1956.64; Fig 11.1, 6)

The following description comes from the published excavation report: 'Large, tinned, bronze brooch with hinge-pin on an iron axis inside a long tubular cross piece. The bow is strongly arched and is slightly concave on the inside surface. It has lateral wings terminating in knobs projecting outwards and downwards. The bow has a shallow groove along the margin, and near the centre is a rivet which originally may have held a stud. The bow is expanded into trumpet-like plates where it meets the cross piece and the foot. The latter is a plain triangular plate and there is a deep solid catch-plate.' (Murray Threipland 1957, 72). It is now in a poorer state than when drawn so nothing can be added to this description. Metal analysis has however demonstrated that the conventional designation of 'bronze' in this case correctly identifies the alloy.

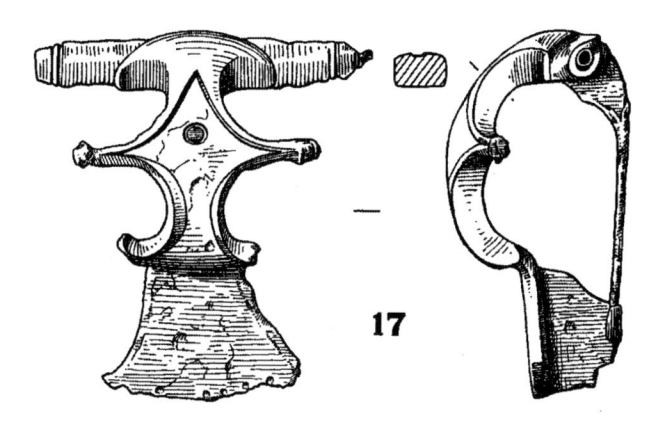

FIG 11.1, 6: THE BROOCH FROM ST. MAWGAN-IN-PYDAR (AFTER MURRAY THREIPLAND 1957, FIG 34).

Charterhouse (BRSMG: Fb8973; Fig 11.1, 7)

This leaded bronze brooch has lost its foot and the ends of its arms but is otherwise in reasonably good condition. The central hollow in the bow does not go all the way through, unlike the other brooches described above, but probably originally held some decorative attachment.

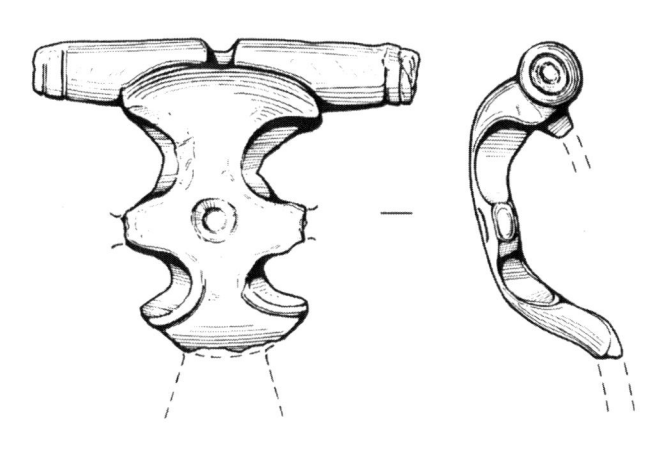

FIG 11.1, 7: THE BROOCH FROM CHARTERHOUSE.

Kingsdon (PAS ref: SOM-183E93; Fig 11.1, 8)

Leaded bronze brooch of which only the foot and lower part of the bow survive. On the bow is a domed stud, as on the brooches from St. Hilary and Constantine, but here it is cast in one with the brooch and has fine engraved cross-hatching surviving on its lower edge. Traces of enamel survive in at least three of the six fields on the foot. The design is clearly visible and confirms the reinterpretation of the design of the less well preserved fields on the brooches from St. Hilary 2 and Constantine. The front surface of the foot is tinned all over. Semi-quantitative XRF analysis found little lead or copper in the enamel, suggesting it was not originally red or orange in colour, though its present dark green appearance is a result of decay and burial.

Ludgvan 1(PAS ref: CORN-459FB7; Fig 11.1, 9)

Only the head and upper part of the bow of this lightly-leaded bronze brooch survive but it can be identified as another example of the type discussed here from the length of the crossbar and the form of its junction with the bow. However it appears to be a variant of the type as the bow lacks a central perforation, is far thinner and flat rather than curved in profile, and apparently more circular than lozenge-shaped in plan. It is deeply corroded and has lost

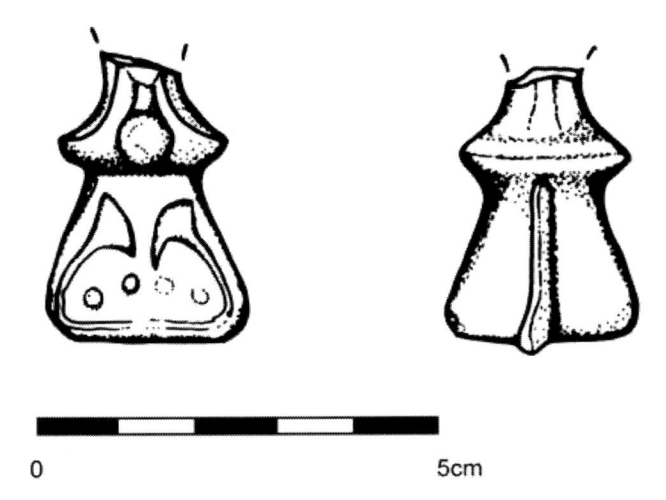

FIG 11.1, 8: THE BROOCH FROM KINGSDON.

much of its original surface but tinning and perhaps traces of an overlay survive on the disc of the bow.

Ludgvan 2 (PAS ref: CORN-51A8A7; Fig 11.1, 10)

This brooch fragment is made of leaded bronze. The crossbar is almost completely lost, as are most of the foot and any wings. A single hole is present in the centre of the

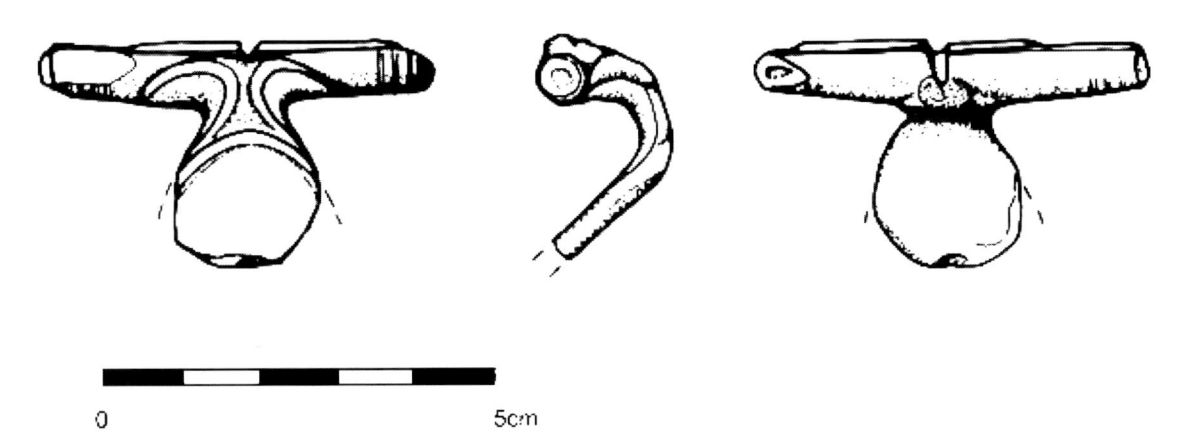

FIG 11.1, 9: THE FIRST BROOCH FROM LUDGVAN.

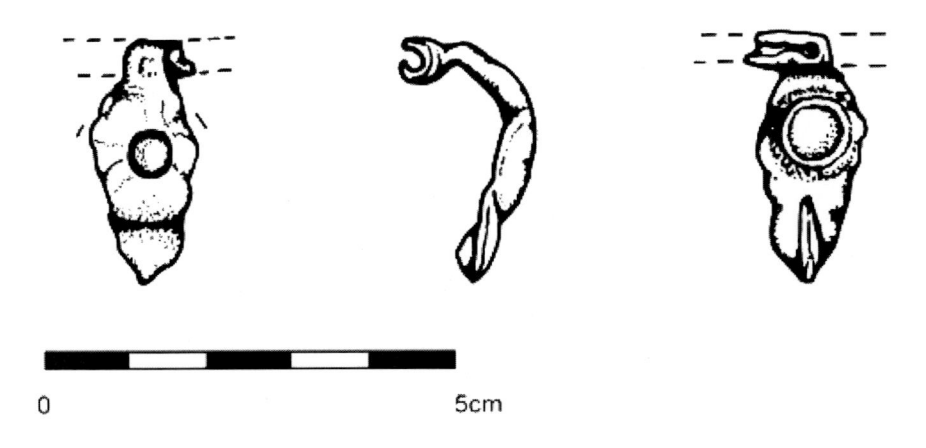

FIG 11.1, 10: THE SECOND BROOCH FROM LUDGVAN.

bow, suggesting that it originally carried riveted-on studs like the brooches described above. Like Ludgvan 1 it is a variant of the main type: the typical trumpet-like junction of bow and crossbar appears not to be present, and the back of the bow has circular depression, suggesting that its front may also have been circular rather than lozenge-shaped in outline.

Old Man, Isles of Scilly (Fig 11.1,11)

The location of this brooch is no longer known. Tebbutt's illustration (1934, fig 3a) shows the head and upper part of the bow of a brooch that in many ways is similar to Ludgvan 2. The bow is shown as far thinner than most of the other examples described here, but the distinctive junction of the head and bow is present as is a central perforation in the bow.

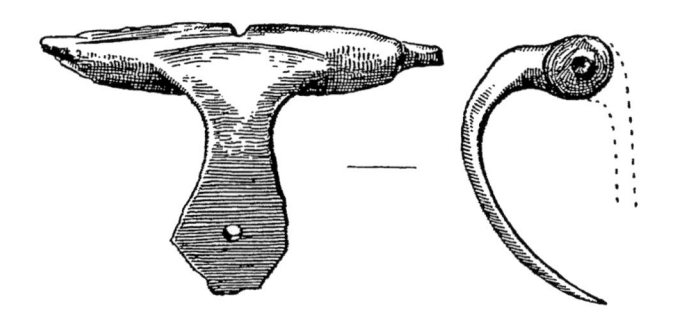

FIG 11.1, 11: THE BROOCH FROM OLD MAN (AFTER TEBBUTT 1934, FIG 3A).

Results of scientific investigation

Most brooch types have a preferred alloy composition which allows parallels to be drawn on technical as well as typological grounds. The compositions of this group of brooches were thus determined at the English Heritage Laboratories in Portsmouth in the expectation that a preferred alloy would emerge, and help in suggesting an origin for the brooches.

The surfaces of the brooches were initially analysed non-destructively by X-ray fluorescence (XRF) which detected varying quantities of lead, tin and zinc in addition to copper.[1] These initial analyses demonstrated that almost all the bosses appeared to have the same composition as the brooch to which they were attached; the only exception was the copper alloy rivet on the Sennen brooch which appears to contain less tin than the brooch, but it was deeply corroded so this result is not definitive. The surface XRF analyses also detected elevated levels of tin in areas where a distinct white metal coating was visible, allowing its unequivocal identification as tinning. The suggestion (above) that traces of thicker deposits on the fantails of several brooches may be the remains of a lead-tin solder that would have attached a decorative metal overlay is also based on the results of surface XRF analyses.

Because the brooches showed significant corrosion, the surface XRF analyses represent the composition of the corrosion products rather than that of the original metal of which they were made. All the brooches were therefore sampled by drilling a 1mm diameter hole into their backs. These drillings were then analysed by the same technique. The results were compared to those obtained from ten copper alloy standards of known composition, so the figures given in Table 11.3 are a reliable guide to the composition of the alloys from which the brooches were made. The drillings were retained so they remain available for future analyses.

---

[1] When analyses are made by XRF there is a problem in detecting traces of arsenic when significant amounts of lead are present. This is because the major XRF peaks (the lead L_α and the arsenic K_α) overlap and the spectrometer cannot fully deconvolute them. The XRF analyses of the drillings suggested traces of arsenic were present in the Charterhouse and two St. Hilary brooches. The spectra were therefore examined to see if the minor arsenic XRF peak (K_β) was present as its position in the spectrum does not overlap with peaks from any of the major elements detected. The minor arsenic peak could not be seen, so it is likely that the arsenic 'detected' by XRF was only present, if at all, at very low levels, well below those suggested by the calibration of the XRF system. Arsenic has therefore been omitted from Table 11.3, as have other elements that were sought but not detected.

	St Hilary 1	Charter-house	St Hilary 2	Constantine	Marazion	St Mawgan	Sennen
Cu%	72.3	75.6	75.9	77.1	88.3	88.1	87.8
Zn%	2.3	0.7	1.5	1.2	0.5	0.7	0.1
Sn%	5.5	7.3	7.8	13.4	6.6	9.9	11.5
Fe%	0.1	0.1	0.1	0.1	0.1	0.1	0.3
Pb%	19.9	16.3	14.7	8.2	4.5	1.2	0.3
Alloy	leaded bronze/gunmetal	leaded bronze	leaded bronze	leaded bronze	(leaded) bronze	bronze	bronze

Cu = copper, Zn = zinc, Sn = tin, Fe = iron, Pb = lead
See footnotes 1 and 2 for discussion of the calibration of the XRF data.

TABLE 11.3: COMPOSITION OF THE DRILLINGS TAKEN FROM THE BROOCHES (NORMALISED WT%)

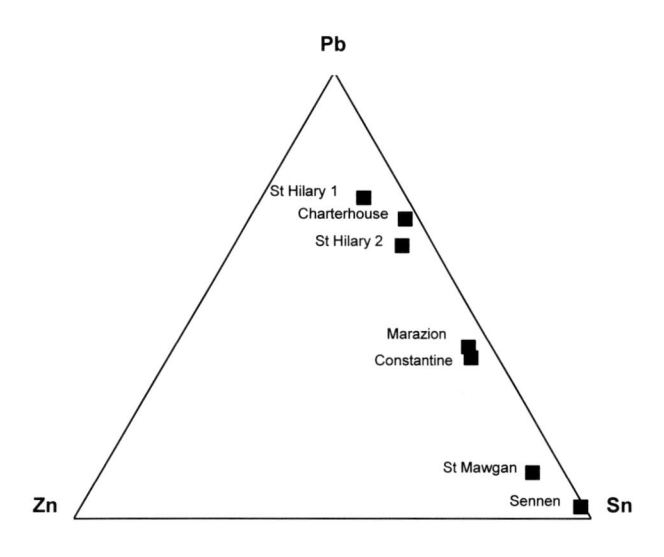

FIG 11.2: TERNARY DIAGRAM SHOWING THE RANGE OF ALLOY COMPOSITIONS OF THE ANALYSED BROOCHES.

It is clear from Table 11.3 that all the brooches are basically copper-tin alloys with varying amounts of lead. The alloy names assigned follow those defined by Bayley and Butcher (2004, table 5). The variable proportions of lead and tin are shown in Figure 11.2, which also shows the greater zinc to tin ratio of St. Hilary 1, which leads it to be classified as a leaded bronze/gunmetal rather than a leaded bronze. Traces of iron (and possibly arsenic, see note 1) are unintentional impurities, present at levels commonly found in Roman copper alloys; it is likely these elements came mainly from the copper.

The data in Table 11.3 is presented in a different way in Figure 11.2 which shows the relative amounts of the three main alloying elements: tin, lead and zinc. This approach has been used by Bayley and Butcher (2004) and allows easy visual comparison to be made between the compositions of different objects. The nearer to a corner a data point lies, the higher is the proportion of that element present. The three brooches plotting nearest to the lead (Pb) corner are the heavily leaded alloys while the brooches from St. Mawgan-in-Pydar and Sennen are unleaded bronzes; the main alloying element present in them is tin (Sn).[2]

The three brooches that were recognised after this paper had been written could not be analysed in the same way as the others, due to a combination of lack of time and the condition of the Ludgvan brooches. Instead the surface XRF analyses kindly carried out by Duncan Hook at the British Museum have been interpreted to allow broad comparisons to be made with the earlier analyses, though in the absence of quantitative results these three brooches cannot be added as Figures 11,1, 12 and 11,1,13. The Kingsdon brooch is almost certainly a heavily leaded bronze as is Lugdvan 2, though in the latter case percentage levels of zinc were also detected. These results suggest that the two brooches probably have similar compositions to those from St. Hilary and Charterhouse. Lugdvan 1 appears to be a bronze containing only a few percent of lead and so its composition is probably intermediate between those of the Constantine and St. Mawgan brooches.

Discussion

These Cornish brooches appear to be related to the Hook Norton (Hull forthcoming) or Aesica variant (Mackreth 1982) types; they share with them an arched bow with sideways expansions and a fantail foot. These types show a great deal of variation in shape, in decoration, and in the method of pin attachment – which led Mackreth (1982) to suggest they were local products of different parts of Britain, most probably dating to the later 1st century. Some of this broad group of brooches have elements of 'Celtic' styles of decoration, most notably the original Aesica brooch from Great Chesters in Northumberland (Charlesworth 1973). They form part of a flourishing of late La Tène decoration in the mid Roman period and seem to have a western and northern distribution in the British Isles. In terms of decorative motifs, broad parallels for the pattern of the enamel fields on the fantail foot of the brooches from St. Hilary, Constantine and Kingsdon can be found in the classic 'Celtic' fantail brooch (Hull Type 36), though normally the pattern on these is in reserved metal in an enamelled field (e.g. Bayley and Butcher 2004, fig 79 no 238) rather than in the enamelled fields.

There is considerable variation at a detailed level between the brooches described here. Those from Sennen and St. Mawgan in Pydar have a crispness of execution and well-defined detailing, while on the other enamelled examples the fields are less precisely cut and overall the brooches have a more casually-made feel to them. It is difficult to know how much of this apparent lack of precision is due to corrosion and abrasion before or during burial, but many other brooch types also show a degeneration in design that has been associated with copying or mass-production. It is therefore tempting to see the smaller, simpler and less highly decorated examples of these Cornish brooches as later in date than the more elaborate ones. When it comes to an absolute rather than relative chronology we have little to go on other than Mackreth's suggestion (above) that related brooch types probably date from the later 1st century, though the brooch from St. Mawgan in Pydar comes from an assemblage that can be dated – to the middle half of the 1st century (Murray Threipland 1956, 43). If we are right in seeing this as one of the earlier examples in our group, the overall dating may well stretch on towards the end of the 1st century, with the possibility that heirlooms may have had an even longer life.

---

[2] There is a further slight problem in calibrating the XRF data as the maximum lead content in the copper alloy standards was just over 11%. The higher lead values given in Table 11.3 therefore have an increased uncertainty associated with them as the calibration had to be extrapolated. However, lead contents of over 20% are not uncommon for brooches made in south-western Britain so the high values quoted are not unexpected.

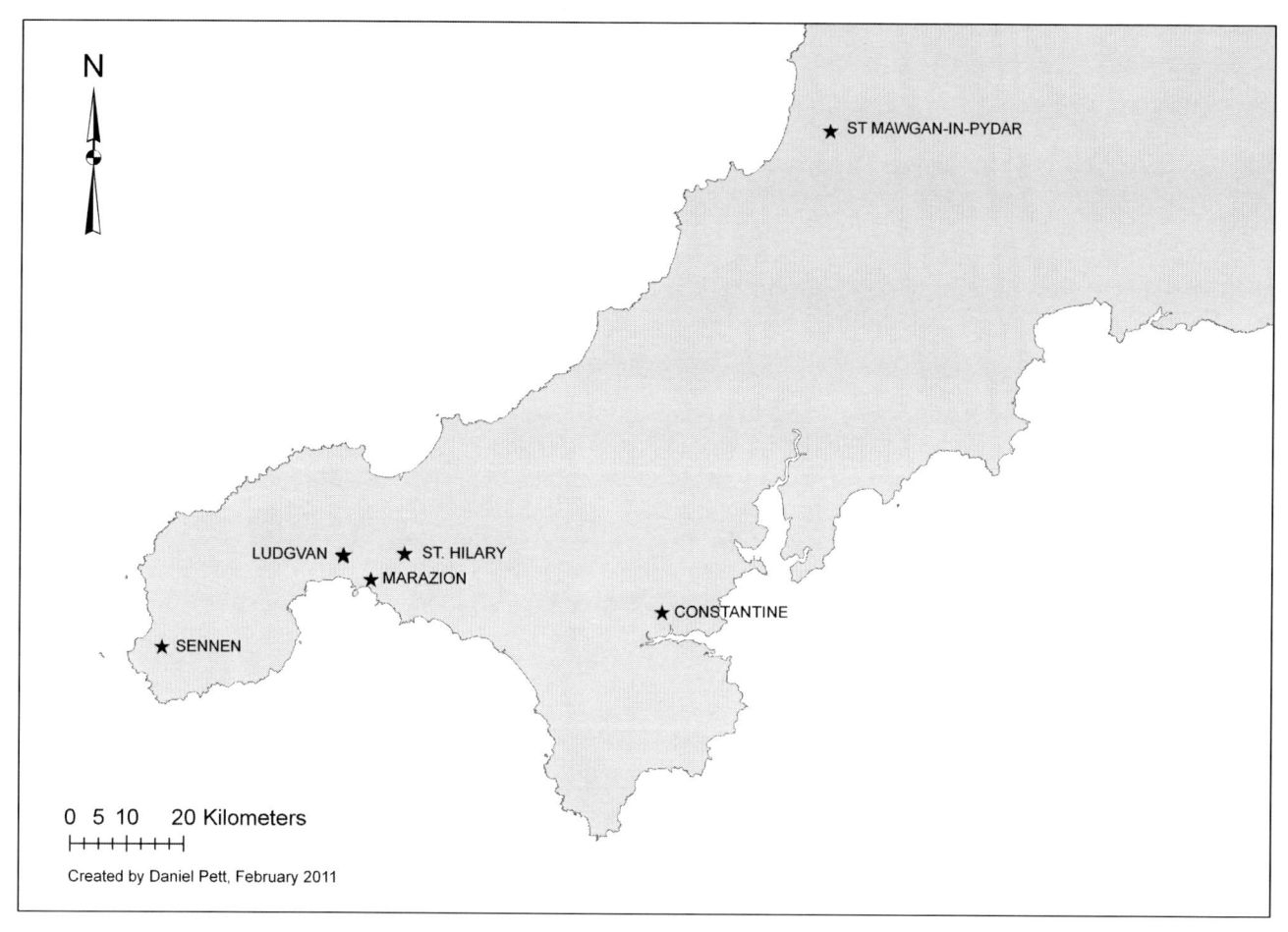

FIG 11.3: MAP OF WEST CORNWALL SHOWING THE FINDSPOTS OF THE BROOCHES.

Having so far concentrated on the brooches themselves, on how they were made and decorated, we should perhaps take a broader view and consider where they were found. The map (Fig 11.3) shows how closely grouped the majority are in the far west of Cornwall, with the one from St. Mawgan-in-Pydar 40km away on the north coast, and only two known so far from outside the county, from on or near the Mendips. This close geographic cluster is intriguing, so we need to consider if there is any evidence they could have been made locally.

The final strand of this study is the composition of these brooches which we hoped might help identify their area of manufacture. Given their distribution and the features they share with many of the T-shaped brooches that are generally accepted as being made in the south-west (in a general rather than a specifically Cornish context), the results are somewhat unexpected. Not only is there no single preferred alloy type (though the sample is small) but when compared with the main group of T-shaped brooches, these Type 31 brooches have a consistent, small, but significant zinc content (average 1.0%). If Figure 11.13 is compared with ternary diagrams for 'initial' and 'developed' T-shaped brooches (Bayley and Butcher 2004, figs 125 and 139) it can be seen that the compositions of the leaded bronzes and (leaded) bronzes fall on the fringes of the main distributions rather than within them. Even those brooches that do not contain enough zinc to alter the name given to the alloy contain more zinc than most south-western brooches, which typically have under 0.5% zinc.

The large group of south-western T-shaped brooches, which incidentally make up over half the Roman brooches from Cornwall recorded on the PAS database, have a distribution that includes areas as far east as Dorset, Somerset, and in particular the Mendips. The large collection of clay piece moulds for T-shaped brooches from Compton Dando is good evidence that at least some of these types were made there. There are said to be thousands of mould fragments from a gas pipe trench (Gater 1986; Bayley and Butcher 2004, 35), and a smaller number found at the same time were recently reported to the PAS (Adams 2008). However, it is most unlikely to have been the only workshop producing them.

If these Hull Type 31 brooches have a mainly Cornish distribution, is it too fanciful to suggest they may have been made here? Though previously almost unique, our examination of the PAS database show they are the second most common type among the 48 brooches recorded from the whole of Cornwall. Their variable composition can be used to suggest that they may have been made of recycled scrap metal. If we assume only a limited amount of scrap was available, it may not have been possible to sort it as carefully as in other parts of the country where it was more abundant. It could thus be a lack of metal that led to the variation in composition.

The question of exactly where this local manufacture might have been carried out must remain open. No evidence for brooch manufacture has been found in Cornwall, but it is not unique in this as there is little evidence from other parts of Britain (Bayley and Butcher 2004, 35-40). Very little copper alloy working has been identified in Cornwall, particularly if we look only at the Roman period. However, one site where it was present was St. Mawgan-in-Pydar where Hut A was probably used in the middle half of the 1st century as a founder's workshop. The finds included '... droplets of bronze, pieces of crucible, a small ingot of bronze and a folded piece of scrap bronze' – and the brooch described above (Murray Threipland 1956, 43). We are not suggesting that the Type 31 brooches were necessarily made at St. Mawgan-in-Pydar, but finds similar to those from Hut A there would have been present where they were made.

Future work

Further analyses of the metal samples are planned, using inductively coupled plasma mass spectrometry (ICP-MS) at Camborne School of Mines, University of Exeter, Cornwall Campus. Dr Jens Andersen and Dr Gavyn Rollinson plan to isolate the particular isotopes within the metal and may thus be able to demonstrate that it came from Cornish ores. This could throw further light on where the brooches were made.

Conclusions

This paper demonstrates how the new data collected by the PAS is changing our view of particular classes of objects. Before the brooches described here were reported, only three examples of this type were known. Now we have an extra seven examples, all of them from within a 20km radius in the far west of Cornwall. The integration of scientific analyses with their typological study has allowed us to demonstrate that our brooches' alloy composition does not quite fit with that of the main group of south-western T-shaped brooches, allowing us to suggest that they may indeed have been made near where they were found, in the far west of Cornwall.

Bibliography

Adams, K. 2008. GLO-9090B6 A ROMAN mould [from Compton Dando]. Webpage available at: http://finds.org.uk/database/artefacts/record/id/221278 [Accessed: Feb 2011]

Bayley, J. and Butcher, S. 2004. *Roman brooches in Britain: a technological and typological study based on the Richborough collection*. Report of the Research Committee 68, London: Society of Antiquaries of London

Booth, A. 2009. SOM-183E93 A ROMAN Brooch [from Kingsdon]. Webpage available at: http://www.finds.org.uk/database/artefacts/record/id/256505 [Accessed: Feb 2011]

Charlesworth, D. 1973. 'The Aesica hoard [of jewellery, Great Chesters, Northumberland]', *Archaeologia Aeliana* ser 5, 1, 225-34

Gater, J. 1986. Compton Dando, *Bristol and Avon Archaeology* 5, 52

Hattatt, R. 2000. *A Visual Guide of Richard Hattatt's Ancient Brooches,* Oxford: Oxbow

Hull, M. R. Forthcoming. *Brooches in Pre-Roman and Roman Britain* (eds G.M. Simpson, N. Crummy and B. Blance)

Mackreth, D. F. 1982. 'Two brooches from Stonea, Cambs and Bicester, Oxon, and the origin of the Aesica brooch', *Britannia*, 13, 310-15

Murray Threipland, L. 1956. 'An Excavation at St. Mawgan-in-Pyder, North Cornwall', *Archaeological Journal*, 113, 33-81

Tebbutt, C.F. 1934. 'A cist in the Scilly Isles' *Antiquaries Journal* 14, 302-04.

Tyacke, A. 2004. CORN-82B305 A ROMAN Brooch [from Marazion]. Webpage available at: http://www.finds.org.uk/database/artefacts/record/id/63814 [Accessed: Feb 2011]

Tyacke, A. 2005. CORN-459FB7 A ROMAN brooch [from Ludgvan]. Webpage available at: http://www.finds.org.uk/database/artefacts/record/id/84682 [Accessed: Feb 2011]

Tyacke, A. 2007. CORN-51A8A7 A ROMAN brooch [from Ludgvan]. Webpage available at: http://www.finds.org.uk/database/artefacts/record/id/187367 [Accessed: Feb 2011]

Tyacke, A. 2008. CORN-3A58B3 A ROMAN brooch [from Constantine]. Webpage available at: http://www.finds.org.uk/database/artefacts/record/id/216934 [Accessed: Feb 2011]

Tyacke, A. 2009a. CORN-8FDAD6 A ROMAN brooch [from Sennen]. Webpage available at: http://www.finds.org.uk/database/artefacts/record/id/268543 [Accessed: Feb 2011]

Tyacke, A. 2009b. CORN-DE55F7 A ROMAN brooch [from St. Hilary]. Webpage available at: http://www.finds.org.uk/database/artefacts/record/id/266813 [Accessed: Feb 2011]

Tyacke, A. 2009c. CORN-DEC722 A ROMAN brooch [from St. Hilary]. Webpage available at: http://www.finds.org.uk/database/artefacts/record/id/266814 [Accessed: Feb 2011]

Acknowledgements

We are grateful to the owners of the newly discovered brooches for loaning them to us to permit further study, and for their permission to remove samples for analysis. We would also like to thank Gail Boyle of Bristol Museum and Art Gallery for arranging for the loan of the brooch from Charterhouse, and for obtaining permission for us to sample it. We are also grateful to Duncan Hook of the British Museum for analysing the Ludgvan and Kingsdon brooches. Figure 6 is reproduced from The Archaeological Journal Vol 113 by kind permission of the editor, Patrick Ottaway. Figure 11 is reproduced by kind permission of the Society of Antiquaries of London from The Antiquaries Journal Vol 14 for 1934, © reserved. Figures 11.1 and 11.8-10 were drawn by Carl Thorpe, Figures 11.1, 2-5 and 7 by Chris Evans and Figure 11.1, 4 by Daniel Pett.

The Early Medieval Native Pottery of Cornwall (c400-1066 AD)

C.M. Thorpe

Abstract

Pottery production in Cornwall runs from the Neolithic to the present day. This paper reviews its manufacture and use during the Early Medieval period, when, in most parts of Britain, pottery production ceased, and pottery use was restricted.

Introduction

Cornwall is in a position of being one of the few places in the British Isles where pottery production and use has been an almost continuous process from the Neolithic to the present day. The county has played a prominent part in the study of Early Medieval ceramics, especially in the identification and understanding of the imported wares from France and the Mediterranean. Cornwall is also one of the few regions in Britain where it can be demonstrated that local 'Native' wares were being manufactured at this time. No work on the post-Roman ceramics of Cornwall can fail to acknowledge the pioneering work of Professor Charles Thomas who was the first to identify and classify the native wares (Thomas 1960; Thomas 1968; 2005); however our knowledge of these has progressed significantly over the last few years with the publication and study of several important sites including Trethurgy (Quinnell 2004), Boden Fogou (Gossip forthcoming), Gwithian (Nowakowski et al.), Mawgan Porth (Bruce-Mitford 1997), Launceston Castle (Saunders 2006), Hay Close, Newlyn East (Jones forthcoming) and Tintagel (Barrowman et al. 2007). The author has worked alongside and collaborated with Henrietta Quinnell on many of these projects (plus numerous other prehistoric sites) our work leading to the identification of the sequence of material offered in this paper. Though this work is ongoing and will no doubt undergo further refinement it is an honour and privilege present here an interim statement of our findings in celebration of Henrietta's Birthday and career so far.

In the late Roman period between the fourth and fifth centuries AD there was a well developed and flourishing pottery industry within Cornwall. Unlike large parts of Britain where the use or production of ceramics declined or ceased completely in the late fifth and sixth centuries AD, in Cornwall, native pottery became more experimental and innovative and developed rapidly in many directions. Manufactured mostly from gabbroic clays derived from the Serpentine rocks of the Lizard, the principal repertoire of forms produced were slack-profiled jars (Trethurgy Type 4), the Cornish flanged bowl (Trethurgy Type 22), and the flat grooved-rim bowl (Trethurgy Type 21) and large storage jars both with cordons (Trethurgy Type 13) and of large cooking pot form (Trethurgy Type 16). The work at Trethurgy suggested that this suite of domestic wares continued into the fifth and possibly sixth centuries showing that the basic patterns of cooking and eating throughout the Roman period endured until then (Quinnell 2004).

Gwithian Style Ware

This material was first identified by Charles Thomas (Thomas 1956; 1960) during excavations at Gwithian, and the forms were subsequently termed 'Gwithian Style' ware. Many of the types are a continuation of the Cornish late Roman potting tradition. Forms include jars and bowls with curved and everted rims, often with a concave internal rim bevel. The ware also introduces the use of low walled platters (sometimes without a wall at all). These platters are completely new form and unrelated to the Romano-Cornish gabbroic repertoire, perhaps connected to some change in the preparation and serving of food (figs 12.1 and 12.2).

Jars

These are generally similar to Romano-Cornish Trethurgy Type 4 jars, but the rims of which are much less everted (figs 12.1, 11-21 and 12.2, 1-2). A marked feature on some smaller jars is a concave internal rim bevel, something never found on the earlier forms of jar. It does however occur on E-ware E2 imported beakers (Campbell 1991; 1996; 2007; Thomas 1957; 1960; 2005), which may have had an influence on the design of this ware. Some of the rim forms that occur are very complex.

Shouldered jars or bowls with short upright rims

These might relate to Trethurgy Type 6 jars, loosely dated to the third and fourth centuries but the resemblance is not close. Again some of these jars have a concave internal rim bevel (eg fig 12.1, 13).

Large flat-rimmed bowls

These bowls are generally large, with thick curved walls and flat, out-turned rims often with concave internal rim bevels (fig 12.2, 3-6). The rim edge on one example from Gwithian, GME, is heavily thumbed. There is a general resemblance to Roman Trethurgy Type 20 bowls but these

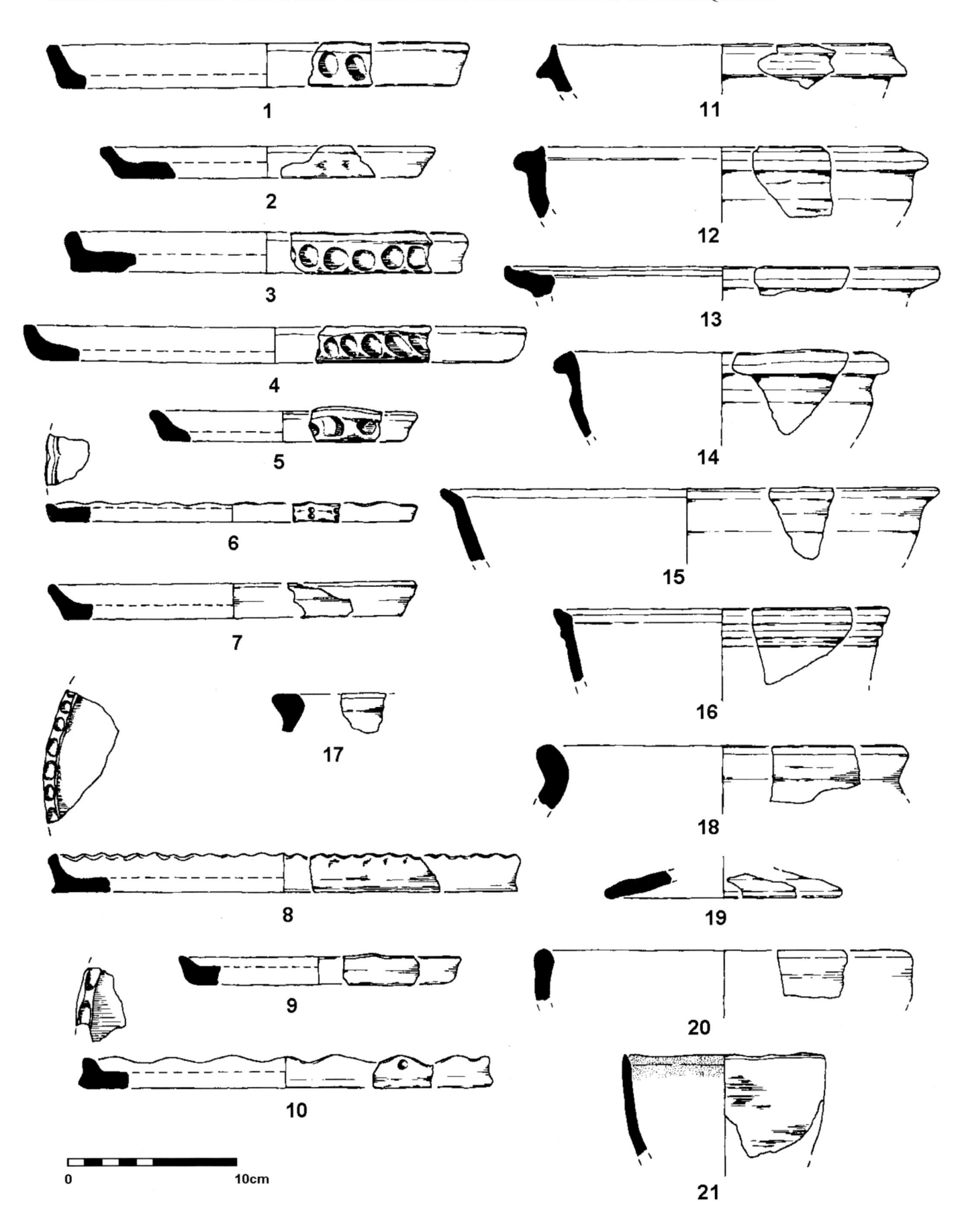

Fig 12.1. Forms of Gwithian Style Ware.

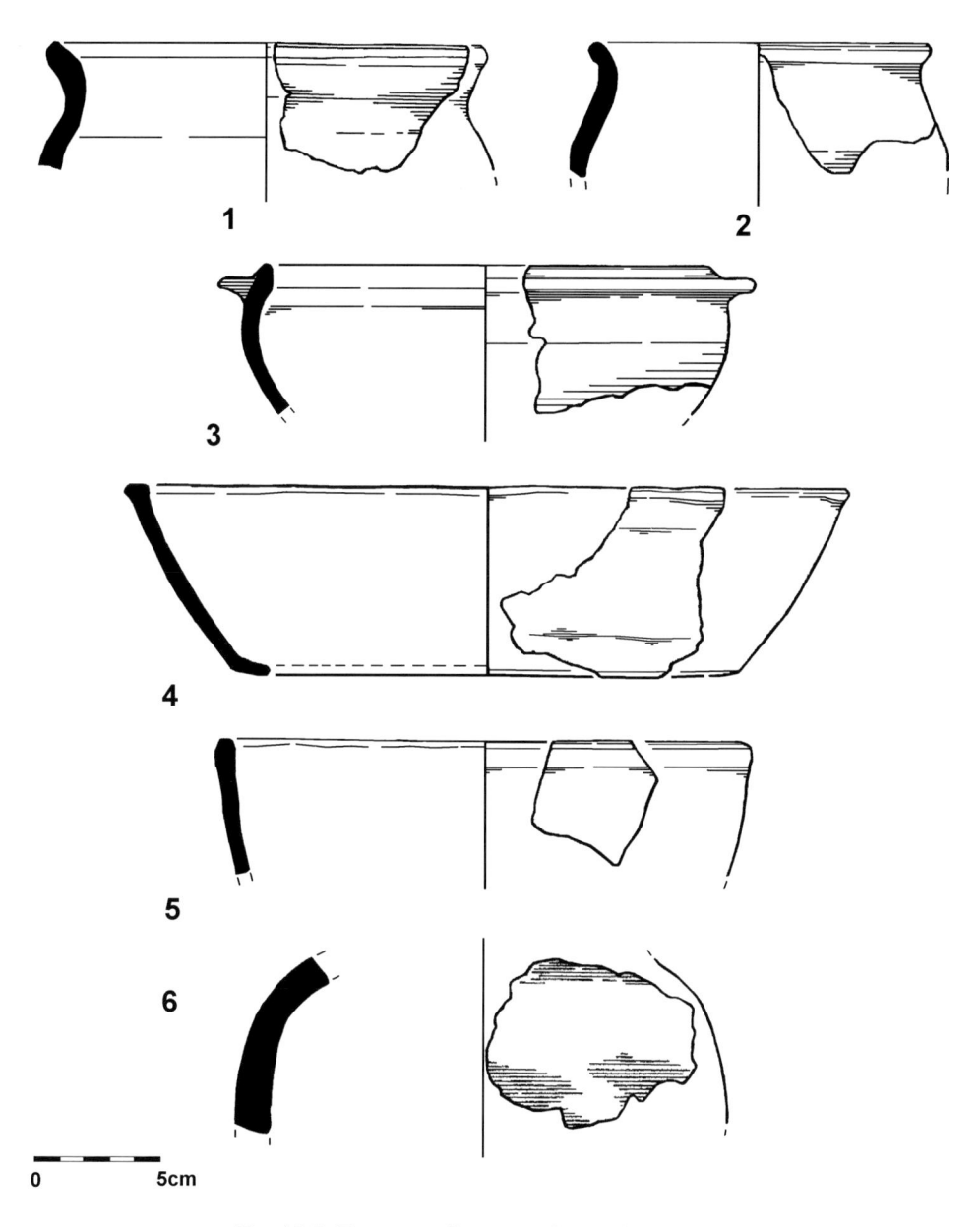

FIG 12.2. FORMS OF CWITHIAN STYLE CERAMICS.

were not thought to continue up until the end of the fourth century. There is some similarity in shape, though not in rim form, to E-ware E3 imported bowls (Campbell 2007; Thomas 2005).

Flanged bowls

These bowls are usually medium sized, with thin curved walls and upright rims with a prominent projecting flange just below the rim (fig 12.2, 3). They appear to be a continuation of the Trethurgy Type 22 Cornish flanged bowls (Quinnell 2004). Examples are known from Hay Close, Boden Fogou, and Tintagel.

Platters

These have very low walls, (a few having none at all), and many appear to be of large diameter. Bases frequently have sand impressions on their undersides and the base angles may be rounded. There is considerable use of thumbed decoration on top of the wall, or around the edge of discs without walls. There is also a range of incised and impressed decoration on the rims and both the inside and the outside of the walls. The decoration is much more extensive than on later, grass-marked, platters (figs 12.1, 1-10).

Miscellaneous

Apart from these categories, other ceramic items have included a large carinated vessel possibly for storage from Hay Close (Jones forthcoming), while lids and an oil lamp (fig. 12.1, 17) have been identified from Boden (Gossip forthcoming).

Gwithian Style ware generally appears to be of a fine, well sorted, highly fired gabbroic fabric, generally finer and more hard-fired than Roman gabbroic ware. Surfaces are often better finished than their Roman predecessors, sometimes wiped, occasionally slightly burnished with some patterning in the burnish. Petrographic examination by Roger Taylor (2004) describes the fabric as 'gabbroic with sparse (c 5%) and generally fine-grained inclusions'. The underside of the bases of the vessels are often sanded, or have been sat on sand prior to firing. There does seem to be some regional variation in fabrics. Those vessels found on the Isles of Scilly such as those from East Porth Samson, are often in a granitic fabric, while those recognised at Tintagel are in a gabbroic fabric with crushed fragments of slate. Further study will hopefully refine these details.

By its association with imported Mediterranean wares such as Late Roman 1 (Bii, and Late Roman 2 (Bi) amphorae, African, and Phocean Red Slipped Wares (i.e. at Gwithian and Hay Close), Gwithian Style ware is dated to the sixth to late seventh centuries AD. This is supported by the radiocarbon (AMS) determination obtained from internal residue on a sanded platter sherd from Gwithian (Nowakowski et al. 2007) GMI context (2210) of cal AD 550-650 (OxA 14528), and a second date from residue within a platter at Boden (Gossip forthcoming) of cal AD 590 - 670 (OxA 14560). A C14 determination (derived from bone) from Hay Close, Newlyn East (Jones forthcoming) from a sealed pit fill, context (6) containing this ware along with associated imported Mediterranean ware gave a date of cal AD 390 – 540 (SUERC-19887).

This date range makes Gwithian Style a contemporary of imported E ware from western France, which may have even influenced its design with the adoption of stylistic features such as concave internal rim bevels. This ware has so far been identified at Gwithian, Boden Fogou, Hay Close, Newlyn East, East Porth, Samson, Scilly and both Goldherring (Guthrie 1969) and Carngoon Bank have platters without grass-marking, while the latter has vessels which may belong to other forms (eg McAvoy 1980, Fig 18, No 73).

Sometime in the late seventh or early eighth centuries AD there appears to have been a major cultural change in Cornwall, which saw a dramatic change in eating habits, with a turning away from individual dining and serving sets common in the Roman period and a change to a more restrictive set of vessels that seems to reflect a more communal way of dining. This material was again first identified and described by Charles Thomas during excavations at Gwithian (Thomas 1956, 1966, 1968). Due to the appearance of the distinctive fabric and surface treatment this ware is called 'Grass-Marked ware'.

'Grass-Marked ware'

Grass-marked ware marked the introduction of a new ceramic production technique, the use of chopped grass to prevent adherence to surfaces prior to firing, leaving clear vegetation marks on the bases and sides of vessels. There appears to be three basic vessel forms (figs. 12.3 and 12.4). There were cooking pots, which are squat flat-based vessels with vertical or slightly incurving sides (fig. 12.3, 1-7); platters, similar in form to those found in 'Gwithian Style' pottery but with grass-marking replacing sanding (fig 12.3, 8-15); and bar-lug vessels with opposed internal suspension bars (or lugs) so that they may be hung over a fire to function as cauldrons (fig 12.4). 'Grass-Marked ware' has been found on numerous sites in Cornwall and the Isles of Scilly. Significant sites in the study of this ware include Gwithian, East Porth Samson Scilly, Tean Scilly, Gunwalloe, Mawgan Porth, and Launceston Castle.

Platters

These are a continuation of the platters found in Gwithian Style ware. They are flat based (the bases being relatively thick in relation to vessel size), with very low walls and rims (some with no wall at all), and many appear to be of large diameter (fig.12.3, 8-15). Rims are either rounded off or flat-topped. Decoration is rare, (especially in comparison to the Gwithian Style platters) but where present consists of 'nicking' of the rim with the back of a knife, fingernail marking also around the rim, or moulding the rim with the fingertips to form a 'pie crust' ornament (Thomas 1963, 1991).

Cooking vessels

These consist of squat, flat based, vertically (or slightly incurving) sided cooking pots. They have simple rims, which may have incised or finger nail decoration. These vessels have no known precursors in Cornwall (fig. 12.3, 1-7). Walls are often thin in comparison to the size of vessel. Rims are either flat topped (levelled by knife or spatula) or slightly beaded, sometimes with a slight eversion. Though often heavily sooted on the exterior, where visible, finger marking, and smoothing using a knife or spatula is common. Decoration where present consists of 'nicking' of the rim with the back of a knife, fingernail marking also around the rim, or moulding the rim with the fingertips to form a 'pie crust' ornament (Thomas 1963, 1991).

Bar-lug vessels

These are medium to large sized vessels identical in shape to the straight-sided cooking vessels however these have opposed suspension bars internally inserted into their rims which may be heavier than previously and pulled out to form an ear shaped 'lip' at the point of attachment (fig 12. 4). These vessels appear to fulfil the same function as cauldrons and are almost invariably heavily sooted on the exterior. Decoration where present consists of 'nicking' of the rim with the back of a knife, fingernail marking also around the rim, or moulding the rim with the fingertips to form a 'pie crust' ornament (Thomas 1963, 1991) This decoration is often continued over the rim of the 'lip' as well. The top of the inserted bar is also often decorated (not always in the same style as the rim) slashed saltires or nicking being common.

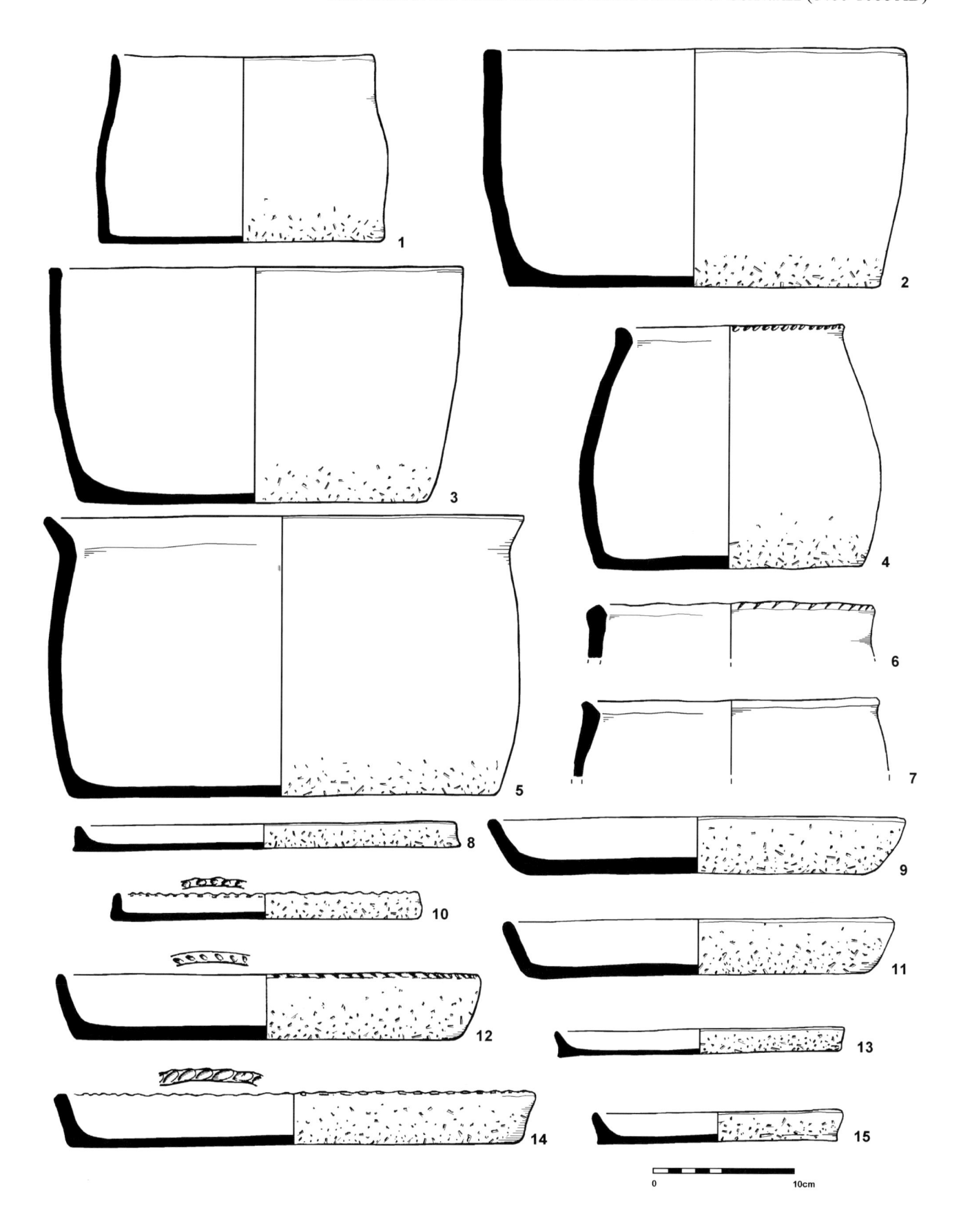

Fig 12.3. Forms of Grass-Marked Cooking Vessels and Platters.

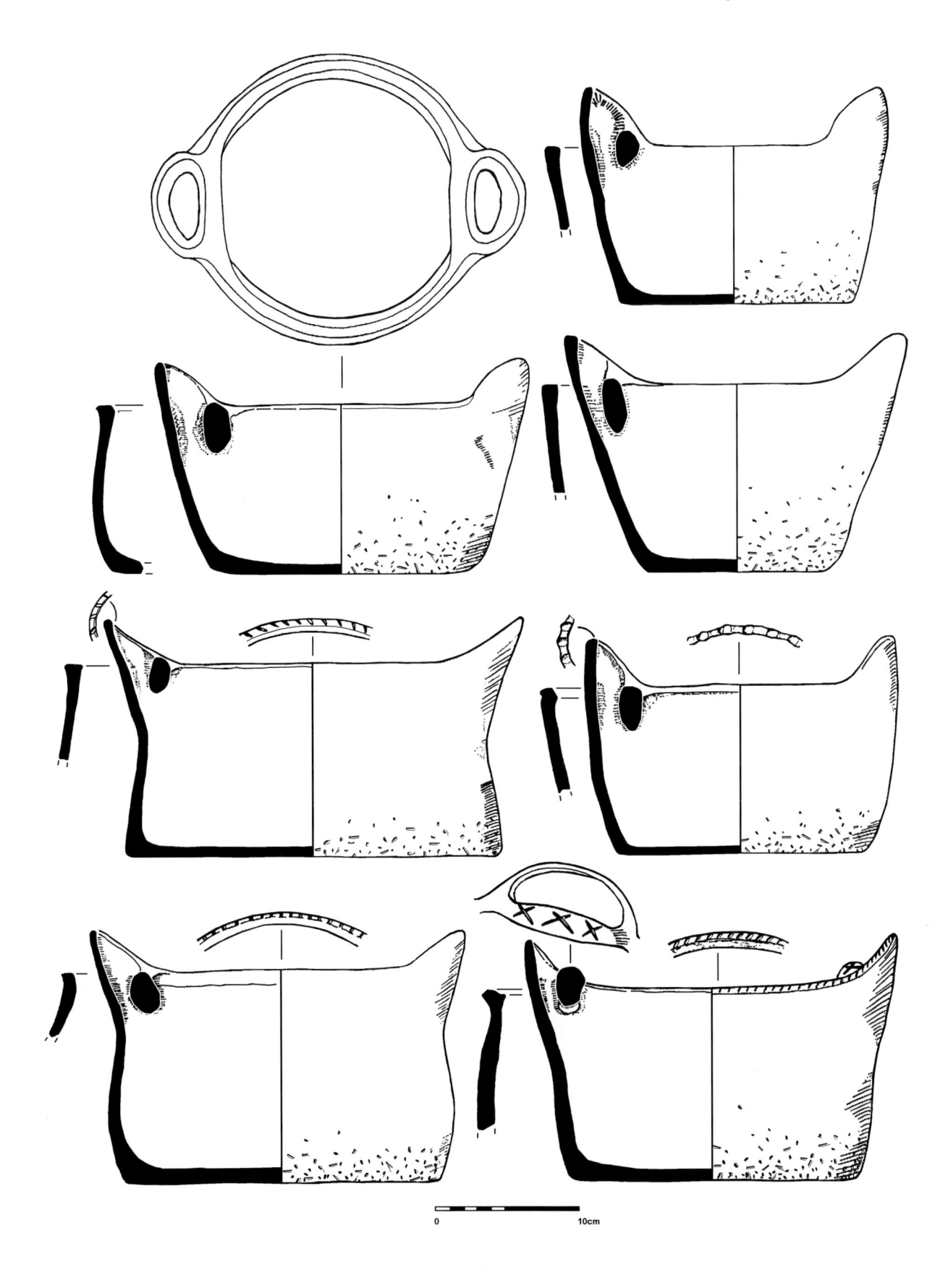

Fig 12.4. Forms of Bar Lug Ceramics.

The vessels are hand made (often ring or coil built), and the fabric is generally gabbroic but softer, thicker and less well finished than that of the Gwithian Style. Four sherds were examined from Gwithian by Dr Taylor (PS53, 54, 55, 56) and described as gabbroic coarse ware with 10-15% inclusions (2004) often with large amounts of feldspar. The firing is variable (often plain body sherds are indistinguishable from prehistoric pottery), but generally well fired with distinctive 'grass marking' - the impressions of chopped grass on the base, sometimes continuing over the exterior and even at times reaching the rim. Again there is some variation, for pieces of this ware found on Scilly are often in a granitic fabric.

When 'grass-marking' was adopted as a manufacturing technique, together with the restriction of vessels to straight-sided cooking pots and platters, is uncertain. Gwithian Style wares are found without grass-marked wares at a number of sites such as Boden (Gossip forthcoming) and Goldherring (Guthrie 1969) suggesting a period of use prior to the introduction of 'Grass-Marked' ware.

Some Concluding Thoughts

'Gwithian Style' may have overlapped with 'Grass-Marked ware' during the seventh century. Unpublished drawings (Thomas 2005) from excavations of a midden on Tean, Isles of Scilly carried out in 1956 and 1960 (Thomas 1985) show at least two Gwithian style jars (though in a granitic fabric) with 'grass-marking'. A radiocarbon date of cal AD 600-770 (OxA 4695) came from the upper part of the midden (Ratcliffe and Straker 1996, 98). This date, together with that suggested above for the Gwithian Style and the possible late importation of Mediterranean wares, allows a date somewhere in the 7th century for the introduction of Grass-Marked wares.

At Gwithian, a sherd obtained from Context (2238), the internal rubble collapse of Structure (2241) in GMI, yielded a radiocarbon date of cal AD 650-780 (SUERC-6168). This determination, the latest obtained, indicated that the structures had collapsed, and been abandoned by the late seventh or eighth centuries AD, marking the end of Phase 3. This has significance for the innovation of the 'bar-lug'. Sherds bearing bar-lugs were discovered within sealed contexts associated with both the use and abandonment of contemporary structures at GMI. This suggests that adoption of the bar-lug element must certainly have been introduced before the end of the 8th century AD (Nowakowski et al. 2007).

'Grass-Marked ware' appears to have had a life of over five hundred years, from the seventh to the eleventh centuries AD. Mawgan Porth saw this ware, including the distinctive bar-lug, in use into the early eleventh century (Bruce-Mitford 1997), and it continued at Launceston Castle into the second half of the eleventh century (Hutchinson 1979, Vince in Saunders 2006). It appears that towards the end of the life of this ware (i.e. within the eleventh century) the use of 'grass-marking' as a pottery technique declined, with very little being observed at Mawgan Porth (about 11% of the entire assemblage) and none at all being present at Launceston Castle. There is some suggestion that undecorated vessels are also more recent.

As stated above, this paper is only an interim statement presenting our current understanding of the early medieval native ceramics of Cornwall. Study is still ongoing with the discovery of new sites providing new information. Older collections of material also need to be re-visited in the light of new ideas (such as Trebarveth, and Carngoon Bank), and this may revise significantly the dates (and perhaps some of the interpretation) of these sites. It is hoped that this may be coupled with a program of scientific dating (especially of internal residues from pottery) that would help to further refine the sequence.

In conclusion, though our knowledge has progressed a great deal over the past few years I would like to end this paper with some important questions that I hope that future researchers will be able to answer.

What happened at the end of the seventh century AD that caused the change from 'Gwithian Style wares' to 'Grass-marked wares' which was a dramatic revolution in the use of ceramics? Was the cause of this change a climatic, social, economic, or political event, or a combination of all? Finally why did the use of these restricted forms of pottery last for over 500 years? Was this due to cultural stability or stagnation?

Bibliography

Barrowman, RC, Batey, CE, and Morris, CD, 2007. *Excavations at Tintagel Castle, Cornwall, 1990-1999.* Reports of the Research Committee of the Society of Antiquaries of London 74, Society of Antiquaries of London.

Bruce-Mitford, R, 1997. *Mawgan Porth. A settlement of the late Saxon period on the north Cornish coast.* English Heritage.

Campbell, E, 1991. *Imported goods in the Early Medieval Celtic West with special reference to Dinas Powis.* Unpublished PhD thesis, Univ Wales, College of Cardiff.

Campbell, E, 1996. 'The archaeological evidence for contacts: imports, trade and economy in Celtic Britain AD 400-800' in Dark 1996, 83-96.

Campbell, E, 2007. *Continental and Mediterranean Imports to Atlantic Britain and Ireland, AD 400 – 800.* CBA Research Report 157. Council for British Archaeology.

Gossip, J, (forthcoming). The evaluation of a multi-period prehistoric site and fogou at Boden Vean, St Anthony-in-Meneage, Cornwall, 2003. *Cornish Archaeology*

Guthrie, A, 1969. Excavation of a settlement at Goldherring, Sancreed, 1958-61. *Cornish Archaeology* 8. 5-39.

Jones, A M, Forthcoming, Hay Close, St Newlyn East: excavations by the Cornwall Archaeological Society, 2007, *Cornish Archaeology*

McAvoy, F, 1980. 'The Excavation of a Multi-period Site at Carngoon Bank, Lizard', *Cornish Archaeology* 19, 31-62

Nowakowski, J, Quinnell, H, Sturgess, J, Thomas, C, and Thorpe, C, 2007. Return to Gwithian: shifting the sands of time. *Cornish Archaeology* 46, 13-76.

Ratcliffe, J, and Straker, V, 1996. *The early environment of Scilly. Palaeoenvironmental assessment of cliff-face and intertidal deposits 1989 - 1993*. Truro. Cornwall Archaeological Unit.

Peacock D, and Williams D 1986. *Amphorae and the Roman economy, an introductory guide*, London and New York.

Quinnell, H, 2004 *Trethurgy: Excavations at Trethurgy Round, St Austell, Community and Status in the Roman and post-roman Cornwall*. CCC/EH monograph

Ratcliffe, J, 1991. *Lighting up the Past in Scilly; Archaeological Results from the 1985 Electrification Project*, Cornwall Archaeological Unit

Saunders, A, 2006. *Excavations at Launceston Castle, Cornwall*. Society for Medieval Archaeology Monograph 24, Leeds.

Thomas, A,C, 1956. Excavations at Gwithian, Cornwall 1955. *Proc West Cornwall Field Club*. Vol. 1.

Thomas. A,C, 1960. People and pottery in Dark Age Cornwall. Old Cornwall Vol V, No 11.

Thomas, AC, 1963. Unpublished material from Cornish Museums: 2 Gunwalloe pottery, Helston Museum. *Cornish Archaeology* 2, 60 - 64

Thomas, A,C, 1968. 'Grass marked pottery in Cornwall', in *Studies in Ancient Europe*. Eds Coles and Simpson. Leicester.

Thomas, AC, 1991. Early Medieval Pottery, in Ratcliffe 1991, 87-92

Thomas, A,C, 2005. *An interim assessment of Post 400, Pre 1200 Native Pottery, and Mediterranean and Gaulish Imported wares in Cornwall and Scilly*. Unpublished Background Paper No 3.

Multiple Identities in Cornwall

Peter Herring

Abstract

Like all identities, Cornish identity is not a single or simple state. This paper suggests a range of nesting relationships which interlock in each individual, within the over-arching sense of Cornishness. Within this, attention is drawn to the significance of the Cornish rural pays.

Introduction

This paper is a contribution to the debate on the nature of former, current and future perceptions of Cornish identity in which Henrietta Quinnell has been closely and productively involved (Quinnell 1986; 1993; 2004). I focus here on the medieval and post-medieval periods, but most of the themes considered have relevance to earlier and later periods, including present-day Cornwall.

There is not space here to set out the extent to which medieval and post-medieval Cornwall was culturally separate from the England that had absorbed it politically in the ninth century. For the purposes of this paper I ask the reader to accept that medieval Cornwall was a distinct place, regarded as not England by some English writers as well as by more Cornish ones. It had its own language, and at times maintained an uneasy relationship with England. Cornish Studies, as exemplified by the Institute of Cornish Studies and their annual journal, continue to explore the centre-periphery relationship between England and Cornwall, especially when considering the industrialisation and post-industrialisation of certain parts of Cornwall in more recent centuries.

Recent academic work on Cornish identity has largely depended on historical documents for its sources; most are now familiar to Cornish historians (see Payton 1992; Deacon 2007). How can archaeology, landscape history and characterisation, help us shed fresh and independent light on Cornish identity in the medieval period? Archaeologists have rarely fully engaged in this debate, not doing much beyond identifying types of features that seem peculiarly Cornish, like the late 8th to 11th-century bar-lug pottery (Hutchinson 1979), or the 12th to 15th-century wayside crosses, whose distributions stop pretty much at the Cornish border with Devon (Preston-Jones and Rose 1986).

Archaeologists and landscape historians could point out other medieval cultural features that seem to straddle the border with Devon. It is perhaps significant that Cornwall's dispersed settlement pattern, dominated by small hamlets, was shared by Devon (Herring 1999; Shorter et al, 1969, 99-111); that Devon also had similar small-scale strip field systems associated with these hamlets, and that the dominant farming regime in medieval Cornwall, ley or convertible husbandry, is also called denshering, or Devonshiring (Herring 1986; 2006a; 2006b; Fox 1971; Stanes 1990). It could be noted that the late medieval long-houses of Devon and Cornwall, from Dartmoor to the north Cornish coast and Bodmin Moor, appear to reveal a very similar design and use of social space, as suggested by the arrangements of principal doors, doors to inner rooms, fireplaces, fixed furniture etc (Austin and Thomas 1989; Herring 1986). The density of the distribution of small medieval market towns, and their form, in Cornwall is similar to that of Devon, but different from that of most of England (Beresford 1988; Kirkham and Cahill, forthcoming).

It seems possible, then, that an argument could be developed for there being a weakening of cultural distinctions between Devon and Cornwall in the later medieval period, as reflected in tenurial arrangements, agricultural (and, incidentally, also tinning) practice, domestic architecture, market and urban life, and through them in typical ways of going about one's daily business. Of course, this separateness of Cornwall, Devon and parts of west Somerset, could also be regarded as a survival of Dumnonia, an earlier and perhaps more significant political entity (for which, see Pearce 2004; Turner 2006; Rippon 2007).

But the intention here is not to confirm or refute claims to either a weakening of Cornish identity at the regional level in the medieval period, or a more fundamental survival of Dumnonian identity, although both of these must be of some interest to those undertaking Cornish Studies. Instead it is to suggest that the modelling of social structure that archaeologists, anthropologists and landscape historians do should allow us to add to the debate on Cornish culture the predictions that Cornish individuals in the medieval and post-medieval periods would have possessed identities that were more diverse, complex and multi-layered than those sometimes portrayed, and that for most of the period, for most people, a specifically Cornish identity would often have been nested with those others.

Fig 13.1 Treligga, St Teath. A hamlet with a complex mix of spaces reflecting the intimacy of knowledge and identity: private or personal spaces attached to particular households enmeshed with communal ones (townplaces, lanes). Beyond are the now enclosed strips of formerly communal subdivided fields. For the inhabitants of medieval and post-medieval Treligga, this world would have been the basis of their identity. (Photo, Steve Hartgroves, Cornwall Council)

This is especially so if we see identity being defined not only by 'difference from', but also by 'belonging to' (see Cohen 1982), and if these defining exclusions and inclusions refer to groups of people as much as to areas of land, although in many medieval arenas relationships between people would have coincided with relationships with land and place.

When archaeologists and ethnographers enter the debate they re-enrich the study of Cornwall by suggesting how complex patterns of local, temporary and intersecting identities can be concealed by emphasis on Cornishness. This is especially important in places like Cornwall where modern political marginality in relation to a perceived more powerful centre can encourage historians and commentators towards cultural reduction and oversimplification.

Identities in Medieval Rural Cornwall

Rural life has probably always been more complex than urban life, at least in terms of social inter-connectedness, intricacy of relationships, and the depth and familiarity of people's knowledge of each other. To illustrate this, we may very briefly consider a range or sample of the groups and areas that a typical medieval Cornish individual is likely to have belonged to, and the social arenas they would have known. Each form of belonging and, conversely, of separation would have impinged on an individual's world-view and contributed to the rich variety of identities and associations that can be expected to have existed in medieval Cornwall.

Household

A person would have had strong attachments with the everyday and familiar, both the people of the household and its associated holding, the steading and the land, however extensive that was. The routine, intricate, intimate and privileged knowledge of the plants, animals, natural features and people on the land where they worked ensured that the household defined their central identity; all others reflecting on it but being ultimately secondary to it. The lyrical writings of the peasant authors of the Great Blasket (Co Kerry) powerfully demonstrate this centrality (O'Crohan 1951; Sayers 1962; O'Sullivan 1953).

Hamlet/cooperative group

The ubiquity of strip fields in the farmed land of medieval Cornwall confirms that agriculture and rural life was cooperative and communal (Herring 1986; 1999; 2006a).

The individual and their household would be closely entwined with others in the hamlet. Essential and deeply embedded commitments and dependencies would have reinforced familiarity and identity with the hamlet as both place and community (fig 13.1). We should not, however, imagine stress-free, blissful medieval hamlets; the Blasket authors (see above) also vividly display the tensions between households in such hamlets, as well as communal pleasures. The latter included the bonding developed from sharing al fresco working meals in the fields and on the hills, and evening gatherings in the houses for gossip, stories, music and play.

Estate

Medieval Cornwall was notably less manorial (especially in terms of relationships between payment of labour services and money rents for land) than the much more widely described and discussed Midlands of England (Hatcher 1970), but land was still largely held from what might best be described as estates. The several hamlets, and their households and individual people, in these estates would have been regularly involved with each other in the organisation and use of shared commons, cliffs, sanding ways etc. Again, the sharing of feudal obligations would have been reinforced by shared feudal pleasures. The estate, then, was the locus of another important determiner of individual identity.

Parish

Hamlets, households and individuals living in a defined area were linked by ceremony, ritual and communal support through the medium of the church (fig 13.2. Many of an individual's rites of passage were marked by church ceremonies, witnessed by gatherings of parishioners. 'It is this little country, this parish, which bounds our emotion, and is the territory of that pack or tribe into which we are born' (Grigson 1954, 13). Strong parish identities developed, revealed by the rivalries implied by giving neighbouring parishes mocking nicknames, the Zennor goats, Towednack cuckoos and St Gennys wreckers or wrestlers (Parnall 1973).

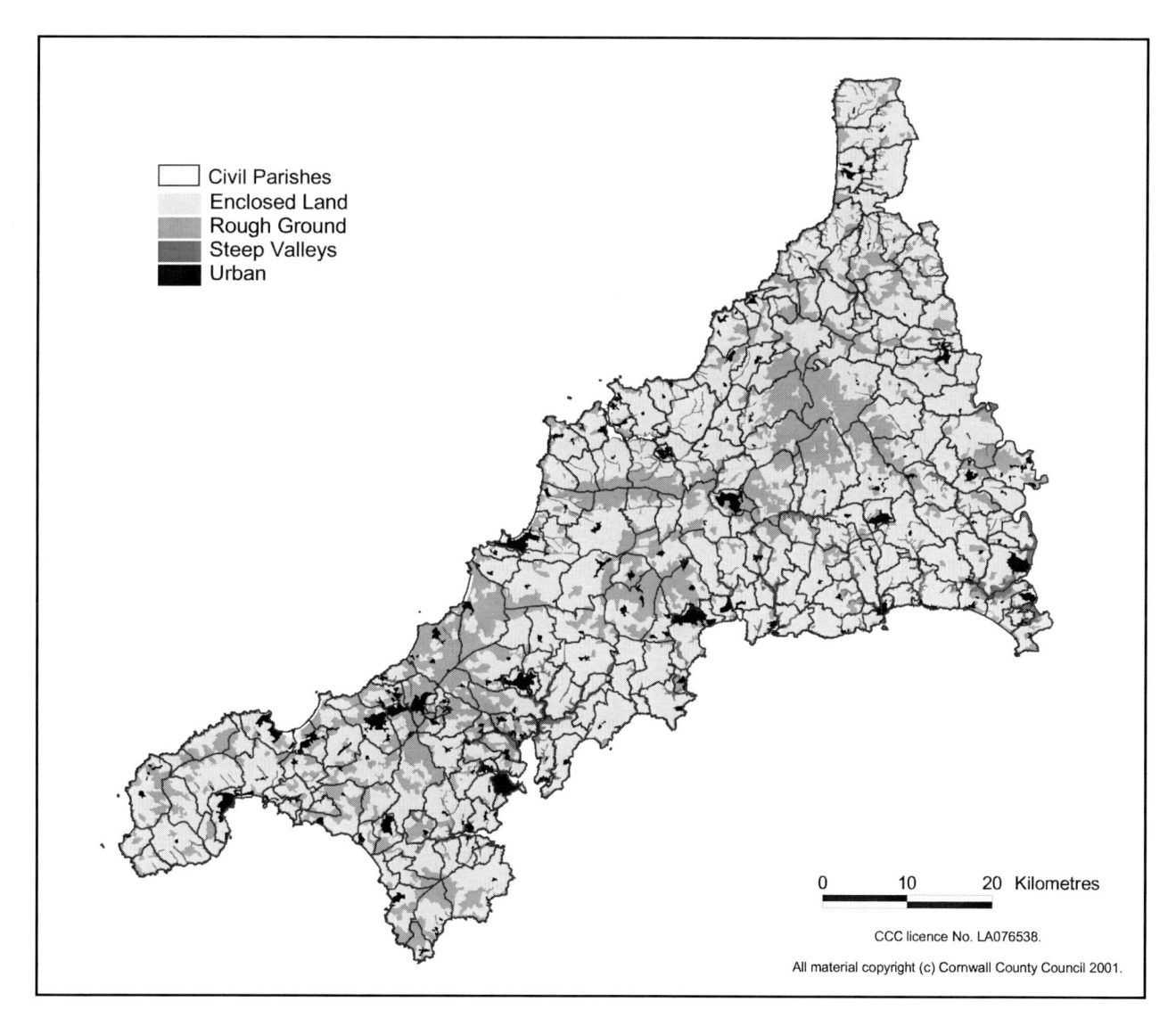

FIG 13.2 CORNWALL'S CIVIL PARISHES, MOSTLY MEDIEVAL IN ORIGIN, AND STILL KEY LOCI OF PERSONAL IDENTITY. (BASE IS A SIMPLIFIED HISTORIC LANDSCAPE CHARACTERISATION; SEE HERRING 1998)

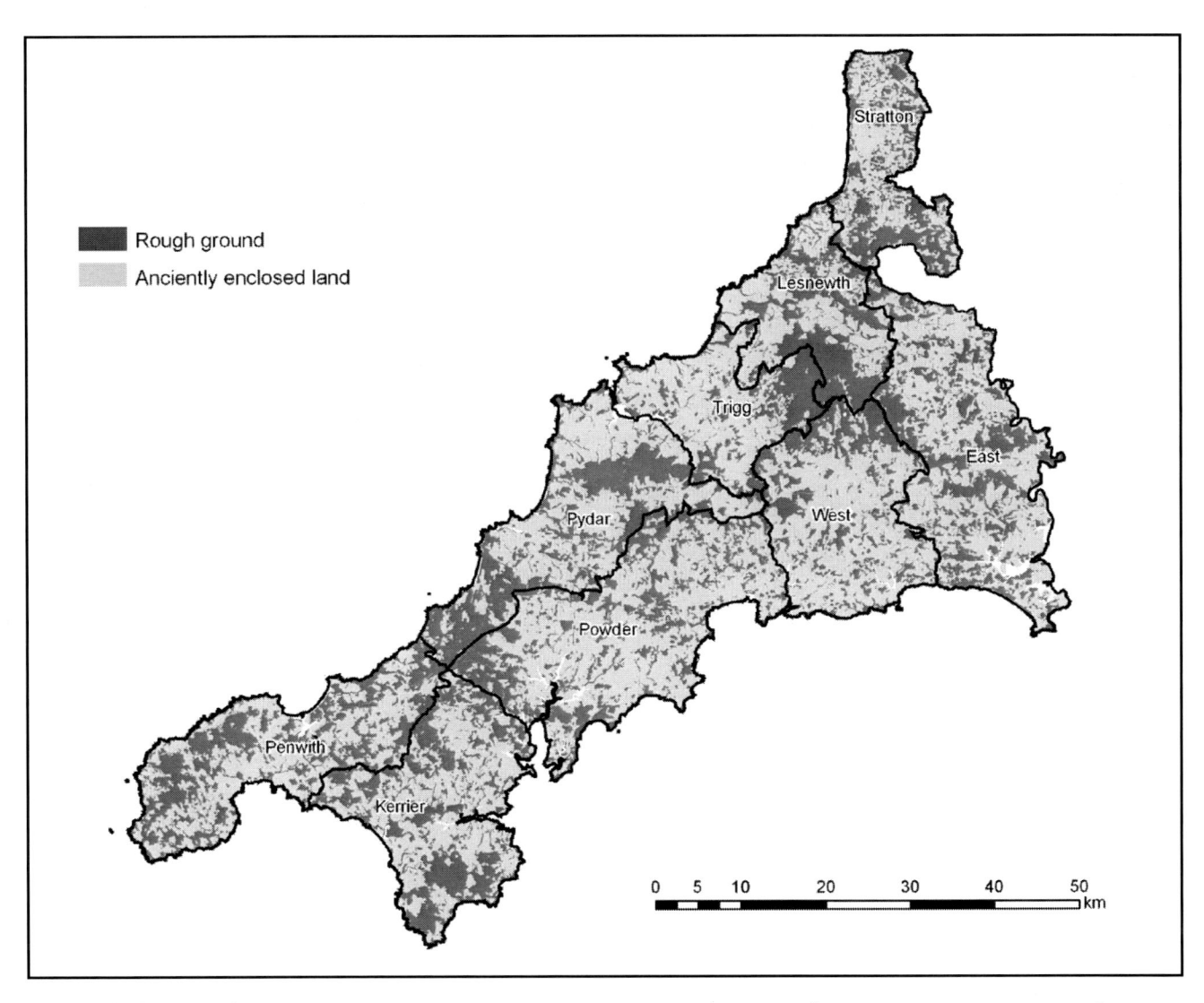

FIG 13.3 CORNWALL'S ANCIENT HUNDREDS IN RELATION TO THE EXTENSIVE RESOURCES (ROUGH GROUND AND THE COAST) WHICH THEY ADMINISTERED (MAPPING DERIVED FROM CORNWALL HISTORIC LANDSCAPE CHAARCTERISATION. FARMING COMMUNITIES DEPENDED ON REASONABLE POLICING OF ACCESS TO THESE RESOURCES AND WOULD PROBABLY HAVE IDENTIFIED WITH THEIR HUNDREDS TO EXTENTS WE NOW FIND DIFFICULT TO IMAGINE. (FROM HERRING 2009; COPYRIGHT CORNWALL COUNCIL)

Hundred

In Cornwall, from at least as early as the post-Roman period, these large administrative units organised aspects of economic and social life, such as access to extensive common resources like upland pastures and the sea, shared among groups of estates (Thomas 1964; Herring 1986) (fig 13.3). A person's relationship with their hundred is likely to have been meaningful, as suggested by the jurymen of Pydar and Powder hundreds protesting in the 13th century against blocking of public highways by the creation of the Bishop of Exeter's deer parks at Pawton and Lanner (Henderson 1935, 159).

Tithings

These medieval groupings of people responsible for upkeep of law and order were often different groups occupying different areas from both estates and parishes and so provided different associations and identities (Pool 1981; Harvey 1997). Other, later communal obligations or impositions included group responsibility for preparing and lighting warning beacons.

Kin groups. Individuals were joined by marriages and births with their own highly particular networks of contacts, some local and some more distant in terms of relationship and place. The strength of such networks cannot be underestimated in Cornwall where people still call to mind convoluted inter-relationships of family in Cornwall and the wider world (Deacon 2004).

Friendships

Being gregarious animals, people can be expected to have formed individual and affectionate alliances in the medieval and post-medieval periods. We can see these in the records of local gentry like the sisteenth century

FIG 13. 4 MEDIEVAL TIN STREAMWORKS BETWEEN LESKERNICK AND BUTTERN HILLS ON WEST MOOR, ALTARNUN. HARD BUT COOPERATIVE WORKING AT SUCH EXPOSED AND REMOTE PLACES MUST HAVE REINFORCED IDENTITY WITH WORKMATES AND PLACE. (PHOTO, STEVE HARTGROVES, CORNWALL COUNTY COUNCIL)

William Carnsew of Bokelly (Pounds 1978), but should expect them to have developed at all levels of society. These personal relationships were perhaps more fluid or less permanent than those others noted above, but they would nevertheless have contributed much to the definition of an individual's identity.

Workplaces

The medieval Cornish economy was famously diversified and while most people seem to have preferred, and aimed, to work the land, many would have spent time tinning, quarrying, fishing, cloth-making, ship-building etc (Hatcher 1969), and so would have developed relations with other people sharing particular crafts and skills, and with the often peculiar and dramatic places their work took them to (fig 13.4).

Cornish Pays and their Significance

That is not all. We have already noted that the economy of medieval and post-medieval Cornwall was more diversified and its society more complex than many others in Britain. Cornwall's landscape is also diverse, and fragmented, with a large number of clearly definable areas whose distinctiveness extended from topography to differing soils, vegetation communities, and differing ways of undertaking mixed agriculture. Many such areas were separated from each other by fairly significant natural features like ridges of hills and creeks (most of which, pre-silting, were considerably longer than today). These areas can be likened to the French localities or pays (see also Fox 1989; Turner 2007; Rippon 2007).

That they existed as identified areas in the medieval period is revealed by the number of names of localities that transcend and do not equate with hundreds, estates, single parishes, or other administrative areas. These names can best be regarded as those of pays (fig 13.5):

Meneage, recorded at least as early as AD 967 (Padel 1988, 118).
Penwith, the peninsular part of the larger hundred of the same name, by 997 (ibid, 136).
Petherwin, encompassing the parishes of North and South Petherwin, and probably the land between, by 1171, but probably substantially earlier, predating the Norman conquest (ibid, 138).
Fawymore (now Bodmin Moor) by 1185 (known in Cornish as Goon Bren), and probably including the ring of parishes whose lands reach up onto the uplands. Again, probably conceived of as an area significantly earlier, being the focus of much transhumance activity from later prehistoric times (ibid, 55; Herring 1996).
The Roseland by 1201 (Padel 1988, 150).
Goonhilly by c1240 (ibid, 89).
Hensbarrow by 1261 (ibid, 96).

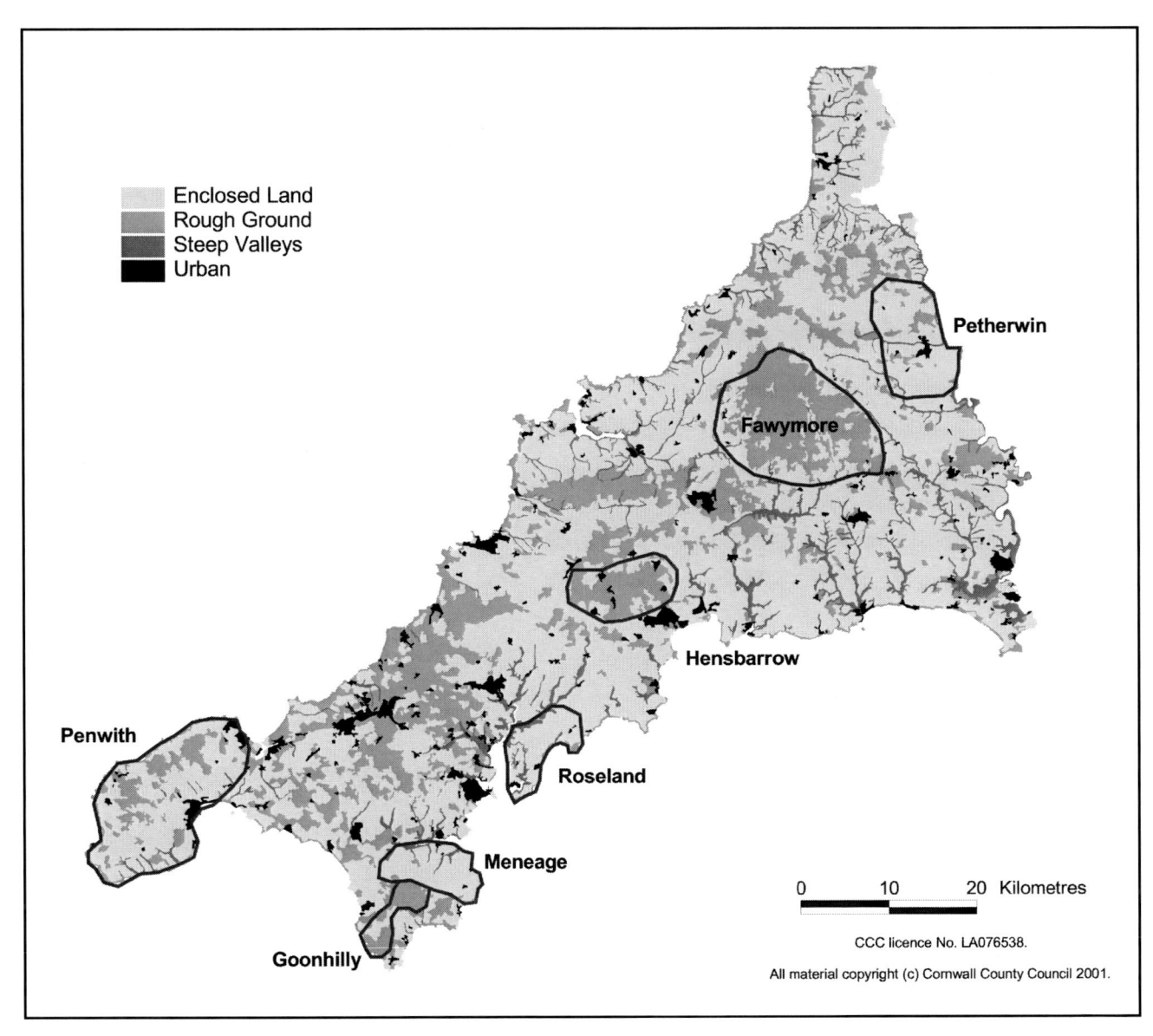

FIG 13.5 CONSERVATIVE EXTENTS OF NAMED MEDIEVAL PAYS, PLOTTED ONTO THE SIMPLIFIED 1994 HISTORIC LANDSCAPE CHARACTERISATION (COPYRIGHT CORNWALL COUNCIL)

Some of these – Meneage, Penwith, Petherwin, the Roseland – were in anciently enclosed land and were probably permanent homes. The others were areas of rough ground, summer pastures that would have been used seasonally or occasionally. Those who lived in or used these areas would have known how to cope with the particular conditions found within them. Shared knowledge and shared ways of 'going on' in these pays would have reinforced associations with both place and people, creating another layer of identity. Through differences with neighbouring pays, they would have increased their sense of belonging.

We can use the 1994 Historic Landscape Characterisation (HLC) of Cornwall to map these known pays, and then tentatively identify others. The Cornish HLC, the first of the many that are now being done throughout Britain, mapped the predominant historic landscape character of each part of Cornwall. As well as graphically demonstrating that all of Cornwall is historic; it is a useful tool for landscape historians wishing to understand the spatial dynamics of historic Cornwall (see Herring 1998 for details). The HLC types have been simplified to generate a mapping of the human geography of medieval and early post-medieval Cornwall in which the following four main differences in land use can be identified, some of them closely related to topography:

Enclosed Land that has been farmed from at least the later medieval period, and mostly from later prehistoric times.

Rough Ground (including the Recently Enclosed Land taken in during the last three centuries).

Steep-sided valleys and creeks, which were natural topographic barriers, and the main areas of ancient woodland in medieval Cornwall.

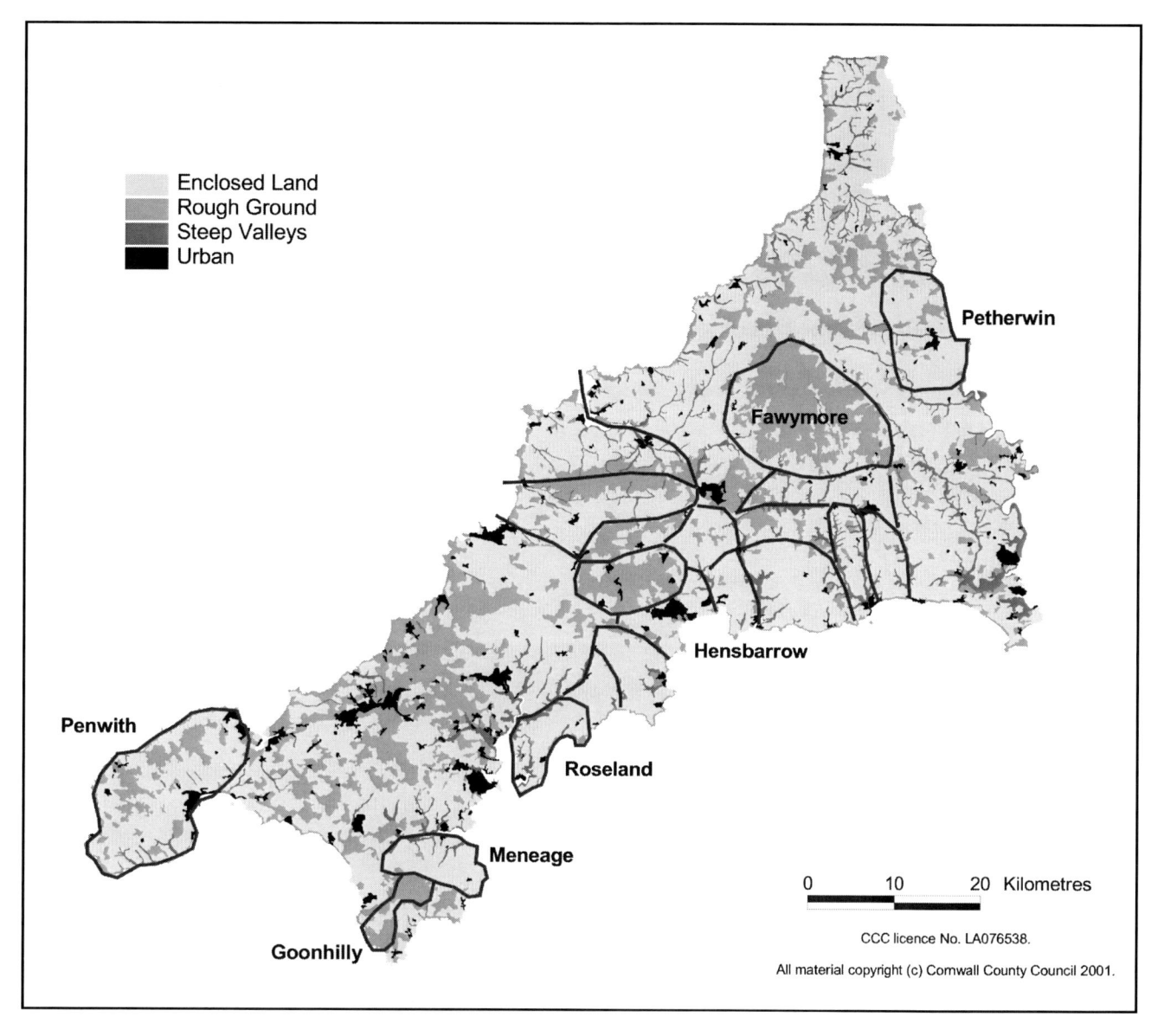

FIG 13.6 OTHER SUGGESTED PAYS IN CENTRAL CORNWALL, BASED ON THE HLC AND LOCAL KNOWLEDGE. THE READER FAMILIAR WITH CORNWALL COULD IDENTIFY OTHERS, AND INSTIGATE SEARCHES FOR LOCAL NAMES (COPYRIGHT CORNWALL COUNCIL).

Towns and larger villages. (NB This mapping captures present extents and so shows towns much larger than they were in the medieval period, and also includes a few post-medieval towns, like Camborne, Porthleven, Torpoint and Bude.)

We notice in fig 13.5 how some of the named pays are defined by valleys or ridges of hills – lines of difference – and can suggest that this reinforces commonality of experience of the similar conditions in the pays themselves. We can tentatively identify numerous other medieval pays (see fig 13.6 for some, and the reader who knows Cornwall can add more). It is likely that people felt close attachments to these areas and identified closely with them, as well as with all the other groupings and areas already mentioned.

In a complex, mobile and ever-changing society like that of medieval Cornwall, people had regular contact with those possessing other identities, whether Cornish or alien. Rather than having a diluting influence, such contacts could have reinforced the feelings of difference and belonging that polish identities. Medieval and post-medieval Cornwall, like modern Cornwall, is therefore misunderstood if regarded as anything other than very heterogeneous, with fluidity of identity mirroring the variety of associations and attachments experienced by its constituent people.

Now, all this need not weaken the case for a distinct Cornish identity in the medieval period, in the same way that the late nineteenth and early twentieth century Blasket community's multiple identities did not diminish their identification with Ireland, as revealed by their responses to the struggles against English occupation (O'Crohan 1951). The fleeting early references drawn together by Payton and others suggest that all the local identities appear to have been overarched, as they are now, by a Cornish identity, the source of which may be sought in the staged contraction of Dumnonia in the face of the Saxon expansion westwards that left Cornwall separate for nearly a century when Devon was taken in the 8th century (Padel 2010), and in the low level of Roman involvement in affairs west of the Tamar (Quinnell 1986).

In the later medieval and post-medieval periods, however, for most of the time, and in most circumstances a person's Cornish identity would have been buried beneath many other more immediately relevant layers. No doubt Cornishness was burnished by a shared culture of stories in the same way that it may be today and there were, of course, occasions when the overarching Cornish identity dominated, the times of rebellion most obviously (Deacon 2007).

Concluding Thoughts

The approach taken here encourages us to understand, celebrate and value the differing perceptions of Cornishness that exist not only among Cornish farming, clayworking, mining, and fishing families or among members of different parishes or pays, but also among those now working in new technologies, arts and crafts, the service industries, tourism. These different perceptions are coloured by people's own local identities, by their own knowledge and ignorance.

To apply to complex medieval and modern worlds only the largest collective label of the many that we know existed greatly diminishes our understanding of Cornwall and the Cornish. But recognising and celebrating not only the common Cornish identity, but also the great differences among the Cornish, will not only ensure that Cornish history is reinvigorated by the search for and understanding of multi-layered meanings, but will also ensure that all Cornish communities, past and present, are properly valued.

Bibliography

Austin, D., and Thomas, J., 1989. The 'proper study' of medieval archaeology: a case study, in D. Austin and L. Alcock (eds), *From the Baltic to the Black Sea: Studies in Medieval Archaeology*, Unwin, London.

Beresford, M., 1988. *New Towns of the Middle Ages*, second edition, Sutton, Gloucester.

Cohen, A.P., 1982. Belonging: the experience of culture, in A.P. Cohen (ed) *Belonging. Identity and Social Organisation in British Rural Cultures*, Manchester University Press, Manchester.

Deacon, B., 2004. *The Cornish Family, the roots of our future,* Cornwall Editions, Fowey.

Deacon, B., 2007. *Cornwall: the Concise History*, University of Wales Press.

Fox, H.S.A., 1971. *A Geographical Study of the Field Systems of Devon and Cornwall*, PhD thesis, University of Cambridge.

Fox, H.S.A., 1989. Peasant farmers, patterns of settlement and pays: transformation in the landscapes of Devon and Cornwall during the later middle ages, in R. Higham ed., *Landscape and Townscape in the South West,* University of Exeter Press, Exeter.

Grigson, G., 1954. *Freedom of the Parish*, Phoenix House, London.

Harvey, D., 1997. The tithing framework of West Cornwall: a proposed pattern and an interpretation of territorial origins, *Cornish Studies*, NS 5, 30-51.

Hatcher, J., 1969. A Diversified Economy: Later Medieval Cornwall, *Econ Hist Rev*, 22, 208-227.

Hatcher, J, 1970. Non-Manorialism in Medieval Cornwall, *Agr Hist Rev* 18, 1-16.

Henderson, C., 1935. *Essays in Cornish History*, Clarendon, Oxford.

Herring, P., 1986. *An exercise in landscape history. Pre-Norman and medieval Brown Willy and Bodmin Moor, Cornwall*, unpublished MPhil thesis, University of Sheffield.

Herring, P., 1996. Transhumance in medieval Cornwall, in H.S.A. Fox (ed) *Seasonal Settlement*, University of Leicester, Leicester

Herring, P., 1998. *Presenting a method of historic landscape assessment*, Cornwall County Council and English Heritage, Truro

Herring, P., 1999. *Farming and Transhumance in Cornwall at the turn of the First Millennium AD, Parts 1 and 2,* Journal of the Cornwall Association of Local Historians, Spring and Autumn 1999.

Herring, P., 2006a. Cornish Strip Fields, in S. Turner (ed.) *Medieval Devon and Cornwall, Shaping an Ancient Countryside,* Windgather Press, Macclesfield, 44-77.

Herring, P., 2006b. medieval fields at Brown Willy, Bodmin Moor, in S. Turner (ed.) *Medieval Devon and Cornwall, Shaping an Ancient Countryside*, Windgather Press, Macclesfield, 78-103.

Herring, P., 2009. Early medieval transhumance in Cornwall, Great Britain. In J. Klapste (ed) *Medieval Rural Settlement in Marginal Landscapes,* Ruralia VII, Brepols, Turnhout, Belgium, 47-56.

Hutchinson, G., 1979. The Bar-Lug Pottery of Cornwall, *Cornish Archaeol*, 18, 81-104.

Kirkham, G. and Cahill, N., forthcoming. Medieval towns, *Cornish Archaeol*, 50.

O'Crohan, T., 1951. *The Islandman* (translated by Flower, R), University Press, Oxford.

O'Sullivan, M., 1953. *Twenty Years A-Growing*, University Press, Oxford.

Parnall, R., 1973. *Wreckers and Wrestlers*, Warne, St Austell.

Payton, P., 1992. *The Making of Modern Cornwall*, Dyllansow Truran, Redruth.

Pearce, S., 2004. *Southwestern Britain in the Early Middle Ages*. Lericester University Press/Continuum.

Pool, P.A.S., 1981. The Tithings of Cornwall, *Jnl Royal Institution of Cornwall*, 8.4, 275-337.

Pounds, N.J.G, 1978. William Carnsew of Bokelly and his Diary, 1576-7, *Jnl Royal Institution of Cornwall*, 8.1, 14-60.

Preston Jones, A., and Rose, P., 1986. Medieval Cornwall, *Cornish Archaeol*, 25, 135-185.

Quinnell, H., 1986. The Iron Age and the Roman period in Cornwall, *Cornish Archaeol*, 25, 113-134.

Quinnell, H., 1993. A sense of identity: distinctive Cornish stone artefacts in the Roman and post-Roman periods, *Cornish Archaeol*, 32, 29-46.

Quinnell, H., 2004. *Trethurgy, Excavations at Trethurgy Round, St Austell: Community and Status in Roman and Post-Roman Cornwall,* Cornwall County Council, Truro.

Rippon, S., 2007. Emerging Regional variation in Historic Landscape Character: the Possible Significance of the 'Long Eighth Century', in M. Gardiner and S. Rippon, (eds) *Medieval Landscapes, Landscape History after Hoskins, Volume 2*, Windgather Press, Macclesfield, 105-121.

Sayers, P., 1962. *An old woman's reflections*, University Press, Oxford.

Shorter, A.H., Ravenhill, W.L.D., and Gregory, K.J., 1969. *South West England*, Nelson, London.

Stanes, R., 1990. *The Old Farm: a history of farming life in the West Country,* Devon Books, Exeter.

Thomas, A.C., 1964. Settlement History in early Cornwall: 1, the Hundreds, *Cornish Archaeol* 3, 70-79.

Turner, S., 2006. *Making a Christian Landscape: the countryside in early medieval Cornwall, Devon and Wessex,* University of Exeter press, Exeter.

Turner, S., 2007. *Ancient Country. The Historic Character of Rural Devon*, Devon Archaeological Society, Exeter.

Acknowledgements

I would like to acknowledge the benefit I received from informally chatting about various aspects of this paper with Cathy Parkes, Caradoc Peters and Graeme Kirkham. Thanks too to Bryn Tapper for help with maps.

A Guinea Pig's Testimony

Judith Cosford

One evening in January 1991 twenty three people, mostly strangers, met to begin this new two year course. Our tutor was Henrietta Quinnell. That evening nobody, including Henrietta and the friends we all became, expected we would meet every year afterwards for a party to catch up on archaeological exploits and other aspects of our lives.

Being in the right place at the right time to tackle this course run to University standards were mature people from a variety of backgrounds and experiences. Our ages spanned about forty years from youngest to eldest, with pre-course archaeological knowledge from none to AO Level Examinations. After that first meeting we realised what a task we faced. In fact one member was never seen again! Later the loss of another just before our last term left us greatly saddened.

We worked one evening a week for six terms, attended Saturday day schools and two summer school weeks, all of which were necessary to success. We had site visits, became avid note-takers, wrote essays, sat examinations and finished with a short dissertation on a relevant subject of our own choosing. Henrietta managed to turn this disparate group into knowledgeable archaeological enthusiasts by her own hard work, stimulating approach and amazing ability to persuade at least twelve high-powered experts in their own field of study to give up a Saturday or part of their summer vacation to drill information into us mortals. Some of these experts were excavating archaeologists, and others worked in areas relating to site and finds analysis, like pollen identification, geography, methodology, and post excavation artefact analysis to mention just a few.

Final results proved how successful this venture had been. From twenty one students, five gained Distinctions and most achieved Merits. We hoped the "powers that be" would agree with our view that this achievement by Henrietta and her team would lead to the Course running for many years. Along with all the information we had absorbed, we had also developed personal study techniques and disciplines broadening our outlook and encouraging our self confidence. With this new-found passion for the subject and Henrietta's support, we felt able in small ways to contribute to the study of Devon archaeology as well as venturing into other counties.

At our first party, held as soon as we finished our last examination, our immediate thought was of leaving hard work behind to lead more leisurely lives. This did not happen. During the party someone suggested, in fun, that we had been Henrietta's "Guinea Pigs" and the name has somehow remained with our group. We began to recall memories of the course: our invention of personal note-taking shorthand in order to keep up; how we could be found in libraries sharing books for further information; and how occasionally Henrietta gave us access to her own bookshelves as well. Midnight oil was burnt to meet deadlines and revise for examinations. The weather only affected practical sessions but we experienced everything from soaking rain to scorching sun.

As prehistory leaves no evidence written during its time, we learnt that absence of evidence was not necessarily evidence of absence, and not to accept statements at face value –much could have changed over the centuries. Site visits illustrated this problem of interpretation. We looked at monuments, some highly visible in the landscape, some lumps and bumps in the turf or crop marks visible only in certain weather conditions. One outstanding memory is of gathering on a bridge over a new by-pass to "see" a site now completely invisible! (To be fair, a small part was safe underneath an inaccessible adjacent garden). Other serious practical activities came in our summer schools. We tried exercises like field walking, surveying and planning sites with a view to their preservation or recording. Pictorial evidence emphasised the way sites were used. One person was put into a burial cist to prove a human fitted. Another was stood in a grain storage pit to show its depth in a photograph. Both had to be hauled out! From all this activity we began to read landscapes as a whole area not just considering single sites on their own.

Since we finished the course, we have done many different things. Site visits continued, some with Henrietta, some on our own. Twice we visited Brittany. Then we became more active. Some took degrees, BA's and MA's (one in regional history), one person achieved a Doctorate in Classics and another became ordained and helps out with archaeology in the Exeter Diocese. This shows that we have diversified as well as continuing with archaeology in many other ways. People have passed on knowledge through teaching, giving talks, leading walks, publishing studies in areas like flint working research, so encouraging more people to become involved in archaeological activities.

Many joined societies including Devon and Cornwall Archaeological Societies, Devon History Society and the Prehistoric Society. Individuals have supported both Devon and Plymouth Record Offices and several local Museums. More helped to form new groups like Dartmoor Tinworking Research Group and Local History Groups in their own areas. Other small groups or individuals have joined excavations, surveyed moorland valleys, farms and prehistoric remains, completed a village sites and monuments register, listed churchyard graves and researched church histories. Relatives have caught the "bug" becoming involved in their own places too.

So Henrietta's passion for and knowledge of her profession taught her students how to use their skills not only in prehistoric activities but other aspects of archaeology and history. They have also been able to introduce others to this fascinating subject. How far afield the waves she set in motion twenty years ago in 1991 have reached we cannot quantify. We had lots of fun worked hard at the time and are still enjoying the outcome.

Thank you Henrietta and your team for setting the ball rolling, from all of us on the 1991/92 Certificate Course.

A Student's Progress

Susan Watts

I first met Henrietta Quinnell in July 1997 at an open evening at the University of Exeter, which was held to discuss the forthcoming Certificate in Archaeology course, of which she was director. The course was due to begin that autumn as part of the programme of studies offered by the University's former Department of Continuing and Adult Education. The general information for those interested in enrolment stated that the course was 'for those with an interest in archaeology who wish to undertake a programme of systematic study leading to a recognised qualification'. This summed up exactly what I wanted to do. I came to the certificate course with a long-standing interest in querns, which was borne out of an even longer interest in watermills and windmills, but I was keen to put the knowledge I had gained on a more formal basis, and to understand more about the archaeological background and contexts of these everyday but nevertheless important objects.

The course duly went ahead, and I consider that we were so fortunate to have the benefit of Henrietta's enthusiasm and knowledge, together with that of Derek Gore and also Mark Corney and Tina Tuohy, as over the course of the next two years we studied the Prehistoric and Roman periods, interspersed with sessions on the more practical aspects of archaeology. Comprehensive notes accompanied each lecture (I still have them all) and what made the classes particularly vibrant and interesting was not only the high standard of teaching but also the fact that questions were positively welcomed. The majority of my fellow students were mature people, which made for some lively and stimulating discussions. Help was also at hand with regard to writing essays, something many of us had not had to tackle for a long time. But the certificate was not all classroom based and we enjoyed some fascinating field trips to Dartmoor, Hod Hill, Salisbury Plain and Caerleon and Caerwent, to name but a few.

The certificate course not only gave me a good grounding in archaeology but I also made some good friends, Henrietta included. However, it was also to have a greater impact on my life than I originally anticipated. When I began the course, I had no thought of going on to take a degree in archaeology (the course being the equivalent of the first year), let alone consider researching for a PhD, but as the course progressed I realised, with Henrietta's encouragement, that I could do so and that, furthermore, I would be able to study part-time. Although querns were (and still are) my main interest, it was Henrietta's suggestion that I should write about something different for the Independent Study Module, a piece of original written research, which completed the certificate course. This was good advice, as I was able to develop my research interest in querns over the following four years while working for my degree, writing my under-graduate dissertation on Cornish querns. I am now completing my PhD research on the structured deposition of querns.

It is regrettable that the Certificate Course no longer runs in Exeter. For those like me who came to archaeology as mature students, it provided an excellent entry into the world of archaeology and, as the course consisted predominantly of evening classes with field trips organised at weekends, it was well suited to those who worked full time.

Henrietta's deep knowledge of the archaeology of south-west England and her enthusiasm for the subject has had a profound affect, not just on me but upon many who took her certificate course and who, as a result, are still involved in archaeology in one way or another. On a more personal level I have benefited greatly from Henrietta's own interest in querns. She has both stimulated and encouraged my researches and I was particularly pleased to be asked to work with her on the querns from Trethurgy Round, the small Roman settlement near St. Austell, Cornwall, excavated and published by Henrietta. This was a collaboration that I found both instructive and rewarding.

Bibliography of Henrietta Quinnell's Published Work

'Excavations at Fisherwick, Staffs., 1968 – A Romano-British Farmstead, and a Neolithic Occupation Site' *Trans S Staffs Archaeol Hist Soc* X 1968-9, 1-23

(with T J Miles) 'Settlement Sites of the Late Pre-Roman Iron Age in the Somerset Levels' *Somerset Archaeol Nat Hist* 113 1969, 17-55

(with T J Miles) 'Excavations on Longstone Downs, St Stephen-in-Brannel and St Mewan' *Cornish Archaeol* 10 1971, 5-28

'Excavations at Rhuddlan, 1969-71: Interim Report' *J Flints Hist Soc* 25 1971-2, 1-8

(with T J Miles) 'A Romano-British Site at King's Bromley, Staffs.' *Trans S Staffs Archaeol Hist Soc* XV 1973-4, 29-32

'Barrows on the St Austell Granite' *Cornish Archaeol* 14 1975, 5-82

'Excavations at Woodbury Castle, East Devon, 1971' *Proc Devon Archaeological Soc* 33 1975, 183-208

(with T J Miles) 'Pilton, North Devon' *Proc Devon Archaeol Soc* 33 1975, 267-295

'Flint Scatters and Prehistoric Settlement in Devon' *Proc Devon Archaeol Soc* 34 1976, 3-16

(ed) *The Sites and Monuments Register and Parish Check-Lists.* 1976. Devon Archaeological Society Occasional Paper No 1.

'Early Medieval Occupation at Honeyditches, Seaton' *Proc Devon Archaeol Soc* 34 1976, 73-6

(with P Trudgian) 'An Excavation at Lesquite Quoit, Lanivet' *Cornish Archaeol* 15 1976, 7-10

(with G King) 'A Bronze Age Cist Burial at Trebartha, Northill' *Cornish Archaeol* 15 1976, 27-31

'The Honeyditches Roman Villa, Seaton, Devon' *Britannia* VII 1977, 107- 148

'The A38 Roadworks 1970-73' *Proc Devon Archaeol Soc* 35 1977, 43-52

'Excavations at Killibury Hillfort, Egloshayle 1975-6' *Cornish Archaeol* 16 1977, 89-121

(with D Harris, S Pearce, M Irwin) 'Bodwen, Lanlivery: a Multi-period Occupation' *Cornish Archaeol* 16 1977, 25-42

'The Flints' in S Butcher 'Excavations at Nornour, Isles of Scilly, 1969-73: the Pre-Roman Settlement' *Cornish Archaeol* 17 1978, 87-91

(with D Harris) Castle Dore: the Chronology Reconsidered' *Cornish Archaeol* 24 1985, 123-132

'Cornwall during the Iron Age and the Roman period' *Cornish Archaeol* 25 1986, 111-134

'The Local Character of the Devon Bronze Age and its Interpretation in the 1980s' *Proc Devon Archaeol Soc* 46 1988, 1-12

'The Late Mrs E.M.Minter's Excavation of Hut Circles at Heatree, Manaton in 1968' *Proc Devon Archaeol Soc* 49 1991, 1-24

'The Villa and Temple at Cosgrove, Northants' *Northants Archaeol* 23 1991, 4-66

'A Late Iron Age Decorated Object from Cosgrove' *Northants Archaeol* 23 1991, 67-8

'Prehistoric and Roman Pottery' in Ratcliffe J, 1991, *Lighting up the Past in Scilly*, 73-84, Cornwall Archaeological Unit, Cornwall County Council

'Radiocarbon dating, pottery and stone objects' in Appleton-Fox, N., 'Excavations of a Romano-British Round: Reawla, Gwinnear', *Cornish Archaeol* 31, 92-113

'A Sense of Identity: Distinctive Cornish Stone Artefacts in the Roman and Post-Roman Periods' in M.Carver (ed) *In Search of Cult: Archaeological Investigations in Honour of Philip Rahtz* 1993, 69-78 Boydell Press. Reprinted in *Cornish Archaeology* 32 1993 with some additional material

New Perspectives on Upland Monuments - Devon in Earlier Prehistory' *Proc Devon Archaeol Soc* 52 1994, 49-62

'Becoming Marginal ? Dartmoor in Later Prehistory' *Proc Devon Archaeol Society* 52 1994, 75-84

(with M. Blockley) *Excavations at Rhuddlan, Clwyd 1969-73 Mesolithic to Medieval* 1994 Council for British Archaeology Research Report No 95

'The pottery and other artifacts in Ratcliffe, J. 'Duckpool, Morwenstow: A Romano-British and early medieval industrial site and harbour' *Cornish Archaeol* 34 1995, 120-136

'Excavation of an Exmoor Barrow and Ring Cairn' *Proc Devon Archaeol Soc* 55 1997, 1-39

(with F.M.Griffith) 'Neolithic settlement, land use and resources' 'Barrows and ceremonial sites in the Neolithic and Earlier Bronze Age' ' Settlement c. 2500BC - c. AD600' 'Iron Age to Roman buildings, structures, and coin and other findspots' in R. Kain and W.Ravenhill (eds) *Historical Atlas of South-West England* 1999, 51-4, 55-61, 62-68, 74-76

(with T.H.Gent) 'Excavations of a Causewayed Enclosure and Hillfort on Raddon Hill' *Proc Devon Archaeol Soc* 57 1999, 1-76 (with T.H. Gent) 'Salvage Recording on the Neolithic site at Haldon Belvedere' *Proc Devon Archaeol Soc* 57 1999, 77-104

'Introduction' in Keene, B. & Newman, P. (eds) *A Gazeteer of Flint Arrowheads from South-West Britain*, i-v. Devon Archaeological Society Occasional Publication 19

'The Pottery and Stone Artefacts' in A Jones 'The Excavation of a Later Bronze Age Structure at Callestick' *Cornish Archaeol* 37-8 1998-9, 19-36

'The Artefacts' in D. Johnston et al, 'Excavations at Penhale Round, Fraddon, Cornwall, 1995/6', *Cornish Archaeol* 37-8 for 1998-9, 85-93

(with J.Roberts) 'The potential for a rapid, minimally-destructive method for the identification of archaeological ceramics – the results of a pilot study on gabbroic ware' *Cornish Archaeol* 37-8 for 1998-9, 126-29

'The prehistoric pottery' in A.Jones, 'The excavation of a Bronze Age enclosure at Liskeard Junior and Infant School' *Cornish Archaeol* 37-8 for 1998-9, 63-5

'First Millennium BC and Roman Period Ceramics', in Herring, P, *St Michael's Mount: Archaeological Works, 1995 -8*. 39-46. Cornwall County Council

'Artefacts' in A. Jones, 'The Excavation of a Multi-period Site at Stencoose, Cornwall, *Cornish Archaeol* 39-40 2000/1, 44-72

'The Pottery, lithics and stone artefacts' in Young, A. 'Time Team at Boleigh fogou, St Buryan' *Cornish Archaeol* 39-40 2000/1, 139-44

(with M. Watts) 'A Bronze Age Cemetery at Elburton, Plymouth' *Proc Devon Archaeol Soc* 59 2001, 11-45

'Pottery, stone artifacts and flints' in C. Johns, 'An Iron Age sword and mirror cist burial from Bryher, Isles of Scilly, *Cornish Archaeol* 41-2 2002/3, 44-52

'Devon Beakers: New Finds, New Thoughts' *Proc Devon Archaeol Soc* 61 2003 , 1-20

Trethurgy: Excavations at Trethurgy Round, St Austell: Community and Status in Roman and Post-Roman Cornwall, 2004, Cornwall County Council, 302 pp

'Prehistoric and Roman Period Pottery and Stonework' in Jones, A.M & Taylor, S.R., *What Lies Beneath.. St Newlyn East & Mitchell: Archaeological Investigations Summer 2001*, 55-63. Cornwall County Council

'The Prehistoric Pottery' in Jones, AM, 'Settlement and Ceremony: Investigations at Stannnon Down, St Breward, *Cornish Archaeol* 43/4 2004/5, 72-87

'The Stone Artefacts' in Jones, AM, 'Settlement and Ceremony: Investigations at Stannnon Down, St Breward, *Cornish Archaeol* 43/4 2004/5, , 87-99

(with Andy M Jones) 'Redating the Watch Hill Barrow, Cornwall', *Archaeol J* 163 2006, 42-66

(with Andy M Jones) 'Cornish Beakers: new discoveries and perspectives' *Cornish Archaeol* 45 2006, 31-70

'Neolithic Pottery' in A.M.Jones & S.J.Reed, 'By Land, sea and air: an Early Neolithic pit group at Portscatho', Cornwall, *Cornish Archaeol* 45 2006, 5-9

'Pottery and Stone' in Reynolds, A. 'An Early Bronze Age pit at Tenoweth, Portreath' *Cornish Archaeol* 45 2006, 83-5

(with Roger Taylor) 'A Peterborough Sherd from the Beach at Westward Ho!', *Proceedings Devon Archaeological Society* 65 for 2006, 231-3

'Milestones in the Archaeology of Lundy', *Proc 60th Anniversary Symposium of the Lundy Field Society* 2007, 9-14

'Prehistoric, Roman and early medieval pottery' in Gossip, J & Jones, AM, *Achaeological Investigations of a Later Prehistoric and a Romano-British Landscape at Tremough, Penryn, Cornwall*, 2007, 51-78. BAR Brit Ser 443

'Stonework' in Gossip, J & Jones, AM, *Archaeological Investigations of a Later Prehistoric and a Romano-British Landscape at Tremough, Penryn, Cornwall*, 2007, 81-88. BAR Brit Ser 443

'Bronze Age Material Culture' and 'The Iron Age and Roman Period' in J.A.Nowakowski et al, 'Return to Gwithian: shifting the sands of time' *Cornish Archaeol* 46 2007, 33-8

(with A M Jones) 'The Farway Barrow Complex in East Devon Reassessed' *Proc Devon Archaeol Soc* 66 2008, 1-26

(with R Taylor) 'Petrological Examination of the Broadsands Pottery' in A Sheridan & R Shulting 'Revisiting a Small Passage Tomb at Broadsands, Devon' *Proc Devon Archaeol Soc* 66 2008, 12-14

(with P Manning) 'Excavation and Field Survey at the Iron Age Hillfort of Berry Ball, Crediton Hamlets' *Proc Devon Archaeol Soc* 67 2009, 99-132

'The Prehistoric Pottery' in T Green 'Excavation of a Hillslope Enclosure at Holworthy Farm, Parracombe displaying Bronze Age and Iron Age Activity' *Proc Devon Archaeol Soc* 67 2009, 66-73

'Prehistoric and Roman pottery, stonework and ironwork' in A M Jones & S R Taylor *Scarcewater, Pennance, Cornwall: Archaeological Investigation of a Bronze Age and Roman landscape*, 2010, 93-133. BAR Brit Series 516

'Prehistoric and Roman artefacts from Lundy' Proc. *Devon Archaeol. Soc.* 68, 2010

(with J A Nowakowski) *Trevelgue Head, Cornwall: the importance of CKC Andrew's 1939 excavations for prehistoric and Roman Cornwall, 2011*. Cornwall County Council Monograph

Unpublished reports (gray literature)

Isles of Scilly Coastal Erosion Project, 1989-93. Cornwall County Council HES Electronic Report 557

Finds from Watching Brief behind St Martin's Hotel, Isle of Scilly, 1993. Cornwall County Council HES Electronic Report 502

'The Pottery' in Hulka, S and Valentin, J, The proposed Hodge Ditch Extension to Chard Junction Quarry, Thorncombe, Dorset: Results of archaeological trench evaluation, 1999. AC Archaeological Report 0198/3/30

'Pottery and Stonework' in Nowakowski, J, Archaeology beneath the Towans,

Excavations at Gwithian, Cornwall 1949-1969:Updated Project Design, 2004. Historic Environment Service, Cornwall County Council/English Heritage

'The prehistoric pottery' in Cole, D, St Piran's Church, Perranzabuloe, Cornwall: Archaeological excavation, conservation and management works, 2007. Historic Environment Service, Cornwall County Council. Report No 2007R050

'Bronze Age Pottery and Fired Clay' in Hollinrake, C. & Hollinrake, N., n.d.,

An Archaeological Watching Brief on a Wessex Water Renewal Pipeline between Williton and Watchet, Somerset; Wessex Water Scheme D1297. Hollinrake report 278. Glastonbury